PT 153 · B56
DAV

OXFORD MODERN LANGUAGES AND LITERATURE MONOGRAPHS

Editorial Committee

The Tale of Bluebeard in German Literature

From the Eighteenth Century to the Present

MERERID PUW DAVIES

CLARENDON PRESS · OXFORD

OXFORD
UNIVERSITY PRESS

Great Clarendon Street, Oxford, OX2 6DP

Oxford University Press is a department of the University of Oxford.
It furthers the University's objective of excellence in research, scholarship,
and education by publishing worldwide in

Oxford New York

Athens Auckland Bangkok Bogotá Buenos Aires Cape Town
Chennai Dar es Salaam Delhi Florence Hong Kong Istanbul Karachi
Kolkata Kuala Lumpur Madrid Melbourne Mexico City Mumbai
Nairobi Paris São Paulo Shanghai Singapore Taipei Tokyo Toronto Warsaw

and associated companies in Berlin Ibadan

Oxford is a registered trade mark of Oxford University Press
in the UK and certain other countries

Published in the United States
by Oxford University Press Inc., New York

British Library Cataloguing in Publication Data

Data available

Library of Congress Cataloging in Publication Data

Davies, Mererid Puw.
The tale of Bluebeard in German literature : eighteenth century to the present / Mererid
Puw Davies.
p. cm. — (Oxford modern languages and literature monographs)
Includes bibliographical references and index.
1. German literature—History and criticism. 2. German literature—18th
century—History and criticism. 3. German literature—19th century—History and criticism.
4. German literature—20th century—History and criticism. 5. Bluebeard (Legendary
character) in literature. I. Title. II. Series.
PT153.B56 D38 2001   830.9'351—dc21   00-050128

ISBN 0-19-924275-5

1 3 5 7 9 10 8 6 4 2

Typeset by Regent Typesetting, London
Printed in Great Britain
on acid-free paper by
Biddles Ltd, Guildford and King's Lynn

To my family
and in memory of my grandmother
Marjorie Winifred Davies
(1903–1998)

PREFACE

It is difficult to be sitting comfortably when contemplating that most murderous of *Märchen*, 'Blaubart'. This tale in which a series of young women are slaughtered by a mysterious, monstrous husband, and their bodies hidden away in a horrible chamber, is one of the most hair-raising of the fairy tale repertoire. And yet, in addition to being a tale about the savage and extreme imposition of authority, this tale, too, is about (among many other things) intellectual independence and initiative, articulacy, quick wits, a close shave, and an unexpected triumph over tyranny. Thus, while 'Bluebeard' has often been used to frighten and subdue children in the nursery, in many of its versions it also has a utopian force, because it shows the ending of a cycle of vicious violence.

Just as the plot of the Bluebeard tale is driven by curiosity, this study was also motivated by a desire to explore some dark corners and forgotten spaces in European culture, since the *Blaubartmärchen* has been neglected in scholarship. This therefore is the first monograph entirely devoted to the history of 'Blaubart' in German literature from its first emergence to the present day (indeed, full-length studies have yet to be published on 'Bluebeard' in English or in the European tradition in general.) And this exploration, like the exploration undertaken by the tale's heroine, finds many skeletons in Bluebeard's closet. Such tales as 'Bluebeard' represent some of our most essential narratives about ourselves, our cultures and histories, and thus an understanding of 'Bluebeard' and the meanings of his private crypt provide us with keys for an understanding of culture and the history that formed it. And crucially, too, the tale tells us that everything changes—or rather, that things can be made to change for the better—given determination, language, knowledge, and courage. At the turn of a century where such need for change is not only fictional, this study hopes to bear that utopian horizon of the tale in mind.

With its focus on a relationship between a woman and a man, 'Blaubart' has consistently been a seismograph of gender politics, and it is on that theme which this study will focus most extensively. But like all tales, this *Märchen* tells us many stories simultaneously, and the meanings of these narratives change with time and place. Therefore, an exploration of Bluebeard's bloody chamber provides us with insights into many other matters—for example, the nature of the *Märchen*; what the sociologist Norbert Elias called the 'process of civilization'; and issues of cultural memory and national identity.

Chapter 1 examines scholarly views of the *Märchen* genre and demonstrates that the *Märchen* is in no sense a timeless form; argues that our perception of it is formed by a canon biased in favour of masculinist values; and shows ways in which some women writers have sought to challenge those values by exploiting the genre's subversive potential. In other words, the opening chapter sets out the reasons why this study examines not only canonical works but also texts which fall outside the canon, and pays particular attention to texts by women and to texts which do not fit the classic generic mould. Chapter 2 discusses the subversive potential of Charles Perrault's original *conte*, 'La Barbe bleue' (1697), a potential which is obfuscated in many German versions of the material. Commentary on this *Märchen* forms a fascinating body of work in itself, and to treat it as a primary, not secondary part of the tradition is highly productive. Therefore, Chapter 3 analyses scholarship on 'Blaubart' and shows how such scholarship dovetails with more obviously literary texts in the way it covers over both the tale's disruptive elements and its contemporary relevance. Chapter 4 looks at early German translations of Perrault's *conte*, and at the familiar, classic versions by the Grimms (1812) and Ludwig Bechstein (1845), all of which seek to cover over the material's explosive potential in similar ways. But Chapter 5 addresses an alternative, nineteenth-century comic and romantic Bluebeard tradition represented by E[ugenie]. Marlitt's novella 'Blaubart' (1866), the first German Bluebeard text known to be written by a woman. Chapter 6 identifies a sea change in a group of texts from the turn of the last century in which the traditional focus on the heroine is replaced by a focus on Bluebeard, who becomes a tragic hero, a Don Juan, and an *Übermensch* who subjects his women to unprecedented savagery. But another strand of the twentieth-century Bluebeard tradition imagines Bluebeard neither as a tyrannical husband nor a hero, but as an oppressive, psychological principle internalized by women, as discussed in Chapter 7 with reference to a group of texts by women written in the later twentieth century, notably the Surrealist Unica Zürn's *Das Haus der Krankheiten: Geschichten und Bilder einer Gelbsucht* (1977). Chapter 8 draws conclusions from the material studied; analyses the formation of the Bluebeard canon; and summarizes how 'Blaubart' reflects changing issues in gender politics, the process of civilization and national identities.

I use the German term *Märchen* consistently, as opposed to the perhaps more euphonic English 'fairy tale'. This choice is due to a slipping of meaning when the word *Märchen* is translated as 'fairy tale', since these two terms have quite different overtones and undertones. Therefore, it is more accurate to refer to *Märchen*. However, the consistent use of the adjective 'German' to describe the texts and traditions in question is regrettably less precise, since reference is made here to texts written in German by authors not only from or in Germany, but elsewhere besides. Thus, what is meant by this term is 'German-language', and it has been chosen for concision.

I should like to express my gratitude to several institutions and foundations for financial support in the work on this study. In chronological order these are: the Alfred-Toepfer-Stiftung FVS, Hamburg; the Humanities Research Board of the British Academy; St John's College, Oxford; Magdalen College, Oxford; and the *Fachbereich Germanistik* of the Freie Universität Berlin.

Thanks are due, too, to many individuals. Above all, my debt to Professor Richard Sheppard, who has been the most inspiring and generous of teachers and friends, is very great indeed. I am also most grateful to Professor Ruth B. Bottigheimer for her invaluable counsel. I thank too many other friends and colleagues who have been unfailingly helpful in discussing and reading this work; the examiners who made constructive comments on the work in its various stages as a thesis at Oxford and my D.Phil. examiners, Professor Elizabeth Boa and Dr Karen Leeder; and most recently, my colleagues in the German Department at University College London for their advice.

I am grateful to the President and Fellows of Magdalen College, Oxford, for providing me with not only academic support but also friendship; and my gratitude to many more friends for support in many forms defies expression. Finally, I thank my family. This book is dedicated to them and to the memory of my grandmother, Marjorie Winifred Davies.

MPD

CONTENTS

BIBLIOGRAPHICAL NOTE

The abbreviation *KHM* refers to Jacob and Wilhelm Grimm, *Kinder- und Hausmärchen*, edited by Heinz Rölleke (3 vols., Stuttgart: Reclam, 1980) on the basis of the Grimms' final edition of 1857. Where the abbreviation is followed by an arabic number in the text, that number refers to the tale number in this edition.

'UNENDLICHE GESCHICHTE'?[1]
READING *MÄRCHEN*

'UNENDLICHE GESCHICHTE'

Wußten wir, Bruder, nicht immer schon, welche Macht unsere Märchen über die Menschen haben?[2]

This remark by a fictional Wilhelm Grimm to his brother Jacob in Günter Grass's novel *Die Rättin* (1986) sets out why the study of *Märchen* matters, for here the fictional Wilhelm is identifying the sheer power of the genre. This is not only the power to fascinate or to entertain, but the power to educate, and to inscribe social and moral standards. Fairy tale is a powerful medium in any Western culture, as those brought up with either the most traditional of Mother Goose picture books or the latest generation of Walt Disney extravaganzas will testify. The very use of the adjective 'fairy-tale' itself has a most potent resonance (evident, for instance, in its consistent evocation by the media at the time of the wedding, in London in 1981, of the Prince and Princess of Wales, an event crucial to the support of some key cultural myths). No wonder, then, that to study fairy tale is to illuminate some of the most central narratives of our culture.

But over and above that general level of significance in Western culture, in German in particular, the *Märchen* is a quite extraordinarily powerful point of reference. It was in German-speaking lands and for a German-speaking public that modern conceptions of folk-tale were first codified, by such writers as Johann Gottfried Herder (1744–1803) and Jacob (1785–1863) and Wilhelm Grimm (1786–1859), and while this 'national' preoccupation dates back to the eighteenth and nineteenth centuries, recently, too, Jack Zipes, a prominent *Märchen* scholar, has written of a 'German obsession with fairy tales'.[3] That perception took root early and strongly, so that it

---

[1] Michael Ende, *Die unendliche Geschichte* (Stuttgart: Thienemann, 1979). On this *Märchen* novel's phenomenal success, see Walter Filz, *Es war einmal . . . Elemente des Märchens in der deutschen Literatur der siebziger Jahre* (Frankfurt am Main: Lang, 1989), 144–64.

[2] Günter Grass, *Die Rättin* (Darmstadt: Luchterhand, 1986), 348.

[3] Jack D. Zipes, 'The Grimms and the German Obsession with Fairy Tales', in Ruth B. Bottigheimer (ed.), *Fairy Tales and Society: Illusion, Allusion and Paradigm* (Philadelphia: University of Pennsylvania Press), 271–85.

soon reached as far as Britain, where in 1828 a translator of *Märchen* could describe the genre as epitomizing 'the genius of German romance'.[4] And the association made between *Märchen* and German identity was preserved in the twentieth century. For example, after 1945 the Allies banned the Grimms' *Kinder- und Hausmärchen (KHM)*, albeit briefly, for fear of its pernicious influence as used and abused by National Socialist cultural policy.[5] And it is this same perception of the *Märchen* as a privileged vehicle for saying something significant about the history, nature, and culture of the nation that is evoked in the film *Deutschland im Herbst* (1978), which presented a psycho-gramme of West Germany during the turbulent events of the *Deutscher Herbst* of 1977.[6] At one point, that important film, which seeks to document cultural memory, and to challenge some conventional historiographies of Germany, turns to the *Märchen* for a possibly more truthful account. As Zipes puts it, 'the Germans . . . have repeatedly used fairy tales to explain the world to themselves'.[7] Therefore, the study of the *Märchen* can go to the heart of German culture and thought.

However, in order to use the study of *Märchen* in this way, one of the most common conceptions about the genre must be dispelled. This is the notion that the *Märchen* emanates from the (implicitly aesthetically and morally superior) past, and has been made extinct or irrelevant by the (implicitly more debased) modern era. In other words, *Märchen* are frequently identified with the past; and frequently, too, are held to represent threatened or lost values to which the present may be exhorted to return. It was in this spirit that the Grimms themselves noted, for example, in the 'Vorrede' to the 1819 edition of the *KHM*:

Es war vielleicht gerade Zeit, diese Märchen festzuhalten, da diejenigen, die sie bewahren sollen, immer seltener werden. Freilich, die sie noch wissen, wissen

[4] 'Preface', in George Godfrey Cunningham, *Foreign Tales and Traditions Chiefly Selected from the Fugitive Literature of Germany* (1828), quoted in Martin Sutton, *The Sin-Complex: A Critical Study of English Versions of the Grimms' 'Kinder- und Hausmärchen' in the Nineteenth Century* (Kassel: Brüder Grimm-Gesellschaft, 1996), 60.

[5] Jack D. Zipes, 'The Struggle for the Grimms' Throne: The Legacy of the Grimms' Tales in the FRG and GDR since 1945', in Donald Haase (ed.), *The Reception of Grimms' Fairy Tales: Responses, Reactions, Revisions* (Detroit: Wayne State University Press, 1993), 167–207 (167).

[6] *Deutschland im Herbst* (1978), dir. Alf Brustellin, Bernhard Sinkel, Rainer Werner Fassbinder, Alexander Kluge, Maximiliane Mainka, Edgar Reitz, Beate Mainka-Jellinghaus, Peter Schubert, Hans-Peter Cloos, Katja Rupé, Volker Schlöndorff.

[7] Zipes, 'The Grimms and the German Obsession with Fairy Tales', 273.

gemeinlich auch recht viel, weil die Menschen ihnen absterben, sie nicht den Menschen: aber die Sitte selber nimmt immer mehr ab, wie alle heimlichen Plätze in Wohnungen und Gärten, die vom Großvater bis zum Enkel fortdauerten, dem stetigen Wechsel einer leeren Prächtigkeit weichen.[8]

Here, the Grimms are stating that they see the *Märchen* as being eternal and superior to transient, degenerate human society ('weil die Menschen [den Märchen] absterben, sie nicht den Menschen: aber die Sitte selber nimmt immer mehr ab'). Reflections on the *Märchen*, since the late eighteenth and early nineteenth centuries, are often characterized by such a sense of loss, which is deemed to bode ill for an increasingly impoverished Western civilization—that phenomenon which the sociologist Max Weber termed 'die Entzauberung der Welt'.[9] That message associated with the *Märchen* marked the twentieth century too, as in Hans Arp's most famous poem, 'kaspar ist tot' (1953):

> jetzt vertrocknen unsere scheitel und sohlen und die feen liegen
> halverkohlt auf dem scheiterhaufen.[10]

More recently, in Barbara Frischmuth's novel *Die Mystifikationen der Sophie Silber* (1976) the fairy characters themselves admit, in view of the increasing barbarism of humanity:

> uns [bleibt] nichts mehr, als der Rücktritt, Schritt für Schritt, der Auszug aus ihrem [the humans'] Bewußtsein, rückwirkend noch und zuerst aus allem Geschriebenen bis zu den ältesten Quellen, bis keine Buchstabe mehr von uns erzählt und nur mehr Großmütter und Kinder eine Erinnerung an uns haben, die immer mehr verblaßt.[11]

And Grass too expressed this sense in a poem included in *Die Rättin*:

> Weil der Wald
> an den Menschen stirbt,
> fliehen die Märchen,
> weiß die Spindel nicht,
> wen sie stechen soll,
> wissen des Mädchens Hände
> die der Vater ihm abgehackt,

---

[8] 'Vorrede', *KHM* i. 15–24.
[9] See Edith Weiller, *Max Weber und die literarische Moderne: Ambivalente Begegnungen zweier Kulturen* (Stuttgart: Metzler, 1994), 9.
[10] Hans Arp, *Gesammelte Gedichte*, ed. Marguerite Arp-Hagenbach and Peter Schifferli, 3 vols. (Zurich: Limes, 1963), i. 26.
[11] Barbara Frischmuth, *Die Mystifikationen der Sophie Silber* (1976) (Munich: Heyne, 1993), 287.

keinen einzigen Baum zu fassen,
bleibt der dritte Wunsch ungesagt. (p. 49)

Such a view of the *Märchen* as a superior, almost irretrievable artefact from a golden past has been taken up by contemporary scholars of the form too, such that the closing chapters of secondary texts dealing with more recent, twentieth-century *Märchen* often bear titles such as 'Das letzte Märchen'[12] and 'Zerbröckelnde Form'.[13]

In other words, the *Märchen* is popularly associated with an idealized past; or, where that idea is taken to an extreme, the genre is even believed to be timeless or archetypal in nature. Such nostalgic beliefs go hand in hand with another, tremendously important perception of the *Märchen*: that it is a pure, authentic, and auratic document of a natural, oral culture. That conceptualization of the *Märchen* supposes it to be a neutral transcription of a genuine folk artefact, free of writerly or editorial interventions and interests. All this means that the *Märchen* is frequently thought to tell a story which, somehow, stands outside history. If indeed it stood outside history in this way, it would be a poor source of insight into the historical and social construction of culture and its myths. Equally, if the *Märchen* could only tell us about the past, there would be little sense in using it to study contemporary times; and if it were not literary, but rather an unchanged part of oral culture, it would fall, too, beyond the reach of the methods of literary criticism.

However, a closer look at the history of the *Märchen* as we know it demonstrates that such ideas about the timelessness and purely oral nature of the genre are in fact due to some carefully constructed theoretical conventions, generated by the earlier practitioners of the form, and based on what the folklorist Jennifer Fox, for instance, has called the founding 'script' of folklore as set down by Herder, and enthusiastically taken up in the interests of a German Romantic Nationalism.[14] A closer examination of the history of the *Märchen* will also show that the nostalgia traditionally invoked with it derives, above all, from an unease about modernity which, it is hoped, can be dispelled by the evocation of a narrative which is allegedly unchang-

---

[12] Filz, *Es war einmal*, 267.

[13] Paul-Wolfgang Wührl, *Das deutsche Kunstmärchen: Geschichte, Botschaft und Erzählstrukturen* (Heidelberg: Quelle & Meyer, 1984), 283.

[14] Jennifer Fox, 'The Creator Gods: Romantic Nationalism and the En-Genderment of Women in Folklore', in Susan Tower Hollis, Linda Pershing, and M. Jane Young (eds.), *Feminist Theory and the Study of Folklore* (Urbana: University of Illinois Press, 1993), 29–40.

ing or archetypal;[15] and that *Märchen* are indeed most appropriately viewed as literary creations.

In formulating his seminal concept of folk culture, which was to include the *Märchen*, Herder was responding to the condition of eighteenth-century Germany, which was politically and culturally fragmented and in which '[m]embers of the German nobility viewed their own cultural heritage with contempt and looked instead to France for cultural inspiration'.[16] Herder's theories aimed to remedy this state of affairs by valorizing a culture which could be understood as being specifically German, and thereby promoting a new, positive German consciousness based on the idea that the Germans constitute an organic and homogeneous group, that is, a *Volk*. Fox notes that '[l]anguage occupies a privileged position in the Herderian framework, and its expressive forms—folksong, poetry, proverb, and the like—are perceived as voicing the collective consciousness and embodying the shared tradition of a *Volk*' (p. 32). Herder's aim was, then, to draw his contemporaries' attention to what he perceived to be the high moral value of the *Volk*, a belief which accounts for the popular perception that such 'folk' products as the *Märchen* represent archetypal values. And it is the work of Herder, and work inspired by him, which has produced the nostalgic, regressive mood often associated with *Märchen* too. Fox notes:

Viewed against the foil of Enlightenment thought, which elevated human reason as the agent of progress, Herder's ideas take on a nostalgic cast. His doctrine glorified what he considered to be a more basic form of social organisation and salutary way of life that he saw passing with Europe's urbanisation and industrialisation. (p. 32)

Therefore, the idea that the *Märchen* is the legacy of an older culture, stands for older values, and is as such endangered, if not already defunct, is a fiction generated by an influential school of thought which followed Herder and like-minded thinkers. The present study will, however, demonstrate that the genre, with its associated ideas and motifs, continually takes on new and often apparently unconventional forms.[17] Indeed, the *Märchen* maintains a

[15] See e.g. Ruth B. Bottigheimer, *Grimms' Bad Girls and Bold Boys: The Moral and Social Vision of the Tales* (New Haven, Conn.: Yale University Press, 1987), 171.

[16] Fox, 'The Creator Gods', 32.

[17] Cf. e.g. Hermann Bausinger, *Märchen, Phantasie und Wirklichkeit* (Frankfurt am Main: Dipa, 1985); Rebecca Sue Bohde, 'The German Märchen from 1970 to 1985: Versions of a Literary Genre in Areas of Topical Interest', Ph.D. thesis (Ann Arbor: Dissertation

prominent position in the contemporary imagination since *Märchen* elements demonstrably occur in the most heterogeneous contexts. In fact, the real situation of the *Märchen* is more akin to an 'unendliche Geschichte', since *Märchen* and their motifs are still used to express important ideas, just as they were in the eighteenth and early nineteenth centuries. In recent literature in German, for instance, there is the satire on the Grimm tale 'Frau Holle' in Elfriede Jelinek's *Die Liebhaberinnen* (1975),[18] or the incantatory quotation from the Grimms' 'Aschenputtel', 'Blut im Schuh', in the opening lines of Christa Wolf's *Kein Ort. Nirgends* (1979).[19] Such contemporary evocations of the *Märchen* not only undermine any notion that the form is dying out, but also show that formally, too, familiar *Märchen* plots are not limited to the form and diction codified by the Brothers Grimm. Rather, the stories constantly take on new literary shapes.

So, in the wake of thinkers like Herder who believed in the importance of organic, national culture, and after the Napoleonic occupation of Germany, it became urgently important to produce evidence of an indigenous, German folk culture. But while Germany in the eighteenth century, like any society, did possess its own vernacular culture, the writing and literature inspired by Herder's theory of oral culture were very specific, self-conscious creations informed by his ideals and aims, rather than a truly faithful, unembellished record of real oral cultural practices, untouched by writerly hand. One such self-conscious creation is the *Märchen* itself as we know it. It is usually thought that *Märchen* have existed in the specific form familiar today for centuries, but in a recent study, Manfred Grätz shows that such a belief is questionable, since evidence for the existence of such *Volksmärchen* in Germany before the eighteenth century is meagre.[20] Grätz goes on to show that it is more likely that the German *Märchen*

Abstracts International, 1992); Filz, *Es war einmal*; E. W. Funcke, 'Das Märchen in Deutschland heute', *Acta Germanica*, 15 (1982), 131–47; Wolfgang Krömer, 'Märchen, Legende, phantastische Geschichte—oder der bittere Unernst als Wesenszug der Moderne', *Sprachkunst*, 15 (1984), 212–26; Jens Tismar, *Das deutsche Kunstmärchen im 20. Jahrhundert* (Stuttgart: Metzler, 1981); Jack Zipes, *Fairy Tales and the Art of Subversion: The Classic Genre for Children and the Process of Civilisation* (London: Routledge, 1991); Jack Zipes, 'The Grimms and the German Obsession with Fairy Tales', and 'The Struggle for the Grimms' Throne: The Legacy of the Grimms' Tales in the FRG and GDR since 1945', in Haase, *The Reception of Grimms' Fairy Tales*.

[18] *KHM* 24, i. 150–3; Elfriede Jelinek, *Die Liebhaberinnen* (Reinbek bei Hamburg: Rowohlt, 1975).

[19] *KHM* 21, i. 137–44; Christa Wolf, *Kein Ort. Nirgends* (1979) (Berlin: Aufbau, 1980), 5.

[20] *Das Märchen in der deutschen Aufklärung* (Stuttgart: Metzler, 1988).

were in fact modelled on the highly fashionable, seventeenth- and eighteenth-century French *contes de fées*, which were sophisticated literary products of a high salon culture, rather than unsullied transcriptions of peasant narrative, although their authors, as in the case of Perrault, did sometimes make such claims. Thus, the way in which the *KHM* and similar texts (some of them earlier, but less known today) naturalized the fashionable, upper-class, literary *conte* and invested it with national value, creating a *Volksmärchen*, can be understood as part of the Herderian project. Such insights have led to a re-evaluation of the distinctions long believed to distinguish the two conventionally separate genres of *Volksmärchen* and *Kunstmärchen*; and all this means that the *Volksmärchen* as epitomized by the *KHM* is in reality the product of a complex fabric of explicitly literary inter-textuality. This will prove to be the case with 'Blaubart', since the German version written down by the Grimms in the early nineteenth century was in fact a direct descendant of Charles Perrault's French literary *conte* 'La Barbe bleue' (1697), which had initially become popular through literary transmission and gradually made its way into German oral culture.

A closer look at the Grimms' *Märchen* in particular, too, is helpful towards an understanding of the ways in which our modern percep-tion of the genre has been constructed, because the Grimms' tales are firmly established today as our educational, popular, and scholarly *Märchen* model.[21] In 1969 the critic Ingrid Merkel wrote: 'Was ist ein Märchen? . . . [Die] bündigste Antwort lautet: Märchen sind "die Geschichten, die die Brüder Grimm in ihren *Kinder- und Hausmärchen* vereinigt haben" ';[22] and Shawn C. Jarvis writes: 'We are forced by the sheer synergy of Grimm scholarship to view Jacob and Wilhelm's work as the standard by which all other German fairy tales are judged.'[23] Jarvis therefore describes any reading of a *Märchen* which does not explicitly conform to the Grimmian model to be 'the work of a Procrustes' because all the models available to us for interpreting *Märchen* are defined by our awareness, conscious or not, of the *KHM*.

Recently, scholarship on the *KHM* has shown that both the text itself and the mythology around it are complex, artificial construc-tions. For instance, the *KHM* has often been seen as the original

---

[21] See Zipes, 'The Struggle for the Grimms' Throne'.

[22] 'Wirklichkeit im romantischen Märchen', *Colloquia Germanica*, 3 (1969), 162–83 (162).

[23] 'Literary Legerdemain and the *Märchen* Tradition of Nineteenth-Century Women Writers', Ph.D. dissertation (University of Minnesota, 1990), 166.

Märchen collection. And it has often been thought that the *KHM* style, that is, its characteristically simple, monodimensional and paratactic narrative, is the purest expression of the *Märchen*; and of course that the tales in the *KHM* are essentially German, oral products. According to these traditional ideas, any *Märchen* which shows international or non-German traits, or linguistic, stylistic, or thematic differences, is thought to be less authentic, or even inferior. However, none of these ideas is accurate. The Grimms' *Märchen* were preceded by others, by such authors as Benedike Naubert (1753–1819), Johann Karl August Musäus (1735–87) and Christoph Martin Wieland (1733–1813), and were contemporary with other collections more influential at the time, above all Ludwig Bechstein's (1801–60) *Deutsches Märchenbuch* (1845). Therefore, the *KHM* has no claim to historical priority. And the seemingly purely oral nature of the *KHM* texts is questionable for fundamental reasons over and above those suggested by Grätz, for in the very process of being committed to paper by a writer, such tales must inevitably become self-conscious, literary products. In *Grimms' Fairy Tales: A History of Criticism on a Popular Classic* (1993), James M. McGlathery sets out various approaches to 'folk literature' that have developed over the last two centuries and shows that this issue was anticipated by the Grimms themselves, only to be occluded until Alfred Wesselski's work in the 1920s.[24]

Moreover, the *KHM* was subject to other, more clearly literary processes also which distanced the tales further still from oral culture. The publication of the earliest, 1810 manuscript of the *KHM* by Heinz Rölleke in 1975 made a more extensive comparison of various drafts of the collection possible and exposed the considerable textual adjustments deliberately made by the Grimms in the interest of nascent, middle-class ideals.[25] Put briefly, Rölleke's work revealed that the Grimms' authorial and editorial activity and increasing stylization of their material make the *KHM* a text of its time, produced by intellectually sophisticated middle-class authors who were working on material provided initially (in the case of the first volume of the *KHM*) by educated middle-class collaborators. And analyses like those by Ruth B. Bottigheimer demonstrate just how firmly the

---

[24] (Columbia, SC: Camden House, 1993), 31–2, 46–51.
[25] Heinz Rölleke, *Die älteste Märchensammlung der Brüder Grimm. Synopse der handschriftlichen Urfassung von 1810 und der Erstdrücke von 1812* (Cologny-Genève: Fondation Martin Bodmer, 1975).

Grimms put their own stamp on the *Märchen*, adjusting and rewriting them in many ways in each subsequent version of the *KHM* from 1810 up to 1857.[26] Thus, the characteristic thematic and formal features which we associate with the *KHM* are the product of the Grimms' literary imagination. Furthermore, a comparison with other earlier or contemporary *Märchen* shows that the *KHM* diction and themes are very idiosyncratic, rather than being typical reflections of a common, familiar style. And, as Grätz has shown, it is a mistake to suggest that the *KHM* are purely, or even mainly, German, for they are the product of a complex intercultural process incorporating, in a German form, international influences. Here too, 'Blaubart' is a case in point, for its French origins are indisputable. Therefore, Zipes can comment:

Undoubtedly, the Grimms knew that most of their sources for the material they used were not 'older, untainted, and untutored German peasant transmitters of an indigenous oral tradition but, instead, literate, middle-class, and predominantly young people, probably influenced by books more than by oral tradition—and including a very significant presence of people who were either of French origins or actually French-speaking'.[27]

Finally, Bottigheimer has also shown, in her work on the 'mythicized' publishing history of the *KHM*, that the very idea of the 'uninterrupted triumphal progress' of the *KHM* in German culture is illusory.[28] In fact, in the nineteenth century, popularly believed to be the golden age of the *KHM*, Ludwig Bechstein's *Märchen* collections 'outsold Grimm from every point of view' (p. 85). The Grimms' texts were initially unpopular, and 'reactions to them were mixed at best and heartlessly critical at worst' (p. 79), such that from a commercial point of view their publication was 'disastrous' (p. 83). This initial failure only came to be replaced by success at the very end of the nineteenth century and above all in the twentieth century, so that Bottigheimer calls the text's success 'a quintessentially twentieth-century publishing phenomenon' (p. 95). She ascribes this pattern to

---

[26] See Bottigheimer, *Grimms' Bad Girls and Bold Boys*; John M. Ellis, *One Fairy Tale Too Many* (Chicago: University of Chicago Press, 1983); Maria M. Tatar, *The Hard Facts of the Grimms' Fairy Tales* (Princeton: Princeton University Press, 1987); James M. McGlathery (ed.), *The Brothers Grimm and Folktale* (Urbana: University of Illinois Press, 1989).

[27] 'The Grimms and the German Obsession with Fairy Tales', 273. Zipes is quoting critically from Ellis, *One Fairy Tale Too Many*.

[28] Bottigheimer, 'The Publishing History of Grimms' Tales: Reception at the Cash Register', in Haase, *The Reception of Grimms' Fairy Tales*, 78–101 (79, 85).

a number of factors, for instance that the 'folk' style created by the Grimms was not liked or valued by most readers in the greater part of the nineteenth century, whereas Bechstein's tales with their more bourgeois tone were popular. The illusion that the *KHM* embodied a much-loved and familiar nineteenth-century genre has been fostered by changing market conditions, 'utterly impossible claims . . . inserted into the secondary literature' (p. 79), the inclusion of the *KHM* in school syllabuses, thus enforcing their familiarity, and a new style of 'panegyric and polemic' in writing on folklore and children's literature at the turn of the century which valorized the *KHM* in the name of a new-found 'folk-based nationalism' (p. 89). By the turn of the century, this 'folk-based nationalism' of the Grimms and the Romantics, for which the Grimms had created a literary expression in the *KHM*, had changed from being an avant-garde manifesto espoused by a minority of intellectuals to a powerful political rhetoric which changed public taste, concomitantly with rising German nationalism at the turn of the century and later fostered by the Great War. Bottigheimer's insights make clear that the notion that the *KHM* represent an unchanging and authentic cultural standard is a retrospectively constructed fantasy which nonetheless dominates our understanding of the *Märchen*.

In sum, then, the *Märchen* familiar to us today, as codified in the *KHM*, is a complex construct, and the Grimms' tales are best viewed as literary documents. Accordingly, the *Märchen*'s literary nature has been increasingly recognized in criticism on the genre from the 1960s onward, in tandem with the decline among many literary critics of the view, deriving ultimately from Kant's Third Critique, that true 'literature' is somehow above history, and with the impact of such movements as Marxist, feminist, and socio-historical criticism on literary studies. Thus, in the last two or three decades a socio-historical discussion has arisen around the Grimms' work, for example, which focuses on the demystification of its traditional status as a timeless ideal, and which sets the *KHM* in its cultural and historical context, as in the work of Bottigheimer and Zipes, who has read *Märchen* in the light of what Norbert Elias called 'the process of civilization'.[29] More recent criticism has uncovered, too, obscured texts and writers, as in the work of Shawn C. Jarvis and Jeannine

---

[29] Norbert Elias, *Über den Prozeß der Zivilisation: Soziogenetische und psychogenetische Untersuchungen* (1939), 2 vols. (Frankfurt am Main: Suhrkamp, 1997).

Blackwell.[30] And some further developments in *Märchen* scholarship use other, relatively new theoretical approaches: Roland Barthes's concept of mythology,[31] Mikhail Bakhtin's concept of speech genres,[32] or ideas about postmodernism.[33]

GENDER AND THE *MÄRCHEN*

Once traditional ideas about the ahistoricity of *Märchen* have been discarded, the *Märchen* becomes a rich source for literary criticism and the study of the history of culture. Given this, it is fruitful to examine ways in which *Märchen* illuminate the 'process of civilization', for among other roles it has had an important function in the changing processes of modern education and socialization, something that is apparent in the Grimms' *KHM* 'Vorrede' of 1819:

> Das ist der Grund, warum wir durch unsere Sammlung nicht bloß der Geschichte der Poesie und Mythologie einen Dienst erweisen wollten, sondern es zugleich Absicht war, daß die Poesie selbst, die darin lebendig ist, wirke und erfreue . . . also auch, *daß es als ein Erziehungsbuch diene*. (pp. 16–17, my emphasis)

And the Grimms' view undoubtedly influenced later writers, for in 1975, Bruno Bettelheim stated: 'Fairy tales depict in imaginary form *the essential steps in growing up* and achieving an independent existence' (my emphasis).[34]

And second, since the inculcation of gender roles and expectations has always been a key factor in the process of civilization, because of the *Märchen*'s key role in that process, it is especially appropriate to examine the genre for changing ideologies of gender and civilization. In 1979, the pioneering feminist critics Sandra M. Gilbert and Susan Gubar deconstructed the normative assumptions implicit in the

[30] Jarvis, 'Literary Legerdemain', and Blackwell, 'Fractured Fairy Tales: German Women Authors and the Grimm Tradition', *Germanic Review*, 62 (1987), 162–74.

[31] Jack D. Zipes, 'Fairy Tale as Myth/Myth as Fairy Tale', in *The Brothers Grimm: From Enchanted Forests to the Modern World* (New York: Routledge, 1988), 147–64.

[32] Jack D. Zipes, 'Henri Pourrat and the Tradition of Perrault and the Brothers Grimm', in *The Brothers Grimm*, 96–109.

[33] Cristina Bacchilega, 'Folk and Literary Narrative in a Postmodern Context: The Case of the *Märchen*', *Fabula*, 29 (1988), 302–16; and *Postmodern Fairy Tales: Gender and Narrative Strategies* (Philadelphia: University of Pennsylvania Press, 1997).

[34] Bruno Bettelheim, *The Uses of Enchantment* (1975), quoted in Ellen Cronan Rose, 'Through the Looking Glass: When Women Tell Fairy Tales', in Elizabeth Abel, Marianne Hirsch, and Elizabeth Langland (eds.), *The Voyage In: Fictions of Female Development* (Hanover, NH: University Press of New England, 1983), 209–27 (209).

Grimms' and Bettelheim's statements when they wrote that fairy tales 'often both state and enforce culture's sentences with greater accuracy than more sophisticated literary texts' inasmuch as they present the complexities of the socialization process in paradigmatic form.[35] In other words, Gilbert and Gubar reveal that the standards and role models provided by *Märchen* are not archetypal or essential, but rather result from being 'enforced'. But such an examination of fairy tale from a feminist perspective is, of course, not new, and its progress to date may usefully be recapitulated.

In 1947 Simone de Beauvoir remarked in *Le Deuxième Sexe*:

La femme c'est la Belle au bois dormant, Peau d'Âne, Cendrillon, Blanche Neige, celle qui reçoit et subit. Dans les chansons, dans les contes, on voit le jeune homme partir aventureusement à la recherche de la femme; il pourfend des dragons, il combat des géants; elle est enfermée dans une tour, un palais, un jardin, une caverne, enchaînée à un rocher, captive, endormie: elle attend. Un jour mon prince viendra . . . Some day he'll come along, the man I love . . .[36]

And around the same time as Marxist and other political theories of the *Märchen* began to emerge in the 1970s, several books central to the second wave of the women's movement, outside the conventional domain of literary criticism, saw relatively early on that the imagery of the *KHM* and, more pervasively, the popular selection and perpetuation of the least emancipatory examples of this imagery (for instance in Walt Disney films like *Snow White* as cited by de Beauvoir) involved oppressive, negative models for women. In 1974 Andrea Dworkin devoted two chapters to fairy tale imagery in *Woman Hating*:

We have taken the fairy tales of childhood with us into maturity, chewed but still lying in the stomach, as real identity. Between Snow-white and her heroic prince, our two great fictions, we never did have much of a chance.[37]

Mary Daly's radical feminist text *Gyn/Ecology* (1978) drew attention to the same issues:

The child who is fed tales such as Snow White is not told that the tale itself is a poisonous apple, and the Wicked Queen (her mother/teacher), having herself been drugged by the same deadly diet throughout her lifetime (death-time), is unaware of her venomous part in the patriarchal plot.[38]

---

[35] *The Madwoman in the Attic: The Woman Writer and the Nineteenth-Century Literary Imagination* (New Haven, Conn.: Yale University Press, 1979), 36.

[36] (1949), 2 vols. (Paris: Gallimard, 1976), i. 44.

[37] Andrea Dworkin, *Woman Hating* (New York: Plume, 1974), 32–3.

[38] Quoted in Jennifer Waelti-Walters, *Fairy Tales and the Female Imagination* (St Albans, Vt.: Eden, 1982), 4.

And in 1976 the feminist psychoanalyst Hélène Cixous wrote in her essay 'Le Sexe ou la tête?':

Woman, if you look for her, has a strong chance of always being found in one position: in bed. In bed and asleep—'laid (out)'. . . . Sleeping Beauty is lifted from her bed by a man because, as we all know, women don't wake up by themselves: man has to intervene . . . She is lifted up by the man who will lay her in her next bed so that she may be confined to bed ever after, just as the fairy tales say.[39]

According to the tales evoked by these writers, the classic fairy tale heroine is a negative, helpless role model 'confined to bed ever after'. But as Kay F. Stone has it, 'the feminist view of [fairy tale] heroines has itself become a stereotype'.[40] And while the criticism by earlier feminist writers of the passive roles assigned to these most famous of female fairy-tale characters remains more than legitimate, such a total rejection of the fairy tale is more of a reinscription than a critical exploration of conventional perceptions of the genre. In such evaluations, the traditional view that the fairy tale is a simple, monodimensional narrative is not challenged; only a very limited selection of stories—that is, those based on the Grimm canon with its patriarchal and nationalistic underpinnings—is considered; and the possibility that the tales may use the possibilities of fantasticism to transmit more complex or subversive messages than meet the eye is not entertained.

For the fairy tale can involve magic; and other, more positive moments in feminist writing on the genre reflect the utopian or subversive potential of enchantment. Indeed, further on in 'Le Sexe ou la tête?' Cixous herself put forward an alternative reading of 'Little Red Riding Hood', suggesting that the tale's heroine is not the victim of the big bad wolf but asserting her own sexuality. Such a reading overturns such conventional psychoanalytic readings as Bettelheim's, who insists that the story demonstrates the 'childish innocence' of a 'normally' developing young girl.[41] Bettelheim's tremendously influential interpretations have been shown to be as constricting in their construction of femininity as an Andersen or a Grimm narrative,[42] and by challenging such readings, whether one agrees with her

---

[39] 'Castration or Decapitation?', trans. Annette Kuhn, *Signs*, 7 (1981), 41–55 (43).

[40] 'Feminist Approaches to the Interpretation of Fairy Tales', in Bottigheimer, *Fairy Tales and Society*, 229–36 (230).

[41] Bettelheim, *The Uses of Enchantment: The Meaning and Importance of Fairy Tales* (London: Thames & Hudson, 1976), 166–83.

[42] See Waelti-Walters, *Fairy Tales and the Female Imagination*, 2–3.

interpretation or not, Cixous highlighted the *Märchen*'s more subversive possibilities.

A specifically feminist *Märchen* scholarship developed in the 1970s, too, and feminist work on the *KHM* and other *Märchen* has achieved a certain canonical status of its own today in that retrospective analyses of its development have now been published.[43] (It is important to remember that this feminist project is distinct from studies on the feminine or women in *Märchen* in general, for such commentaries are by no means necessarily feminist and may simply confirm those familiar preconceptions about gender roles and their literary representations which feminists question.) And the gradually changing feminist critique of *Märchen* is similar to the developments in perceptions of the *Märchen* in the feminist cultural criticism and psychoanalysis described above, in that it moves from rejection to reappraisal and reappropriation for critical and subversive ends.

So, while earlier feminist readings of *Märchen* analysed only a very restricted range of familiar *KHM* motifs and dismissed them as pernicious and irretrievably sexist, later readings have pointed to ways in which it is possible to subvert the canon by rereading those tales in different ways, rediscovering less well-known tales and writers, looking at tales which make disruptive or alternative uses of the genre, or introducing a new telling or teller. And the studies by Jarvis and Blackwell make clear that the *Märchen* was used by women, often as a vehicle of subversive utopianism, well before the twentieth century. In contemporary German literature, such evolving attitudes in both literature and criticism are embedded in Svende Merian's

---

[43] See McGlathery, *Grimms' Fairy Tales*, 25–6 and 51–4; Stone, 'Feminist Approaches'; Natascha Würzbach, 'Feministische Forschung in Literaturwissenschaft und Volkskunde: Neue Fragestellungen und Probleme der Theoriebildung', in Sigrid Früh and Rainer Wehse (eds.), *Die Frau im Märchen* (Kassel: Europäische Märchengesellschaft/Röth, 1985), 192–214; Jack Zipes, 'Der Prinz wird nicht kommen: Feministische Märchen und Kulturkritik in den USA und England', in Früh and Wehse, *Die Frau im Märchen*, 174–92; and Zipes's introduction to *Don't Bet on the Prince: Contemporary Feminist Fairy Tales in North America and England*, ed. Zipes (New York: Methuen, 1986), 1–36.

For some German-language feminist interpretations of *Märchen*, see Heide Göttner-Abendroth, *Die Göttin und ihr Heros: Die matriarchalen Religionen in Mythos, Märchen und Dichtung* (Munich: Frauenoffensive, 1980); Renate Steinchen, 'Märchenerzählerin und Schneewittchen—Zwei Frauenbilder in einer deutschen Märchensammlung: Zur Rekonstruktion der Entstehungsgeschichte Grimmscher Märchenfiguren im Kontext sozial- und kulturhistorischer Entwicklung', in Barbara Schaeffer-Hegel and Brigitte Wartmann (eds.), *Mythos Frau: Projektionen und Inszenierungen im Patriarchat* (Berlin: Publica, 1984), 280–308; and Ingrid Spörk, 'Das Bild der Frau im Märchen', in Beate Frakele, Elisabeth List, and Gertrude Pauritsch (eds.), *Über Frauenleben, Männerwelt und Wissenschaft: Österreichische Texte zur Frauenforschung* (Vienna: Verlag für Gesellschaftskritik, 1987), 121–42.

popular Marxist-feminist novel *Der Tod des Märchenprinzen* (1980), in which the protagonist not only writes *Märchen* texts but also works on them as a student of German literature, while she learns to reject the familiar topos of Prince Charming:

> Die Hoffnung auf den Märchenprinzen war der Boden, auf den ich jahrelang gewandelt bin. . . . [Ich] [b]rauche den Märchenprinzen mit seinem Pferd nicht mehr.
>
> Wenn da mal wieder einer ankommt, zu Fuß, und zufällig in die gleiche Richtung will wie ich, dann können wir ja vielleicht zusammen gehen. Aber ich werde nicht mehr stehenbleiben, um auf einen zu warten.[44]

She also appreciates how the *Märchen* may be put to positive feminist use:

> Ich habe sowas im Kopf, mit Märchen auch politische Gedanken ausdrücken zu können. Es als literarische Form für heute zu nutzen, weil die Klischees noch sehr gut in den Köpfen abrufbar sind. Und das ist nicht nur rückwärts gerichtet. (pp. 149–50)

On the whole, though, much feminist *Märchen* criticism originated in the Anglo-American world, a fact which highlights the conservative nature of many academic approaches to *Märchen* in German-speaking countries, which seems to be due to the quasi-religious 'German obsession with fairy tales' identified by Zipes.

SHAHRAZAD AND 'DIE ALTE MARIE': THE *MÄRCHEN* AS A GENDERED NARRATIVE[45]

In a study of *Märchen*, the process of civilization, and gender politics, it is important to examine the changing ways in which the genre has been gendered. A key issue here is the traditional fantasy of the

---

[44] Svende Merian, *Der Tod des Märchenprinzen: Frauenroman* (1980) (Reinbek bei Hamburg: Rowohlt, 1983), 328.

[45] Shahrazad is the protagonist and narrator of the Arabic narrative cycle *The Arabian Nights*, ed. Muhsin Mahdi, trans. Husain Haddawy (New York and London: Norton, 1990). *The Thousand and One Nights*, as they are also known, were translated into French and so introduced to western Europe by Jean Antoine Galland in 1704–17, and translated into German by Talander (ps. August Boße) in 1712. See Wührl, *Das deutsche Kunstmärchen*, 41–2.

See Heinz Rölleke, 'Die "stockhessischen" Märchen der "alten Marie": Das Ende eines Mythos um die frühesten *KHM*-Aufzeichnungen der Brüder Grimm', *Germanisch-Romanische Monatsschrift*, 25 (1975), 74–86, on the fictionality of the Grimms' idealized depiction of this figure, long assumed to be a major *KHM* contributor. Hermann Rebel's article 'Why Not "Old Marie" . . . Or Someone Very Much Like Her? A Reassessment of the Question about the Grimms' Contributor from a Social Historical Perspective', *Social History*, 13 (1988), 1–24, defends the image of the simple peasant woman.

woman narrator. In *Der Tod des Märchenprinzen*, the protagonist is aware that she is taking and adapting a gendered genre. However, like the earlier feminist critics of the *KHM* and other familiar *Märchen*, Merian's character sees the genre solely as a vehicle for the specific, patriarchal ideology of Romantic Nationalism; and furthermore, she nowhere refers to the fact that *Märchen* texts by both women and men have been written within an older tradition of fictional women narrators of fairy tales, or cycles of tales centred on women narrators or groups of women in a tradition which reaches back as far as such early narrative cycles as the *Arabian Nights,* Giovan Francesco Straparola's *Le piacevoli notti* (1550), or Giambattista Basile's *Il Pentamerone* (1634–6).[46] In fact, the image of the woman narrator is equally familiar in German in the modern period too, as in the case of the Grimms' 'alte Marie' and recent scholarly controversies around her. And the eponymous Jewish protagonist of Jurek Becker's novel *Jakob der Lügner* (1969) observes, when he finds himself having to improvise a *Märchen*: 'Mein Gott, wie lange das her ist, fällt ihm ausgerechnet jetzt ein, für Märchen war der Vater nicht zuständig, die waren Mutters Sache.'[47] However, the importance of the woman narrator is a literary convention as much as a historical fact, since men too undoubtedly participated in traditional oral culture as well as women.[48] What is at issue here is, rather, a complex fantasy about the gender of narrative, whereby it has traditionally been imagined that there is something quintessentially feminine about telling fairy tales, and that the most appropriate mouthpiece—or persona—of fairy tale is a female figure. The discussion which follows, therefore, will focus on the literary topos of the *Märchenerzählerin* rather than on the cultural practices of historical women.

While the image of the woman teller of tales is enshrined in culture, her status is as ambivalent as it is sometimes prestigious. Marina Warner, for instance, in her recent study on women as tale-

[46] See Karen E. Rowe, 'To Spin a Yarn: The Female Voice in Folklore and Fairy Tale', in Bottigheimer, *Fairy Tales and Society*, 53–74; Blackwell, 'Fractured Fairy Tales'; Tatar, *Hard Facts*, 106–36; Jarvis, 'Literary Legerdemain', 21–44; and Marina Warner, *From the Beast to the Blonde: On Fairy Tales and Their Tellers* (London: Chatto & Windus, 1994).

[47] Jurek Becker, *Jakob der Lügner* (1969) (Frankfurt am Main: Suhrkamp, 1982), 171. It is a trivial indication of the tragedy and disruption inflicted on the Jewish community that the protagonist finds himself in the unaccustomed position of telling *Märchen*.

[48] See Bengt Holbek, *Interpretation of Fairy Tales* (Helsinki: Suomalainen Tiedeakatemia, 1987); for an account of how tale-telling is gendered and how folklorists have ignored women, see Ines Köhler-Zülch, 'Who Are the Tellers? Statements by Collectors and Authors', *Fabula*, 38 (1997), 199–209.

tellers, emphasizes the misogyny and prejudices which led to the unjust stereotyping of women's oral culture as 'old wives' tales' or *Ammenmärchen*, arguing that in many cases, the use of this female figure explicitly or implicitly serves the interests of the dominant, that is to say patriarchal, discourse. For instance, Warner remarks of male authors' tendency to use a female narrator to tell a story about wicked women:

attributing to women testimony about women's wrongs and wrongdoing gives them added value: men might be expected to find women flighty, rapacious, self-seeking, cruel and lustful, but if women say such things about themselves, then the matter is settled.[49]

And in a different way, Shahrazad in the *Arabian Nights* is another case in point. Shahrazad is intelligent, eloquent, brave, and in many senses a positive figure who becomes a role model for later writers and their female characters, such as Else Lasker-Schüler's Tino in *Die Nächte der Tino von Bagdad* (1907) or Irmtraud Morgner's Bele H. in *Hochzeit in Konstantinopel* (1968).[50] But the frame narrative in which Shahrazad, and by analogy Tino and Bele H., tell their stories is far from being one of straightforward empowerment. Shahrazad is allowed to remain alive only so long as she can entertain the king. Hence, because this constant threat lends a sinister subtext to the most brilliant of these narratives, when women writers like Morgner in *Hochzeit in Konstantinopel* refer to the figure of Sharazad, they are using a literary topos fraught with dangerous meaning, since in imitating Shahrazad, it is implied that Bele H. also lives in existential danger, even though that danger has taken on different forms in the twentieth century.[51]

The history of these women narrator figures and their 'old wives' tales' in European culture has also been traced by such critics as Maria M. Tatar, who suggests mythical and other origins of 'Mother

[49] Warner, *From the Beast to the Blonde*, 209.

[50] Else Lasker-Schüler, 'Die Nächte der Tino von Bagdad' (1907), in *Gesammelte Werke in einem Band: Lyrik, Prosa, Dramatisches*, ed. Sigrid Bauschinger (Munich: Artemis & Winkler, 1991), 112–37; Irmtraud Morgner, *Hochzeit in Konstantinopel* (1968) (Frankfurt am Main: Luchterhand, 1979).

[51] For instance, the analogy with Shahrazad gives the lie to the assessment of *Hochzeit in Konstantinopel* by Annemarie Auer, quoted on the jacket of a recent edition (Frankfurt am Main: Luchterhand, 1989). Auer calls the stories in this collection 'lockere Beischlaf-geschichten' and goes on to say: '[die Autorin geht] daran, ganz ruhig und freundlich und deutlich jene Sachen, die den Leuten Freude machen, beim Namen zu nennen.' Auer overlooks the disturbing intertextual reference of Morgner's stories to the *Arabian Nights*, which suggests that the situation of women in a modern patriarchal society is perilous.

Goose'. For example, in her analysis of nineteenth-century illustrations of the woman narrator of tales, Tatar points out significant iconographical changes. The frontispiece of the first edition of Perrault's *Histoires ou contes du temps passé* showed an old peasant woman spinning and telling tales to children who seem to be of a higher social class, and so appear to be her charges rather than her own children.[52] But while editions of children's tales in the advancing nineteenth century preserve the female figure, she becomes increasingly benevolent in aspect; signs of physical work and lower social class disappear, so that she comes to appear more like a relative of the children; and in Gustave Doré's representation of 1862, in which the woman narrator looks like a kindly grandmother, a book appears on her lap.[53] Tatar interprets the appearance of the book as showing the new dominance of print culture, a shift from recounting to reading, and from the workroom into the parlour and the bosom of the family.

Furthermore, it could be said that this shift undermines women's creativity because the woman narrator can no longer be thought to be making up her own tales, but reads out tales written by a male authority, in this case Perrault. In Doré's illustration, too, the woman narrator acquires spectacles. Among other things, this development seems to indicate that the woman not only needs intellectual and moral help in her duty of telling *Märchen* by means of a text written by a bourgeois, intellectual man, but also technological help to decipher that text. In her analysis of the changing views of the narrator, Jarvis sees such developments as symptomatic of the way in which *Märchen* were often used didactically in the nineteenth century to promote a model of the bourgeois family. With the rise of the nuclear family, the concomitant exclusion of servants from the newly invented *Kinderstube* and a new emphasis on a gender-specific division of labour whereby bringing up children and running a household gained a new moral status as Woman's only true vocation,[54] reading out *Märchen* became a middle-class mother's moral duty. Correspondingly, with the rise of the printed, literary *Märchen*, a jealously guarded masculine province, the previously active and autonomous female narrator-figure is assigned an increasingly passive and harmless role. One

---

[52] Tatar, *Hard Facts*, 108; Warner, *From the Beast to the Blonde*, p. ii.

[53] Tatar, *Hard Facts*, 111; Warner, *From the Beast to the Blonde*, 86.

[54] Cf. Ute Frevert, *Frauen-Geschichte: Zwischen Bürgerlicher Verbesserung und Neuer Weiblichkeit* (Frankfurt am Main: Suhrkamp, 1986).

way of imposing this role upon her is by incorporating her into the bourgeois family, as Tatar's findings show.

But while the woman narrator was domesticated in this manner, Jarvis identifies another strand in the development of the woman narrator figure, specifically within the German tradition. This development will prove intimately related to the founding theories of folk culture and the *Märchen* discussed above, and involves the demonization and defamation of a different kind of woman narrator, who comes to appear ever more suspect. With the institutionalization of the *Märchen* as a didactic instrument and its identification with the biological, nuclear family, the nurse, characterized as ignorant and lower-class, enjoyed an increasingly poor reputation as a being who was inferior to (male) producers of literary high culture. Jarvis quotes Wieland, writing in 1786: 'Ammenmärchen, im Ammenton erzählt, mögen sich durch mündliche Überlieferung fortpflanzen, aber gedruckt müssen sie nicht werden' (p. 35). By 1815, Albert Ludwig Grimm could write in the 'Vorrede für die Aeltern' in *Linas Mährchen-buch*:

> In kindlicher Einfachheit müssen freylich die Mährchen für Kinder erzählt werden. Aber dazu gehört ein ganz idealer Erzähler, den man nicht in der ersten besten Kindermagd unserer Tage findet; und fehlt dieser, so muß der Dichter seine Stelle vertreten.[55]

And in 1837 August Lewald continued and amplified this diffamatory tradition in a manner which corresponds to Jarvis's findings. In the introduction to his *Blaue Mährchen*, he describes 'ein liebes, heimathlich trautes Bild . . . das der guten Frau Gloniek, jener alten Polin, welche die Wärterin meiner jüngern Schwester war'. While this characterization is apparently affectionate, Lewald goes on to say:

> Den Ton jener Mährchen würde ich jedoch Anstand nehmen, hier zu wiederholen. . . . Ich glaube, daß selbst die Kinder von Heute nicht Stich halten würden, wenn eine alte, gelbe und runzelige Polin, im dunkeln Kattunrocke, eine große, bunte Haube auf den Kopfe, nicht unähnlich einer bösen Fee, wie sie in den Mährchen häufig geschildert wird, sich zum Ofen setzte und nun mit scharf prononcirtem slavischen Accente, stark mit plattdeutschen Redensarten untermischt, ihre Geschichten ziemlich weitschweifig anhebt.[56]

Not only is this woman lower-class and associated with the body in a negative way (she is 'gelb' and 'runzelig', and thus a harbinger of

---

[55] Jarvis, 'Literary Legerdemain', 35, 36.
[56] August Lewald, *Blaue Mährchen für alte und junge Kinder* (Stuttgart: Scheible, 1837), pp. v–vii.

mortality, a topos traditionally linked to the female body), but Lewald gives traditional suspicions a couple of new twists. First, this woman is Polish, thus of an ethnic origin which would have been perceived by many in Lewald's German audience as being inferior and 'other'. This ethnic origin helps justify Lewald's rejection of her narratives because of her linguistic failings of a strong, foreign accent and Low German dialect. Second, Lewald makes the implicit demonizing of this figure in the earlier texts quoted by Jarvis explicit, by comparing her to a 'böse Fee'. Third, and presumably as a result of that new explicitness, Lewald portrays Frau Gloniek as a figure from the past, a move designed to neutralize any threat she might pose and to ensure her irrelevance, since Lewald clearly subscribes to the typically nineteenth-century notion of rapid progress which will ensure that even one generation later, children will no longer take an interest in Frau Gloniek's tales. Lewald suggests not only that German children will have superior moral and aesthetic tastes which lead them to reject Polish stories but also that, in the space of just one generation, the woman's narratives will become obsolete. Which is to say that even the children of a later generation, who are implicitly more educated, German, and therefore superior, become legitimate arbiters of taste whose rejection of the adult Polish woman Frau Gloniek is justified.

The demonization of the woman narrator is explicitly and very neatly echoed in the purportedly distinct genre of the *Kunstmärchen*. Here too, women's narratives are repressed as subversive and harmful, as in E. T. A. Hoffmann's *Der Sandmann* (1816–17), where horror stories told by a nurse are identified as one possible cause of Nathanael's madness:

Voll Neugierde, Näheres von diesem Sandmann und seiner Beziehung zu uns Kindern zu erfahren, frug ich endlich die alte Frau, die meine jüngste Schwester wartete: was denn das für ein Mann sei, der Sandmann? 'Ei Thanelchen', erwiderte diese, '. . . Das ist ein böser Mann, der kommt zu den Kindern, wenn sie nicht zu Bett gehen wollen und wirft ihnen Händevoll Sand in die Augen, daß sie blutig zum Kopf herausspringen. . . . Gräßlich malte sich nun im Innern mir das Bild des grausamen Sandmanns aus; sowie es abends die Treppe herauf-polterte, zitterte ich vor Angst. . . . Schon alt genug war ich geworden, um einzusehen, daß das mit dem Sandmann . . . so wie es mir die Wartefrau erzählt hatte, wohl nicht ganz seine Richtigkeit haben könne; indessen blieb mir der Sandmann ein fürchterliches Gespenst.[57]

---

[57] E. T. A. Hoffmann, 'Der Sandmann', in Hoffmann, *Nachtstücke* (1816–17), cited here

The child has subsequently to be comforted by his good mother, who attempts to defuse the horror caused by the bad nurse with a rationalist dismissal. Here then, we see a graphic polarization of 'good' and 'bad' women's narratives, and the moral superiority of the written source over the oral, since the other tales told to the child Nathanael are those read to him from books by his father, which are described in positive terms. Nevertheless, the nurse's demonic narrative cannot be fully eradicated, since it returns uncannily in Nathanael's later life and kills him.

And the negative association of women and frightening, unreliable, or low-quality tale-telling has flourished in the twentieth century too. For instance, it is to this topos which Walter Benjamin implicitly referred in 'Über den Begriff der Geschichte' (published posthumously in 1942) when he wrote:

[der historische Materialist] überläßt es andern, bei der Hure 'Es war einmal' im Bordell des Historismus sich auszugeben. Er bleibt seiner Kräfte Herr: Manns genug, das Kontinuum der Geschichte aufzusprengen.[58]

Here, Benjamin is dramatizing his theoretical proposition by opposing to his hero, the heroic, emphatically male 'historische[r] Materialist', a pernicious female figure who personifies what Benjamin considers to be a dishonest, obfuscatory kind of historical narrative and who is characterized by the classic phrase of the *Märchenerzählerin*: 'Es war einmal'. This female figure is therefore closely related to those described above, but here Benjamin gives her the *coup de grâce* by additionally describing her as a whore. Thus here, the bad female narrator is not only lower-class, non-intellectual and potentially dangerous, she is also venal, and deceptive in her appearance, since, as a caricatured prostitute, she presumably paints her face, too. Accordingly, while the Grimms were still able to idealize the German woman tale-teller in the form of 'die alte Marie', Benjamin's characterization a century later signals a modern crisis in the romanticization of the *Volk* in the figure of the *Märchenerzählerin*.

In sum, the image of the female teller of tales was polarized by the imagination of the modern period, and of the nineteenth century in particular, into an angelic mother or grandmother who keeps to the

from *Sämtliche Werke*, ed. Wulf Segebrecht and Hartmut Steinecke, 6 vols. (Frankfurt am Main: Deutscher Klassiker Verlag, 1985), iii. 11–49 (13).

[58] Walter Benjamin, 'Über den Begriff der Geschichte', in *Gesammelte Schriften*, ed. Rolf Tiedemann and Hermann Schweppenhäuser, 7 vols. (Frankfurt am Main: Suhrkamp, 1991), i. 2, 691–704 (702).

book and a demonic figure, usually of lower social origin. This latter figure is gradually suppressed as a written *Märchen* culture develops, but she does not disappear, and because she is no blood relation to the child, she is under no ideological obligation to be good. The status of such a lower-class figure in the bourgeois sphere is that of a servant or a nurse, who re-emerges in literature as an ominous messenger, and so she stands for the return of those threatening principles that have been repressed by the good narrator.

One evident reason for this domestication, demonization, and occlusion of the traditional image of the female narrator is to be found in Herder's 'script' for folklore. It has been argued that in Herder's view, 'the quintessential nation constitutes a culturally homogeneous, organic whole within a stratified, patriarchal form of social organisation much like the nuclear family on which it is modelled; Herder conceived of the nation literally and figuratively as a family writ large'.[59] And for Herder, since 'patriarchy represents nothing less than the "natural order" of the world',[60] both the nation and the family were to be ruled by fathers. In this view, cultural production, national identity, and even civilization itself were patriarchal; conversely, femininity represented a lack of civilization. Accordingly, Herder imagined that the transmission of authentic culture could occur only in a patrilinear manner, and this idea is reflected in the quotation from the Grimms' *KHM* 'Vorrede' above, which describes a transmission of culture from 'Großvater' to 'Enkel'. That notion is taken up in turn by commentators on the Grimms, who use the image of the 'founding fathers' most explicitly and literally, as when Merkel comments: 'Das Märchen ist ein Schoßkind der Forschung gewesen, seit die Brüder Grimm es aus der wissenschaftlichen Taufe hoben' (p. 202).

These ideas explain why Jarvis concludes: 'anything that smacked of the oral source, i.e. the product of women, had to be improved by men' (p. 35), that is, because feminine narratives can threaten the basic conventions of the patriarchal 'script'. And indeed, it has been shown that this is not only a matter of literary topoi; in terms of fieldwork, too, later German folklorists have tended to obscure women's oral culture in favour of men's in quite spectacular ways.[61] More broadly too, Amy Shuman has demonstrated how the very

---

[59] Fox, 'The Creator Gods', 32.
[60] Ibid. 34.
[61] See Köhler-Zülch, 'Who Are the Tellers?'.

notion of genre in folklore is gendered in a manner which tends to disregard cultural forms associated with women.[62]

WOMEN WRITING *MÄRCHEN*

Die langen Finger

Es lebte einmal eine junge Frau in Australien. Ihre Schreibmaschine aber befand sich in Afrika. Zum Glück hatte diese Frau so lange Finger, daß diese von Australien bis Afrika reichten. Sie mußte sehr viel schreiben auf der so weit entfernten Schreibmaschine. Eines Tages passierte es, daß ein großer, schwerer Riese über ihre Finger ging, und dabei brachen sie. Ach wie war das furchtbar. Nun konnte sie nicht mehr schreiben!

Elisabeth Werthmann, 9 Jahre, Schülerin in Salzburg[63]

Herder's 'script' for a German culture did not only marginalize and demonize the fictional woman narrator and lead German folklorists from the nineteenth century onward systematically to omit and even deny the existence of the oral culture of women.[64] It also affected the way in which the production of literary *Märchen* by women was marginalized and suppressed. Jarvis quotes the following dedication by Gisela von Arnim of a *Märchen* to her prospective father-in-law, Wilhelm Grimm, in 1856. It is a story which Grimm, she writes, addressing him in the second person singular,

als Mährchenvater gütig aufnehmen must. Es ist einer Kinderfrau im Haus hier abgelauscht. Sie hatte zwei große Warzen, in der einen war Pfantasie in der andern Oriegienalietaet, und das Mährchenkind, da es immer alte Weiber zu kennen hat—hat sich an diesen beiden Brüsten recht satt getrunken,—und ist zu beifolgender Geschichte gekommen, die ich Dir hier zu Füßen lege. (p. 1)

Not only is the *Märchenamme* now made dependent on a male, academic authority figure for her legitimization, but this quotation is interesting too because of what it tells us about the woman author herself. It is clear that she wants to distance herself explicitly from the production of *Märchen*, and so invents another, lower-class source for it. More precisely, it seems to me that in this quotation von Arnim is actively splitting off from her own persona as author all those aspects

---

[62] 'Gender and Genre', in Hollis et al., *Feminist Theory and the Study of Folklore*, 71–85.

[63] Folke Tegetthoff (ed.), *Das rot-weiss-rote Wolkenschiff: Märchen aus unser Zeit* (Vienna: Österreichischer Bundesverlag, 1985), 11.

[64] See Köhler-Zülch, 'Who Are the Tellers?'.

of femininity which appear traditionally suspect and projecting them onto the nurse figure: 'Pfantasie', 'Oriegienalietaet' (i.e. eccentricity and irrationality), maternity, and the body. That is, von Arnim is sensing that there is something wrong with being a woman writer of tales and so she denies her own authorship. And it seems that the idea of women writing *Märchen* in Germany today (or indeed writing at all) is still stigmatized, since a contemporary authority such as Marcel Reich-Ranicki seems to be permitted such remarks as: 'In Deutschland sind Literatinnen doch nur verhuschte Wesen, die ständig in Ohnmacht fallen und Lyrisch-Märchenhaftes von sich geben. Gräßlich!'[65] While this comment does not have a wholly reliable source, since it was quoted without chapter and verse in *Der Spiegel*, the point is less whether or not it was actually made and in what context, but more that it is clearly thought plausible that it *could* have been made.

Despite the influential activity of women writers, there is no doubt about the real historical suppression of *Märchen* by women, as bibliographies in some studies make clear.[66] For instance, the many *Märchen* texts by the women in the von Arnim family were ignored until recently,[67] as were such writers as Naubert, Elsa Bernstein (alias Ernst Rosmer) (1866–1949), Hermynia Zur Mühlen (1878–1951), and Irmtraud Morgner (1933–90). As a recent study notes of Naubert:

> a certain anonymity still surrounds the *Neue Volksmährchen der Deutschen*. . . . Even scholarship on the *Märchen* of this period fails to recognize the implications of Naubert's combined work with *Volksmärchen* and historical fiction. Frequently her *Volksmärchen* are eclipsed by the wider reputation of works by Musäus or later, Romantic, authors.[68]

---

[65] Quoted in *Der Spiegel*, 47 (40) (4 Oct. 1993), 279.

[66] Dorothea Bäuerle, 'Das nachromantische Kunstmärchen in der deutschen Dichtung', Ph.D. dissertation (Würzburg, 1937); Ellen Pröpstl, 'Neuromantische Prosamärchendichtung', Ph.D. dissertation (Munich, 1950); Brigitte Ewe, 'Das Kunstmärchen in der Jugendliteratur des 20. Jahrhunderts', Ph.D. dissertation (Munich, 1965); Bernd Dolle-Weinkauff, *Das Märchen in der proletarisch-revolutionären Kinder- und Jugendliteratur der Weimarer Republik, 1918–33* (Frankfurt am Main: Dipa, 1984); Wührl, *Das deutsche Kunstmärchen*; Blackwell, 'Fractured Fairy Tales'; Grätz, *Das Märchen in der deutschen Aufklärung*.

[67] Jarvis, 'Spare the Rod and Spoil the Child: Bettine's *Das Leben der Hochgräfin Gritta von Rattenzuhausbeiuns*', and Edith Waldstein, 'Romantic Revolution and Female Collectivity: Bettina von Arnim's *Gritta*', *Women in German Yearbook*, 3 (1986), 77–91 and 92–101 respectively; Blackwell, 'Fractured Fairy Tales'; Gisela and Bettine von Arnim, *Das Leben der Hochgräfin Gritta von Rattenzuhausbeiuns: Erste vollständige Ausgabe, mit 17 Zeichnungen von Gisela von Arnim und Herman Grimm*, ed. Shawn Jarvis (Frankfurt am Main: Insel, 1987); Gisela von Arnim, *Märchenbriefe an Achim*, ed. Jarvis (Frankfurt am Main: Insel, 1991).

[68] William Wilton Anthony, 'The Narration of the Marvelous in the Late Eighteenth-

And on the occasion of a new production of the neglected opera *Königskinder*, Peter Skrine has recently observed of its librettist Elsa Bernstein:

What is inexplicable and deeply disturbing is the fact that her dramatic output has sunk almost without trace. The reason can hardly lie in the plays themselves. Their quality and scope make her the finest woman dramatist in German literature. Could their neglect be due to an anti-feminist bias in a literary culture which even today is undeniably male-dominated? Here, today, *Königskinder* will be billed as the work of Humperdinck . . . But it is worth remembering that when Elsa's father secured him to write the music for his daughter's play, the composer was only too pleased to accept the challenge.[69]

Of course, the voice of Bernstein, who, as a Jewish woman, was in later life persecuted and interned in Theresienstadt by the National Socialists, has been suppressed in the most scandalous of ways due to anti-Semitism. However, her obscurity today does fit in also with the marginalization of writing by women described here. And of the GDR authorities' reception of Morgner it has been said:

Mit der *Amanda* . . . habe es massive Probleme bei der Veröffentlichung gegeben . . . Ungestraft konnten Aussagen wie: Auch die DDR sei eine patriarchale Gesellschaft, oder: Patriarchale Gesellschaften seien an Kriegen interessiert—nicht passieren. Zweieinhalb Jahre seien zwischen der Fertigstellung und dem Erscheinen der *Amanda* vergangen, sie habe vieles ändern müssen und sei schließlich so fertig gewesen, daß sie massive Sehstörungen bekommen habe . . . So habe genau zu ihrem 50. Geburtstag ein 'Kollege' im *Neuen Deutschland* verkündet, das Thema der Frauenbefreiung sei nun passé . . . Und alle, die weiter über dieses Thema schrieben, seien Männer- und Kinderfeinde.[70]

Given this background, it is unsurprising that, despite the existence of a rich corpus of *Märchen* texts by women writers, the canon of familiar primary texts shows a bias towards masculinity, in terms both of the authors it favours and of the themes involved. Because of that canon, the literary *Märchen* that are best known today are by not

[69] Peter Skrine, 'Elsa Bernstein and *Königskinder*', in the programme to the English National Opera production of *Königskinder or The Prince and the Goosegirl*, ed. Nicholas John (London: ENO, 1991–2).

[70] Dorothee Schmitz-Köster, 'Hexen, Weltfahrer und die schöne Melusine: Annäherung an Irmtraud Morgner', in *Irmtraud Morgners hexische Weltfahrt: Eine Zeitmontage*, ed. Kristine von Soden (Berlin: Elefanten-Press, 1991), 16. See also Alice Schwarzer, *Warum gerade sie? Weibliche Rebellen: 15 Begegnungen mit berühmten Frauen* (Frankfurt am Main: Luchterhand, 1989), 22–3.

only by men; they may also function as fantastic *Bildungsromane* for the enactment of masculine concerns or the creation of masculine identities. This tradition is evident as early as the quest of the protagonist in Novalis's novel *Heinrich von Ofterdingen* (1802):

Gewiß ist der Traum, den ich heute Nacht träumte, kein unwirksamer Zufall in meinem Leben gewesen, denn ich fühle es, daß er in meiner Seele wie ein weites Rad hineingreift, und sie im mächtigen Schwunge forttreibt.[71]

And it is perpetuated in the sentimental and political education of all manhood traced in Grass's novel *Der Butt* (1977).[72] Here, female figures are generally instrumentalized constructions of alterity which serve the search for masculine identity; to paraphrase Goethe, 'Das Ewig-Weibliche bildet uns aus'. In Heinrich's prophetic dream referred to above, 'Die Flut schien eine Auflösung reizender Mädchen, die an dem Jünglinge sich augenblicklich verkörperten' (p. 242). And in *Der Butt*, as the protagonist waits at the edge of the sea for his female companion:

Es dämmerte schon, als sich Maria mit dem Butt ausgesprochen hatte. . . . Dann kam sie langsam ihren Spuren entgegen. Doch nicht Maria kam zurück. Es wird Dorothea sein, sorgte ich mich. Als sie mir Schritt nach Schritt größer wurde, hoffte ich auf Agnes. Das war nicht Sophies Gang. Kommt Billy, die arme Sibylle zurück?

Ilsebill kam. Sie übersah, überging mich. Schon war sie an mir vorbei. Ich lief ihr nach. (p. 556)

The similarity between these passages is striking. Both male protagonists are at a liminal point in their search for the meaning of life, formulated as a historical quest: Novalis's hero is at its beginning and Grass's at its end. In both cases, the protagonist, a unified physical and psychological subject, encounters in his search a supernatural or near-supernatural feminine principle, associated with the fluid element of water, which takes on individual identity on coming into contact with the male subject.[73] Thus, as Zipes sums up:

Though we tend to think of fairy tales as part of the female domain, as belonging to the household and childrearing, it is the tailors [a reference to Heinrich

---

[71] Novalis (Friedrich von Hardenberg), *Heinrich von Ofterdingen*, in *Heinrich von Ofterdingen und andere dichterische Schriften* (Cologne: Könemann, 1996), 227–412 (236).

[72] Günter Grass, *Der Butt* (1977) (Frankfurt am Main: Fischer, 1979).

[73] Water is a typical topos for representing Otherness, e.g. the Feminine or the Unconscious: Hartmut Böhme, 'Umriß einer kulturgeschichte des Wassers. Eine Einleitung', in *Kulturgeschichte des Wassers*, ed. Böhme (Frankfurt am Main: Suhrkamp, 1988), 7–42.

Heine's uncomplimentary description of Hans Christian Andersen] who have reigned in the fairy tale tradition. To be sure, there were some remarkable female writers of fairy tales from the beginning . . . But, by and large, the development of the literary genre has taken place within a discourse established by male writers . . . the genre as an institution operates to safeguard basic male interests and conventions against which various writers, male and female, have rebelled. The dialogue remains open, but only under certain institutionalized conditions that have been largely set by men of bourgeois culture.[74]

In the last two or three decades, feminist scholarship has un-covered multiple reasons for the exclusion of women's texts from the canon. These reasons are social, political, and psychological but are often passed off as aesthetic, as Lewald does in the case of Frau Gloniek's accent, which he uses as a pretext for suppressing her voice, which is in fact disruptive for more serious reasons. Jarvis illuminates the political reasons for the suppression of the female voice by quoting Zipes, and concluding that such 'male interests' must be missing from many *Märchen* texts by women, as they docu-ment a non-dominant experience, or may provide a subversive critique, of culture.[75] And in the particular case of *Märchen*, a further reason for the marginalization of women writers is Herder's patri-archal 'script' for the genre; another important related factor is the dominance of one text in this tradition which has been shown to codify most clearly nineteenth-century bourgeois values, i.e. the *KHM*. As scholars have shown, this collection was compiled in the interest of an ideological programme which, following Herder's lead, is in many respects not reconcilable with feminist or proto-feminist aims.[76] As a result, tales which somehow challenge the norms which were codified by the Grimms, by exhibiting formal or thematic features which deviate from that norm, are excluded from scholarly discussion. And given Jarvis's argument that *Märchen* by women are more likely to be eccentric to dominant cultural trends, they are more likely too to deviate from such dominant formal or stylistic norms.

However, Zipes's suggestion that the whole *Märchen* genre is wholly male-dominated and stabilizing is not wholly accurate. Jarvis points out also that more women have produced *Märchen* than men and that, while these texts have not been canonized and are now

[74] Zipes, *The Brothers Grimm*, 23–4.
[75] Jarvis, 'Literary Legerdemain', 171.
[76] e.g. Bottigheimer, *Grimms' Bad Girls and Bold Boys*; Ellis, *One Fairy Tale Too Many*.

forgotten, they were tremendously influential in the popular culture of their day, as in the case of E[ugenie]. Marlitt's writing (albeit ostensibly in a different genre), to be discussed later in this study. And furthermore, as Zipes himself has argued elsewhere, there also exist classic *Märchen* texts by men which deploy the Fantastic and other unconventional narrative modes in a subversive manner.[77] The original Bluebeard tale, Perrault's 'La Barbe bleue', with all its ambivalences and utopian force, is, as we shall see, a case in point, as are Ludwig Tieck's versions of 'Blaubart'. And indeed, the very originary 'script' of German folklore itself is less monolithic and closed to contradiction than meets the eye. Fox points out that in his conceptualization of a patriarchal folk culture, Herder was in fact initiating a major shift in thinking about nature, the nation, and gender (pp. 37–8). On one hand, nature, the (mother)land, and things associated with those concepts, like folk culture and the mother tongue, are traditionally imagined as being feminine, hence the traditional power of the image of Mother Goose or the *Märchentante*. Herder, on the other hand, precisely because these concepts were so important to him, masculinized them, producing the alternative and more innovative notion of the Fatherland and a native, patriarchal, and patrilinear culture. Thus, due to his influential theoretical intervention and successful regendering of oral culture as masculine rather than feminine, Herder's theory in fact inadvertently reveals the cultural, constructed nature of both the old and the new views— and therefore the fact that the relationship of gender and culture is in no way fixed but, rather, constantly open to changes.

It can be argued, too, that the *Märchen* is particularly well suited to the subversion of dominant cultural conventions. This genre, and by analogy the feminine narrative voice of the *Märchentante*, is closely linked with the Fantastic, a narrative mode which often explodes the familiar boundaries of culture. Rosemary Jackson suggests that

> fantastic literature points to or suggests the basis upon which cultural order rests, for it opens up . . . on to disorder, on to illegality, on to that which lies outside the law . . . the fantastic traces the unsaid and the unseen of culture: that which has been silenced, made invisible, covered over and made 'absent'.[78]

This 'unsaid' and 'unseen' is traditionally the domain identified with

[77] Jack D. Zipes, 'The Revolutionary Rise of the Romantic Fairy Tale in Germany', *Studies in Romanticism*, 16 (1977), 409–50.

[78] Rosemary Jackson, *Fantasy: The Literature of Subversion* (1981) (London: Routledge, 1988), 4.

the feminine in Western culture, a 'dark continent' to Sigmund Freud and even to such recent theoreticians as Jacques Lacan.[79] And the demonic old narrator and her tales, although repressed, 'unsaid', and 'unseen', do not, as my opening quotation from the Grimms suggests, simply disappear. There is always a disruptive return of the repressed, as the passage quoted above from *Der Sandmann* illustrates. Similarly, Grass's poem in *Die Rättin* on the demise of the *Märchen* quoted above ends not with closure but with a suggestion of precisely such a return of the *Märchen*:

> die Märchen [gehen] zufuß in die Städte
> und böse aus.

The submerged or repressed tales told by the old woman narrator, far from being silenced or unsaid, may, like the Fantastic, have a powerful subversive potential. For example, the editors of an anthology of English-language fairy tales by women reveal how that demonic figure may unexpectedly re-emerge in the civilized world of the nursery in a suggestive reading of the scene in Virginia Woolf's *To the Lighthouse* (1927) in which the docile, civilized Mrs Ramsay tells fairy tales:

Woolf . . . makes us aware of moralistic male revisions of female journeys. Like the fictional Shahrazad . . . and like the imaginative woman punished in the Grimm tale, Mrs. Ramsay struggles against male narrative power. She invests herself with magic by promising her son a 'passage' to a distant tower in a 'fabled land', but her magic and the promised voyage are illusory. Mrs. Ramsay is not one of those weavers and spinners traditionally associated with the fairies or fays and their pagan ancestors, the Fates. Her knitting and her journey will be left undone until her husband claims them. . . . The dissipation of Mrs. Ramsay's magic into a cautionary tale punishing an overweening wife is a symptom of the violated female tradition whose restoration Woolf urges in her great address to the next generation of women writers, 'A Room of One's Own'.[80]

However, despite the domestication of Mrs Ramsay, Woolf's narrative subverts the canonical discourse because it involves the return of a repressed which was never truly absent, with attendant

---

[79] Jacques Lacan, *Le Séminaire livre XX: Encore*, ed. Jacques-Alain Miller (Paris: Seuil, 1975); Kaja Silverman, *The Subject of Semiotics* (Oxford: Oxford University Press, 1983), 126–93, esp. 186–7.

[80] Nina Auerbach and Ulrich C. Knoepflmacher, *Forbidden Journeys: Fairy Tales and Fantasies by Victorian Women Writers* (Chicago: University of Chicago Press, 1992), 7. The 'Grimm tale' referred to is *KHM* 19, 'Von dem Fischer un syner Fru', i. 119–26, a narrative to which *Der Butt* and *Die Rättin* also refer.

subterfuges and displaced narrative strategies. In this scene of the novel, too, there is a submerged counterpoint to the figure of Mrs Ramsay, 'an old woman in the kitchen with very red cheeks, drinking soup out of a basin', and it is argued that this figure, the polarized opposite of the angelic Mrs Ramsay, is a 'herald of restoration' of a tradition involving strong female figures who defy the convention of tamed femininity.

The final part of this chapter will consider how, in the hands of women writers in particular, the *Märchen* may seek to change or subvert dominant cultural 'scripts', theoretical reflections to which this study will return. When women write *Märchen*, they are appropriating a genre or narrative which is gender-marked and which in its more familiar, recent manifestations often promotes masculinist ideology and consciousness. But at the same time they are also entering a narrative tradition which involves the powerful if problematic fantasy of the woman narrator, and a submerged tradition of women writers. There is a broad range of possible responses to this situation, and of course many women authors of *Märchen* may reproduce dominant conventions. However, feminist critics like Jarvis and Blackwell have shown compellingly with reference to *Märchen* by women writers of the eighteenth and nineteenth centuries that women may, like Woolf, often challenge such dominant conventions in the *Märchen* in various ways. For instance, women writers may be aware of the subversive potential of enchantment and use the *Märchen* to encode messages opposing or subverting the dominant discourse *à la* Grimm. They may, for example, write *Märchen* in such a way as to highlight patriarchal conventions critically. One more recent instance of such a case, demonstrating the consistency of the tradition highlighted by Jarvis and Blackwell, is Morgner's novel *Leben und Abenteuer der Trobadora Beatriz* (1974), which picks up familiar *Märchen* motifs and reverses them, for instance in retelling the tale of 'Dornröschen' from the point of view of the sleeping beauty Beatriz. And another woman teller of *Märchen* in that novel actively defends the subversive potential of tales which she writes herself, significantly enough, on the back of scientific papers. It is important to note that for that character, this medium is a counterpoint to, not a rejection of, rationalist scientific discourse, since she is a scientist herself who would reject the idea that rationality and femininity might be opposed. When her partner criticizes her for her interest in *Märchen* she defends herself as follows:

Er sagte: 'Phantasterei ist Flucht, ein Zeichen für Kapitulation.' Ich sagte: 'Im Gegenteil, sie ist ein Zeichen von Souveränität. Ja, von souveränem Wirtschaften mit den Gegenständen der Realität, wie Kinder es beispielsweise in ihren Zeichnungen tun.' . . . Meine Märchen nannte er 'Gegenbilder'. Es war ein erbitterter Streit. . . . Ich antwortete ihm zum Beispiel, meine Märchen wären Aktionen, keine Modelle.[81]

The emphasis on 'Aktionen' here is a reminder that, just as culture is always in process, so too must strategies of resistance against its negative aspects be.

Finally, Jarvis and Blackwell have identified a conscious or unconscious awareness among women writers that *Märchen* can be imagined as feminine narrative property, and a corresponding emphasis in writing by women on the act of tale-telling by women. This awareness may involve a stress on the figure of the woman narrator, or on an alternative feminine or feminist community, as in the works of such writers as Bettine and Gisela von Arnim and Benedikte Naubert. And again, demonstrating the continuity of that tradition, a contemporary instance of the same phenomenon is to be found in Helke Sander's book *Die Geschichten der drei Damen K.* (1987), in which a supportive female narrative community is invoked when three women spend a holiday together:

Nachts aber, wenn sie sich gegenseitig schlafend glaubten, war bisweilen das leise Weinen der Frau K. aus der Kammer zu hören, oder Frau K. im Wohnzimmer schrie in ihrem Alptraum nach dem Mann, der sie verlassen hatte, und auch die dritte Frau K. wälzte sich stöhnend im Bett. Jede der drei Damen K. behielt das von den anderen Preisgegebene für sich, aus Takt. . . . Um sich vor den grausamen Nächten zu schützen und sie so lange wie möglich hinauszuschieben, begannen sie, sich an den Abenden Geschichten zu erzählen. . . . Die Geschichten sollten im Kern wahr sein, und den traurigen sollten die lustigen Seiten abgewonnen werden.[82]

This situation recalls the frame narrative of the *Arabian Nights*, in which a woman uses narrative to protect herself and other women from the dangers of the night, and the sociable frame narratives of the early Italian cycles of tales, as well as the seventeenth-century feminine French salon culture which produced the *conte de fées* on which German *Märchen* were modelled. Here, Sander adapts those traditional conventions in order to demonstrate a model of feminist

---

[81] Irmtraud Morgner, *Leben und Abenteuer der Trobadora Beatriz nach Zeugnissen ihrer Spielfrau Laura* (1974) (Berlin: Aufbau, 1989), 332–3.

[82] Helke Sander, *Die Geschichten der drei Damen K.* (Munich: Frauenbuchverlag, 1987), 7–8.

solidarity. Thus, it seems that while the feminine voice has been suppressed in the *Märchen* canon, women nonetheless make productive and sometimes subversive use of the *Märchen*. Consequently, the chapters of this study which look at texts by women will ask whether strategies such as those outlined here are implemented.

This chapter has shown that the *Märchen* is a literary creation and that, like all literary texts and genres, it changes over time and reflects its historical period. To overlook this aspect of the *Märchen* is to occlude its potential both as an account of its time and as a potentially critical or subversive narrative, issues which will be addressed in this study. Moreover, the familiar *Märchen* canon is skewed, in terms both of the authors on which it focuses and of the forms, themes and values which it privileges. Most broadly, albeit with exceptions, it can be said that to engage with the *Märchen* is to engage with a gendered tradition which in the past has tended to promote a masculinist canon, to suppress or discredit the feminine narrator as well the female author, and often to socialize the female reader in a manner which serves patriarchal interests. This study will challenge those conventions by including in my discussion texts which fall outside the traditional canon.

So, despite the familiar topos of the 'death', fragmentation or redundancy of the *Märchen*, to address the genre today is to enter into a dialogue with an immense, flourishing literary and critical tradition. Thus, just as Hans Arp's Kaspar in the poem 'kaspar ist tot', quoted above, proves ultimately not to be dead but to have been transformed into more elusive forms, so too has the *Märchen*. And now, this study of such transformations of the tale of Bluebeard will begin at the beginning, with a discussion of Perrault's original *conte*.

2

BLUEBEARD—A SUBVERSIVE NARRATIVE: SOME THEORETICAL IDEAS

Bluebeard as we know him first appeared in Paris in 1695 as 'La Barbe bleue', in the manuscript version of Charles Perrault's *Histoires ou contes du temps passé*, a collection which was to become a seminal influence on the evolution of fairy tale. In this most murderous of tales, the third in Perrault's volume, the eponymous villain is a wealthy *grand bourgeois* who has a blue beard: 'cela le rendait si laid et si terrible, qu'il n'était ni femme ni fille qui ne s'enfuit de devant lui.'[1] And young women's initial fears of him turn into a more emphatic disgust: 'Ce qui les dégoûtait encore, c'est qu'il avait déjà épousé plusieurs femmes, et qu'on ne savait ce que ces femmes étaient devenues' (p. 257). Nonetheless, by dint of a display of wealth, Bluebeard persuades the younger daughter of his lady neighbour to overcome her fear and marry him. After a month of marriage, Bluebeard announces that he must leave for some weeks and makes a great show of generosity in giving his wife his keys and urging her to make use of all that is his. This generosity is, however, accompanied by a prohibition on one room, to which the wife is nonetheless given the key. On Bluebeard's departure, the wife's female friends and relatives arrive, but her own first thought is to examine the forbidden room—which proves to be full of blood and to contain the dead bodies of Bluebeard's previous wives hung up on the walls in a perverse display.[2] In her fright the woman drops the key into the blood on the floor. As the key is 'Fée', it cannot be cleaned, and, on Bluebeard's alarmingly sudden return, he sees what has occurred. He

---

[1] Charles Perrault, *Contes*, ed. Marc Soriano (Paris: Flammarion, 1989), 257–62 (257), including an account of the minor differences between the MS and the first edition.

[2] This image is practically never included in illustrations; cf. Maria Tatar, *The Hard Facts of the Grimms' Fairy Tales* (Princeton, NJ: Princeton University Press, 1987), 162–3. This omission is an aspect of the selective censorship of the *Blaubartmärchen*, but one exception in the German tradition is in Ernst Lausch, 'Vom Ritter Blaubart', in *Das Buch der schönsten Kinder- und Volksmärchen, Sagen und Schwänke* (Leipzig: Spamer, 1876), 221–4 (223). Examples of illustrations are in Tatar, *Hard Facts*; Hartwig Suhrbier, *Blaubarts Geheimnis* (Cologne: Diederichs, 1984); Marina Warner, *From the Beast to the Blonde: On Fairy Tales and Their Tellers* (London: Chatto & Windus, 1994).

threatens to kill his bride, but she persuades him to grant her a brief respite for prayer, which she is able to prolong in the hope of rescue. But during this respite, the woman does not pray at all, but, less resignedly, conducts a highly dramatic dialogue with her helpful sister Anne, who is posted on the tower to watch for the women's two brothers who are due to visit. Just as time finally seems to be running out and Bluebeard has caught his wife by the hair and is swinging his cutlass, the brothers burst in and kill him; his widow inherits and buys her brothers officers' commissions; enables her sister to marry; and finally makes a good marriage herself to 'un fort honnête homme, qui lui fit oublier le mauvais temps qu'elle avait passé avec la Barbe bleue' (p. 262).

Perrault adds two verse 'Moralités' to this account. In the first he criticizes curiosity in both men and women, and in the second he stresses that his tale '[e]st un conte du temps passé', since in present-day marriages it is hard to tell who is master. Bluebeard's first emergence in manuscript form was followed in 1697 by the publication of *Histoires ou contes du temps passé* and, due to that volume's immediate popularity and its influence on popular culture, Perrault's codification of the Bluebeard material remains the most familiar one to the present day, not only in French but in German and English versions as well.

CURIOSITY, KNOWLEDGE, AND POWER

Whilst Perrault was eager to stress, in the first verse *moralité* appended to 'La Barbe bleue', that curiosity is a vice deplorable in both sexes, his tale actually involves a strongly gendered cultural narrative about curiosity and knowledge in Western culture, and it is to these resonances that the text owes much of its fascination. In the modern period, what is a heroic drive for knowledge in a man is either vicious curiosity or madness in a woman, for which she will be punished, as the juxtaposition of two quotations from Goethe's *Faust II* (1832) and Ludwig Tieck's (albeit parodic) play *Ritter Blaubart* (1797) shows:

MEPHISTOPHELES.   Versinke denn! Ich könnt' auch sagen: steige!
'   's ist einerlei. Entfliehe dem Entstandnen
'   In der Gebilde losgebundne Reiche!
'   Ergetze dich am längst nicht mehr Vorhandnen;
'   Wie Wolkenzüge schlingt sich das Getreibe,

Den Schlüssel schwinge, halte sie vom Leibe!

FAUST.   Wohl! fest ihn fassend fühl ich neue Stärke,
                Die Brust erweitert, hin zum großen Werke.³

Das Weib, das neugierig ist, kann ihrem Mann nicht treu sein. Der Mann, der ein neugieriges Weib hat, ist in keiner Stunde seines Lebens sicher. Neugier ist die Sünde, die jede andere nach sich zieht . . .⁴

In both *Faust II* and 'Bluebeard', privileged access to knowledge is provided by a highly symbolic key. Thus, the key which Faust is given has amazing tumescent qualities:

MEPHISTOPHELES.   . . . Hier diesen kleinen Schlüssel nimm.
FAUST.   Das kleine Ding!
MEPHISTOPHELES.   Erst faß ihn an und schätz ihn nicht gering.
FAUST.   Er wächst in meiner Hand! (p. 192)

Because the key serves as a weapon to protect Faust from 'die Mütter' whom he is about to visit, it functions as a masculine talisman against an archaic, possibly castrating feminine power. Indeed, the physical reality of this threat is implicit in the expression 'vom Leibe halten' in the first quotation from *Faust II*. And in German the key is a particularly appropriate symbol for Bluebeard, since in German the 'bit' (on the business or penetrating end of a key) is known as a 'Bart', and generations of pre- and post-Freudian writers and illustrators have interpreted it as a phallic symbol.⁵ The Grimms' *Deutsches Wörterbuch* also makes clear that the beard is a marker of masculine authority, both divine and societal.⁶ In other words, in Goethe's text and 'Bluebeard' knowledge appears to be gendered because it is intimately associated with powerful phallic symbols owned by a male figure; and it is no coincidence that the phallic beard and phallic key should be singled out as the magical elements in the 'Bluebeard' narratives.

³ Johann Wolfgang von Goethe, *Faust. Zweiter Teil*, in *Werke, Kommentare und Register. Hamburger Ausgabe*, ed. Erich Trunz, 14 vols. (Munich: Beck, 1981), iii. 146–364 (193).

⁴ Ludwig Tieck, *Der Blaubart. Ein Märchen in fünf Akten* (1797) in *Schriften*, ed. Manfred Frank et al., 12 vols. (Frankfurt am Main: Deutscher Klassiker Verlag, 1985), vi. 394–483 (477).

⁵ In *Die Traumdeutung* (1900), referring to the key as the most obvious of phallic symbols, Freud wrote: 'Welcher Schlüssel das Zimmer aufsperrt, braucht dann nicht ausdrücklich gesagt zu werden': *Studienausgabe*, ed. Alexander Mitscherlich, Angela Richards, and James Strachey, 11 vols. (Frankfurt am Main: Fischer, 1989), ii. 349. See also Warner, *From the Beast to the Blonde*, 244.

⁶ Jacob Grimm and Wilhelm Grimm, *Deutsches Wörterbuch*, 16 vols. (Leipzig: Hirzel, 1804–78), i. 1142.

While in the early modern, anonymous *Historia von D. Johann Fausten* (1587) the masculine search for knowledge was condemned, from Goethe's *Faust* onwards this pattern was reversed and the curious Faust became a hero. But the West also knows a parallel tradition which marks out as a sinner a woman who seeks knowledge and in which no comparable moral reversal takes place. This tradition is exemplified in the early sixteenth-century Dutch mystery play *Mariken van Nieumeghen*, in which the eponymous protagonist makes a pact with the Devil to acquire knowledge. Although she is saved by divine intervention at the last minute, within the metaphysical schema of the Christian play there is no doubt that she has perpetrated evil.[7] And, in contrast to the case of *Faust*, this fraught relation of women and knowledge is not resolved even today. For instance, in the Dutch author Connie Palmen's acclaimed novel *De Wetten (The Laws)* (1991), a modern reworking of *Mariken van Nieumeghen*, the protagonist, a woman philosopher, is driven to a near-annihilating breakdown in her pursuit of knowledge which only men possess.[8]

A similar theme runs through the film *Picnic at Hanging Rock* (1975, dir. Peter Weir), based on a novel (1968) by Joan Lindsay, who drew in turn on real historical events at the turn of the century in Australia.[9] In that film, two schoolgirls and their teacher are apparently spirited away by supernatural forces whilst on a school outing during which the girls are impelled by curiosity to venture onto the eponymous rock, territory which has been expressly forbidden them. Furthermore, the girls' penetrative curiosity (and the structure of the rock is so convoluted that penetration is an apt description of the girls' exploration) is inseparable from their collective identity as part of a girls' school, that is, an institutionalized body of women in search of knowledge. The retribution is terrible. As a result of these events, the school has to close because it has become the object of profound suspicion and disapproval; the headmistress and another pupil die unnatural deaths soon after the picnic; and finally, the school burns down, a historical fact mentioned in the novel (p. 185) but not the film. And in a lighter vein, in the cinema blockbuster *The Mummy* (1999, dir. Steven Sommers), when a female

---

[7] See Warner, *From the Beast to the Blonde*, 247–8, who makes the connection between 'Bluebeard' and the mystery play.

[8] Connie Palmen, *De Wetten* (1991), trans. Richard Huijing as *The Laws* (London: Minerva, 1992).

[9] Joan Lindsay, *Picnic at Hanging Rock* (1968) (Harlow: Longman, 1991).

archaeologist, in her eagerness for knowledge about Ancient Egypt, opens and reads a forbidden magic book, the seven plagues of Egypt are released anew.

Both Hartwig Suhrbier and Maria Tatar demonstrate forcefully that 'Bluebeard', up to and into the twentieth century, has been presented by countless authors, illustrators, and commentators as a tale about the evils of female curiosity that is duly and harshly punished.[10] The German Bluebeard tradition is no exception. In illustration of this, a recent reference work on *Märchen* sums up 'Blaubart' as '[das] Märchen von der jungen Frau, die sich nicht bezähmen kann, die Mordkammer ihres Mannes zu betreten'.[11] The formulation 'sich nicht bezähmen können' implies that the young woman's curiosity is wilfulness rather than legitimate enquiry, and this reference is just one example from a very rich German tradition which interprets the *Blaubartmärchen* to the detriment of the wife. Indeed, in a more recent publication the same author describes the wife as 'etwas leichtfertig', rather than, say, brave, and therefore implicitly deserving of punishment.[12]

Thus, if Faust's phallic key marks him out as a hero, and if in 'Der goldene Schlüssel' (*KHM* 200), a tale to which Wilhelm Grimm was 'especially devoted',[13] the discovery of a key and the opening of a mysterious box by a poor boy leads him to the confident expectation of good fortune in a reversal of the Pandora myth, the same key catalyses the temptation and nearly causes the downfall and punishment of Bluebeard's wife. (The Grimms harboured no comparable affection for the feminine equivalent of 'Der goldene Schlüssel', 'Blaubart', since that tale was omitted from the *KHM* after its first edition.) Indeed, in the Grimm tradition the only key which a female character can legitimately possess and use is one which she has cut from her own body. In 'Die sieben Raben' (*KHM* 25) (i. 154–6), the little girl must cut off her own finger and use it as a key in order to enter the mountain in which her brothers are imprisoned. Here, in other words, the act of entering a secret domain and the physical punishment or disfigurement (or, indeed, the symbolic castration)

---

[10] And by extension, when the *Blaubartmärchen* is used as children's literature, the prohibition on curiosity also applies to children.

[11] Walter Scherf, *Lexikon der Zaubermärchen* (Stuttgart: Kröner, 1982), 21–5 (21).

[12] Scherf, *Das Märchenlexikon*, 2 vols. (Munich: Beck, 1995), i. 94–8 (95).

[13] *KHM* ii. 429–30. In *Grimms' Bad Girls and Bold Boys: The Moral and Social Vision of the Tales* (New Haven, Conn.: Yale University Press, 1987), Ruth B. Bottigheimer stresses Wilhelm Grimm's affection for 'Der goldene Schlüssel' (p.27).

which ensue for a female character are condensed most economi-
cally. The severed female finger also emerges in 'Der Räuberbräutigam' (*KHM* 40) (i. 219–23), a tale which is closely related to
'Blaubart', and in which a finger chopped from the body of a victim
flies into the lap of the concealed, observing bride. She has the good
fortune to be able to use it as evidence of the crime: that is, the
severed finger represents in both 'Die sieben Raben' and 'Der
Räuberbräutigam' a redemptive physical sacrifice on the part of their
female owner.

It is no coincidence that the bodily part sacrificed here, while not
the head, is nonetheless intimately connected with intellectual
endeavour and power (traditionally identified with masculinity) and
expression, being used for pointing, writing, gesticulating, and so
forth. The analogy between finger and key, and the chilling sacrifice
of the finger, are also echoed in the recent film *The Piano* (dir. Jane
Campion, 1993), in which the protagonist, Ada, is dumb and her only
self-expression is through her fingers and the keys of her piano.[14]
When Ada's husband, Stewart, takes away the piano (and its keys)
and gives it to an associate of his called Baines, Ada is devastated,
since this is the equivalent of losing her voice. When Stewart discovers Ada's adultery with Baines, in which she engages in order to
retrieve her piano, he hacks off one of her fingers. It is no coincidence
that *The Piano*, with its competition between the male and female
characters for the possession of keys, explicitly cites 'Bluebeard' in the
form of a melodramatic play that is performed within the film.

In the fairy tale, however, Bluebeard responds even more violently
than Ada's husband to his wife's transgression. Most emphatically,
Bechstein's Ritter Blaubart warns: 'Würdest du dieses Kabinett
öffnen, so erwartet dich die schrecklichste Strafe der Neugier. Ich
müßte dir dann mit eigener Hand das Haupt vom Rumpfe
trennen!'[15] This threat is emphasized in illustrations of the Bluebeard
tale, since by far the most dominant visual image presented alongside
the text involves Bluebeard holding his wife by the hair and swinging
his cutlass towards her throat. And in *Picnic at Hanging Rock*, the one

---

[14] Jane Campion, *The Piano* (London: Bloomsbury, 1993). For a detailed reading of the
'Bluebeard' narrative in the film, see Cristina Bacchilega, *Postmodern Fairy Tales: Gender and
Narrative Strategies* (Philadelphia: University of Pennsylvania Press, 1997), 129–38.

[15] Ludwig Bechstein, 'Das Märchen vom Ritter Blaubart', in *Deutsches Märchenbuch*
(1845), ed. Hans-Heino Ewers (Stuttgart: Reclam, 1996), 374–7 (375). In the illustration to
Lausch's 'Vom Ritter Blaubart' mentioned above too, it is only the severed heads which
are on view.

girl who survives reappears with a mysterious, diabolical mark on her forehead, so while she is not decapitated, her head nonetheless bears the physical inscription of her transgression.

This punishment means that the feminine desire for knowledge is self-defeating inasmuch as it involves the loss of the head, the physical locus of knowledge, and Hélène Cixous identifies such a consequence as a fundamental cultural myth:

It's a question of submitting feminine disorder . . . to the threat of decapitation. If man operates under the threat of castration, if masculinity is culturally ordered by the castration complex, it might be said that the backlash, the return on women of this castration anxiety is its displacement as decapitation, execution, of woman, as loss of her head.[16]

This tremendously powerful prohibition on feminine appropriation of knowledge, diminished and dismissed as 'curiosity' in 'Bluebeard', often correlates with a suspect sexuality, and is at the very roots of Western culture. In classical culture, for instance, Pandora and Psyche offer parallels to Bluebeard's wife, and in Gerd Winkler's television play *Mike Blaubart* (1968) the narrator says:

Psyche würde heute noch in Amors Armen glücklich sein, wenn sie es dabei belassen hätte, ihren Geliebten unter dem Schleier zu lieben. . . . Aus reiner Neugierde lüftete sie ihn und ward in die Unterwelt gestoßen.[17]

The same narrative informs much of Western thought. This is the case, for instance, in Freudian and Lacanian psychoanalytic theories of subjective development, according to which entry into full consciousness and subjective knowledge is accompanied by the traumatic threat of real or symbolic castration, another wounding which is also intimately connected to sexual identity. Similarly, just as Bluebeard's wife suffers in a physical and sexualized manner, so Freudian psychoanalysis identifies Woman in particular with the body and describes her as already castrated, so that her passage into conscious subjecthood is more fraught than her male counterpart's. But as many authors, illustrators, and commentators point out, the most powerful and familiar codification of this prohibition is to be found in the Book of Genesis, in which God warns Adam that to eat from the tree of knowledge of good and evil will entail death. Nevertheless, Eve succumbs to Satan's temptation to eat from that tree, and by so doing drags Adam and all humanity with her into

[16] 'Castration or Decapitation?' (1976), trans. Annette Kuhn, *Signs*, 7 (1981), 41–55 (43).
[17] Gerd Winkler, *Mike Blaubart* (Frankfurt am Main: Heine, 1968), 47.

disaster. And while both Adam and Eve are punished, God then metes out more punishment separately and gender-specifically. While Adam will be cursed and will have to labour, gaining his bread by the sweat of his brow, Eve's punishment involves physical suffering which is explicitly connected with the sexualized female body:

in labour you shall bear children. You shall be eager for your husband, and he shall be your master (Gen. 3: 16)

Or in other words, the case of Eve particularly emphasizes that the female body is a locus of bloody suffering and accursed female sexuality—and, paradoxically, she is now condemned to a sexual curiosity or 'eagerness'. A similar fate befalls Lot's wife when she defies God's angels' prohibition on looking back at the doomed city of Sodom (Gen. 19: 15–26), for she is also physically punished by being changed into a pillar of salt. In the context of the Genesis narrative, the name of the girls' school in *Picnic at Hanging Rock* is particularly significant since it is called after its principal, Mrs Apple-yard; and strikingly, too, the curious woman archaeologist in *The Mummy* is called Evelyn.

Therefore, 'Bluebeard' refers to a theology in which a woman who wants to know too much precipitates the Fall of Man and is punished in an emphatically physical manner. Just as God threatens Adam and Eve with death if they disobey, so Bluebeard warns his wife of death. For instance, in Perrault's tale he says (albeit after the fact), 'il faut mourir'. Perrault's tale also echoes and undermines a further Biblical formulation, for after passing judgement, God speculates: 'The man has become like one of us, knowing good and evil; what if he now reaches out his hand and takes fruit from the tree of life also, eats it and lives forever?' (Gen. 3: 22). This is precisely the scenario enacted in Perrault's tale, where the woman does indeed acquire knowledge of good and evil and outlives her husband. In the case of both 'Bluebeard' and the biblical narrative, this is an asymmetrical power relationship which is weighted against the female transgressor. Just as in the Bible Eve's physical punishment is sexualized, so 'Bluebeard', being a tale about the immediate consequences of marriage, is very commonly read as a tale about entry into feminine sexuality and the bloody physical dangers and curses it involves.[18] And just as Eve's

[18] Such an interpretation is proposed, albeit in different ways, by Warner, *From the Beast to the Blonde*; and Bruno Bettelheim, in *The Uses of Enchantment: The Meaning and Importance of Fairy Tales* (London: Thames & Hudson, 1976), 209–303.

transgression is the original sin which will haunt all future generations, so the Bluebeard tale concerns the serial punishment of one
woman after the next, and in both narratives a cycle of suffering and
punishment is produced which appears irredeemable.

But Christian theology involves a tripartite model of history in
which the Fall of Man by the fault of Woman is eventually followed
by salvation through Christ the man, and in the tale, the bride is also
saved by her brothers. Nevertheless, the parallel here is imperfect, for
while in the biblical narrative Eve can hardly be said to be the victor,
in the tale the woman does triumph and is rewarded. Not only does
the heroine survive, but Perrault writes that she has the phenomenal
luck to inherit everything, and that her new marriage allows her to
forget 'le mauvais temps qu'elle avait passé avec la Barbe bleue'. As
Marina Warner points out, such an inheritance, possible only when a
husband had no children from previous marriages whose claims
would take precedence over his widow's, would have been an almost
unheard-of stroke of luck in seventeenth-century France (p. 264).

Thus, far from being a tale about feminine subjection and suffering, 'Bluebeard' is a tale about a woman who flouts patriarchal
authority, acquires knowledge in the face of terrifying adversity, and,
with the assistance of her sister and brothers, is rewarded for it. And
if Christian salvation is achieved only through the human sacrifice of
Christ himself, in 'Bluebeard' the agents of salvation, the brothers,
survive unscathed. So whereas in the Bible redemption through
Christ involves terrible human sacrifice and remains a distant, future
prospect in another life only, in Perrault's tale the happy ending is
remarkable because it is *material* and *immediate*. Such immediate,
unpunished, and material rewarding of disobedience proves that the
status quo, whether in terms of knowledge, material property, or
gender identity, can occasionally be changed by disobedience, not
obedience. However, in the case of 'Bluebeard', it is clear too that
transgressive intervention on the part of a woman is not always a
successful strategy, since it has ended in death for all the other
women. The difference seems, at least partly, to lie in the family
support Bluebeard's wife possesses (Adam, on the other hand, reports
Eve to God). But it is precisely the way in which the odds are against
the wife and her family which makes her success in 'Bluebeard'
remarkable.

'Bluebeard', then, involves the retraction of a fundamental cultural
narrative about the punishment of feminine knowledge, and as

such is a subversive narrative, not only because it is part of the traditionally disruptive genre of fantasy, or because of its uncompromising exposure of the material basis of marriage—that only money can buy you love—which contradicts the idealized and socially stabilizing notion of romantic love which the fairy tale has been used to promote from the nineteenth century onward. We can also read 'Bluebeard' as an account of gender trouble, or rather crisis, in which traditional and clearly defined gender roles are undermined. This is the argument made by Philip Lewis in his account of 'La Barbe bleue' as a tale of a 'mimetic rivalry' so powerful that it has to end in death for one party.[19] If, at the outset, gender distinctions are clearly marked by Bluebeard's possession of privileged knowledge, symbolized by the phallic key, which incorporates the 'Bart' itself, his wife's (castrating) appropriation of the key's power and Bluebeard's closely guarded knowledge precipitates crisis.

The synecdochal transfer of the 'beard'/'bit' is of central significance here. The beard is prominent in popular representations of the Christian God, and is in general an important symbol of masculine authority, but it is also a marker of the very physical presence of that authority. In the *Deutsches Wörterbuch* the Grimms wrote: '*vor dem bart*, drückt, wie unter den augen, das coram, nähe und gegenwart aus.' This idea gives rise, for instance, to Luther's disapproving formulation in his *Tischreden* which the Grimms quote too: 'unserm herrgott in bart greifen' (i. 1142). And in the *Handwörterbuch des deutschen Aberglaubens* we read: 'Im Bart vermutete man, wie im Haar überhaupt, die Lebenssubstanz; darum beschwört man durch Berührung des Bartes den Angerufenen gleichsam bei seinem Leben.'[20] For women, however, facial hair signifies unnatural deviancy. Just as Bluebeard's disobedient wife acquires a 'Bart' along with the key, so the *Deutsches Wörterbuch* also refers to the belief that girls or women involved in some kind of sexual or sexualized transgression will grow beards, and boys who behave inappropriately may lose theirs:[21]

---

[19] *Seeing Through the Mother Goose Tales: Visual Turns in Perrault* (Stanford, Calif.: Stanford University Press, 1996), 203–6.

[20] *Handwörterbuch des deutschen Aberglaubens*, ed. Hanns Bächtold-Stäubli with E. Hoffmann-Krayer, 10 vols. (Berlin: de Gruyter, 1927–42), i. 930–1.

[21] Cf. Warner, *From the Beast to the Blonde*, 353–69, on the association of inappropriate female body hair such as beards with disobedience and deviancy. Drawing a physiological conclusion from Warner's mythological and cultural examples, hairy women appear to be suspect because hairiness accompanies infertility, increasing e.g. after the menopause and in old age, in anorexia, or in hormonal disturbances. The real implication therefore is not

mädchen mit dem taufwasser eines knaben getauft, bekommen davon *bart*; eine frau, die einen knaben über taufe hält kann davon *bart* bekommen; kleine mädchen, die sich von männern küssen lassen, bekommen *bart*; das mädchen musz die mutter, der knabe den vater zuerst küssen sonst bekommt das mädchen *bart*, der knabe keinen. (i. 1143)

Given this association between feminine deviancy, knowledge (sexual or otherwise), and beards, it is unsurprising that in 'Beobachtungen über das Gefühl des Schönen und Erhabenen' (1764), Immanuel Kant should have noted two intellectual and therefore transgressive women:

Mühsames Lernen oder peinliches Grübeln, wenn es gleich ein Frauenzimmer darin hochbringen sollte, vertilgen die Vorzüge, die ihrem Geschlechte eigentümlich sind und können dieselbe wohl um der Seltenheit willen zum Gegenstande einer kalten Bewunderung machen, aber sie werden zugleich die Reize schwächen, wodurch sie ihre große Gewalt über das andere Geschlecht ausüben. Ein Frauenzimmer, das den Kopf voll Griechisch hat, wie die Frau DACIER, oder über die Mechanik gründliche Streitigkeiten führt, wie die Marquisin v. CHASTELET, mag nur immerhin einen Bart dazu haben; denn dieser würde vielleicht die Miene des Tiefsinns noch kenntlicher ausdrücken, um welchen sie sich bewerben.[22]

The wife's unnatural appropriation of the key, which combines both key and beard, involves a particularly strong challenge, as it is highly disrespectful and violates the husband's vitality, phallic power, and immediate physical presence. This threat to Bluebeard's authority is expressed particularly graphically in an obscure nineteenth-century text, Armand Vestris's *Blaubart. Großes romantisch-pantomimisches Ballett* (1832). Here, once the wife has transgressed by using the forbidden key to look in the chamber, that key breaks in a particularly symbolic manner: 'Aber wehe! der Bart ist abgebrochen . . .'[23] Bluebeard's horrifically violent response to this challenge is therefore unsurprising because he is, in effect, responding to the threat of castration.

Moreover, Perrault's tale challenges conventional cultural myths in its deployment of a further feature: the two interpretations appended by the author as *moralités*. These little verses tend either to

so much that disobedient women are hairy, but that hairy women may be infertile and therefore 'abnormal' and suspect.

[22] Immanuel Kant, 'Beobachtungen über das Gefühl des Schönen und Erhabenen' (1764), in *Werke*, ed. Ernst Cassirer et al., 11 vols. (Berlin: Bruno Cassirer, 1922), ii. 243–300 (271).

[23] Armand Vestris, *Blaubart. Großes romantisch-pantomimisches Ballett in drei Abtheilungen* (Berlin: Lassar, 1832), 14.

be omitted in translations and interpretations of the *conte*, or to be treated in superficial ways, such that the critical ambivalences produced when the morals are read against the main body of the tale are overlooked.[24] Yet the discrepancy between the force of the *conte* itself and the *moralités* is one of the most striking features of Perrault's tale.

While Perrault is depicting the patriarchal society of his time, his *conte* is far from reflecting a man's world in which women have no autonomy or agency. Specifically, the bride's family is headed not by a tyrannical father, but by a mother who gives her daughters a large degree of freedom, and so the daughter's decision to marry Bluebeard is her own. Perrault's text implies too that the bride is shrewd enough to recognize that 'love' is a cover for material expediency in marriage, or, more subtly and provocatively still, the text may imply that affection in marriage is a necessary fiction which makes bearable the mercenary nature and sometimes the brutality of that institution, another potentially pro-feminist point. Furthermore, the wife transgresses of her own volition and is rescued not only by her articulate strategies for distracting Bluebeard but also by the solidarity of her sister, who is with her in Bluebeard's house, as well as by the intervention of her brothers. And other female company (the 'bonnes amies') too is given a central place in the narrative. Finally, the woman's family benefits royally both from her transgression and from their support of her.

Given these potentially proto-feminist features, the *moralités* are perplexing with their apparently more sexist and thus contradictory implications. The first *moralité* reads:

> La curiosité malgré tous ses attraits,
> Coûte souvent bien des regrets;
> On en voit tous les jours mille exemples paraître.
> C'est, n'en déplaise au sexe, un plaisir bien léger;
> Dès qu'on le prend il cesse d'être,
> Et toujours il coûte trop cher. (p. 262)

This verse seem to reiterate the powerful prohibition on feminine knowledge and autonomy described above, belittling them as curiosity. At the same time, curiosity is described as a vicious attribute in both men and women, and by redefining the principal

---

[24] For instance, Jack D. Zipes in *Fairy Tales and the Art of Subversion: The Classic Genre for Children and the Process of Civilisation* (1983) (London: Routledge, 1991) and Tatar in *Hard Facts* perceive no ambiguities, interpreting the tale as a straightforward moral lesson to girls not to be curious.

moral problem exposed by the *conte* as curiosity (not murder), this *moralité* trivializes the force of Perrault's tale and retracts its stark gender politics. Yet a closer look reveals that the *moralité*'s relationship to the body of the text is riddled with contradictions, and that it is difficult to identify the curiosity criticized in the verse with the behaviour of the tale's heroine. While curiosity is connected with the story's heroine, it is notable that the word 'curiosité' is used once only in the text of the *conte* itself, and then with reference to the heroine's desire to open the chamber. Up to that point, the word 'impatience' had been used to describe her feelings, indicating that curiosity is a particularly heightened and exceptional state of mind; and the tale stresses that the heroine has an extraordinary and unique experience. Yet the verse claims that curiosity is unacceptable in both women *and* men, and is a trivial, commonplace, and repetitive phenomenon ('On en voit tous les jours . . .'). And whilst the *moralité* implies that the text cautions against curiosity on the grounds that 'il coûte trop cher', curiosity is in fact richly rewarded there, both individually and socially. Finally, although the penultimate line of the moral implies that curiosity is an ephemeral phenomenon which leaves only regret in its wake, in the *conte* itself the benefits are clearly lasting and empowering.

Despite such discrepancies, many authors and commentators from Perrault's time onward have taken the *moralité* at face value and at the same time unquestioningly accepted the idea that the *conte* is about the evils of *feminine* curiosity, since the reference in the *moralité* to men's curiosity seems redundant, having no evident correspondence in the main body of the tale. In defence of this reading it could be argued that Perrault sensed the explosive potential of his denial of the Genesis myth in 'La Barbe bleue' and so attempted to re-stabilize the text by adding such conventional and less pro-feminist *moralités* to it. But it could also be argued that this conclusion simplifies a more complex reading experience, for, in a recent study of the French *contes de fées*, Lewis C. Seifert has argued that the *moralités* commonly attached to the *contes* were not to be taken at face value as mere summaries of the tale which they accompanied. Rather, they were designed to challenge readers or listeners to interpret further, enciphered meanings in the tales.[25]

In this light, the apparent inconsistencies between the *conte* and the

---

[25] *Fairy Tales, Sexuality and Gender in France 1690–1715: Nostalgic Utopias* (Cambridge: Cambridge University Press, 1996), 51–8.

moralité take on a new dimension. The very fact that the *moralité* does not explicitly associate women and curiosity, while the *conte* does, might be a warning *against* understanding the *moralité* as a simple indictment of feminine curiosity. What if this moral were in fact not directed at the woman at all, but at Bluebeard? After all, the description of vicious and inappropriate curiosity neatly fits his behaviour. Whilst the wife's curiosity is a distinctly isolated and profitable incident, Bluebeard's behaviour is the expression of a repetitive (or in modern terms, pathological) curiosity about how his next wife will respond to his prohibition. It is Bluebeard therefore who seeks fulfilment in a curiosity which 'coûte trop cher' for his victims and, ultimately, for himself. Such curiosity seems, until the extraordinary triumph of the final wife, ultimately pointless in its relentless repetition of identical events, and thus trivial or 'léger'. And it is not the wife's, but Bluebeard's curiosity which has to be constantly restaged, a repetition which Perrault sums up in the paradox 'dès qu'on le prend il cesse d'être'.

The second *moralité* was not included in the manuscript of 1795 but appeared in the first edition of 1797, and so was presumably written later, a chronology which also justifies the assumption that text and moral do not necessarily form a monolithic whole. The second *moralité* is as ambivalent as the first and reads:

> Pour peu qu'on ait l'esprit sensé,
> Et que du monde on sache le grimoire,
> On voit bientôt que cette histoire
> Est un conte du temps passé;
> Il n'est plus d'Époux si terrible,
> Ni qui demande l'impossible,
> Fût-il malcontent et jaloux.
> Près de sa femme on le voit filer doux;
> Et de quelque couleur que sa barbe puisse être,
> On a peine à juger qui des deux est le maître. (p. 262)

Far from opening with an assurance that its potential reader is a rational, well-informed subject who may be relied upon to draw proper conclusions, this *moralité* undermines such assumptions by opening with the doubtful '[p]our peu' and the subjunctive of uncertainty. Furthermore, while the expression 'savoir le grimoire' commonly meant 'to understand contemporary *mores*',[26] on another

---

[26] Perrault, *Contes*, ed. Jean-Pierre Collinet (Paris: Gallimard, 1981), 329–30.

level that expression undermines rational certainty, since a 'grimoire' is literally a book of spells. Thus it is implied that the 'Monde' which the moral describes may not be ruled by rational principles ('seeing is believing') and familiar rules of etiquette, but by more arcane and hermetic laws.

This *moralité* claims that the *conte* is an account of a distant, and therefore harmless, past. Yet the main body of the text itself involves a wealth of contemporary detail and is concerned with a thoroughly modern marriage.[27] Here too, then, it is perplexing that this *moralité* should have been read literally by authors and critics who have no difficulty in taking the second moral at face value and understanding the tale as a 'conte du temps passé'. But the moral's claim to refer to the past might just as easily be read ironically. While the second *moralité* claims on the one hand that such marriages as Bluebeard's no longer exist, on the other it goes on to describe a contemporary marriage which in fact has striking similarities to Bluebeard's. While the husband described in the second *moralité* is said to appear harmless, it is also stressed that an observer would have trouble passing judgement on the marriage described ('On a peine à juger . . .'). It may be that the point of this *moralité* is to highlight the discrepancy between the urbane appearance of Bluebeard's marital behaviour and its reality, and the difficulties involved in the Enlightenment assumption that 'seeing is believing'.[28] After all, it was a false appearance of sociability and 'honnêteté' which seduced the wife in the first place, and so it may be that the superficially harmonious marriage described in this *moralité* is no different from Bluebeard's.

THE PROCESS OF CIVILIZATION

Perrault's 'La Barbe bleue' encodes the utopian and transgressive possibility of usurping patriarchal authority. Bluebeard's wife, for example, gains knowledge of good and evil by discovering that the man she believed, by virtue of his wealth, to be 'honnête', is a monster, and that riches and power do not equate with goodness. This revelation constitutes a challenge to the ideological order of things as set out at the start of the tale; and, by implication, to patriarchal order and even the order of the Christian cosmos. Further-

---

[27] Ibid. 326–30.
[28] On vision in 'La Barbe bleue', see Lewis, *Seeing Through the Mother Goose Tales*, 197–246.

more, the appended verse *moralités* can be read in such a way as to emphasize the complexity of these meanings. Therefore, 'Bluebeard' is fascinating and exciting because of the way it defies a powerful cultural narrative about feminine knowledge and autonomy which goes back to biblical models. And this narrative about transgressive feminine knowledge also dovetails precisely with the yet broader narrative of the 'process of civilization', and in doing so it breaches certain taboos which that process involves.

According to Norbert Elias, 'civilization' is the gradual process through which the modern subject and the modern state interdependently emerged through the early modern and modern periods in Europe.[29] Elias argues that as social organization became more complex and regulated, so the human subject changed; and conversely, that these changes in the subject permitted societal change. For the modern, stable nation-state to emerge, individuals increasingly had to accept and internalize standards of civility or 'civilization' which suppressed instinctual, libidinal, and aggressive behaviour in favour of increasing self-control. This self-control or 'civilization' came to be legitimized and valorized as a mark of good breeding and human value, and can be described as the delegation of responsibility for keeping order, which used to be the role of the king and his forces, to the individual, who now had to learn to police him- or herself. Or, in Elias's terminology, there is a progression from the imposition of 'Fremdzwänge' on the individual by the king or a similar, extraneous authority to the imposition of 'Selbstzwänge'. On the one hand, this process guaranteed greater physical security for individuals within society; on the other, Elias points out that the process of civilization did not eradicate the violence which was such an evident part of behaviour and an important means of social control before the early modern period. Instead, both over the centuries and during the individual's own process of maturation, violence took on new, subliminal, and psychologized forms, resulting in the production of pressures, fears, and struggles within the individual subject.

These influential ideas have been reiterated in important ways by other theorists too, for example by the historian Michel Foucault,[30]

---

[29] *Über den Prozeß der Zivilisation: Soziogenetische und psychogenetische Untersuchungen* (1939) 2 vols. (Frankfurt am Main: Suhrkamp, 1997).

[30] Cf. developments in the treatment of crime and punishment from the early modern period onward, traced by Foucault in *Surveiller et punir: naissance de la prison* (Paris: Gallimard, 1975), who suggests that control of delinquents shifted from external, physical punishments to psychological control.

and Elias's account of violence done within the individual in the interest of maintaining a controlled Symbolic and societal order overlaps also with that in Theodor W. Adorno and Max Horkheimer's influential analysis of modern culture, *Dialektik der Aufklärung* (1944):

Furchtbares hat sich die Menschheit antun müssen, bis das Selbst, der identische, zweckgerichtete, männliche Charakter des Menschen geschaffen war, und etwas davon wird in jeder Kindheit wiederholt.[31]

In this account then, the violence involved in the process of civilization is two-edged. On the one hand, the individual is its *object*, because she or he undergoes an implicitly violent 'civilization'; on the other hand, the individual is also the *subject* or *agent* of civilization, in being involved in imposing the norms of civilization on others. As Hartmut Böhme and Gernot Böhme have written:

Das 'Furchtbare', das nach Horkheimer/Adorno die Bildungsgeschichte des mit sich identischen Subjekts ermöglicht und begleitet, ist psychoanalytisch nach zwei Seiten hin zu entwickeln: als das Furchtbare einer Autonomie, deren undurchdringliche Maskierung und konzentrierte Macht allem Anderen das Fürchten lehrt; und als das Furchtbare einer rigiden inneren Kolonisierung, die das Subjekt im Prozeß seiner Selbstermächtigung sich selbst antun muß—und es darum in eine perennierende Angst vor den Stimmen des ins Unbewußte exilierten Anderen der Vernunft bannt.[32]

Yet, while the process of civilization appears to be all-pervasive in its imposition of authority, nonetheless, there are always resistances to the absolute enforcement of order; more radically, it can be argued that the imposition of rational order inevitably also produces its opposite. As Böhme and Böhme put it, 'mit der Realisierung der Vernunft wird die Unvernunft mitproduziert'. The very act of creating the individual who is defined by 'his' rationality *generates* the complementary notion of the irrational in order to indicate the contours of the 'rational'. Or, as Böhme and Böhme put it in psychoanalytical terms:

Der Preis für den historischen Aufbau eines gepanzerten Selbst ist folglich die *Erzeugung* weiter Räume des Unbewußten, eines 'inneren Auslands' (Freud), das ununterbrochen mit hohem Energieaufwand bewacht werden muß. (p. 17, my emphasis)

---

[31] *Dialektik der Aufklärung: Philosophische Fragmente* (1944), in Adorno, *Gesammelte Schriften*, ed. Rolf Tiedemann, 20 vols. (Frankfurt am Main: Suhrkamp, 1997), iii. 50.

[32] *Das Andere der Vernunft: Zur Entwicklung von Rationalitätsstrukturen am Beispiel Kants* (Frankfurt am Main: Suhrkamp, 1985), 19–20.

The paradox that order generates disorder is evident, for instance, in a nineteeth-century didactic text quoted by Elias, which seems to be particularly appropriate here since it concerns the evils of curiosity about sexuality in little girls. Elias identifies an increasing polite insistence on 'Scham' in sexual and physical matters which culminated during the nineteenth century, and while he notes that such standards of modesty also applied to the education of boys, it is significant that he takes his example from a primer for girls' education, implicitly underlining the more severe limitations imposed upon girls. The pamphlet, *Die Erziehung der Mädchen* (1857) by K. von Raumer, totally lacks the relative openness of earlier tracts on how to discuss sexuality and reproduction with children:[33]

Man berühre alle diese Dinge überhaupt nicht in Gegenwart der Kinder, am wenigsten auf eine geheimnisvolle Art, welche geeignet ist, die Neugier zu reizen . . . Fragen später die Mädchen, wie es denn eigentlich mit den kleinen Kindern zugehe? so sage man: der liebe Gott gibt der Mutter das kleine Kind . . . Wie Gott die Kinder gibt, das brauchst du nicht zu wissen und könntest es auch nicht verstehen. An ähnlichen Antworten müssen sich Mädchen in hundert Fallen begnügen, und die Aufgabe der Mutter ist es, die Gedanken ihrer Töchter so unablässig mit Gutem und Schönem zu beschäftigen, daß ihnen keine Zeit mehr bleibt zum Grübeln über solche Dinge . . . Eine Mutter . . . sollte nur einmal ernst sagen: es wäre garnicht gut für dich, wenn du so etwas wüßtest, du mußt vermeiden davon sprechen zu hören. Ein recht sittsam erzogenes Mädchen wird von da an eine Scheu empfinden, von Dingen der Art reden zu hören.[34]

The prohibition imposed on the little girl is addressed to her in such as way as to make it her individual responsibility, or in Elias's terminology a 'Selbstzwang'. Most interestingly of all, although Elias does not draw attention to this, von Raumer's formulation does *not* assume that 'Neugier' is a natural propensity in little girls, but rather that it is the *result* of a 'geheimnisvolle Art' of discussing intimate matters, such that secrecy *generates* rather than *suppresses* curiosity in sexual matters.[35] Thus, it seems that the imposition of civilization persistently produces its opposite, and forces which undermine it, just

---

[33] Von Raumer's pamphlet appeared 12 years after Ludwig Bechstein's 'Ritter Blaubart' (1845), which is particularly concerned to preach against feminine curiosity.

[34] Elias, *Über den Prozeß der Zivilisation*, i. 246. Reproduced in more detail in *Schwarze Pädagogik: Quellen zur Naturgeschichte der bürgerlichen Erziehung*, ed. Katharina Rutschky (Frankfurt am Main: Ullstein, 1977), 335–6. Rutschky dates this pamphlet at 1815.

[35] Such a conclusion anticipates that drawn by Foucault in *La Volonté de savoir* (Paris: Gallimard, 1976): that the control mechanisms which sought to suppress sexuality in the Victorian era actually *produced* it as we know it today, rather than obscuring it.

as Bluebeard's wife is compelled, by the utterance of a prohibition, to commit an act which might otherwise never have occurred to her.

WOMAN AND THE PROCESS OF CIVILIZATION

Elias does not present a theory of gender relations and neither does his work have much to say explicitly about women. While he does devote a chapter to 'Wandlungen in der Einstellung zu den Beziehungen zwischen Mann und Frau', this is in fact mainly about changing attitudes to sex (in itself a loaded association in that it equates women with sexuality and the body). Otherwise, references to women or gender relations are sparse, although at one point Elias states in a footnote that '[d]ieses Spezialproblem' (ii. 412) is so massive that it would exceed the limits of his current study and notes that he planned to devote a third volume to the 'relations between men and women'. Thus, just as Adorno and Horkheimer specify in the quotation above that the modern rational subject is 'männlich', so too is the subject of civilization in which Elias is principally interested masculine. Indeed, in the chapter 'Wandlungen in der Einstellung zu den Beziehungen zwischen Mann und Frau', Elias makes this point specifically: 'Am geradlinigsten tritt diese Ver-änderung [civilization] hervor, wenn man sie an den Männern der jeweiligen Oberschicht beobachtet' (i. 349). In other words, this observation makes clear that Elias's concept of 'civilization' is a very specific one, meaning a particular process which does not apply in equal measure to all human subjects.

The suggestion that Elias is principally concerned with a certain type of masculine subject is indirectly corroborated by much of the content of the chapter in question. First, while he allows that the process of civilization permitted a certain degree of emancipation for aristocratic ladies, this emancipation did not equal that of aristocratic men, and in later, bourgeois society women were increasingly subjugated to male authority (i. 345–8), with a double standard applying to women's sexual freedom in particular. Second, women and girls have a more ambivalent status than boys and men in the educational tracts like that by von Raumer discussed by Elias. The early tracts concern the education of boys only, suggesting that in this early stage of civilization girls were not considered to be important subjects of the process. And while Elias goes on to discuss later

nineteenth-century educational tracts which do deal with girls' education, here, girls and their mothers are presented as subordinate to
male authority, indicating that women were not accepted as moral
teachers. This shift seems to indicate that there was an increasing
sense that girls and women were in particular need of civilization, but
too uncivilized themselves to act as its agents. Hence Elias's comparison elsewhere of women's traditional status with that of 'Unter-
worfene, Besiegte oder Leibeigene', none of whom were traditionally
perceived as being subjects in their own right, is also significant.

Consequently, the position of women in Elias's theory of the
process of civilization is ambiguous. While the upper-class, adult,
male individual is split into both the subject and the object of civilization, and so is subjected to violence as well as being permitted to
wield authority himself, the female individual of any class seems to be
assigned less subjectivity or agency, remaining more the object of the
process.[36] And the process of civilization is gendered on a deeper,
symbolic level too, since in our culture such powerful concepts as the
conscious and unconscious, and the rational and the irrational, are
traditionally thought of in gendered terms. Historically, the rational
consciousness and order of civilization have been commonly
identified with masculinity and irrational unconsciousness and disorder with femininity, so in this respect too the position of feminine
subjects in the 'process of civilization' is a fraught one. The implication is that Woman and femininity will always be particularly closely
associated with disorder.

BLUEBEARD AND THE PROCESS OF CIVILIZATION

However, despite Elias's apparent omission of gender, his ideas can
be used productively to analyse the gender issues in the *Blaubartmärchen*, as two critics have already demonstrated. Jack Zipes has
made connections between Elias's observations and the French
upper-class *contes de fées* tradition in which Charles Perrault partici-

---

[36] Ute Frevert, in *Frauen-Geschichte: Zwischen Bürgerlicher Verbesserung und Neuer Weiblichkeit*
(Frankfurt am Main: Suhrkamp, 1986), highlights the manner in which women came
increasingly to be objects of patriarchal control in the modern period. See also Klaus
Theweleit, *Männerphantasien*, 2 vols. (Reinbek bei Hamburg: Rowohlt, 1980), which sets out
to expand on Elias's theory of the process of civilization by examining its gender politics up
to the mid-twentieth century and finding an increasing fear of the 'Other', imagined as
feminine and projected onto women, who become objects of male violence in literature.

pated, arguing that the *contes* became an instrument in the process of civilization and were used to inculcate the standards of civilization in children. Zipes shows how fairy tales were used to teach children self-discipline in a seventeenth-century society which was increasingly concerned with control:

Restraint and renunciation of instinctual gratification were part of a socio-religious code which illuminated the proper way to shape human drives and ideas so that children would learn docilely to serve church and state. Perhaps one of the main reasons for the rise of a 'state of childhood' by the end of the seventeenth century was the rise of a greater discrepancy between adult and child as the civilizing process became geared more instrumentally to dominate nature. The entire period from 1480 to 1650 can be seen as a historical transition in which the Catholic Church and the reform movement of Protestantism combined efforts with the support of the rising mercantile classes to rationalize society and literally to exterminate social deviates [*sic*] who were associated with the devil such as female witches, male werewolves, Jews, and gipsies. In particular, women were linked to the potentially uncontrollable natural instincts, and, as the image of the innocent, naive child susceptible to wild natural forces arose, the necessity to control and shelter children became more pronounced. Social non-conformism and deviation had to be punished brutally in the name of civility and Christianity. (p. 22)

Zipes makes it clear that the *contes* are the product of an upper-class ideology which sought to control not only children but, in a broader way, all elements which appeared unruly and potentially threatening, including Woman. One consequence of this view of Woman was an insistence on gender-specific models of socialization for children, which involved a passive role for girls. Zipes argues that 'La Barbe bleue' is one of a group of tales which presented an ideal role model for girls by warning them about the consequences of disobedience, so that they would learn to control themselves:

Here the heroine is beautiful, well-bred, but too curious. Again the moral explains that it is a sin to be curious and imaginative for a woman and that she must exercise self-control. . . . the female role is dictated by conditions that demand humility and self-discipline.[37]

So according to Zipes, 'La Barbe bleue' is an instrument in the process of civilization because it teaches little girls standards of self-control by threatening them with murder. This interpretation fits

---

[37] Zipes, *Fairy Tales and the Art of Subversion: The Classic Genre for Children and the Art of Civilisation* (1983) (London: Routledge, 1991), 22.

well with Elias's concept of the transformation of 'Fremdzwang' into 'Selbstzwang', as versions of 'Bluebeard' which follow Perrault's focus increasingly on psychological, not physical coercion. If we accept this idea, we can go on to argue that Bluebeard's crimes are therefore not to be read as dreadful aberrations in gender relations or in the process of civilization, but rather as their necessary dark side. The seventeenth century in France experienced, in tandem with the Enlightenment, a phenomenon which historians have called the 'grand refermement', that is, the imposition of more repressive social rules on women, and Lewis C. Seifert has written of this period:

Historians have characterized the seventeenth century as a period of rising 'paternalism'. . . . In both religious and political discourse, the *paterfamilias* was included in a continuum of authority that stretched to the king and, ultimately, God. The individual father was to be master of his family as the king was master of his kingdom and God was master of the universe. This pyramid of paternal authority was a topos frequently used during this period to justify fatherly hegemony in the emerging bourgeois nuclear family. Although paternal benevolence was a common refrain in political and religious texts, images of the 'père terrible' were a no less frequent means of driving home the authority of fathers. Several political theorists went to great lengths to prove the necessity of paternal violence in many circumstances of family life. In the end, this renewed valorization of paternal authority exceeded the bounds of textual images; in fact, it was likely an integral part of the concentration of the powers of fathers and husbands in matrimonial, inheritance, and artisanal practices at this time.[38]

In that sense the 'terrible' husband Bluebeard is not a perverse individual flouting the demands of civilized behaviour, but is in fact upholding those standards. Thus, the real scandal and transgression of the tale lie less in the fact that it involves violence in the family than in that it *reveals* that violence, necessarily present but usually hidden, which in more recent times especially has become a taboo subject. One detail in Perrault's text underlines this point nicely. During the initial courtship, the bride decides that Bluebeard is 'honnête'—a cardinal virtue of 'civilization' in seventeenth-century French polite society—and thus worthy of her, despite his blue beard. And at the end, the woman marries a new husband who is also 'honnête'. On a superficial reading, it could be inferred that in the first case the woman is taken in by a false appearance and that in the second she has learnt to identify true 'honnêteté', corresponding to traditional notions of fairy tale in which the protagonist undergoes a learning

[38] *Fairy Tales, Sexuality and Gender*, 157–8.

process and which ends in satisfying closure. On another reading, however, the conclusion may be more ambiguous. It may equally be inferred that 'honnêteté' as embodied by Bluebeard is just that: a necessarily two-edged quality with inseparable and interdependent 'civilized' and 'violent' sides. The second marriage may in fact be as identical with the first, as the repetition of 'honnêteté' implies. And it might be said that the end result of Perrault's tale, a new, more conventional marriage in which the woman's second husband 'lui fit oublier le mauvais temps qu'elle avait passé avec la Barbe bleue', constitutes not so much the abolition of violence as its repression, or the re-establishment of a stabilizing silence about it. In sum then, 'La Barbe bleue' is both a conventional instrument of civilization, as Zipes argues, and yet at the same time, less conventional and transgressive, in that it is a dramatic and scandalous exposition of how that violent process works.

Hartwig Suhrbier, who draws on Zipes's use of Elias, also comments on the ways in which the plot of 'La Barbe bleue' reflects the workings of the process of civilization. While the French Bluebeard tradition is older than the German, since the first German Bluebeard texts emerge only towards the end of the eighteenth century, Suhrbier's use of Elias's ideas is in no way anachronistic. The notion of the 'process of civilization' may be used to illuminate the German Bluebeard tradition too, since not only did the processes of modernization which characterized seventeenth-century France take place later in Germany but, more importantly, civilization is an ongoing process and so the phenomena observed by Elias do not cease to obtain in later centuries. As Elias notes, 'Die Zivilisation ist noch nicht abgeschlossen. Sie ist erst im Werden' (ii. 465). Suhrbier suggests that Bluebeard, the man from the dominant class, may be read as the epitome of the subject of civilization. On one hand Bluebeard is subjected to violence himself, since Suhrbier suggests that he has been cut off from his 'feminine' side, symbolized by his murder of women. On the other hand Bluebeard also exerts violent control over others: his wife and, by analogy, in the world at large. Moreover, Suhrbier demonstrates how the story of a husband attempting to control his wife reflected the culture of the seventeenth century in broader ways, for instance in the control of nature, Woman, and the newly imposed colonies. Carolyn Merchant has shown how the seventeenth century saw changes in perceptions of the natural world which redefined Man not as part of an animate, organic cosmos but as the knowing master over subordinate matter. The earth which came to be the object of control was traditionally perceived as feminine, and thus the process of controlling a suspect, because potentially unruly, Nature went hand in hand with increasing control over the potentially unruly Woman.[39] Suhrbier writes:

> Die . . . Unterwerfung, Beherrschung und Ausbeutung der Natur erstreckte sich gleichermaßen auf die Umwelt wie auf die Organisierung der Gesellschaft und die Anpassung menschlichen Verhaltens: . . . Ein besonders düsteres Kapitel dieser Entwicklung waren die Hexenverfolgungen vom 15. bis 17. Jahrhundert, die die extremste Form der Zurichtung und Anpassung der Frau an die Bedingungen der entstehenden bürgerlich-patriarchalischen Gesellschaft gewesen sind. . . . Ziel war es, das 'Naturwesen' Frau zu unterwerfen und zu zähmen, in dessen Gestalt dem Mann all das entgegentrat, was er bei sich unterdrückte und bekämpfte. . . . Mit dem Unterwerfungsversuch über die Gehorsamsprobe befindet Blaubart sich in Übereinstimmung mit den Leitwerten der bürgerlich-patriarchalischen Gesellschaft. (pp. 17–19)

On the basis of Suhrbier's argument, 'Bluebeard' is thus a transgressive narrative in that it tells the savage truth about the dark side of civilization on a more global level too.

So Zipes's and Suhrbier's readings of Perrault's *conte* tally with the seventeenth-century process of civilization in France as summarized above. However, both critics overlook the way in which 'La Barbe bleue' is not only a tale about control and self-control, and as such an effective, repressive instrument of civilization, but also a 'literature of subversion' *par excellence*. While Suhrbier does point out the subversive potential of Perrault's text, he considers that potential to be increasingly covered over by successive generations of writers, and assumes that the Bluebeard order is ever more firmly asserted in the course of the nineteenth century. Neither Zipes nor Suhrbier takes account of the way in which the process of civilization also produces its own disruptive opposite. Because Bluebeard asserts his authority by making a secret out of the forbidden chamber in a manner that serves to provoke his wife's curiosity, the imposition of order ultimately generates a disobedience which overturns his authority. In fact, this narrative tradition is explicitly concerned with an attempted imposition of order which proves, over and over again, to generate its own opposite and ultimately to fail.

---

[39] Carolyn Merchant, *The Death of Nature: Women, Ecology and the Scientific Revolution* (New York: HarperCollins, 1983), 2.

Therefore, the scandal of the tale lies not only in its stark revelation of the usually hidden truths about marriage or similar relationships between men and women, and the violent control of women. 'Bluebeard', as it emerges at the beginning of modernity, also breaks taboos on expressing profound doubts about the apparently rational, nominally masculine subject of Western civilization and the processes which produce it: in short, with the projects of modernity and civilization themselves, by revealing their deeply irrational and dangerous sides. At the same time, on one reading the tale draws its excitement from the way it hints that the cycles of violence inherent in the process of civilization may be broken. Thus, the tale may be read as a critique of civilization and its discontents; as part of an evolving, complex, and gendered mythology about civilization and disorder; and ultimately as a challenge to that very mythology.

THE RECEPTION OF 'BLUEBEARD'

For these reasons, the Bluebeard material has exercised a strong fascination. The *Enzyklopädie des Märchens* states that the *Märchen*'s literary impact in Europe was 'enorm';[40] one critic has gone so far as to write of an 'obsession' with the figure of Bluebeard in nineteenth-century English literature;[41] and Warner suggests that the tale has 'entered secular mythology' (p. 269). Moreover, the term 'Bluebeard' has gone into popular usage in Western Europe. Georges Doutrepont points out the currency of the term 'Barbe-bleue' (*sic*) in everyday French usage for a 'mari féroce et sanguinaire (désignation souvent ironique)'.[42] And Karl Voretzsch claims that 'Bluebard' (sic) is in general English usage to designate an 'Ehetyrann'.[43]

---

[40] Walter Puchner, 'Mädchenmörder', in Kurt Ranke et al. (eds.), *Enzyklopädie des Märchens: Handwörterbuch zur historischen und vergleichenden Erzählforschung*, to date 8 vols. (Berlin: de Gruyter, 1975–   ), viii. 1407–13 (1410).

[41] Sherrill E. Grace, 'Courting Bluebeard with Bartók, Atwood and Fowles: Modern Treatments of the Bluebeard Theme', *Journal of Modern Literature*, 11 (2) (July 1984), 245–62 (248).

[42] *Les Types populaires de la littérature française*, 2 vols. (Brussels: Lamertin, 1926), i. 57.

[43] 'Blaubart', in *Handwörterbuch des deutschen Märchens*, ed. Lutz Mackensen with Johannes Bolte, 2 vols. (Berlin: de Gruyter, 1930–3), i. 266–70 (267). There does not, however, appear to be an equivalent expression either in nineteenth- or twentieth-century German. The *Deutsches Wörterbuch* does not refer to 'Blaubart' as a colloquial expression, only as the German translation of the name coined by Perrault and as the name for a type of shellfish: ii. 83. It does, however, point out that the adjective 'blau' may be used to describe the growth of a beard or stubble. A further selection of German dictionaries makes no mention

However, while 'Bluebeard' was popular in the nineteenth century, in the twentieth century, unlike other tales ultimately deriving from Perrault's work, it no longer has a privileged place in contemporary popular affection and the culture of childhood, one index of which today is, for example, the Disney film. In a culture which privileges *Märchen* as communicative symbols, Bluebeard is most conspicuous by his absence, while mermaids and dwarfs, for instance, often feature in advertising.

Indeed, a comparison with Hans Christian Andersen's celebrated tale 'The Little Mermaid' (1837) and such precursors of that tale as Friedrich de la Motte Fouqué's *Undine* (1811) is most interesting in this context. Although there are considerable thematic similarities between the Bluebeard and the mermaid tales, there is a discrepancy in their popularity and familiarity in modern times.[44] Both tales comment on a marital relationship or the hope for one, and both have been used didactically to distinguish between ideal and deviant models of women's marital behaviour. In both, a crisis is precipitated by feminine curiosity with sexual overtones: in the case of the little mermaid, a desire for legs so that she can discover the human world and undergo marriage. This entry into knowledge is acquired at the price of suffering and great cruelty, for the mermaid has her tongue cut out (recalling the sacrifice of the finger in 'Die sieben Raben' and other tales) and acquires legs in exchange for her voice and the sensation of always walking on sharp knives.

Nonetheless, the mermaid tales, as epitomized by Andersen's, are considerably better known. The difference between 'Bluebeard' and those other narratives seems to lie in the *nature* of the tale's popularity as the twentieth century progressed. Rather than being consistently included in children's culture, 'Bluebeard' seems to have been increasingly considered to be adult material, so that the Bluebeard material has inspired not Disney films but highbrow operas like *Ariane et Barbe-bleue* by Paul Dukas and Maurice Maeterlinck (1899) and *Duke Bluebeard's Castle* by Béla Bartók and Béla Balász (1910–11); adult literature, plays like the Gridiron Theatre Company's adaptation of

of 'Blaubart' in colloquial usage either. However, there is one exception, since Joachim Heinrich Campe's *Wörterbuch der deutschen Sprache*, 4 vols. (Brunswick: Schulbuchhandlung, 1807–11), gives the following definition: 'eine Person mit einem blauen d.h. ins Blaue fallendem Barte, nicht völlig schwarz' (i. 554). However, Campe's definition does not refer to any *Märchen* connotations of the term or colloquial usage for a tyrant or murderer.

[44] In Ovid's *Metamorphoses* sea deities are blue-bearded. John Lemprière, *A Classical Dictionary* (London: Routledge & Kegan Paul, 1948), 567–8.

Angela Carter's *The Bloody Chamber* (1997) and puppet shows like the Little Angel Theatre's *Bluebeard* (1999); and, according to Warner, pornographic films (pp. 269–70). In German too, the tale is used in the theatre not for children's entertainment but for dark adult drama, as in the case of Dea Loher's play *Blaubart—Hoffnung der Frauen* (1997) or Walter Bickmann's *Blaubart. Die letzten Männer* (1997).

Therefore, in the twentieth century 'Bluebeard' is treated with some circumspection; and this may be due to the potentially subversive power of its meanings which seem to call for selective use, or even suppression, more than to its violent content, which has its equal in 'The Little Mermaid' for instance. Moreover, the 'Bluebeard' material has an especially problematic status in Germany, where the tale's noticeably chequered career reflects a particularly strong cultural ambivalence towards it. That ambivalence, and the concomitant suppression of at least some aspects of the tale, goes back to the work of the Grimms and appears to be due to the way in which the tale breaches a series of specifically German *Märchen* taboos as codified in the *KHM*. And in turn, due to the influence of the Grimmian *Märchen* on the international fairy-tale tradition, that suspicion of 'Bluebeard' is reflected both in the tale's reception beyond German-speaking areas and in the ways in which scholarly and adult, literary treatments of the material in German often use repressive strategies to stabilize Perrault's disruptive text.

BLUEBEARD IN GERMANY

If we examine the *Blaubartmärchen* via the standard works of fairy-tale scholarship, we discover a concern with very exact classification, since traditional *Märchenforschung* has used a complex system of 'tale types' which are numbered and aim to codify all folk tales according to the salient features of their plots. These 'tale types' are to be found in the extensive *Motif-Index of Folk-Literature*, compiled by Antti Aarne and revised by Stith Thompson, which comprises six large volumes and refers to thousands of individual tale variants.[45] This approach permitted the identification and comparison of what are perceived to be variants on the same story from very diverse international and historical sources.

[45] *Motif-Index of Folk-Literature* (Copenhagen: Rosenkilde & Bagger, 1958).

Such scholarship associates the story of Bluebeard with three distinct tale types which are nonetheless acknowledged to be closely related. The most familiar of these types derives from the best-known Perrault version and so is most widely disseminated in France and francophone areas, but corresponds also with the version of 'Blaubart' included by the Grimms in the first edition *only* of the *Kinder- und Hausmärchen* (1812).[46] This tale type, which German scholars have also referred to as the 'Blaubarttypus', includes, according to Karl Voretzsch in a standard work of folklore scholarship, 'alle diejenigen Märchen, welche den Typ des vielfachen Frauenmörders in Verbindung mit der verbotenen Kammer und der glücklichen Errettung der bedrohten Frau festhalten'.[47] This type of tale is given the classification number 312 in the Aarne–Thompson index (which can also be expressed as AT 312). Paul Delarue went on to make finer distinctions within this category.[48] According to Delarue's classification, Perrault's *conte* can be classified as 312A; he identifies a second, related and yet distinct tale type which he numbers as 312B, in which a more emphatically Christian influence is perceptible and the villain is diabolical or demonic rather than human.

There is also a third cognate narrative category which both Delarue and Aarne–Thompson classify as No. 311 and which corresponds to *KHM* 46, 'Fitchers Vogel' (i. 235–9). In 'Fitchers Vogel', three sisters are magically carried off in turn by a *Hexenmeister* to his richly appointed home. The *Hexenmeister* forbids each sister to enter a particular room and, additionally, gives each an egg to look after. On entering the forbidden room and seeing a large bowl full of dismembered human bodies, the first two sisters drop the egg into the bowl and the egg becomes bloody. The wizard therefore discovers the sisters' disobedience and murders them. But the third sister has the foresight to put the egg away safely before she explores the house. Thus, on discovering the forbidden chamber and its contents, including her sisters' corpses, she is not only able to avoid incriminating herself, but also succeeds in resurrecting her sisters and tricking the wizard into smuggling them home, along with a good deal of his gold. The third sister then escapes her planned wedding with the

---

[46] Jacob Grimm and Wilhelm Grimm, *Kinder- und Hausmärchen* (1812–15), ed. Ulrike Marquardt and Heinz Rölleke, 3 vols. (Göttingen: Vandenhoeck & Ruprecht, 1986), i. 285–9; also in *KHM* i. 235–9.

[47] Voretzsch, 'Blaubart', 266.

[48] Paul Delarue, *Le Conte populaire français*, vols. 2–4 with M. L. Ténèze, 4 vols. (Paris: Érasme, 1957), i. 182–99.

wizard by covering herself in honey and feathers and reaching home disguised as a bird; the girls' brothers and relatives return to the wizard's house and burn him alive inside. A further, related category of narrative is AT 955, the Grimms' 'Räuberbräutigam' (*KHM* 40) (i. 219–23), in which a girl is engaged to a stranger and secretly observes him chopping up, salting, and eating another young woman before she can escape and ensure retribution. And in AT 710, 'Marienkind' (*KHM* 3) (i. 36–41), a girl is brought up in heaven by the Virgin Mary but severely punished with exile and the loss of speech for opening a forbidden door. Subsequently, the girl narrowly avoids being burnt at the stake in error for alleged infanticide. Finally, the so-called *Mädchenräuber* ballads are often linked with the *Blaubartmärchen* in that they involve a girl being carried off by a man who proves to be a serial murderer.[49]

However, the usefulness of such scrupulous differentiations and classifications is limited, since authors, tellers, and anthologists tend not to, or cannot, respect such hard-and-fast distinctions absolutely consistently. Furthermore, such apparently neutral and transparent categories in fact reflect the interests and values of their inventors, and are therefore not always objective.[50] And these fixed classifications tell us little about the *significance* and morphology of the tales themselves. Indeed, I would argue that the formalistic nature of traditional systems of *Märchen* classification itself may represent an attempt to deflect attention from their often problematic content and significance, with 'Blaubart' being a particularly relevant example. Finally, there is no evidence that even those tales considered to be the most authentic, and therefore used as a basis for such classifications (such as the Grimms' 'Fitchers Vogel'), are in fact more archetypal or 'uncontaminated' than other versions. For instance, Marina Warner describes the 'feel' of 'Fitchers Vogel' not as a harmonious and unadulterated whole but as 'a rummage bag of scraps', including elements from many traditions or tales (p. 255); and Voretzsch too notes: 'Schon in *Fitchers Vogel* . . . ist mancher Zug, der kaum ursprünglich ist' (p. 267).

But while all classifications of *Märchen* are thus problematic, the *Blaubartmärchen* is even more elusive than some other tales. First,

[49] See Ulrike Blaschek, 'Einführung', in Blaschek (ed.), *Märchen vom Blaubart* (Frankfurt am Main: Fischer, 1989), 9–37.

[50] e.g. Torborg Lundell, 'Gender-Related Biases in the Type and Motif Indexes of Aarne and Thompson', in Ruth B. Bottigheimer (ed.), *Fairy Tales and Society: Illusion, Allusion and Paradigm* (Philadelphia: University of Pennsylvania Press, 1986), 149–64.

many writers resist seeing 'Bluebeard' as a *Märchen* at all. For instance, Warner writes: 'The story can hardly be said to be a fairy tale' (p. 269); Ulrike Blaschek states: 'Blaubart . . . ist keine wirklich märchenhafte . . . Gestalt' (p. 12); and, most categorically, Bruno Bettelheim asserts: 'Actually this story is not a fairy tale' (p. 299). Such resistance to calling 'Bluebeard' a fairy tale or *Märchen* is usually justified on the grounds that the tale contains only two supernatural elements, the blue beard and the magic key, and Bettelheim also adds that the wife's character does not develop, a process which he considers a prerequisite of the genre. Many, notably earlier, commentators express suspicion in referring to the *Blaubartmärchen*, objecting to Perrault's urbane narrative tone, its 'profan' character, as Hedwig von Beit puts it,[51] or the apparently recent date of some of its features, such as the allegedly inauthentic or extraneous motif of the forbidden chamber which may come from the 'Tale of the Third Calender' in the *Arabian Nights*. Voretzsch calls this motif an 'orientalische Beimischung' (p. 269), and Emil Heckmann in his dissertation of 1930 agrees with him.[52] Such criticisms imply that a corruption of a putative, more authentic and therefore superior oral tale has taken place.

And second, 'Blaubart' tends to evade traditional classification. For instance, in the prestigious *Enzyklopädie des Märchens*, Bluebeard is included under 'Mädchenmörder', while in Bolte's and Polívka's important commentary on the Grimm tales, 'Blaubart' is subsumed under 'Fitchers Vogel'.[53] Other works of reference which include *Märchen* also omit the tale or bury it under another heading.[54]

So, even the way 'Blaubart' is classified and discussed by scholars reflects a certain unease about the tale. But there is more easily quantifiable evidence, too, for the suppression of 'Blaubart' in Germany. That tradition of suppression begins with the Brothers

---

[51] *Symbolik des Märchens: Versuch einer Deutung* (1952), 2nd rev. edn., 2 vols. (Berne: Francke, 1960), i. 611–17 (616).

[52] Emil Heckmann, 'Blaubart: Ein Beitrag zur vergleichenden Märchenforschung', Ph.D. dissertation (Heidelberg, 1930), 136–7 (Schwetzingen: Moch, 1932).

[53] Johannes Bolte and Georg Polívka, *Anmerkungen zu den Kinder- und Hausmärchen der Brüder Grimm* (1913), 5 vols. (Leipzig: Dieterich'sche Verlagsbuchandlung Theodor Weichen, 1913–32), i. 398–412.

[54] For instance, Scherf follows the Grimms and Bolte and Polívka in including 'Blaubart' in his entry on 'Fitchers Vogel' in his *Lexikon der Zaubermärchen*, 124–7; Franz Anselm Schmitt includes a wide range of *Märchen*, but not Bluebeard, in *Stoff- und Motivgeschichte der deutschen Literatur* (Berlin: de Gruyter, 1976); and Claude Aziza, Claude Olivieri, and Robert Sctrick smuggle him into their *Dictionnaire des symboles et des thèmes littéraires* (Paris: Nathan, 1978), under the heading 'Châteaux'.

Grimm. After including 'Blaubart' in the first edition of the *KHM* in 1812, the Grimms realized that the tale, which they had collected from the Hassenpflug family, was not an indigenous German tale, but a retelling in German of Perrault's literary French *conte*; they subsequently dropped it in favour of 'Fitchers Vogel' (provided by Friederike Mannel and Dortchen Wild), which shared certain motifs with 'Blaubart', since they considered that tale to be more authentically German. And today, too, 'Blaubart' has become relatively unfamiliar in twentieth-century Germany. Of the *Volksmärchen* anthologies published in West Germany during the postwar period (with the exception of scholarly editions of the *KHM* edited by Heinz Rölleke, complete editions of Bechstein's *Deutsches Märchenbuch*, which included 'Das Märchen vom Ritter Blaubart', and collections on specific themes such as witches) and available in the Deutsches Literaturarchiv in Marbach am Neckar in 1995, only four out of eighteen feature 'Blaubart'.[55] Clearly, following the Grimms' verdict, 'Blaubart' is not universally considered by anthologists to be a German *Volksmärchen*. Apparently quite anomalously, then, no fewer than three German anthologies devoted to the Bluebeard material have appeared in the last fifteen years.[56] However, at least two of these are aimed specifically at an adult audience, rather than at re-instating 'Bluebeard' in *Märchen* culture in general; and the very fact that these are specialized anthologies including variants of only one tale does not indicate that their editors are seeking to undo the special treatment 'Blaubart' has received.

Similarly, 'Blaubart' has not attracted the same volume of critical and scholarly attention as some other classic *Märchen*.[57] Bibliographies of secondary literature on Bluebeard contain only an insignificant number of secondary texts. In this respect 'Bluebeard' cannot compete with the most popular tales such as 'Little Red Riding Hood' or 'Hansel and Gretel', whose reception history alone attracts full-length studies. Furthermore, most of the secondary references to 'Blaubart' in such bibliographies are not studies

[55] And one of these anthologies (*Die schönsten Märchen der Welt für 365 und einen Tag*, ed. Lisa Tetzner, 12 vols. (Darmstadt: Luchterhand, 1981)) is exceptional in that it consists of 12 volumes and is not an anthology of specifically German *Märchen*.

[56] These are Hartwig Suhrbier, *Blaubarts Geheimnis: Märchen und Erzählungen, Gedichte und Stücke* (Cologne: Diederichs, 1984); Ulrike Blaschek (ed.), *Märchen vom Blaubart* (Frankfurt am Main: Fisher, 1989); and Felicitas Feilhauer (ed.), *Blaubärtchen: Märchen und Geschichten für neugierige Leser* (Munich: Hanser, 1990).

[57] Most recently, Scherf's *Märchenlexikon*; the *Enzyklopädie des Märchens*; and Suhrbier's anthology list only a small number of secondary texts.

exclusively of that tale, but rather are part of larger works on topics which happen to include it, such as works on *Märchen* in general or on Perrault's tales. For instance, almost all the items on Suhrbier's bibliography answer this description. And of the four longer studies cited by Suhrbier which are devoted to 'Blaubart', two date from the prewar period, and all are doctoral or MA dissertations, and thus have a limited circulation. It is also noteworthy in this context that until very recently the author of the only serious recent work on 'Bluebeard' in German, Suhrbier, was not a university academic at the time of writing his essay. And while it might appear that in 1995 the first postwar, published, book-length study of German 'Blaubart' texts at last appeared, with Winfried Menninghaus's *Lob des Unsinns. Über Kant, Tieck und Blaubart*, in fact its author is principally interested in Kant and Tieck, and theoretical issues connecting their writing as exemplified in one of Tieck's Bluebeard texts, rather than in the German 'Bluebeard' tradition.[58]

Several explanations can be proposed as to why this should be so, and yet none explains the situation fully. First, while the *KHM* has been central in the definition of what constitutes a *Märchen*, the first edition of 1812, the only one to contain the *Blaubartmärchen*, is hardly ever used as a basis for anthologies. This situation certainly explains the subordination of 'Blaubart' to 'Fitchers Vogel' in such works of reference as Bolte's and Polívka's. But although it is tempting to assume that this alone would account for the omission of 'Blaubart' from the contemporary German *Märchen* canon, the issue is more complex, particularly since 'Fitchers Vogel' too is missing from the anthologies explored above. Moreover, Ludwig Bechstein's *Deutsches Märchenbuch* (1845), which did include 'Das Märchen vom Ritter Blaubart', was better known and more popular than the Grimms' book in the nineteenth century, and a wealth of other nineteenth-century 'Blaubart' texts exists too.[59] Therefore it cannot be assumed that the tale was simply forgotten. Second, it could also be argued that 'Bluebeard' has been omitted from the popular canon because

---

[58] Winfried Menninghaus, *Lob des Unsinns. Über Kant, Tieck und Blaubart* (Frankfurt am Main: Suhrkamp, 1995). In 1999, a further book which deals partly with Bluebeard, Jürgen Wertheimer's *Don Juan und Blaubart: Erotische Serientäter in der Literatur* (Munich: Beck, 1999), appeared. Due to its very recent publication, however, it has not been possible to discuss this study in the present work.

[59] See Ruth B. Bottigheimer, 'The Publishing History of Grimms' Tales: Reception at the Cash Register', in Donald Haase (ed.), *The Reception of the Grimms' Fairy Tales: Responses, Reactions, Revisions* (Detroit: Wayne State University Press, 1993), 78–101.

its content is more violent than that of other tales. But this argument is not convincing either, since 'The Little Mermaid' or 'La Belle au bois dormant', the latter also included in *Histoires ou contes du temps passé*, contain equally gruesome material, and the twentieth century on the whole has not shied away from the literary depiction of violence and has sanctioned its presence in *Märchen* for children, due to the influence of Bettelheim, for instance. Third, the argument that 'Blaubart' is inadequately supernatural is also unconvincing, since a tale like 'Le Petit Chaperon rouge' from Perrault's collection is just as short on magic, the only instance of the supernatural in that tale being that the wolf can speak.

It may be inferred, then, that the caution surrounding the *Blaubart-märchen* is more than a formal question. From the outset, 'Blaubart' and the question of its classification and dissemination have had political implications. For instance, the Grimms' omission of the tale from the *KHM* in favour of 'Fitchers Vogel' and 'Der Räuber-bräutigam', and the subsequent subsumption of 'Bluebeard' under the heading of 'Fitchers Vogel' in works such as Bolte's and Polívka's, were based on perceptions of what constituted an authentically national culture. And the resistance to seeing 'Bluebeard' as a *Märchen*, the uncertainty about its classification, scholars' and antho-logists' apparent lack of enthusiasm for it, and the desire to distance and implicitly devalue it by identifying it with another, non-German culture are related not only to issues of national identity but also to the tale's gender politics, issues which the influential Grimms in par-ticular perceived to be incompatible with an ideal German culture.

Not only does the motif of the forbidden door come in for criticism by scholars for its perceived inauthenticity, recalling as it does the non-European *Arabian Nights* (a misleading judgement, since the *Arabian Nights* represents one of the origins of what we think of as European tale-telling); but Suhrbier has shown that a persistent association is made between Bluebeard and the Orient which permits a Eurocentric condemnation of his brutality as essentially 'other' and foreign. Where Bluebeard is orientalized, issues of gender and race meet, in that the brutality of the tale's gender politics provokes a denial that such things could happen in Europe. How-ever, Suhrbier also points out that this connection is made mainly in English texts and is rare in German ones. But even without such vivid Orientalizations, doubts as to Bluebeard's true nationality have been a consistent feature of the tale's history in German, with a desire to make him into an authentic German folk product on one hand competing on the other with a desire to distance him from home. In 1850, for instance, Alexander von Ungern-Starnberg's 'Blaubart' is (parodically) 'der vollkommenste Kavalier', and that term is enough to Frenchify him, as is the revelation that he is an effeminate user of wigs, make-up and the like. Alfred Döblin's eponymous protagonist in 'Ritter Blaubart' (1911) is exotically called Baron Paolo di Selvi, and in Richard von Kralik's patriotic Austrian play *Zarathustra Blaubart und der liebe Augustin* (1927), the evil Bluebeard is a Persian. In 1968 Winkler's *Mike Blaubart* is a 'Deutsch-Amerikaner'; and in 1982 Peter Rühmkorf sent his Bluebeard back to France. However, the latter part of the twentieth century has revised that perception of Bluebeard's nationality to a certain extent, as the final chapter of this study will show.

The possibility that 'Bluebeard' has been a particularly problematic text for the German tradition is suggested to me at least in part by the manner in which the tale breaches a series of gendered cultural taboos which traditionally operate in the German *Märchen*, following the lead of the *KHM*. First, there is the taboo on the use of a key and the acquisition of knowledge by a female character discussed above. Second, Ruth B. Bottigheimer has also pointed out that there is a particular *KHM* taboo on the acquisition of riches by a woman,[60] which does not seem to have concerned Perrault, for instance, when he granted a rich reward to Bluebeard's widow. Bottigheimer shows too that the Grimms inscribed into the *Märchen* a resistance to autonomous and, above all, successfully disobedient heroines like Perrault's. This would explain why, although 'Fitchers Vogel' and 'Der Räuberbräutigam' were taken up by the Grimms as alternatives to 'Blaubart' in the collection which was to shape our perception of *Märchen*, these tales too are seldom included in anthologies. 'Fitchers Vogel' in particular involves a considerably more resourceful and less tearful heroine than Perrault's or the Grimms' versions of 'Bluebeard'. She manages to save herself and her sisters and absconds with the villain's fortune to boot, and it seems that this challenging characterization has offset the prestige acquired by 'Fitchers Vogel' through being seen by the Grimms as a more 'German' story because of the passive and submissive ideal for German womanhood set up by the *KHM*.[61]

---

[60] Bottigheimer, *Grimms' Bad Girls and Bold Boys*, 130.

[61] Reasons for the comparable obscurity of 'Marienkind' (*KHM* 3, i. 36–41) are less

Third, the particularly problematic status of 'Bluebeard' in German appears to be bound up with its breaking of a *KHM* taboo on depicting irrational, human, male evil. 'Bluebeard' presents a brutal reflection of patriarchal power in the form of savagery inflicted by a man who appears to be fully human (rather than supernatural) and socially integrated. But in the German *Märchen* canon which is familiar today, gruesome crimes practised by older, apparently solid, bourgeois men do not have a prominent place, while frightful mutilations practised by older, supernatural, female figures like the mother-in-law of 'La Belle au bois dormant' ('elle était de race Ogresse'[62]) are practically a generic prerequisite. Bottigheimer has demonstrated how the image of the cannibal ogre with whom Bluebeard is frequently associated, while being initially and traditionally male, was systematically feminized from the nineteenth century onward in visual representations of ogredom in the Grimms' tales. And as a general principle, Bottigheimer shows that if we trace the image of the cannibal from English and French texts to the *KHM*, there is a consistent pattern of gender mutation whereby ogres who are initially male turn into females:

The male cannibal tradition did not die out with classical antiquity, but lived on in many tale traditions. In England children learned to associate a fearsome appetite for young English flesh with the Fee-Fi-Fo-Fum of a male giant, while French children grew up learning about ogres and ogresses, both of whom had a keen appetite for ragout fin à l'enfant. But Wilhelm Grimm, chiefly responsible for editing the collection of tales that bear his and his brother's name, codified a very different identity for cannibals. German youngsters reading *Grimms' Tales* came to associate the desire for . . . human flesh primarily with females.[63]

evident, for there, the prohibiting and punishing authority is the female Virgin Mary. Presumably this narrative has become equally unpalatable since it contradicts the virtues usually expected of Mary, depicting as it does an unmerciful character.

    [62] Bottigheimer, *Grimms' Bad Girls and Bold Boys*, 249.
    [63] Bottigheimer, 'The Face of Evil', *Fabula*, 29 (1988), 326–35 (328). In *Off With Their Heads! Fairy Tales and the Culture of Childhood* (Princeton, NJ: Princeton University Press, 1992), Maria Tatar uses the theories of Sigmund Freud and Melanie Klein to illuminate these cannibalistic fantasies. Tatar describes how, in *Totem and Taboo* (1913), Freud suggested that the root of his narrative about masculine, patrilinear conflict 'is probably the result of the transformation of oral aggressive tendencies directed upon the mother' (203); and Klein replaces that story about fathers with one about maternity in describing the mother's breast as the object of the child's cannibal fantasy, which is projected back onto the mother, producing a dread in the child of being eaten. Both psychoanalysts suggest that the origins of cannibalism somehow lie with the mother; and Klein's adaptation of Freud's theory seems to me to resonate with Bottigheimer's observation that female cannibals come to replace males in recent cultural history.

Therefore, while visual images of female cannibalism abound, a tale like 'Der Räuberbräutigam', with its uncompromising depiction of the bridegroom hacking into human flesh, is almost never illustrated.[64] And Bottigheimer fits this observation into a broader pattern:

The face of evil is incontrovertibly feminine, with much-vitiated male entries into the lists of evil a relatively recent phenomenon. This conclusion both complements and corroborates a content analysis of *Grimms' Tales*, where an unrelenting editorial pressure existed to incriminate female and to exonerate male figures. But whereas Grimm acted individually, this study suggests that his editorial tendencies formed part of a socially broad, geographically diverse, and historically extensive phenomenon. (pp. 334–5)

Thus, because 'Bluebeard' treats male violence and gendered power relations in a way which is culturally uncomfortable in Germany, it is treated with circumspection by authors and commentators alike.

For example, although writers have long been aware of parallels between the Bible and 'Blaubart', they have subtly changed the analogy in order to exonerate divine power. For example, no less an author than Frederick the Great focused on the affinity between the two narratives in his anti-clerical satire *Commentaires apostoliques et théologiques sur les saintes prophéties de l'auteur sacré de Barbe-bleue* (1779), whose narrator, masquerading as an ecclesiastical authority, claims that Perrault's 'La Barbe bleue' is a biblical book and comments:

Dieser Mann ist reich, er ist eitel, er hat einen blauen Bart. Das ist das charakteristische Zeichen des Teufels. Dieser Urheber alles unseres Elends kann keinen Bart haben, wie die Kinder der Menschen, er muß blau sein. Denn der Teufel, der unter der Gestalt einer Schlange, *Eve'n* im Paradiese versuchte, hatte eine bläuliche Farbe. Ich unterstützte diese Behauptung mit einem physischen Grunde. Die Lampen, worin man Oel brennt, werfen einen bläulichen Widerschein; die Teufel, welche die Verdammten in großen Kufen voll siedenden Oels untertauchen, färben unvermerkt ihren Bart mit dieser Farbe, so wie die Arbeiter in Vitriolwerken in die Länge grünliche Haare zu bekommen pflegen.[65]

Nevertheless, Frederick's identification of Bluebeard with Satan

---

[64] The only exception which Bottigheimer mentions shows him asleep, rather than red-handed.

[65] Friedrich II, König von Preußen, *Commentaires apostoliques et théologiques sur les saintes prophéties de l'auteur sacré de Barbe-bleue* (Berlin, 1779). Suhrbier has recently edited the first German translation (1787) as *Das Buch Blaubart: Eine Satire* (Frankfurt am Main: Insel, 1987), 26–7 quoted here.

involves an imperfect parallel between the biblical text and Perrault's, since he chooses to overlook the fact that while in the *Märchen* Bluebeard is both the speaker of the prohibition and the tempter, these roles are separated in the Bible. While the Bible ostensibly assigns these roles to God and Satan respectively, thus diminishing God's responsibility for the loss of Paradise, the parallel with the *Märchen* makes it abundantly clear that God can also be seen as the true tempter, for it is he who sets up the prohibition in an irresistible manner, and Satan must, in any case, be his creation. But to draw a direct parallel between God and Bluebeard, even in satire, would seriously challenge God's status as a benevolent patriarchal authority, a move which a king of Prussia who was committed to the divine right of kings, in a culture where Providentialist theology was dominant, would be concerned to avoid. And such exoneration of patriarchal power is quite typical of Bluebeard texts up to the present day. For example, a character in Rühmkorf's 'Blaubarts letzte Reise' states: 'denn so wahr wie die Menschenmutter Eva dem Rat der Schlange nicht widerstehen konnte, wird noch die klügste ihrer Töchter sich von ihrer unbezähmbaren Ausspählust verleiten lassen.'[66]

Rühmkorf's analogy, like Frederick's, not only permits the implicit shift of blame away from patriarchal authority, it also exculpates Bluebeard by blaming both his biblical mother, Eve, and his biological mother. Rühmkorf's narrator comments:

Nun hängen die lieben Mütter oft länger an den Schürzenbänder der Kinder als denen gut tut, und auch des Blaubarts Mutter hatte ihren Sohn so fest in ihr Herz geschlossen, daß sie ihn um nichts in die Welt hätte geben mögen, schon gar nicht in die Fänge eines fremden Frauenzimmers. (p. 110)

And Suhrbier too has shown (yet without arguing, as I have done here, that there is a peculiarly German tradition at work here) how many German literary versions blunt the tale's pro-feminist or subversive potential in one of three ways. They may reinterpret the moral of the story as a warning against feminine curiosity, thus discrediting the heroine and justifying her punishment. Alternatively, they may transpose the tale into a distant social or historical context, most popularly the Middle Ages, in order to undermine any sense that the tale may reflect aspects of contemporary society and civiliza-

---

[66] Peter Rühmkorf, 'Blaubarts letzte Reise' (1982), in *Der Hüter des Misthaufens: Aufgeklärte Märchen* (Reinbek bei Hamburg: Rowohlt, 1983), 110–22 (114).

tion. Or authors may seek to exculpate Bluebeard explicitly, by saying outright that he is innocent, rather than implicitly, by simply blaming his wife.

And finally, just as patriarchal power is exonerated, so too is the assertive heroine suppressed in the German tradition, as in the case of 'Fitchers Vogel'. This is the case in modern texts like Ingeborg Bachmann's *Das Buch Franza* (1977) too, which uses 'Blaubart' to comment on the suffering of women under patriarchy. Bachmann chooses to omit the utopian force of the happy ending in Perrault's version, leaving her eponymous female protagonist helpless in the face of, and ultimately destroyed by, the consequences of her 'Blaubartehe', which in turn symbolizes patriarchal society in general. That pessimistic conclusion is in striking contrast to recent English-language versions of 'Blaubart' and its variants by women writers, who also use the tale to make feminist points. In Angela Carter's *The Bloody Chamber* (1979), the heroine is saved by family solidarity, as in Perrault's text, except that here it is her mother, alerted by good sense, who comes dramatically to the rescue. In Margaret Atwood's *The Robber Bride* (1993), the female protagonists, for all their faults and weaknesses, are not passive and tearful. And even in Atwood's short story 'Bluebeard's Egg' (1983), while Bluebeard's wife is hurt by her husband, who resembles Franza's in significant ways—both are doctors, unfaithful, powerful, and willing to abuse the advantages bourgeois marriage gives them—she is not destroyed by him. In conclusion, the *Märchen*'s subversive messages are only rarely taken up affirmatively in German. The next chapter will show in more detail how that tradition is reflected in German secondary texts on 'Blaubart'.

3

NARRATIVES OF ORIGIN

A characteristic feature of traditional, notably older commentaries on *Märchen* is the attempt to identify origins—to establish what the original meaning of a particular tale must have been—or to locate where and when it originated. Commentaries on 'Blaubart' are no exception, and thus such older studies of 'Blaubart' as exist are generally concerned with establishing the origins and original meaning of the tale by drawing on ideas from mythology, anthropology, social history and folklore studies. More recently, similar attempts to identify an origin have been made using the idiom of psychoanalysis.

However, a survey of such studies reveals no consensus as to the origins of 'Blaubart'. Indeed, even the issue of whether its origins are oral or literary remains open. In studies on 'Bluebeard', the traditional view until very recently was that in committing 'La Barbe bleue' to paper, Perrault must have been responding to and recording a tale of oral origin, since his is its first known codification and no evidently similar written source was known on which he could have drawn directly. Therefore, it was with supreme confidence that an expert could state the accepted view in 1968: 'Personne, à vrai dire, ne prétend sérieusement que "La Barbe Bleue" pourrait venir de sources écrites.'[1] But the belief that an ancient oral culture is the sole origin of *Märchen* has been challenged in recent years; and there is little evidence for an obvious source in oral culture before Perrault.[2]

Today, therefore, there is no clear scholarly consensus as to the origin of the tale. On one hand, a recent German reference work (1995) believes that Paul Delarue's claim to have discovered a variant older than Perrault's is conclusive, and that Perrault's version is therefore not 'original'.[3] The *Enzyklopädie des Märchens* (1996), on the

---

[1] Marc Soriano, *Les Contes de Perrault: culture savante et traditions populaires* (Paris: Gallimard, 1968), 161.

[2] Nonetheless, studies which suggest possible antecedents are Paul Delarue, *Le Conte populaire français*, 4 vols. (vols. ii–iv with Marie-Louise Ténèze) (Paris: Érasme, 1957), i. 197–8; Marina Warner, *From the Beast to the Blonde: On Fairy Tales and Their Tellers* (London: Chatto & Windus, 1994), (261), who gives her sources as Charlotte Velay-Vallantin, *L'Histoire des contes* (Paris: Fayard, 1992), 85–7, and the *Bulletin archéologique de l'association bretonne*, 2 (1850), 133.

[3] Walter Scherf, *Das Märchenlexikon*, 2 vols. (Munich: Beck, 1995), i. 94–8.

other hand, takes the opposing view: 'Die Geschichte selbst wie der sprechende Name des frauenmordenden Reichen dürften eine Erfindung von Perrault sein.'[4] This observation is of great importance, for it represents the first instance of a *Märchen* scholar suggesting that the origin of the tale may not be either oral or ancient in a major, or indeed any, reference work.

Thus, recent literary studies too may compete with more traditional folkloristic theories to cast new light on the old question of the origin of the *Blaubartmärchen*. Recently, for instance, Marina Warner has highlighted similarities between Perrault's *conte* and a slightly earlier tale by his cousin Marie-Jeanne Lhéritier, 'La Princesse adroite' (1694), which Perrault would have known and which was probably inspired by Giambattista Basile's 'Sapia Liccarda', in his narrative cycle *Lo cunto de li cunti* (1634–6), better known as the *Pentamerone*.[5]

In Lhéritier's *conte*, the eponymous princess is the youngest of three sisters. Her sisters succumb to the sexual temptation of a villainous prince, a trangression which comes to light because the glass spindles which they possess as symbols of their virginity are broken. The third sister, however, not only resists temptation by the same prince but also succeeds in tricking—and killing—him. The similarities between the plots of 'La Princesse adroite' and 'La Barbe bleue' are striking. In each case there is a powerful, wicked suitor; a (possibly sexualized) prohibition; and the last intended female victim of a series triumphs over a male villain, breaking a cycle of violence. It can be argued, therefore, that the genesis of Perrault's text can be located not in ancient myth or superstition but in contemporary intertextuality. It is certainly well established that the attribution of some *contes de fées* to an individual author can be difficult, since it was common practice among the *salon* authors to imitate the style of one of their peers, or even to cite verbatim from other texts:

> Or une des traditions de cet esprit salonnier, c'est justement la pratique des citations interpolées qui constituent une sorte d'hommage à l'ami que l'on veut honorer. À noter que Mlle Lhéritier ne procède pas autrement quand elle veut honorer Charles Perrault.[6]

---

[4] Walter Puchner, 'Mädchenmörder', in Kurt Ranke et al. (eds.), *Enzyklopädie des Märchens: Handwörterbuch zur historischen und vergleichenden Erzählforschung*, to date 8 vols. (Berlin: de Gruyter, 1975–   ), viii. 1407–13 (1410).

[5] Warner, *From the Beast to the Blonde*, 249–52.

[6] Soriano, *Les Contes de Perrault*, 65.

And Warner notes too that 'as Perrault's version postdates his cousin's, his changes can be taken as emending hers, even teasing her for her treatment' (p. 249). It seems that, along with the traditional assumption that the origin of the tale is purely oral, scholarly bias against the women writers of *contes* has been responsible for the late discovery of this possible literary source. Indeed, 'La Princesse adroite' has frequently, although erroneously, been attributed to Perrault himself, although Warner notes that 'Perrault would never have created such an Amazon trickster for a heroine' (p. 249).

While such recent literary thories of origin are compelling, an exploration of other secondary texts which provide alternative, more traditional narratives of origin for 'Blaubart' is rewarding too, partly because literary authors responding to the material are often aware of such theories of origin which then come to inform their writing, with the result that this tradition of exegesis and commentary not only responds to primary texts but also influences them. Further-more, quests for an originary meaning, beginning with the Grimms' own commentary on the *KHM*, are most informative about the tale's meaning—not in prehistoric times, but at the time of their composi-tion.[7] And ultimately this tradition of exegesis is most fruitfully examined not in order to establish which theory of origin is correct but as a series of interpretations, or indeed retellings, of the *Märchen* in their own right. These ostensibly secondary texts are in fact part of the complex and evolving fabric of intertextuality which forms the tale of 'Bluebeard'.

ORIGINS IN HISTORY

Several attempts have been made to read 'Bluebeard' as folk historio-graphy of real events and characters. Two such characters who have been identified with Bluebeard are King Henry VIII of England and Ekkehard of Naumburg,[8] and a further possible historical antecedent for Bluebeard is 'ein gefürchtete[r] englische[r] Kämpfer namens "Blue Barb", der im Hundertjährigen Krieg von sich reden gemacht haben soll'.[9] Most commonly, however, the historical origins of the

---

[7] See *KHM* iii. 85–8.

[8] Ulrike Blaschek, 'Einführung', in Blaschek (ed.), *Märchen vom Blaubart* (Frankfurt am Main: Fischer, 1989), 9–37 (27); Elisabeth Frenzel, *Stoffe der Weltliteratur* (Stuttgart: Kröner, 1992), 107–11.

[9] Hartwig Suhrbier, 'Blaubart: Leitbild und Leidfigur', in *Blaubarts Geheimnis: Märchen und Erzählungen, Gedichte und Stücke* (Cologne: Diederichs, 1984), 11–79 (13).

tale are said to come from France, more specifically from Brittany, and the figures of Comor and Gilles de Rais (or Retz) have become popularly associated both with one another and with the Bluebeard tradition.[10]

It is thought that Comor was a minor Breton chieftain who seized power in c.540 CE. To do this, he murdered the ruling chieftain, Iona, and married his widow. Iona's son Judwal eventually returned to oust Comor, and killed him in 554–5 CE at the battle of Brank-Halleg. It is also recorded that Comor married Triphine of the Vannetais, daughter of the chieftain Wéroc or Guérok. Comor is mentioned in accounts of the life of St Gildas in two hagiographical volumes, Alain Bouchard's *Les Grands Croniques de la Bretaigne* (1514) and Albert Le Grand's *Les Vies des Saints de la Bretagne Armorique* (1636).[11] The latter is more frequently mentioned in the secondary literature on Bluebeard, perhaps because it accentuates Comor's cruelty and thus makes more dramatic reading. Bouchard writes that Gueroch (Bouchard's orthography) was forced to surrender Triphine to Comorus (Bouchard's orthography), reassured by St Gildas's promise that he would be able to restore his daughter to him alive and healthy on request. But after her marriage, Triphine discerned that she was pregnant and learnt that her husband was used to killing his wives once they were with child, whereupon she attempted to escape to her father, but was caught and beheaded by Comor. However, St Gildas kept his promise to Gueroch and restored his daughter to life.

Gilles de Rais (1404–40), a Maréchal de France who was married once only, is a historical figure about whom more is known, since many contemporary documents survive, and the records of his trials were recently edited by Georges Bataille.[12] Gilles's early feats of arms in the service of Joan of Arc are recorded, after which he returned to his Breton properties where he allegedly experimented with black magic. He was eventually condemned to death on charges of satanism and the murder of 140 children, although the legal docu-

---

[10] Harriet Angell Hobson Mowshowitz, 'Bluebeard and French Literature', Ph.D. thesis (University of Michigan, 1970). Different variants of the name Comor (such as Comorus, Comorre, Conomor, or Cunmar) are used in various texts and sources; Mowshowitz has Comor. Sometimes the name is given the Breton supplement 'ar Miliguet', 'the accursed'.

[11] Alain Bouchard, *Les Grandes Croniques de Bretaigne Composées en l'an 1514* (Nantes: Société des Bibliophiles Bretons et de l'Histoire de Bretagne, 1886), livre ii, feuillet 62; Albert Le Grand, *Les Vies des Saints de la Bretagne Armorique* (1636–7), 5th edn. (2 vols., Quimper: J. Salaun, 1901), i. 17–29.

[12] Georges Bataille, *Le Procès de Gilles de Rais* (Paris: Pauvert, 1972).

ments which survive are hardly likely to be reliable. As early as the eighteenth century, Voltaire questioned the judgement on Gilles as the probable product of unenlightened superstition and inquisition, and in the nineteenth century the historian Jules Michelet emphasized that Gilles was more likely to have been the victim of his political enemies than the vassal of Satan. In 1885, the Abbé Eugène Bossard made the first serious biographical study of Gilles which claimed an explicit connection between Gilles and Bluebeard on the basis of oral testimonies collected from peasants in the areas around Gilles's castles of Tiffauges and Machecoul, in which the two figures seemed to be linked.[13] The twin figures of Gilles and Bluebeard, and possible connections between them, influenced much French literature, such as Joris-Karl Huysmans's important novel *Là-bas* (1891), and is represented in German by Georg Kaiser's play *Gilles und Jeanne* (1923) and two prose narratives, Carl Felix von Schlichtegroll's *Gilles de Rais: Das Urbild des Blaubart* (1938) and Hans Natonek's posthumous novel *Blaubarts letzte Liebe* (1988). However, no definite link between Gilles and Bluebeard can be substantiated, and their association is best described as a confluence of narrative traditions.[14] Indeed, as early as 1930, Karl Voretzsch could state: 'die historische Ableitung darf als erledigt gelten.'[15]

ORIGINS IN MYTHOLOGY

Other theories of origin have been proposed which draw on perceived connections between various mythologies and the *Blaubartmärchen*, following the Grimms' notion that *Märchen* were 'abgesunkene Mythen'. In 1901 Paul Kretschmer referred to Italian, Greek, and Slavonic variants in which the obedience test of the forbidden chamber is replaced by a test in which the bride has to eat human flesh and in which, on failing to be obedient, she is murdered.[16] And there are echoes of the cannibalism motif in a

[13] Eugène Bossard, *Gilles de Rais, Maréchal de France dit Barbe-bleue* (1885) (Paris: Champion, 1886). While the glorification of Gilles was initiated by the Marquis de Sade in *Justine* (1791), Bossard's theory became influential in literary developments of the Bluebeard theme, e.g. in Joris-Karl Huysmans's novel *Là-bas* (1891), ed. Yves Herlant (Paris: Gallimard, 1985). [14] Mowshowitz, 'Bluebeard and French Literature', 54.

[15] Karl Voretzsch, 'Blaubart', in Lutz Mackensen with Johannes Bolte (eds.), *Handwörterbuch des deutschen Märchens*, 2 vols. (Berlin: de Gruyter, 1930–3), i. 266–70 (268).

[16] Paul Kretschmer, 'Das Märchen vom Blaubart', *Mitteilungen der anthropologischen Gesellschaft*, 31 (1901), 62–70.

Dutch variant provided by the Grimms in their commentary on 'Fitchers Vogel'. In the cellar of the husband's castle, the bride comes upon an old woman: '"Ei Mütterchen" sprach das Mädchen, "was macht sie da?" "Ich schrappe Därme, mein Kind, morgen schrappe ich eure auch"' (iii. 87–8). It could be that the entrails are being pre-pared for culinary purposes (of course, in the Western tradition culinary and sexual appetites often correlate, for instance in 'Little Red Riding Hood'). In these versions described by Kretschmer, the husband or abductor seems more demonic than human.

Kretschmer, and in 1930 Emil Heckmann, argued that these variants demonstrated that the tale had originated in Hellenic mythology and reflected classical fantasies about such underworld deities as Hades (under the name of Eurynomos) or Hecate, who ate the flesh of the dead.[17] The figure of Hades gradually mutated during antiquity from being a demon of the underworld to being its king, and since the image of a king consuming human flesh came to be considered inappropriate, that proclivity was later transferred to an inferior demon, Charon or Charos, who, along with his wife, Charóndissa, ate the dead. According to Heckmann, the pair were still used in Greek folklore at the time of his study, and he believed that this mythology may have been used in Mediterranean and Southern Europe as a possible explanation for the untimely death of young women:

In unseren Märchen . . . finden wir leicht die Antwort auf diese Fragen (warum holt sich der Tod immer wieder eine neue Braut, warum ist er mit keiner zufrieden?): 'Weil keine seine Gemahlin werden und die ekle Speise mit ihm teilen will.' (p. 135)

Furthermore, as memories of such myths involving the consumption of human flesh became culturally unintelligible and receded, the obedience test of eating human organs or limbs was replaced by the test of the forbidden chamber, which Heckmann thus regards as a corruption. However, the *Handwörterbuch des deutschen Märchens* points out that there is no evidence for the assumption that such *Menschen-fresservarianten* antedate the more familiar 'Bluebeard' versions which involve a forbidden chamber.

[17] Emil Heckmann, *Blaubart: Ein Beitrag zur vergleichenden Märchenforschung*, Ph.D. thesis (Heidelberg, 1930) (Schwetzingen: Moch, 1932). In *Symbolik des Märchens: Versuch einer Deutung* (1952), 2nd rev. edn., 2 vols. (Berne: Francke, 1960), i. 611–17, Hedwig von Beit also refers to the cannibalistic variants. More recently, Blaschek also refers extensively to this tradition.

Other theories of mythological origin current in the early twentieth century involved astrology. For instance, according to Émile Gabory in 1926:

Barbebleue serait le Dieu soleil anthropomorphisé à des époques relativement récentes; la petite clé serait l'Aurore qui ouvre les portes de l'Orient; les sept femmes seraient les sept Pléjades [*sic*], épouses du Dieu soleil.[18]

An alternative astrological model was provided by Marie Pancritius (1930), who interpreted the tale and related folk songs as a residual memory of a prehistoric, matriarchal astrology which was covered over by later, patriarchal models.[19] According to this theory, the original number of wives must have been twelve (as it is in some folk material about serial murders of women, notably the *Mädchen-räuberballaden*), since the bride represents the new moon who is eclipsed or murdered by her husband, the dark phase of the moon, twelve times a year. In this drama however the ultimate authority is not the murderous husband but his mother, the moon goddess, who ordains the series of murders. Pancritius accounted for the forbidden chamber as follows:

Da die auf uns gekommenen . . . Mythen im Schatten von Tempeln und Heiligtümern entstanden sein müssen, und hier verbotene Räume eine Hauptrolle spielten, so lag das Betreten des verbotenen Raumes als straf-würdiger Frevel nahe, und dieses *verbotene Gemach* bewahrte, als der Schwarz-mond zum Blaubart wurde, die Opfer—die elf Mondhäupter. (p. 897)

There are, however, problems with this ingenious explanation. First, all the evidence is extremely disparate, and none of the individual texts cited by Pancritius provides any consistent confirmation of her schema. Indeed, she arrived at such confirmation only by associating many pieces of undated evidence of diverse geographical provenance and correcting their many 'inaccuracies' (e.g. 'Die drei Schwestern werden ursprünglich wohl zwölf an der Zahl gewesen sein' (p. 904)). Second, the popular nineteenth-century theory of the existence of a prehistoric matriarchy is no longer generally accepted.[20] Due to their highly speculative nature, such mythological theories are no longer accepted today.

[18] Quoted by Heckmann, *Blaubart*, 170–1.

[19] Marie Pancritius, 'Aus mutterrechtlicher Zeit: Blaubart', *Anthropos*, 25 (1930), 879–909.

[20] See Sarah B. Pomeroy, 'Selected Bibliography on Women in Antiquity', *Arethusa*, 6 (1973), 127–57; Lucia Nixon, 'Gender Bias in Archaeology', in Léonie J. Archer, Susan Fischler, and Maria Wyke (eds.), *Women in Ancient Societies: An Illusion of the Night* (London: Macmillan, 1994), 1–23.

ORIGINS IN SOCIAL PRACTICE

Other commentators have suggested that the tale is an account of social or linguistic practice which has become unfamilar with the passing of time. Earliest of all, the Grimms suggested that the tale may originally have referred to a case of leprosy which was once thought to be curable by bathing in the blood of virgins.[21] And since, according to some superstitions, leprosy was also thought to be a sign of excessive sexual appetite, the Grimms' theory seems to have a faint echo in the twentieth century's fascination with Bluebeard as a serial sexual murderer. The Grimms also made linguistic observations according to which the possible origins of the uncanny blue beard were located in some familiar element in the language of daily life, a classic case of what Freud was to call 'das Unheimliche' originating in a repression of 'das Heimliche'.[22] Thus, they pointed out:

> In Hamburg sagt man von einem Starkbärtigen, es sei ein Blaubart . . . dasselbe gilt von dem ehemaligen Hessen; hier in Cassel ist ein verwachsener, halb alberner und toller Handwerksbursch unter dem Namen bekannt genug. (iii. 526)

But of course it may well be that the 'Handwerksbursch' acquired his name from the familiar *Märchen*, rather than the name's being evidence for the common use of the expression 'Blaubart' independently of the *Märchen*. Furthermore, while the Grimms located the origins of 'Blaubart' in France, they, like other commentators who refer to the idea of the black beard, do not provide evidence for a similar expression in French which, on this argument, Perrault must have been echoing. Such expressions do not seem to be registered in French dictionaries of the seventeenth century or of more recent times.[23] But although the interpretation of Bluebeard as a 'Stark-

---

[21] Voretzsch calls this 'eine bloße Mutmassung', 268. But Warner too associates Bluebeard and a deforming, anti-social illness related to sexuality, quoting Italo Calvino's 'Il naso d'argento' (1956), based on Italian tales in which the villain has a silver nose, which might cover a deformation caused by syphilis (256).

[22] Sigmund Freud, 'Das Unheimliche' (1919), in Freud, *Studienausgabe*, ed. Alexander Mitscherlich, Angela Richards, and James Strachey, 11 vols. (Frankfurt am Main: Fischer, 1989), iv. 241–67.

[23] While the *Dictionnaire de l'Académie* (1694)—contemporary with Perrault's text—lists expressions involving beards, it does not mention blue beards. Neither does the modern *Grand Larousse de la langue française*, 6 vols. (Paris: Larousse, 1971). However, reflecting the influence of Perrault, the *Trésor de la langue française: dictionnaire de la langue du 19e et du 20e siècle (1789–1960)*, 16 vols. (Paris: Éditions du CNRS and Gallimard: 1971–94) makes the following reference: '*Barbe bleue* (p. allus. au principal personnage du conte de Perrault *Barbe Bleue*). "Un mari cruel, et parfois même un assassin"' (iv. 165).

bärtiger' may be a misleading explanation as far as Perrault's work goes, its relative plausibility has made it a popular topos in literary versions. In secondary literature the idea was picked up in 1883 by K. Hofmann, who made explicit the sexual subtext implicit in the association made with leprosy when he added a further twist by interpreting the profuse growth of hair as a symbol of potency and masculinity:

Nach den Sprichwörtersammlungen des sechszehnten Jahrhunderts bedeutet Blaubart einen Mann, der einen dichten schwarzen Bart hat, der ins bläuliche schimmert. Nach der Meinung jener Zeit wurde ein solcher *Blaubart* für einen geborenen *Don Juan* und *Frauenverführer* gehalten.[24]

These joint, explicit associations of beardedness with potency and Bluebeard with Don Juan were a new development in the tale in the late nineteenth century, and they tally with those literary reworkings of the tale from that time onward which interpret it as an account of an often admirable, potent, and sexually active masculinity, an important change in emphasis.

However, none of these ideas accounts fully for the sheer weirdness, indeed the apparently supreme unaccountability, of the *blue* beard, which (for all that it may have merely been Perrault's amusing invention, as the *Enzyklopädie des Märchens* suggests), positively gleams with more suggestive possibilities. There exists a wealth of commentary in German on the colour blue, demonstrating that this is no ordinary colour, but symbolically exceptionally powerful, since no other colour has inspired such critical interest or similar collections of reflections published in German.[25] The colour has unsettling associations in German culture. Briefly, its conceptual range includes all kinds of suggestive, supernatural elements: it is the colour of the Virgin Mary, of the Romantic *blaue Blume*, as well as diabolical in its connotations. The *Lexikon der sprichwörtlichen Redensarten* (1973) states: 'Blau ist sodann (vor allem in der älteren Sprache) die Farbe der Täuschung, Verstellung und Lüge', as in the expression 'das Blaue vom Himmel herunterlügen'.[26] This work of reference also points to

[24] 'Über die älteste Quelle der Blaubartsage', *Romanische Forschungen*, 1 (1883), 434–5.

[25] Hans Gercke (ed.), *Blau: Farbe der Ferne* (Heidelberg: Wunderhorn, 1990), esp. Regina Keil, 'Von Blaustrümpfen und Blaumäulern: Linguistische Betrachtungen zu einem plümeranten Thema' (209–33); Angelika Overath, 'Azurne Scherben', *Merkur*, 38 (1984), 619–28; and Angelika Lochmann and Angelika Overath (eds.), *Das blaue Buch: Lesarten einer Farbe* (Nördlingen: Greno, 1988).

[26] Lutz Röhrich, *Lexikon der sprichwörtlichen Redensarten*, 2 vols. (Freiburg im Breisgau: Herder, 1973), i. 136. See also Hanns Bächtold-Stäubli and E. Hoffmann-Krayer (eds.),

the use of the colour blue in women's costume as signal of sexual transgression:

> blau tragen und *es ist nur eine blaue* beziehen sich auf einen in manchen Orten üblichen Brauch: gefallene Mädchen durften keine weiße Schürze mehr tragen und mußten auch bei Prozeßionen in einer blauen erscheinen. (i. 137)

Interestingly, this observation returns us to the punishment of feminine sexual curiosity. In short then, the colour blue is remarkable for its symbolic versatility and association with the intangible; as Goethe wrote in his *Farbenlehre* (1810):

> Blau, Rotblau und Blaurot . . . stimmen zu einer unruhigen, weichen und sehnenden Empfindung . . . So wie Gelb immer ein Licht mit sich führt, so kann man sagen, daß Blau immer etwas Dunkles mit sich führe . . . Diese Farbe macht für das Auge eine sonderbare und fast unaussprechliche Wirkung. Sie ist als Farbe eine Energie; allein sie steht auf der negativen Seite und ist in ihrer höchsten Reinheit gleichsam ein reizendes Nichts. Es ist etwas widersprechendes von Reiz und Ruhe im Anblick . . . Wie wir den hohen Himmel, die fernen Berge blau sehen, so scheint eine blaue Fläche auch vor uns zurückzuweichen . . . Wie wir einen angenehmen Gegenstand, der vor uns flieht, gerne verfolgen, so sehen wir das Blaue gerne an, nicht weil es auf uns dringt, sondern weil es uns nach sich zieht . . . Das Blau gibt uns ein Gefühl von Kälte, so wie es uns auch an Schatten erinnert. Wie es vom Schwarzen abgeleitet sei, ist uns bekannt . . . Blaues Glas zeigt die Gegenstände im traurigen Licht . . .[27]

The hue of the beard is not only mysterious, but evokes a massive range of symbolic possibilities. As such the beard remains ultimately impervious to, or in excess of, the insistently realist interpretations proposed here by commentators seeking to locate its meaning in real historical practices.

On another tack, with reference to 'Fitchers Vogel', the Grimms also noted the similarity between the bride's escape strategy, which involves disguising herself as a bird by covering herself in honey and feathers, and the contemporary punitive practice of tarring and feathering. They cited two real, near-contemporary instances in which women had been punished in this manner and made to imitate animals. The most recent of these incidents cited by the

---

Handwörterbuch des deutschen Aberglaubens, 10 vols. (Berlin de Gruyter, 1927–42), i. 1366–86; Gercke, *Blau*, esp. Keil, 'Von Blaustrümpfen und Blaumäulern'; Overath, 'Azurne Scherben'; and Lochmann and Overath, *Das blaue Buch*.

[27] Johann Wolfgang von Goethe, *Werke, Kommentare und Register. Hamburger Ausgabe*, ed. Erich Trunz, 14 vols. (Munich: Beck, 1981), xiii. 498.

Grimms had happened in Spain in 1824 to 'eine Frau[,] die sich unehrerbietige Reden gegen den König erlaubt hatte' (iii. 86).

And in 1905, J. A. Macculloch saw the tale with its cannibalistic variants described above as a folk memory of genuine, historical cannibalism as opposed to descriptions of it in mythology as proposed by Kretschmer and Hoffmann.[28] In 1923 Pierre Saintyves, referring to a very wide range of sources which went far beyond relatively recent, West European narratives, suggested that the tale depicted pre-Christian initiation rites.[29] While it is acknowledged that Saintyves provided valuable comparative evidence from Eastern sources, his syncretic views are rejected today because, as Paul Delarue put it, 'On reste confondu devant de telles méthodes de comparaison et de recherche' (i. 199).

A more recent theory uses language to explain the term 'Barbe bleue'. In 1988, Jean-Louis Picherit suggested that the term is derived from the Old French 'barbeu' meaning 'werewolf'.[30] On this reading, Perrault's seventeenth-century codification preserves only vestiges of earlier, more monstrous tales which involved a semi- or inhuman character more akin to the ogre or demon of the cannibal variants. To substantiate his suggestion, Picherit referred to similarities between medieval accounts of werewolves and the *Blaubartmärchen*. Just as Bluebeard seems to lead a double life, so a werewolf undergoes transformation; both figures are bloodthirsty and fierce; and some werewolf stories hold the werewolf's wife responsible for his transformations. Furthermore, once in monstrous form, the werewolf in such stories returns to wreak revenge upon his wife, just as Bluebeard attempts to take revenge on his wife for discovering his double identity as both generous husband and serial killer. Picherit's idea recalls further connections too, for in Brittany, Comor is described in local legend as a werewolf.[31] And the image of Bluebeard the werewolf may also possibly hark back to the image of Bluebeard the leper, for the linguistic imagery surrounding leprosy is linked to wild beasts. The disease's Latin name is *leonine facies*, for in the final stages leprosy can disfigure the sufferer's face in such a way that (it has been thought) it resembles a lion's.

[28] J. A. Macculloch, *The Childhood of Fiction* (London: Murray, 1905).

[29] Pierre Saintyves (ps. Émile Nourry), *Les Contes de Perrault et leurs récits parallèles, leurs origines* (Paris: Librairie Critique, 1923), 353–96.

[30] Jean-Louis G. Picherit, 'Qui était Barbe bleue?', *Neuphilologische Mitteilungen / Bulletin de la société néophilologique / Bulletin of the Modern Language Society*, 89 (1988), 374–7.

[31] Warner, *From the Beast to the Blonde*, 261.

In 1989 Ulrike Kindl made the suggestion that the motif of wife murder can be understood as an effort on Bluebeard's part to avoid paternity, since a father may perceive his children as a threat to his authority, as in the Oedipus myth for instance.[32] Bluebeard's murders also eliminate the father's potential fear of matrilinear inheritance, which is, of course, the conclusion of Perrault's tale where the wife and her blood relatives take possession. The logic of this second point seems suspect, since Bluebeard's wife can be expected to produce Bluebeard's legitimate children, unless she is, rightly or wrongly, suspected of adultery. And yet there is no evidence for the wife's adultery in Perrault's tale. Furthermore, if Bluebeard *is* so afraid of matrilinearity, it is unclear why he should marry in the first place: as a rich man, sex would be easily available to him without marriage. But most recently, and less sensationally, the series of dead brides has been interpreted as a representation of women's fear of death in childbirth, an occurrence so frequent before the nineteenth century that the family constellation of an older multiple widower marrying yet another young wife was not unusual.[33] Such an interpretation reverses that suggested by Kindl according to which the husband sought to avoid becoming a parent through the use of violence. Here, it is the wife who evades maternity by means of the violent death of Bluebeard, a far more illicit idea in a Christian culture which traditionally considered motherhood to be the highest feminine vocation, and which recalls the perplexingly unmotherly (and seldom mentioned) Madonna of the Grimms' 'Marienkind'.

Among the theories locating the meaning of *Blaubartmärchen* in social reality, this is one of the more plausible, and while it cannot be accepted as a certain identification of the *Blaubartmärchen's* origin to the exclusion of all other possibilities, it does help explain the tale's traditional appeal. And the reading of 'Bluebeard' as a story about a young woman who escapes the frequently fatal consequences of marriage and sex, i.e. childbirth, tallies with the idea that tales told by women functioned to calm fear and provide comfort.[34] And finally, and perhaps most plausibly, it has been suggested that in 'La Barbe bleue' Perrault was consciously and supportively contributing to the

[32] 'Blaubarts Mord-Motiv oder: Wie neugierig darf Märchendeutung sein?', *Lendemains*, 53 (1989), 111–17.

[33] Warner, *From the Beast to the Blonde*, 263.

[34] Ibid. 259–65; Jeannine Blackwell, 'Fractured Fairy Tales: German Women Authors and the Grimm Tradition', *Germanic Review*, 62 (4) (1987), 162–74.

condemnation by radical, proto-feminist, salon women in contemporary Paris of the lack of legal and property rights for married women, double standards of marital behaviour for men and women, and the common practice of arranged marriage for material gain.[35]

PSYCHOLOGICAL ORIGINS

In the twentieth century, interest in the mythological or historical origins of 'Blaubart' has been increasingly replaced by psychoanalytic theories. In particular, Jungian thinking has dominated psychoanalytic readings of the *Blaubartmärchen* and influenced both literary studies and literary production: examples are Mowshowitz's dissertation, Suhrbier's article, and Karin Struck's novel *Blaubarts Schatten* (1991). The frequency of Jungian readings can be explained either in terms of a tradition which, once established, gains its own momentum or, alternatively, in terms of a particular compatibility between a certain perception of the *Märchen* and Jungian thinking. As C. G. Jung himself wrote:

In Mythen und Märchen wie im Traume sagt die Seele über sich selbst aus, und die Archetypen offenbaren sich in ihrem natürlichen Zusammenspiel.[36]

And a recent Jungian commentator has compared that view of the unconscious with Max Lüthi's classic definition of the *Volksmärchen* in a way which highlights their alleged structural similarity:

Während zum Beispiel der Roman lebensvolle Personen beschreibt, mit widersprüchlichen Regungen und Anlagen, zerlegt das Märchen in eindeutige und isolierte Figuren. Der sichtbaren Isolation der Gestalten und Geschehnisse entspricht aber eine Allverbundenheit, d.h. die isolierten Figuren fügen sich, unsichtbar gelenkt, zum harmonischen Zusammenspiel. Das Märchen ist eine Dichtung, die den Zufall nicht kennt. Die Koordination des Geschehens ist nicht Zufall, sondern Präzision. Das sichtbare Märchengeschehen erscheint als Gipfel eines Landes, das im Nebel liegt.[37]

According to this widely accepted definition, there is a remarkable

---

[35] Warner, *From the Beast to the Blonde*, 169.

[36] Quoted in Mario Jacoby, 'Märcheninterpretation aus der Sicht C.G. Jungs: Allgemeine Überlegungen zu einer tiefenpsychologischen Hermeneutik', in Mario Jacoby, Verena Kast, and Ingrid Riedel (eds.), *Das Böse im Märchen* (1978), 2nd rev. edn. (Fellbach: Bonz, 1980), 12–23 (22).

[37] Max Lüthi, *Das europäische Volksmärchen* (Berne: Francke, 1960), cited here by Jacoby, 'Märcheninterpretation', 15.

consonance between the structure of the *Märchen* and the workings of the unconscious (the 'Land, das im Nebel liegt'). The affinity perceived between psychoanalysis and that type of *Märchen* has proved tremendously influential in the twentieth century. Indeed, it has been argued that the Grimmian *Märchen*'s extraordinary usefulness to psychoanalysis has helped form the foundation of the *KHM*'s contemporary success.[38]

In 1952 another Jungian, Hedwig von Beit, analysed 'Blaubart' and its related tales as expressions of archetypal patterns under the heading 'Die Fahrt der Jungfrau'. Here, 'Blaubart' is understood as a tale about the maturing process of the feminine subject in which male figures, Bluebeard and the wife's brothers, represent, respectively, negative and positive aspects of the animus in the feminine psyche.[39] Consequently, the bride's confrontation with Bluebeard does not represent an encounter with another, hostile being but rather with 'die negative Seite des eigenen Animus . . . die Abgründe des eigenen Wesens' (p. 614).[40] Thus, von Beit concludes: 'Dieser dämonische Aspekt des weiblichen Logos ist nur durch ein starkes, sich ihm entgegenstellenden Bewußtsein oder durch Opfer zu überwinden' (p. 643).

In 1978 Verena Kast came to similar conclusions in using Jungian theory to explain the *Märchen* as an account of processes in the feminine psyche, depicting Bluebeard as a destructive animus figure.[41] However, Kast goes further than von Beit by introducing a societal dimension to her reading. She sees the tale as an account of blind power-seeking on the part of Bluebeard—patriarchal man—to which women submit equally blindly for the sake of wealth and status, thus forfeiting their naturally unmaterialistic femininity. Accordingly, the dead wives represent the high spiritual price that is paid by women for such wordly goods. When the woman protagonist opens the chamber, she realizes what she has done to herself, and realizes also that by virtue of this behaviour she too is 'irgendwo Blaubart' (p. 100), dominated by her negative animus. As with von Beit, the solution lies in the appearance of the brothers, the positive

---

[38] Ruth B. Bottigheimer, 'The Publishing History of Grimms' Tales: Reception at the Cash Register', in Donald Haase (ed.), *The Reception of Grimms' Fairy Tales: Responses, Reactions, Revisions* (Detroit: Wayne State University Press, 1993), 78–101.

[39] Von Beit, *Symbolik des Märchens*, ii. 586.

[40] Ibid. i. 616.

[41] Verena Kast, 'Der Blaubart: Zum Problem des destruktiven Animus', in Jacoby et al., *Das Böse im Märchen*, 90–108.

animus figures, and at the end, where the woman is said to be almost dead from fright, this is interpreted as symbolizing her rebirth as another person. While women suffer from being involved in such arrangements, Kast stresses at several points that what she considers to be the feminist analysis of such relationships is wrong in that it makes a neat distinction between victims and aggressors: 'Mir scheint es gerade auch für die Frauenbewegung wichtig zu sein, daß wir Frauen . . . Blaubart in uns erleben und in uns bekämpfen, wenn es ihn gibt' (p. 105). That is, she argues that gender is not central to the tale's account of power relations, because the sado-masochism that causes the victim to maintain the pattern is, like Bluebeard, present in both men and women.

Both von Beit's and Kast's approaches suffer from a-historicity and overgeneralization to the extent that their characterizations of what is properly masculine and feminine and how these principles ideally work take no account of historical, regional, class-based, or other specific circumstances. In fact, their schema reinscribes a modern, bourgeois ideal of gender roles (propagated, for instance, by the nineteenth-century *Märchen*) which is then applied indiscriminately to all of history, regardless of the specific issues which Perrault showed to be central in the gender politics of the late seventeenth century, such as the status in law of a wife. Thus, for instance, von Beit and Kast do not consider the wife's subjugation to her husband in terms of historical, legal, or material issues, but only as masochism, with the complex interrelations between real legal or material oppression and the production of a psychological masochism in their subject left unexamined. Furthermore, their interpretations take the edge off the gender politics of 'Blaubart' by making the violence purely symbolic and recasting the tale, ironically enough, as an account of a normative healing process. Finally, the notion of a potentially harmonious co-existence of anima and animus dull the edge of the text's commentary on the violence that is inherent in real gender divisions as they are inscribed in Perrault's tale. Subtly, too, these readings imply that the tale may be, at bottom, about the potential of women's imaginations to run riot and project negative thoughts onto men, irrationally or hysterically imagining them to be murderers.

The most recent Jungian study of 'Blaubart' is Helmut Barz's *Blaubart: Wenn einer vernichtet, was er liebt*.[42] While Barz shares certain basic assumptions with von Beit and Kast, his work involves interest-

[42] (Zurich: Kreuz Verlag, 1987).

ing differences. First, he refers to the Grimms' rather than to Perrault's version of the tale; second, his account explicitly claims to be pro-feminist and describes 'Blaubart' as a tale about the cata-strophic effects of patriarchy; third, he uses the tale principally to examine the personalities of men rather than women. In this context, the choice of primary text is significant. Not only is the Grimms' 'Blaubart' more clearly a tale about feminine helplessness than is Perrault's 'La Barbe bleue', it also lacks Perrault's sharp observations about the material basis of marriage. These two features enable Barz to concentrate on an idealistic notion of essential femininity and propagate an ideal heterosexual relationship based on a romantic notion of complementarity rather than, as Perrault suggests, material expediency.

Barz claims that the female protagonist of the *Blaubartmärchen* is motherless because, in the patriarchal family, the presence and posi-tive influence of the mother are erased.[43] As a result the daughter is dominated by her father and has no positive anima, or strongly developed feminine, i.e. intuitive and emotional side. Her union with Bluebeard indicates that she comes to be dominated by her negative animus, and her further development hinges on her response to the corpses in the forbidden chamber. She may either regress further into submission,[44] or reject her husband. Rejection of the murderous husband would make the woman herself a female Bluebeard, a type of unfeeling and therefore unfeminine woman whom Barz criticizes elsewhere. Therefore, only few women respond adequately to the discovery of the secret chamber:

ohne darüber in Panik oder in Schulmeisterei zu verfallen . . . Sie können erschrocken stillhalten und sich fragen, ob ihnen diese quälenden Grausamkeiten wirklich ganz fremd sind. Gibt es nicht auch in ihren Herzen eine Mördergrube? Kennen sie nicht die eiskalte Berechnung im Umgang mit Männern, die gerade deren Sehnsüchte aus verständlicher Rache ausnutzt? Spüren sie nichts von der Grausamkeit der verschlingenden Mutter in sich . . .? Haben sie nicht selber ein wenig Angst vor dem Weiblichen, von dem sie nur die angenehmen Seiten sehen möchten . . .? Es gibt Frauen, die sich so fragen, und

[43] This is a familiar observation in earlier feminist commentaries on *Märchen*. For instance, Andrea Dworkin in *Woman Hating* (New York: Plume, 1974) pointed out that, where mother figures are influential, they tend to be wicked; and 'When [the fairy-tale mother] is good, she is soon dead' (41).

[44] This helplessness may be, Barz suggests, an anima projection on the part of men, who may be so alienated from their feminine side that they project their negative perception of it onto their female partner.

die deswegen zu zweifeln beginnen, ob das Schicksal und die Untaten des
Blaubarts wirklich nur Männersache seien. Sie können vielleicht, wenn sie ihm
trotz allem zu lieben vermögen, den Blaubart erlösen—gerade deswegen, weil
sie an ihm Anteil haben. (pp. 52–3)

Barz then examines what Bluebeard represents for contemporary
men. Just as the wife's weakness is the result of her motherless childhood, so parental relationships are also responsible for Bluebeard's
hatred and fear of his partner and his own anima. However, Barz
here reverses the family constellation which he considered to apply to
Bluebeard's wife:

Nicht selten sind es Männer, die einen schwachen Vater und eine dominierende
Mutter hatten (denn es liegt vielen vom Patriarchat dominierten Müttern
nahe, sich 'liebevoll' an ihre Söhne zu klammern) und die deswegen später ein
besonders zwiespältiges Verhältnis zum Weiblichen entwickelten: Sie sind ihm
einerseits verfallen und spüren andererseits die Notwendigkeit, sich daraus zu
befreien. Sie haben ein unersättliches Bedürfnis, zu lieben und geliebt zu
werden, und fühlen sich doch dem riesigen Anspruch, den sie an ihre Liebes-
fähigkeit stellen, nie gewachsen—sondern erleben sich als jenen Blaubart, der
seine Frauen aus verzweifelter Liebe tötet. (pp. 96–7)

Blame for Bluebeard's development is ascribed *not* to his father but to
his mother, a shift that is necessary to distract attention from the male
as oppressor and to direct it towards the male as victim who kills out
of 'verzweifelter Liebe', not hate, and deserves women's love and
sympathy. Thus, because such men long to be saved by a perfectly
loving, forgiving woman, Barz interprets Bluebeard's entrusting her
with the keys both as an attempt to gain her attention and as a
gesture that is riddled with fear and aggression, hence the book's sub-
title 'wenn einer vernichtet, was er liebt'. In other words, Bluebeard
is no longer his wife's but his own worst enemy, saying to his partner:

Ich bin gar nicht so, wie ich mit aller Anstrengung versuche zu erscheinen und
wie du mich vielleicht siehst. Ich bin gar nicht stark; sondern erbärmlich
schwach. . . . Du glaubst, daß ich dich liebe. Aber glaub mir lieber, daß ich überhaupt nicht lieben kann . . . ich [habe] die größte Angst vor dem Orgasmus . . .
Da ist nur Auflösung und Chaos—und du glaubst, das habe etwas mit Liebe zu
tun. Eines Tages werde ich sterben darin oder wahnsinnig werden, oder dich
umbringen. *Du weißt nicht, wie verwirrt ich bin, wie viele Wahnsinnige, Mörder,
Selbstmörder, Perverse, Halsabschneider, Gotteslästerer, Schwachsinnige, Schauspieler und
Krüppel in mir auf der Lauer liegen. Versteh mich endlich, sonst bring ich dich um. Du mußt
mich lieben, sonst bring ich dich um. Du darfst mich nicht lieben, sonst bring ich dich um.*
(p. 51, my emphasis).

In other words, Bluebeard's desire to murder his partner is embedded in, and a secondary effect of, his self-pity, and so can be presented as its natural and unsurprising consequence. The sympathetic tone and the structure of the argument here are extraordinary, since they implicitly sanction a man's desire to murder his partner as a normal punishment for his own inadequacies.

Consequently, Barz's claim to be pro-feminist is fissured. Although he claims that he is dealing with historical truths and contemporary societal arrangements, and suggests that archetypal formations can change in the course of history, the idealized gender roles which inform his account are thoroughly traditional, since they involve a polarized complementarity between the sexes in which the feminine is 'ernährend, pflegend, schützend, fördernd' and the masculine is 'anspornend, fordernd, unterweisend, ordnend, klärend' (p. 65). Thus a woman who, like Perrault's heroine, is frightened by or rejects her murderous husband, or who may not always put her man's needs before her own, is considered threatening and unfeminine because she shatters this schema. Barz's arguments place masculinity at centre stage and implicitly erase the notion of women's agency, corresponding to the Grimm tale with its helpless heroine. In addition, as in most traditional conceptualizations of femininity, a double standard is operating, since Barz suspects too that many, or even all, men may be egocentric Bluebeards, but that the ideal woman is far rarer because the demands made on her are much higher, not to say impossible. According to Barz's view of the *Blaubartmärchen*, the victim must overcome her predicament and save not only herself but also her oppressor. While the topos of woman as man's endlessly patient complement and salutary educator is familiar from an old mystical tradition which personified Divine Wisdom as a feminine figure, Saint Sophia, in union with whom man can achieve some kind of completeness, Barz articulates that topos in terms of the Romantic ideals of the late eighteenth century which came to dominate the nineteenth and twentieth centuries as well.[45]

So, while in the biblical model the Fall is precipitated by a woman and salvation is achieved by the sacrifice of a man, and while in Perrault's *conte* the woman is saved by male rescuers, Barz appears to be proposing an alternative model of redemption which involves

---

[45] Cf. Friedrich Schlegel's novel *Lucinde* (1799) (Frankfurt am Main: Ullstein, 1980); and *Ob die Weiber Menschen sind: Geschlechterdebatten um 1800*, ed. Sigrid Lange (Leipzig: Reclam, 1992).

forbearance and guidance on the part of the feminine agent rather than the physical sacrifice of Christ the Son. But on another, less explicit reading,, it seems that Barz's commentary may also imply a schema that differs from both of the above, according to which the bloody sacrifice is preserved but displaced onto the feminine ('Du mußt mich lieben, sonst bring ich dich um. Du darfst mich nicht lieben, sonst bring ich dich um'). Woman must become the sacrifice to redeem the initial fall from grace and correct present imbalances, a conclusion which ties in with von Beit's conclusion quoted above that those demonic aspects of femininity are only 'durch Opfer zu überwinden'.

Turning to a different psychoanalytic approach, in his influential classic about child psychology, *The Uses of Enchantment* (1975), Bruno Bettelheim stated that *Märchen* have a fundamental role in child development because they provide a creative field in which the child may live out his or her sadistic and destructive fantasies without being consumed by guilt.[46] Bettelheim is critical of attempts to domesticate *Märchen* on the grounds that such censorship limits the power of the tale to give the child imaginative autonomy. Accordingly, he emphasizes that children should be provided with the earliest known version of any given *Märchen* since such versions tend to be less bowdlerized, and also insists that, despite the rigid gender roles which they apparently propose, children's reception of *Märchen* is non-gender-specific. But while *The Uses of Enchantment* thus initially seems to break with many taboos on what children are supposed to think and dream, it actually uses a model of personality development which is strongly normative, gender-specific, and conservative.

Bettelheim's reading of 'Bluebeard' in fact causes him to contradict his initial claim that *Märchen* should uncover the dark side of experience since, when he examines the dark side of 'Bluebeard', it provokes him into denying and contradicting not only features of the text itself but also points that he had made elsewhere in *The Uses of Enchantment*. For instance, he is severely critical of tales like Perrault's 'Le Petit Chaperon rouge', which he perceives to have explicitly sexual overtones (p. 169). Yet his response to 'Bluebeard' does introduce an explicit and yet relatively unmotivated sexual reading of the tale. While this reading could be understood on one hand as an

---

[46] *The Uses of Enchantment: The Meaning and Importance of Fairy Tales* (1975) (London: Thames & Hudson, 1976), 299–303. The title of the German translation, *Kinder brauchen Märchen*, is an even more emphatic mission statement.

example of the more serious confrontation with the dark side of experience which Bettelheim initially advocates, it could on the other be in fact the lesser of two evils, enabling the author to deflect attention from an even more shocking issue: serial murder committed by a male figure. While in Bettelheim's view the most savage mother figures are necessary in *Märchen* to permit the child to deal with 'his' antagonism towards his mother, he makes no equivalent statement on fathers and threatening male figures, whom he ignores.[47] However, as Ruth B. Bottigheimer pointed out in 1989, Bettelheim's insistence on an Oedipal model of child development should also involve a threatening father figure to be blamed and destroyed, as well as an equivalent mother figure. This omission constitutes an inconsistency in Bettelheim's writing which resonates with the Grimmian tendency to shift blame from male to female characters.[48] Indeed, Bettelheim is so unaccepting of the dangerous male figure of Bluebeard that, while he is fascinated enough to include the *Blaubartmärchen* in his book, he opens his account by claiming: 'Bluebeard is the most monstrous and beastly of all fairy-tale husbands. Actually this story is not a fairy tale' (p. 299). The paratactic juxtaposition of these two statements is no coincidence: the monstrous and beastly husband or father figure is so scandalous that he provokes an impulse to exclude him altogether.[49]

Bettelheim's presents an idiosyncratic interpretation of the tale, claiming that it 'present[s] in the most extreme form the motif that as a test of trustworthiness, the female must not inquire into the secrets of the male' (p. 300). In this account, if the woman opens the door, she is neither a heroine nor a victim, nor something between the two, but morally dubious—'untrustworthy'. Bettelheim justifies his view that it is the woman, not Bluebeard, who is the villain of the piece, by stating: 'if one thinks over the story's events for a moment, strange discrepancies become apparent' (p. 301) (although elsewhere in his

[47] For Bettelheim, fathers are at worst ineffectual, never antagonistic. In tales involving threatening father figures whom Bettelheim cannot ignore, e.g. those who attempt to marry (or rape) their daughters, the aggression of the fathers is played down and dismissed as a figment of a daughter's fantasy, as in Sigmund Freud's later, problematic accounts of paternal incest in which he sought to account for analysands' accounts of sexual abuse in the family by dismissing them as wishful thinking (356).

[48] Bottigheimer, 'Bettelheims Hexe: Die fragwürdige Beziehung zwischen Märchen und Psychoanalyse', *Psychotherapie—Psychosomatik—Medizinische Psychologie*, 39 (1989), 294–9.

[49] In support of this view, Bettelheim says that the tale was invented by Perrault, rather than taken from oral tradition. Given Bettelheim's usual acceptance of the traditional view that *Märchen* are products of an oral tradition, the suggestion that it is inauthentic reflects his unease with the Bluebeard material.

book (p. 53), he insists that appealing to rationality is inappropriate in reading *Märchen*.) Nonetheless, this is precisely what he does here, asking why the wife does not call to her guests for help on discovering the bloody chamber, escape or disguise herself, and concluding: 'The behaviour of Bluebeard's bride suggests two possibilities: that what she sees in the forbidden closet is the creation of her own anxious fantasies; or that she has betrayed her husband' (p. 301). The unequivocal term 'betrayal' (rather than the morally more ambivalent 'disobedience') leaves no doubt as to who is in the wrong. Bettelheim then interprets this betrayal:

the nature of the betrayal may be guessed by the punishment: execution. In certain parts of the world in times past, only one form of deception on the female's part was punishable by death inflicted by her husband: sexual infidelity . . . It is left to our imagination what went on between the women and her guests with Bluebeard away, but the story makes it clear that everybody had a high time. The blood on the egg and the key seems to symbolize that the woman had sexual relations. Therefore we can understand her anxious fantasy which depicts corpses of women who had been killed for being similarly unfaithful . . . it immediately becomes obvious that the female is strongly tempted to do what is forbidden to her. (pp. 300–11)

Despite Bettelheim's claim elsewhere that children are sexually unaware, and the possibility that blood on the key or the egg (the equivalent object in 'Fitchers Vogel') could, more innocently, represent, say, menstrual blood, he sees it as an umambiguous symbol of defloration, supporting the idea that the deception here might be sexual. But if the same 'rational' mode of deduction as Bettelheim's is followed, it could be objected that since the 'high time' everyone allegedly has in Perrault's text *follows* the wedding night, it is unlikely that any presumed infidelity which took place would have been the wife's first sexual experience. Also, there is no festive scene in 'Fitchers Vogel', and therefore no opportunity for the wife to be unfaithful. And to substantiate this view, Bettelheim has to misread Perrault's description of the 'high time' in Bluebeard's absence, since Perrault describes the wife's guests as 'les voisines et les bonnes amies', that is, as explicitly female neighbours and friends. Bettelheim, however, assumes that they are male or mixed company (and given his insistence on normative, heterosexual gender roles, it is unlikely that lesbian encounters might be meant). There is confusion here too, inasmuch as sexual infidelity is deemed a crime and serial murder a socially accepted punishment.

For Bettelheim the moral of the story is: 'Women, don't give in to your sexual curiosity; men, don't be carried away by your anger at being sexually betrayed' (p. 302). This formulation implies that men must always expect to be sexually betrayed, since women are all fundamentally prone to 'sexual curiosity' construed as infidelity and dishonesty, especially since all the murdered wives must have behaved in the same way and done the same thing. And this conclusion contradicts Bettelheim's initial claim that the relevance of the *Märchen* is not gender-specific, since it works with gender-specific personality ideals and notions of what little women have to learn in order to become good wives, rather than what all children have to learn in order to become adults. Bluebeard is cleared of murder and becomes the wronged husband of an unfaithful wife given to hysterical imaginings in a way which contrasts with Bettelheim's acceptance of maternal or feminine cruelty or deceitfulness as a necessary part of life.

A contrasting, feminist, psychoanalytic reading is provided by Annemarie Dross in her essay of 1980, 'Blaubarts Schloß steht im Wald'.[50] Dross's essay is informed by theories of *écriture féminine* which enjoyed currency among some West German feminists in the 1970s and 1980s and strove to break out of the perceived phallogocentric and rationalist discourse of conventional criticism.[51] As a result, there is no single, structured line of argument, but rather a loosely associative or rhapsodic sequence of analyses of various *Märchen* phenomena and family constellations. Therefore, in classic Freudian manner,[52] the woods in which Bluebeard's castle stands represent the process of subjective development which the child must undergo on leaving the parental home and/or infantile security; and the castle at its centre represents the oppressive psychological complexes generated in the individual under patriarchy, from which the 'Bluebeard' heroine is hopelessly trying to escape, when she finds the forbidden door:

Führt die Tür hinaus ins Freie oder öffnet sie sich zur verbotenen Kammer, zum Schlachterraum? Denn die Gewaltherrscher, auch wenn sie souverän sich

---

[50] Annemarie Dross, 'Blaubarts Schloß steht im Wald', in Brigitte Wartmann (ed.), *Weiblich-Männlich: Kulturgeschichtliche Spuren einer verdrängten Weiblichkeit* (Berlin: Ästhetik & Kommunikation, 1980), 134–49.

[51] Cf. Toril Moi, *Sexual/Textual Politics: Feminist Literary Theory* (London: Routledge, 1988), 108–26.

[52] See Jack Zipes, *The Brothers Grimm: From Enchanted Forests to the Modern World* (London: Routledge, 1988).

dünken, verbergen gern ihre Folterkammer und -keller, wer Ahnung vom KZ erhält und nicht daran beteiligt ist, kommt selbst hinein . . . Wer aber hat die Schlüsselgewalt in Blaubarts Schloß? Der Gemahl auf Reisen, die Frau geht durchs Haus. Die letzte Kammer birgt das Geheimnis seiner Macht. Und wenn sie es entdeckt, so muß sie sterben. Das Geheimnis der Macht des Mannes ist der Tod, die zerstückelten Leiber seiner Frauen, der Boden voller Blut. (p. 147)

Three issues are important here. First, Dross acknowledges that 'Blaubart' is a tale about patriarchy and misogyny. Second, while she pays attention to the potentially monstrous nature of motherhood under patriarchy as Barz does, she relativizes that monstrosity by comparison with that of the father. And third, she equates universal patriarchy and National Socialism in a way which was not anomalous in feminist thinking in West Germany in the 1970s and early 1980s.[53] We saw above that 'Blaubart', from the Grimms onward, has been caught up with issues of national and ethnic identity, and Dross provides a most problematic variation on this connection, since the extermination camps were primarily (albeit not exclusively) the location of racialist genocide, rather than of the oppression of women.

CONCLUSION

In the last analysis, these studies of the Bluebeard material are best read not as expositions of its *origins*, but as *interpretations* or even retellings of that material which tell us less about its putative past meanings than about its contemporary significance and the way it reflects contemporary ideas about marriage, *Märchen*, and civilization. Although the theories of origin discussed in this chapter appear at first sight to form an extremely disparate and inconclusive body, in fact they involve significant underlying similarities, from which symptomatic conclusions may be drawn that reveal much about the changing meanings of the *Blaubartmärchen* over the last hundred years. For instance, the clear shift from philological and anthropological interpretations to psychoanalytic accounts tallies with Elias's theory of the increasing psychologization of civilization over time. And while the pursuit of origins is a standard component of *Märchen* scholarship, it seems to me that in the case of 'Blaubart' one of its

---

[53] Cf. Ann Taylor Allen, 'The March Through the Institutions: Women's Studies in the United States and West and East Germany, 1980–1995', *Signs*, 22 (1996), 152–80 (171).

most important functions has been to deflect attention from the brutality and potentially subversive character of Perrault's tale. Ultimately, this *Verharmlosung* of the material takes the form of telling the tale in such a way that it seems to have no contemporary relevance, exculpating Bluebeard and blaming another character, either his wife or another woman. It seems that we can speak of an agenda of domestication here, as in the case of the insistence that Bluebeard's beard is not inexplicably or disturbingly blue at all, but in fact just plain black. So in addition to being part of a respected and important tradition of criticism, the search for Bluebeard's origins is also a search for reassuring explanations in the face of the unsettling, or 'das Heimliche' in 'das Unheimliche', and for control over it by naming it.

Paradoxically, while these texts clearly reflect their authors' historical and cultural contexts, they imagine the tale as being relevant not for contemporary experience, either at the time of writing or in Perrault's time, but rather as a reflection of long-past historical events (Comor, Gilles de Rais), of quite obsolete and fanciful social practice (leprosy cures, capital punishment for adultery, cannibalism, unfamiliar linguistic expressions), or of far-fetched mythological or astrological beliefs (Saintyves and Pancritius). In a similar way, while the Jungian and Freudian quests for an originary psychological meaning do not *displace* the *Blaubartmärchen* in history, they do *replace* history with universalizing hermeneutic theory, or with mysticism. Such simplifying strategies exclude history and any local—i.e. regional, societal, political—specificities from the *Märchen*. And this move goes hand in hand with the erasure of gender politics from the tale, for instance in the cannibalism theory, which extrapolates 'universal', apparently ungendered meanings from a text which in the Perrault or Grimm versions was emphatically concerned with gender conflict. Or Jungian readings also eliminate gender issues from the *Märchen*, as they universalize its gender roles in terms of anima and animus. In other words, such readings exclude the possibility that the tale is a commentary on contemporary reality, civilization, and the relationships of men and women, and neutralize the *Märchen*'s potentially subversive meanings of Perrault's telling with its contemporary societal reference.

Furthermore, these texts are striking in the way they often contain and normalize the events of a tale which in Perrault's and other well-known versions is about excess and violence. They seek to enshrine

Bluebeard's behaviour, which is identified by Perrault as distinctly antisocial and exceptional, in social practices which they consider to have been at one time quite acceptable and normal (leprosy cures, cannibalism, the death penalty for adulterous women). Or Bluebeard's transformation into a mythological character has the same function, inasmuch as it gives him a religiously sanctioned social prestige which is not to be analysed or criticized by humans. And the way in which psychoanalytic commentators rewrite a tale about antisocial, violent excess as an account of a beneficial healing process (and thus neutralize it) is remarkable too.

A further common upshot of these strategies is to diffuse the question of blame in the *Blaubartmärchen*. Ultimately, these narratives tend towards the exculpation of Bluebeard, tallying with the broader tendency to exonerate male cannibals or aggressors in the German *Märchen* tradition. In line with this pattern, Bluebeard is often portrayed as a victim, in the form of Gilles de Rais as defended by Voltaire, for instance. Or else the blame for the crimes is shared by another, female figure like Charon's wife, Charóndissa, or the old woman scraping guts in Bluebeard's castle in the Hanoverian variant given by the Grimms.

But most often Bluebeard is turned into the victim of a woman. The werewolf's transformation from human to monstrous form is said to be precipitated by his wife. Pancritius's idea of a mother goddess controlling the murderous actions of her son is echoed by Barz and Kast, and all three draw attention not only to the archetype of the Great Mother but also to the allegedly narcissistic behaviour of 'real' mothers which damages their sons and which Bottigheimer has convincingly criticized. Dross too buys into this traditional assumption, and echoes can be heard in the work of Peter Rühmkorf for example ('Nun hängen die lieben Mütter oft länger an den Schürzenbändern der Kinder als denen gut tut').[54] Most explicitly, Bettelheim reverses culpability in making the wife's presumed infidelity the real crime (an idea that may well be implicitly echoed by Kindl). It might also be said that the Jungian notion of Bluebeard as the woman's uncontrolled animus projection reflects the same tendency, since such a suggestion is tantamount to the woman perjuring Bluebeard for reasons that derive from her own unbalanced mental state. Bettelheim makes a similar move when he argues that the bloody

[54] Peter Rühmkorf, 'Blaubarts letzte Reise' (1982), in *Der Hüter des Misthaufens: Aufgeklärte Märchen* (Reinbek bei Hamburg: Rowohlt, 1983), 110–22 (110).

chamber is a projection of the wife's guilty conscience, and in this context it is noteworthy that much less is made of the possibility that Bluebeard himself might be imagining things, or that the wife might be *his* anima projection. All in all, while the psychoanalytic theories discussed above are mainly Jungian or Freudian in inspiration, in their starkness they echo the psychoanalyst Jacques Lacan's bleak dictum that 'there is no sexual relation'.[55]

So in these texts it seems to follow, too, that the exculpation of Bluebeard and the inculpation of his wife must culminate in her punishment. In other words, the texts tend to reinscribe the more conventional biblical and cultural narratives involving the savage physical punishment of Eve and her daughters which Perrault's text had so spectacularly reversed. One thinks, for example, of the werewolf's wife who is murderously attacked; Barz's 'Du mußt mich lieben, sonst bring ich dich um . . .'; or the Grimms' description of the woman in Spain who was tarred and feathered for challenging the king, just as the wife challenges Bluebeard. And this association made by the Grimms between the woman's disguise as a bird in 'Fitchers Vogel' and tarring and feathering seems to make an implicit connection between the woman as 'Opfer' (Pancritius; Beit) and a sacrificial animal. So while on one level Barz's text, for instance, recalls the redemptive image of the Divine Sophia, more often the literature examined here evokes a sacrificial redemption in which the sacrifice is not male but female. This recalls too Luce Irigaray's description of the social contract as based on the sacrifice of the feminine, thus reversing the celebrated Freudian contention that the social contract is based on a male sacrifice.[56] Therefore, the dually destabilizing potential of Perrault's 'La Barbe bleue' is often erased in these tellings. First, its accusatory demystification of patri-archal power is glossed over in the exculpation of Bluebeard; second, the subversive implication of the woman's getting away with it with-out being harshly punished like Eve, Pandora, and Psyche is lost. And these narratives of origin, as the next chapter will show, are quite consistent with similar strategies used in the nineteenth-century German *Märchen* tradition which inspired them.

[55] Cf. Malcolm Bowie, *Lacan* (London: Fontana, 1991), 3.

[56] Cf. Luce Irigaray, 'Women on the Market', in *This Sex Which Is Not One*, trans. Catherine Porter (Ithaca, NY: Cornell University Press, 1985), 170–97. Philip Lewis, *Seeing Through the Mother Goose Tales: Visual Turns in the Writings of Charles Perrault* (Stanford, Calif.: Stanford University Press, 1996) gives an Irigarayan reading of the bloody chamber in Perrault, 225–30.

4

THE MORAL(S) OF THE STORY:
EARLY VERSIONS OF 'BLAUBART'

The French Bluebeard material made its way into German literature
in the course of the eighteenth century, and the first known German
version is Friedrich Wilhelm Gotter's poem 'Blaubart. Eine
Romanze' which appeared in 1772, three-quarters of a century after
the publication of the *Histoires ou contes du temps passé*.[1] Thus, although
there is a considerable gap between the first publication of Perrault's
text (1697)[2] and the first appearance of the material in a German
literary version, we can assume that the Bluebeard material must
have been known by the time of that publication, since the comedy of
Gotter's 'Romanze' derives partly from its ironic relationship with a
model that the reader is assumed to know. This apparent paradox is
explicable by the accessibility of fashionable French *contes* to the educated and often aristocratic German reading public, who would have
known French as a matter of course and some of whom would have
preferred to speak French rather than the 'coarser' German. This
would also explain why the first translation of French *contes de fées* into
German, by Friedrich Immanuel Bierling (which is unlikely to have
included 'La Barbe bleue'), appeared as late as 1761–6, when
German was establishing itself as a literary language and French was
being superseded as the language spoken at court.[3]

Bierling's translation was followed by others, the most influential
being Friedrich Justin Bertuch's *Blaue Bibliothek aller Nationen* (1790–
1800), which did include 'Blaubart'. Such translations were
succeeded by Ludwig Tieck's play *Ritter Blaubart: Ein Ammenmärchen in
vier Akten* (later made into five acts and retitled *Der Blaubart*, in Tieck's
collection *Phantasus* (1812–17)) and his prose text *Die sieben Weiber*

---

[1] Friedrich Wilhelm Gotter, 'Blaubart. Eine Romanze', in *Göttinger Musenalmanach auf
1772*, 129–37; and in Gotter, *Gedichte*, 3 vols. (Gotha: Ettinger, 1787–1802), i. 47–56.

[2] Charles Perrault, 'La Barbe bleue', in *Contes*, ed. Marc Soriano (Paris: Flammarion,
1989), 257–62.

[3] *Das Cabinet der Feen. Oder gesammelte Feenmährchen in neun Theilen aus dem Französischen über-
setzt*, ed. and trans. Friedrich Immanuel Bierling (Nuremberg: Raspe, 1761–6). See Manfred
Grätz, *Das Märchen in der deutschen Aufklärung. Vom Feenmärchen zum Volksmärchen* (Stuttgart:
Metzler, 1988), 62 and 362.

des Blaubart: Eine wahre Familiengeschichte (both 1797), which were
inspired by Perrault but given quite distinctive and influential new
characteristics.[4] And it is undeniable that by the beginning of the
nineteenth century the Bluebeard tale was well known in Germany,
since it appeared in the first edition of the Grimms' *KHM* in 1812,
only to be dropped from all subsequent editions when the Grimms
realized that it was a retelling of Perrault's text. Clearly, then,
Perrault's 'La Barbe bleue' was the dominant influence on the
emerging German Bluebeard tradition from the late eighteenth
century onward, and inspired not only Tieck and such German
translators as Bertuch (1790) and August Lewald (1837)[5] but also,
more indirectly, the Grimms' telling of 1812[6] and Ludwig Bechstein's
version of 1845.[7]

'VERFLUCHTE NEUGIER!' TIECK'S BLUEBEARDS

The fact that Ludwig Tieck was the author of not one but two
remarkable Bluebeard texts testifies to the fascination that narrative
must have held for him. The play *Ritter Blaubart* was published in
Volksmärchen herausgegeben von Peter Lebrecht (1797), and was followed
up later in 1797 by the story *Die sieben Weiber des Blaubart*, which
purported both to be a response to the play published under the
pseudonym of Peter Lebrecht and to provide the background to the
plot of that play, detailing how Bluebeard came to be as he is at the
beginning of the action. In the play, the action takes place not in
urbane, modern France but in a fantastical, feudal Germany. In the
version included in *Phantasus*, to which the following reading refers,
Bluebeard is the knight Hugo vom Wolfsbrunn, who has a real,
mystifyingly blue beard and is known to have had other wives who

[4] Ludwig Tieck, *Ritter Blaubart* (1797), in *Schriften*, ed. Manfred Frank et al., 12 vols.
(Frankfurt am Main: Deutscher Klassiker Verlag, 1985), vi. 394–483; *Die sieben Weiber des
Blaubart* (1797), in *Ludwig Tieck's* [sic] *Schriften*, 28 vols. (Berlin: Riemer, 1828), ix. 89–242.
[5] Friedrich Justin Bertuch, 'Blaubart', in *Die Blaue* [sic] *Bibliothek aller Nationen*, ed.
Friedrich Justin Bertuch, 12 vols. (Gotha: Ettinger, 1790), i. 13–21; August Lewald, 'Blaubart', in *Blaue Mährchen für alte und junge Kinder* (Stuttgart: Scheible, 1837), 267–75.
[6] Jacob Grimm and Wilhelm Grimm, 'Blaubart', in *Kinder- und Hausmärchen gesammelt
durch die Brüder Grimm. Vergrößerter Nachdruck der zweibändigen Erstausgabe von 1812 und 1815*, ed.
Heinz Rölleke and Ulrike Marquardt, 3 vols. (Göttingen: Vandenhoeck & Ruprecht,
1986), i. 285–9.
[7] Ludwig Bechstein, 'Das Märchen vom Ritter Blaubart', in *Deutsches Märchenbuch*
(Stuttgart: Reclam, 1996), 374–7.

disappeared. Hugo presses his suit on Agnes, the younger sister of the von Friedheim family, which includes too her sister Anne and three brothers, but no parents. Early on in the text, Agnes expresses her boredom with the limits of her life and a joyful desire for new experience and knowledge as follows:

Die Welt ist so schön und freundlich, alles so mannigfaltig durch einander, daß man nicht genug sehen, nicht genug erfahren kann. Ich möchte immer auf Reisen sein, durch unbekannte Städte gehn, fremde Berge besteigen, andre Trachten, andre Sitten kennenlernen. Dann mich ganz allein in einem Palaste einsperren lassen, und die Schlüssel zu jedem Gemach, zu jedem Schranke in Händen: dann würde eins nach dem andern aufgeschlossen, die Schränke täten sich voneinander, und ich holte von den schönen und seltsamen Kostbarkeiten eins nach dem andern hervor, träte damit ans Fenster und besähe es ganz eigen, bis ich seiner überdrüssig wäre und zu einem andern eilte, und so immer fort, immer fort, ohne Ende. . . . Ich habe mir schon oft gedacht, wenn ich plötzlich in ein fremdes Schloß geriete, wo mir alles neu, alles merkwürdig wäre; wie ich aus einem Zimmer in das andre eilen würde, immer ungeduldig, immer neugierig, wie ich mich nach und nach mit den Sachen und Gerätschaften bekannt machte. Hier weiß ich ja jeden Nagel auswendig. (p. 415)

Pressure to marry the wealthy Hugo is put on Agnes by her brother Anton, despite the misgivings of a more sensitive younger brother, Simon. After the wedding, Agnes and Anne go to live at Bluebeard's castle, and when Hugo goes away, leaving Agnes with his keys, of course her dreams of endless discovery are recalled, prompting her immediately to explore the six rooms permitted to her, while proudly resisting the 'kindisch' temptation of entering the seventh, forbidden room. However, later Agnes is overcome after all in a monologue where she considers the possibility of exploring the rooms, concluding:

Es muß doch irgendeinen Grund haben, warum er es mir so strenge verboten hat, und den hätte er mir sagen sollen, dann wäre meine Folgsamkeit ein vernünftiger Gehorsam, aber so handle ich nur aus einer blinden Unter-würfigkeit, eine Art zu leben, wogegen sich mein ganzes Herz empört. (p. 460)

But she returns on stage devastated by what she has seen off-stage in the forbidden room, she is unable to clean the key, and the plot develops much as in Perrault's *conte*. At the von Friedheims' castle, Simon has a premonition that all is not well with his sister and insists on hurrying to her with the sceptical Anton, just in time for a dramatic rescue. Tieck's plot is very similar to Perrault's, with the addition of more psychological detail, whereby Agnes is made into a sympathetic character and her loyal siblings too (except Anton) regarded positively.

In addition, however, Tieck stresses the comic aspects of the material as well as the gruesome, and adds a considerable amount of material in the form of two Shakespearean-style sub-plots, the first concerning two comic servants and the second the elopement of Leopold von Friedheim with Brigitte von Marloff, whose father intends another marriage for her. That potentially tragic plot, too, is happily resolved. In addition to this action, the play also involves extensive philosophical play and reflection on the notions of 'Verstand' and 'Vernunft', whereby Simon, who rejects conventional rationality and is considered foolish or even mad by Anton, is proved to be the more perceptive brother. Similarly, the comic character of the Ratgeber, who is employed to dispense advice and wisdom, is incapable of any such good counsel, whereas Claus the Fool is wise.

Thus the play, like Perrault's text, indicts marriages arranged for the material gain of women's relatives and the role of the terrible husband or father; furthermore, it questions conventional doctrines about rationality, delighting in nonsense and oddity. That feature seems to be reflected in the texture of the play itself, which appears sometimes disconnected or incongruous in its developments and reflections, and never treats its characters with very great seriousness.

Tieck's second text, *Die sieben Weiber des Blaubart*, is dedicated to Peter Lebrecht, the fictional author of the play. Therefore, this text of necessity deviates more from Perrault's model than the play, and is in many respects odder and more complex in its narrative technique. In this text, which the author claims is based on genuine historical documents rather than mythological tradition, Bluebeard, whose name here is Peter Berner, is once more a feuding knight surrounded by the paraphernalia of Romantic fantasies of the feudal German Middle Ages. Peter is under the tutelage of Bernard, a literary author who attempts to mould Peter's life and career into that of the hero of a *Ritterroman*. In this, Bernard is aided by a powerful fairy who lives underground and intervenes by magic in Peter's life. This fairy allows Peter to select the sources of both his fortune and misfortune; he chooses respectively to be lucky in war and unlucky with women. These ill-advised choices are due to Peter's innate stupidity, which Bernard is unable to influence. To compensate for this deficiency, however, Peter is given by his fairy godmother a head, made of lead, which can dispense good advice on being touched with a magic key.

Peter locks the magic head in a special room in his castle, and gives the key to Mechtilde, his housekeeper and lover, while forbidding her to make use of it. However, Mechtilde enters the room, finds the head and uses it to acquire so much wisdom that she exhausts it. Because of her new magic powers she is able to prevent Peter from punishing her, and he has to return to his protectress for more wisdom, at the same time requesting a beard in order to appear more manly. Unfortunately, however, during this mission he succeeds in insulting the fairy, so that she curses him with a beard which is blue. Peter's life now takes an unfortunate turn. He marries, or coerces into marriage, six wives, each of whom is afflicted with some folly, weakness, or other stereotypical characteristic, fails the obedience test for a different reason, and is killed. Bernard and Peter become increasingly estranged as Bernard realizes that Peter does not have the makings of a glorious hero but behaves repetitiously and unimaginatively, and Bernard retires. The text ends with cursory reference to the events of Lebrecht's play.

An important feature of this text is the presence of its narrator (who is in no way identified with Bernard), who often intervenes with addresses to the reader and his own reflections. These are mainly of a self-reflexive, literary theoretical nature and constitute a sustained critique of much conventional contemporary thinking about literature, for example in the satire on Bernard, who longs for an unrealistic, literary hero in Peter, or the reflections on the unpleasant obligation to include 'Moralitaet' in literature nowadays. In 1995 Winfried Menninghaus considered these literary theoretical issues to be the text's most important feature in his detailed study of the ways in which *Die sieben Weiber des Blaubart* may be understood as a manifesto for nonsense literature.[8]

Tieck's play was to have a seminal, if today generally unrecognized, influence on the German Bluebeard tradition. However, since the Grimms' and Bechstein's texts, along with Perrault's *conte*, conform most closely to what is deemed to be the classic *Märchen*, they therefore are regarded as the essential codifications of the material right up to the present day. But Tieck's texts too are of great importance to our understanding of the career of 'Blaubart' in German, and relativize the status of the Grimms' and Bechstein's versions, since they pre-date the version by the Brothers Grimm by some fifteen

---

[8] Winfried Menninghaus, *Lob des Unsinns: Über Kant, Tieck und Blaubart* (Frankfurt am Main: Suhrkamp, 1995).

years; Tieck's play in particular represents a kind of German *Urtext* for the *Blaubartmärchen*, forming the prehistory of the better-known tradition often believed to have started with the Grimms.

It was Tieck, and not later authors, who first used in literary form many of those features which diverge from Perrault's material and which have come to be considered typically German. Drawing not only on Perrault but possibly too on the French-language opera *Raoul Barbe-Bleue* by Jean-Michel Sédaine and André Ernesto Modeste Grétry (1789), Tieck brings in such elements as the aristocratic status of 'Ritter Blaubart' and the mysterious, pseudo-medieval German past, thus cementing the shift away from the contemporary bourgeois milieu described by Perrault.[9] Tieck, too, sets the tale in a man's world, for if the bride's family is headed by a mother in Perrault's text, here the brides are either orphans under the tutelage of older brothers or at least supposedly dominated by their fathers' will. In other words, it is here that the characteristic German feature of removing feminine authority figures from the *Blaubartmärchen* begins. And it is Tieck who introduces into German literature, in the character of Mechtilde, the menacing, complicit, often older woman accomplice who shares the blame with Bluebeard, or even exculpates him. Tieck also introduced the popular motif of seven wives, with the seventh being fatal to Bluebeard, into German literature, although this detail is not in Perrault's text and was not taken up by the Grimms. In other words, Tieck's *Ritter Blaubart* is an important link between the French and the German traditions.

In addition to sharing features with the slightly later *KHM* version, Tieck's play in particular inspired also a distinct and important strand in the German Bluebeard tradition. That strand consists of usually dramatic texts, and might even be argued to include Bechstein's version, which in some ways shares more features with *Ritter Blaubart* than it does with the *KHM*. Certainly this tradition includes the Bluebeard plays of the earlier twentieth century, which were inspired by Tieck's medieval atmosphere while not treating it as lightheartedly.

Yet despite the importance of Tieck's contribution, both his Bluebeard texts are marginalized in the *Märchen* scholarship which refers to 'Blaubart'. For instance, scholars and commentators have been consistently more interested in the versions by Perrault or the

---

[9] See Hartwig Suhrbier, 'Blaubart: Leitbild und Leidfigur', in Suhrbier (ed.), *Blaubarts Geheimnis: Märchen und Erzählungen, Gedichte und Stücke* (Cologne: Diederichs, 1984), 11–79 (30).

Grimms; and in secondary literature Tieck's contributions tend to be at best relegated to footnotes or treated simply as literary curios, implying that they are somehow unserious or inauthentic. And while the play *Ritter Blaubart* has been an object of some interest for Tieck scholars, *Die sieben Weiber des Blaubart* has been condemned to thorough obscurity, having been printed twice only during Tieck's lifetime, in 1797 and in the 1828 edition of his works, and has not reappeared since in a modern edition.[10] It seems that the ways in which Tieck's two texts fail to fit and thus relativize our understanding of the development of the German Bluebeard tradition may have contributed to their obscurity.

For example, Tieck's texts explicitly undermine the traditional assumption that the older *Blaubartmärchen* was a purely oral phenomenon, not only because their existence suggests that the better-known nineteenth-century versions held to be more closely linked to oral traditions thus appear to have definite literary antecedents, but also because those literary antecedents, in turn, pay explicit homage to their own literary lineage and are self-consciously literary texts.

Tieck's texts, in particular *Die sieben Weiber des Blaubart*, are both strikingly literary in nature, and each makes its debt to literary tradition explicit. *Der Blaubart*, as it appears in Tieck's *Phantasus*, is introduced by a frame narrative which recalls not primitive, oral (and possible feminine) origins and performance but a literate, urbane (and masculine) cultural community. The play is read out from a manuscript by its purported author, Lothar, to a group of men and women, representing the German Romantic intellectual circle. Thus, the text is presented as having an explicitly written form, and is used as part of a sophisticated, intellectual cultural convention. It is of interest to the group for its formal, literary qualities, since it provides material for a theoretical discussion of dramatic theory.[11] And Lothar explains that he was inspired to write it by his reading of Carlo Gozzi, whose work was a key influence on the Romantic German *Märchen*. In other words, Lothar is deliberately inserting himself

---

[10] Menninghaus, *Lob des Unsinns*, 92–3. However, Menninghaus's bibliography reveals that the 1828 edition of Tieck's works was recently reprinted in facsimile (Berlin: de Gruyter, 1974).

[11] The manner in which, as soon as the reading has ended, the group launches into a complex discussion not of the play and its gory themes, but of dramatic theory, suggests not only that the play and its narrative frame were composed separately but also that the highly theoretical debate is an attempt to detract from the play's disturbing aspects by discussing it in formalist terms alone.

into literary traditions (the French *salon* and the Romantic *Kunst-märchen*) and paying homage to those traditions through intertextual reference, as the French *salon* writers did for one another. And at the same time, Tieck in turn is inserting himself into an explicitly literary and intellectual tradition, that of the intellectual Romantic community.

Die sieben Weiber des Blaubart emphasizes its literary antecedents and interests even more strongly. Its author claims that his material is historical, and that he is drawing on original historical records and documents. And if Tieck's play is in homage to Gozzi, this text pays tribute (albeit perhaps ironically) to the French *contes de fées* in the character of Almida, a traditional fairy in the French mould who occasionally drops into the narrative to provide a counterpoint to the views and theories of Bernard. Almida too has a protégée, whom she is bringing up as the heroine of a French *conte*. Almida's approach to this project is diametrically opposed to that of Bernard, who is attempting to guide Peter into the role of the hero of the *Ritterroman*. In other words, the narrator of the text is explicitly concerned throughout with literary theories as personified by Bernard and Almida and their protégés, and uses the Bluebeard material to make points about writing.

In purporting to tell us Bluebeard's past in *Die sieben Weiber des Blaubart*, Tieck both anticipates and answers many of the questions asked years later by authors and scholars as to how Bluebeard has come to be how he is, why his beard is blue, how the forbidden chamber first came to be forbidden, what happened to all the wives, and so forth. And Tieck's answers to all these questions are not historical (for the reference to historical, documentary sources is transparently a convention), mythological, anthropological or psychoanalytical, but literary. That is, Peter's behaviour and blue beard are explained as literary conceits, jokes, or as the results of certain literary theoretical demands. In this way, Tieck not only pre-empts the serious, scholarly questioning of the material described in the previous chapter; he also anticipates and parodies it, revealing the impetus behind the 'Blaubart' plot to be light-heartedly literary, and not religious, astrological, essential, or anything else of that order. It seems that Tieck is less interested in presenting the *Blaubart-märchen* as oral material than later authors have been. This factor must at least partially explain the obscurity of his two Bluebeard texts, which identify themselves as part of a complex fabric of explicitly intellectual, literary intertextuality. Furthermore, *Die sieben Weiber des Blaubart* ridicules precisely those searches for onotological or essential meaning in the material which were later, in the wake of the ideological prestige the supposedly oral German *Märchen* was to acquire in the nineteenth century, to become of great importance.

That being said, the texts are not devoid of reference to oral styles of culture. The play is called a *Kindermärchen*, and its author does not claim to have invented the material, but refers to it as an existing tale. However, no speculation is made as to its origin, oral or not; and of course the material would have been best known to an eighteenth-century audience from Perrault's work. And both texts do refer at one point to a certain convention of oral narrative in an interesting way. Both the play and the prose text form a narrative frame for another *Märchen*, told by Mechtilde. In the play, it is told to Agnes and Anne in the night after Agnes has opened the forbidden chamber, ostensibly for comfort and society, although it later transpires that Mechtilde is complicit in Bluebeard's schemes and knows that her tale will terrify, rather than reassure (pp. 469–70). And in *Die sieben Weiber des Blaubart*, Mechtilde also tells a tale to one of the unfortunate wives, Catharine (pp. 230–3). This tale is near-identical with that told in the play, deviating only in occasional formulations, but longer, for in the play Mechtilde is interrupted by a distressed Agnes. Catharine too interrupts the tale in horror, but after listening for longer. The reason for the women's horror at Mechtilde's *Märchen* is its content, for it is a story about a girl who lives in a haunted forest, and is pursued by nightmarish beings, monstrous bearded faces, dismembered body parts, and the like. The tale is cut short before there is any intimation of closure or rescue. The motifs used by Mechtilde are especially calculated to terrify the women, since they pick up aspects of those women's experiences after marrying Bluebeard, that is, solitude, isolation from their family, threatening beards and dismembered bodies, and the fear that there is no escape. This tale closely resembles those set down by the Grimms in their *KHM*, with such familiar features as paratactic narrative, a dead mother, and the home in the dark woods which is traditionally especially threatening to women characters.

Since Tieck uses this tale twice, he clearly valued it. This must partly be for its dramatic effect, but may also have something to do with its genre, since it is, like the text which frames it, a *Märchen*. But while these episodes each seem to thus highlight oral narrative told by a folk narrator, in fact the nature of Mechtilde's *Märchen* is more complex than first meets the eye. Mechtilde's tale exists, of course, as a written text which corresponds to a certain concept of folk narrative, and is mediated and framed within a complex intertextual work of literature. It is therefore perhaps better understood as one particular variant type of *Märchen* narrative displayed alongside others within the works, which refer also to other fairy-tale styles, such as the *conte de fées*, rather than as a more primal form. And while Mechtilde's tale is important, it is not seen as prestigious. Rather, it is discredited by the demonic character of its narrator and by the unkind motivation behind its telling, that is, to frighten innocent women. Mechtilde's oral narrative is presented as being inferior to its framing text, which in both cases is written and bears masculine authorship and authority. For all the importance Tieck accords to Mechtilde's narrative, that tale is discredited, and takes its place in the distinctly literary tradition of demonizing the *Märchentante*.

Tieck's texts may also appear marginal to the canon because in other ways too they deviate from the code of values which later came to be associated with the German *Blaubartmärchen*. Despite romancing the Middle Ages, or rather, propagating a certain fantasy about a pre-modern, feudal Germany, as *KHM* enthusiasts have done too, Tieck portrays a society which is anything but romantic and superior. It is ruled by such characters as Bluebeard, brutal feudal lords with none of the heroic appeal of Goethe's Götz von Berlichingen, for instance. Bluebeard proves to be a stupid man whose authority is unjustified, as is paternal authority, since both texts are critical of a father's (or an elder brother's) power to arrange marriages for young women. The concept of the 'graumsamer Vater' who demands blind obedience, which matches so well with the Bluebeard figure, is explicitly criticized. On one hand, this negative characterization of the feudal lord can be understood as a distancing strategy whereby the uglier face of modern civilization is suppressed by identifying it not with the present day and the bourgeoisie, as Perrault did, but with another era and another social class.[12] On the other hand, the texts serve to undermine many aspects of patriarchal authority. Elopements and love-matches made by young lovers themselves in the face of paternal disapproval are championed. Almida proves to be a better guardian than Bernard, and Peter's wise fairy protectress is very powerful. Agnes's words quoted above show that insistence on

---

[12] Cf. Suhrbier, 'Blaubart: Leitbild und Leidfigur', 34.

feminine obedience at all costs is also criticized, and the play in particular sympathizes with the women characters. Yet Tieck's is not a simple *parti pris* in favour of women, as is demonstrated by the folly of many of the wives in *Die sieben Weiber des Blaubart* and by the character of Mechtilde, who is complicit in Bluebeard's schemes and shows no sympathy or solidarity towards his victims.

The story of Mechtilde in *Die sieben Weiber des Blaubart* is one of the most interesting aspects of Tieck's adaptation of the Bluebeard material, challenging as it does some of the values upheld by the canonical *Märchen* discussed later in this chapter. For one thing, Mechtilde is not portrayed as being simply evil. Rather, she is given a tragic history of seduction and betrayal which excludes her from the life of a 'good' woman, and leads her to taking up employment with Bluebeard. Mechtilde's ugliness, an outward sign of poor character, is not essential to her nature, but brought upon her by having been poisoned by a wife of Bluebeard jealous of Mechtilde's good looks. Most interestingly, while *Die sieben Weiber des Blaubart* plays down the utopian ending to the story proposed by Perrault and preserved in the play, in Mechtilde's actions it gives an interesting, explicit twist to the themes of the mimetic rivalry between Bluebeard and the woman, and of the dangerous feminine acquisition of knowledge.

Mechtilde's acquisition of knowledge and rivalrous confrontation with Bluebeard take place after Peter has been given his magic head by his fairy protectress and locked it in a room in his castle. When he and Mechtilde become lovers, he 'hielt es für unedel, gegen seine Geliebte mißtrauisch zu sein' (p. 125), and gives her the key to the room when he goes away, while warning her not to make use of it. This occurs early in Peter's history of misfortune with women, before he has become a murderer or a misogynist, and there is a certain generosity about his view. However, the inconsistency of giving Mechtilde the key and yet forbidding her to use it also illustrates Peter's denseness. Unsurprisingly, Mechtilde looks in the room, finds the head, and uses it to increase her own worldly and magical knowledge. Since she is in any case far more intelligent than Peter, she draws great advantage from her tutorial with the head, until 'sie klüger war, als ihr Lehrer' (p. 126). Finally she exhausts the head's store of knowledge, so that it falls silent. When Peter returns to find the head empty of knowledge, he turns on Mechtilde. She is able, however, to defend herself verbally and physically when Peter attempts to kill her, paralysing his sword arm by magic powers. Peter has to accept that he will be unable to take revenge on Mechtilde, and that she has power over him. Given this bitter conflict, it appears odd that Mechtilde should choose to stay in Bluebeard's castle, but this is what she does; and it is this episode which leads Peter to take revenge instead on all womankind.

The implications of this episode are complex. On one hand what we have here is a classic indictment of feminine curiosity as the root of all evil, for this is Mechtilde's verbal self-defence in the face of Peter's accusations:

Warum habt ihr mich . . . so in Versuchung geführt? Wenn ich nicht hätte neugierig seyn sollen, so hättet ihr mir auch keine Veranlassung zur Neugier geben müssen. Was kann ich dafür, daß ich so eingerichtet bin, wie es alle Frauenzimmer sind? Ihr selbst seyd jetzt an eurem Unglücke Schuld. . . . Daß Weiber nicht neugierig seyn sollten, ist eben so unmöglich, als daß die Sonne kein Licht verleiht . . . Und darum muß uns jeder vernünftige Mensch auch diese Neugier zutrauen. (pp. 128–9)

This acceptance of a vicious, essential feminine curiosity which, as in the Bible, leads to the punishment of all women is echoed in the play *Ritter Blaubart*. In that play, Agnes is articulate in her identification of the ridiculousness and weakness of Bluebeard's prohibition. But when she is stricken with curiosity, she identifies it as a specifically feminine trait, and describes herself as 'lüstern' to see into the room. Afterwards, the negative implications of that adjective are amplified by her conclusion: 'O Neugier, verdammte, schändliche Neugier! Ich glaube, es gibt keine größere Sünde als die Neugier!' (p. 462), which concurs with Bluebeard who later, on discovering Agnes's transgression, says: 'Verfluchte Neugier! . . . Durch dich kam die erste Sünde in die unschuldige Welt . . . Die Sünde der ersten Mutter des Menschengeschlechts hat alle ihre nichtswürdigen Töchter vergiftet' (p. 477). The women described by Tieck concur with this unsympathetic condemnation of explicitly feminine curiosity. But at the same time both Mechtilde and Agnes keep a sense of intellectual and moral proportion, identifying both the ridiculous nature of the prohibition and that Bluebeard is the more evil of the couple; and Agnes calls him 'das schändlichste, mir fremdeste Ungeheuer' (p. 462).

While Tieck does not undermine or question the trope of vicious feminine curiosity as Perrault's text does, and does not reward Agnes (her brothers agree to share up Bluebeard's property between them and send her home, apparently empty-handed, beginning the gradual intensification of the woman's punishment in the German tradition),[13] he nonetheless preserves its rewards for Mechtilde. She is miraculously exempted from the fate of all other curious women, and able to defend herself against being murdered (rather than having to rely on the fortuitous help of her brothers), but is rewarded with superhuman knowledge. This reward is as striking as that of riches for Perrault's heroine, for it flies in the face of a powerful taboo on feminine knowledge, precisely that taboo which Tieck's ostensible condemnation of feminine curiosity upholds. Furthermore, Mechtilde's act of self-defence by paralysing Bluebeard's sword arm is worthy of comment, for this is another quite graphic representation of the symbolic castration inherent in the heroine's appropriation of the key and its 'Bart'. Interestingly, at this point in the narrative Peter is still a young man who does not yet have a beard, and it is as a response to his physical humiliation by Mechtilde that he makes the fatal mistake of asking his protectress for a beard as proof of his disputed manhood. And of course this second magical, powerful female figure also humiliates him in that exchange.

It is no wonder that the triumphant, unpunished, and knowledgeable Mechtilde is demonized in both Tieck's texts, as reflected in the scenes where she tells *Märchen*. Her death in both cases is interesting too. In neither text do we see her being killed, as Bluebeard is; it is merely reported that she has jumped off the castle walls. While this is supposed to have killed her, this is an equivocal exit of a type which in German literature seems to be reserved for particularly threatening women who are so powerful that their presence cannot be completely erased, even through death—thus leaving open the fearful prospect that they may return. (Another instance is the final exit of the demonic, dangerous Kunigunde von Thurneck in Heinrich von Kleist's *Das Käthchen von Heilbronn* (1808–10), who is vanquished but threatens to return, railing 'Pest, Tod und Rache! Diesen Schimpf sollt ihr mir büßen!'[14] Similarly, the Kunigunde-like Helmina von Boschau, the eponymous protagonist of Karl Hans Strobl's *Madame Blaubart* (1929), slips out of the narrative and the capture intended for her.[15]) This inconclusive ending for the apparently defeated Mechtilde reflects the potent threat she represents, and is one of the most interesting aspects of Tieck's Bluebeard works.

---

[13] Suhrbier, 'Blaubart: Leitbild und Leidfigur', 24.

[14] *Das Käthchen von Heilbronn oder die Feuerprobe. Ein großes historisches Ritterschauspiel* (1808–10), in *Sämtliche Werke und Briefe*, ed. Helmut Sembdner, 2 vols. (Munich: Hanser, 1984), i. 429–531 (531).

[15] *Madame Blaubart* (Leipzig: Singer, 1929).

In conclusion, then, Tieck's two plays on one hand go less far than Perrault in their messages about femininity and curiosity, being explicitly critical of woman's innate sin. On the other hand, however, in Mechtilde Tieck creates a villainess who is more self-reliant and powerful that Perrault's heroine, so much so that it is implied that she might even be able to resist death. This interesting feature goes hand in hand with a critique of patriarchal authority, although the texts remain deeply suspicious of feminine authority and agency. Such features, along with the texts' explicit literariness, serve to mark off Tieck's writing from the better-known German Bluebeard texts which form the subject of the remainder of this chapter.

EARLY TRANSLATIONS OF PERRAULT: BERTUCH AND LEWALD

Although the two *moralités* appended by Perrault to 'La Barbe bleue' make subtle, complex, and riddling points which do not necessarily inculpate the wife or exculpate the husband, the German *Blaubart-märchen* tradition interprets Perrault's text in precisely this way, relying on a superficial, conservative reading of the morals and making the tale into a rigid morality tale about inappropriate feminine behaviour. Two early German translations of Perrault's 'La Barbe bleue' prefigure precisely this development, albeit in almost imperceptible ways. These two translations are of interest both because they must have been themselves influential in the reception of Perrault in Germany and, on a broader level, because they reflect the same cultural and social standards which gave rise to the indigenous German Bluebeard texts by the Grimms and Bechstein.

Bertuch's *Blaue Bibliothek aller Nationen* opens its first volume with some of Perrault's *contes* and 'L'Adroite Princesse' by Marie-Jeanne Lhéritier, a text which may have served as a model for 'La Barbe bleue' and which Bertuch erroneously attributes to Perrault.[16] Lewald explains that his *Blaue Mährchen* are based on a recent French collection entitled *Cabinet des Fées*, with the addition of writing by Wieland.

Both translators see the main virtue of their tales as lying in their pleasing aspect. However, the charm of the collections is in both

---

[16] A common error, once the prestige of women writers like Lhéritier dwindled. Marina Warner, *From the Beast to the Blonde: On Fairy Tales and Their Tellers* (London: Chatto & Windus, 1994), 249–52.

cases linked to a specifically moral, albeit not heavily didactic, purpose. Bertuch states in his introduction that he intends to provide 'gute amüsante Lectüre zur Unterhaltung und Nahrung des Geistes, und Ausbildung des Geschmacks'. He praises Perrault's 'naife[n], einfältige[n] und leichte[n] Erzählungston, mit der angenehmen Manier, Moral des täglichen Lebens einzukleiden' (p. xxvi), and at one point (where he complains of the cultural degeneration of contemporary Germany) he mentions in particular that 'die Lectüre, sonderlich der weiblichen Welt und der Jugend' (for whom most serious 'Geisteskost' is too hard) 'schlechter wird', so that his intention is to provide 'ein nützlicheres, wenigstens unschädlicheres Spielzeug' for society (unpaginated section of introduction). Lewald's introduction ascribes a more existential character and function to *Märchen*: 'Glücklich der, dessen Kindersinn an Märchen großgesäugt wurde; sein Gemüth bewahrt sich stets den zarten Hauch der Kindlichkeit' (p. iv). It is this state of soul which Lewald seeks to foster in the readers of his collection:

mögen diese wechselvollen und anziehenden Erscheinungen die jugendlichen Gemüther bewegen; denn das jugendliche Gemüth ist unabhängig von dem Alter des Menschen; mögen sie . . . bei den glänzenden, wundervollen Beschreibungen mit jener innigen Lust verweilen, die den wahrhaft kindlichen Sinn charakterisirt, das höchste Glück des Lebens, das ich allen meinen freundlichen Lesern jeden Alters als schönes Eigenthum bis zum Ende wünsche. (pp. xv–xvi)

In other words, both writers legitimize their projects by claiming that they are transmitting moral standards, particularly to children (and, for Bertuch, women too). This is in striking contrast to Tieck's mockery in *Die sieben Weiber des Blaubart* of the belief that literature should be moral. That insistence on morality means that both translators acknowledge the standards and expectations of their times regarding the behaviour of women and men, which in turn must, however obliquely, affect their work.

By and large Bertuch's and Lewald's translations are very faithful to their original. While Lewald states in his introduction that he intends to take liberties in translation, his alterations to 'Blaubart' are minimal, apart from occasional errors in translation; Bertuch's alterations, also limited, are more striking. But in both cases small details point to one consistent interpretation which underlies both translations. In general, the changes in Bertuch's 'Blaubart' involve a heightening of the drama,[17] especially as regards the woman's emotional state, and Lewald's text shares that tendency, albeit in a less striking manner, and, more importantly, softens Bluebeard's character.

For instance, when Bluebeard is making his suit to his lady neighbour and her reluctant daughters, Perrault writes: 'Elles n'en voulaient point toutes deux, et se le renvoyaient l'une à l'autre, ne pouvant se résoudre à prendre un homme qui eût la barbe bleue' (p. 257). Bertuch renders this as follows:

Aber sie wollten ihn alle beyde nicht, und wenn die eine sagte: Nimm du ihn, so sagte die andre: Ey behalte du doch den Blaubart selbst. Genug es konnte sich keine entschließen, einen so häßlichen Mann zu heyrathen. (p. 13)

Bertuch dramatizes the situation by means of explicitly comic direct speech, a change which trivializes the mysterious emotions which the women feel in Perrault's version. Where Perrault's women have powerful if unclearly defined feelings, and the reason why they do not wish to marry a man with a blue beard is not given, here their unease is reduced to a question of aesthetic taste, since Bertuch infers that their unease must be caused by nothing more complex than Bluebeard's ugliness, which Perrault does not mention at all. Thus Bertuch banishes the sense of sinister enigma regarding the beard's effect which was generated by Perrault, and makes the women appear shallow in their response to a purely surface appearance. Then again, when the younger daughter decides to marry Bluebeard, Perrault expresses her decision succinctly:

. . . enfin tout alla si bien, que la Cadette commença à trouver que le Maître du logis n'avait plus la barbe si bleue, et que c'était un fort honnête homme. Dès qu'on fut de retour à la Ville, le mariage se conclut. (pp. 257–8)

But Bertuch writes:

Die Sachen giengen so gut, daß endlich die jüngste Schwester den Bart ihres Wirths so gar blau nicht mehr fand, und daß sie zugab, er sey doch ein recht braver Mann. Mit Einem [*sic*] Worte, die Sache wurde richtig, und da sie wieder in die Stadt gekommen waren, machten sie Hochzeit. (p. 14)

Bertuch indicates his unease at the precipitate and independent way the woman acts in Perrault's original by, on the one hand, making

[17] e.g. the occasional introduction of direct speech, or emphatic, dramatic repetition, as in the depiction of the forbidden room. Whereas in French, the windows are simply closed: 'les fenêtres étaient fermées' (259), in German that fact is stressed more strongly: 'die Fensterladen [waren] alle fest, fest zu' (16).

her decision appear even more hurried ('da sie wieder in die Stadt gekommen waren', rather than 'dès qu'on fut de retour') while, on the other, moderating that haste and emphasizing social propriety by inserting a conventionally approbatory phrase between the woman's decision and the marriage ('Mit Einem Worte, die Sache wurde richtig'). And Lewald's text evinces even greater reservation about the woman's decision and its precipitate implementation:

Die Folge war, daß die jüngere der Schwestern endlich zu bemerken glaubte, der Herr des Hauses habe gar nicht einen so blauen Bart, der ihn entstellte, und die guten Eigenschaften seines Charakters wären auf jeden Fall bei weitem überwiegend. Sie theilte diese Ansicht ihrer Mutter mit, und kaum war man nach der Stadt zurückgekehrt, so wurde auch die Hochzeit vollzogen. (p. 268)

Although this passage restores the time-lapse between the decision and the marriage, Lewald clearly senses that there is something indecorous about the young woman's sudden decision, and ostentatiously introduces the mother as a respectable mediator.

While Lewald's introductory passage makes the woman appear more cautious than Perrault's heroine, that initial impression is soon dispelled by other elements in his text, as happens, with greater force, in Bertuch's as well. In all versions, when Bluebeard goes away the woman is visited by her female friends, and their emotions and behaviour prefigure hers. In the French text the visiting women are driven by 'impatience', which is also the emotion felt by the heroine on thinking about the forbidden room, and this mutates into the less neutral 'curiosité' only on the third reference to the woman's emotional state, when she finally confronts the room itself. According to Bertuch, however, the friends arrive driven by 'Neugierde', and in Lewald's version the women friends are already 'neugierig' on arrival. Moreover, according to Bertuch, the friends' response to the house is more excitedly emotional than in Perrault's text, since they are 'ausser sich', just as the wife herself is when she has seen into the forbidden room, a telling repetition. Bertuch also makes the wife's approach to the forbidden chamber more dramatic and elemental. While in Perrault's text she is 'si pressée de sa curiosité' and while Lewald replaces 'pressée' with the more sensational 'quälte', Bertuch has the more overwhelming 'konnte ihrer Neugierde keine Gewalt mehr antun'. Indeed, Bertuch enlarges on and extends the drama of Perrault's description of the woman running downstairs and almost breaking her neck in her haste to open the room.

A similar intensification happens in the moment of reflection before opening the door. While Perrault writes:

Étant arrivée à la porte du cabinet, elle s'y arrêta quelque temps, songeant à la défense que son Mari lui avait faite, et considérant qu'il pourrait lui arriver malheur d'avoir été désobéissante; mais la tentation était si forte qu'elle ne put la surmonter . . . (p. 259)

Bertuch translates this as:

Da sie an die Thüre kam, bedachte sie sich einige Minuten, ob sie ihrem Manne gehorchen oder ob sie sich seinem Zorne aussetzen wollte. Aber die Versuchung war zu stark, und es war ihr unmöglich, Herr darüber zu werden. (p. 16)

Bertuch's translation implies a less sophisticated degree of reflection on the woman's part, because she does not think about the prohibition and weigh up her chances of being punished ('considérant qu'il pourrait lui arriver malheur'), i.e. take a calculated risk, as Perrault describes her doing. Rather, she sees her situation in a less differentiated manner, as one in which she will either obey, or disobey and definitely be punished. Given which, Bertuch's account makes the woman's decision to enter a good deal more foolish than Perrault's, since she is acting with the certain knowledge that she must be punished. Indeed, in Bertuch's version, the woman's action is no longer formulated as a decision at all, but as something she cannot help ('es war ihr unmöglich, Herr darüber zu werden'). And it is particularly interesting that Bertuch chooses a gendered expression for self-control, that of mastery or 'Herr werden', since this turn of phrase implies that self-control is a masculine attribute and so by definition out of reach of the heroine. Lewald's heroine also seems more foolish than Perrault's, since Lewald's Bluebeard himself utters the prohibition once more often than Perrault's, and just to reinforce that effect Lewald translates 'la défense que son Mari lui avait faite' as a '*warnender* Befehl' (my emphasis), thus adding an element which the woman is even more foolish to ignore.

In Perrault's text and Bertuch's translation, the woman is so overcome by her experience that she is unable to regain her self-possession even when she has returned to her own room: 'elle . . . monta à sa chambre pour se remettre un peu; mais elle n'en pouvait venir à bout, tant elle était émue' (p. 259). In Lewald's translation, however, this detail is amplified and the woman is so shocked that she can hardly even reach her room: 'und stieg in ihr Zimmer hinauf, welches sie kaum erreichen konnte, so sehr war sie von starker innerer Bewegung ergriffen' (p. 270). While this appears to be a mistranslation of Perrault's 'elle n'en pouvait venir à bout', meaning that the woman cannot calm herself, not that she cannot move, the slip is a telling one, stressing as it does Lewald's assumption that the woman's state of debilitation must be so great that she loses control of her body as well as her emotions, something which is not implied in Perrault's description of his comparatively self-possessed heroine. Finally, on his return Bertuch's Bluebeard, too, contributes to the characterization of his wife as emotionally uncontrolled, for while Perrault's Bluebeard says: 'vouz avez voulu entrer dans le cabinet!', Bertuch's puts it in a way which emphasizes the affective nature of her motivation more strongly: 'Du hast also *Lust bekommen* in das Kabinett zu gehn?' (my emphasis). The difference here lies in the subtleties of the way in which the woman's behaviour is described. If, in French, 'vouloir' can merely mean 'to intend' or 'to attempt' as well as 'to want' or 'to desire', the German expression 'Lust bekommen' is more limited in its nuances than Perrault's restrained if ambiguous formulation and can *only* be understood as a description of active desire.

In other words, in the translations by Bertuch and Lewald the woman is more emotional and uncontrolled than in Perrault's original. This seems to be due to the way in which, as the eighteenth century progressed, women were increasingly imagined to be non-rational creatures, with the result that elemental, emotional forces were increasingly imputed to them and shown to motivate their actions. So the suspense and gradual heightening of the woman's emotion, based on her reasonable perceptions and relatively sophisticated, if unfortunate, judgement as portrayed by Perrault are transformed into more elemental responses that are 'essential' in the female character. This occurs most obviously in Bertuch's text. Because the women have lost the power to control their emotions and to discriminate between various sources of excitement (women are 'ausser sich' when confronted with both nice furniture and dismembered bodies), decisions (such as opening the door) are practically taken away from the heroine and made the work of uncontrollable forces. So, given that the woman is controlled by elemental, emotional forces, the idea that she might act as an independent agent becomes tacitly problematic for the translators because such independent agency is apparently irrational and dangerous. And thus, when the woman decides of her own volition to get married, this action has to be moderated and controlled by the new emphasis on social propriety added by the translators.

Perrault's translators also modify the depiction of Bluebeard. Lewald's version, which reflects a certain confusion at the mixed messages he must have sensed in Perrault's text, is more striking and also more contradictory in this respect. At some junctures Lewald's Bluebeard is more horrific than Perrault's, since women and girls flee when they see him *even in the distance*, an added detail, and during Bluebeard's final dialogue with his wife Lewald adds the adjective 'wild' to his characterization. But at others, Lewald's adaptation of Bluebeard's character echoes Bertuch's in that he diminishes Bluebeard's suspicious, terrifying aspects, compared to Perrault's characterization.

While Bluebeard is introduced in all three cases as an undesirable suitor, Perrault calls him 'laid et . . . terrible', Bertuch calls him 'abscheulich häßlich', and Lewald describes him merely as 'häßlich'. That is, Bluebeard's terrifying aspect (the adjective 'terrible') is reduced to an aesthetic category ('häßlich'). Whereas the French text draws much of its power from avoiding naming the precise cause of the women's unease, in the German texts the disturbance Bluebeard provokes is trivialized and subsumed under his ugliness. Similarly, the fact that Bluebeard had many wives who disappeared is introduced by Perrault with 'Ce qui les dégoûtait encore . . .', but this powerful expression of disgust is softened by Bertuch to 'Dazu kam auch noch . . .', and Lewald has the moderate 'Außerdem aber war man dem Blaubart abgeneigt . . .'. Both German formulations replace the insistence on the sisters' disgust by a vaguer, more exculpatory expression. Lewald also attempts to normalize Bluebeard by stressing that the marriage is initially 'eine glückliche Ehe', a conciliatory detail which Perrault does not include. While, in the forbidden room, Perrault reveals that Bluebeard has killed his wives by slitting their throats ('égorgées'), Bertuch renders this more tamely as 'ums Leben gebracht', as does Lewald with 'getödtet'. The magic key is described by Lewald as 'ein Werk der bösen Feen', another original detail which deflects responsibility away from Bluebeard and onto (female) supernatural beings, since Perrault's adjective 'Fée' does not imply the same thing, but simply describes a '[c]hose enchantée par quelque puissance supérieure'.[18] And on discovering that his wife has been in the forbidden chamber, Lewald's Bluebeard says: 'Du

---

[18] Perrault, *Contes*, ed. Jean-Pierre Collinet (Paris: Gallimard, 1981), 328.

wolltest das Kabinet sehen. Nun gut, ich will deinen Wunsch erfüllen und du sollst in der Gesellschaft, die dort versammelt ist, den dir gebührenden Platz erhalten' (p. 272). While this formulation tones down the notion of desire expressed by Bertuch ('Lust bekommen'), it is more stilted than Perrault's 'Hé bien, Madame, vous y entrerez, et irez prendre votre place auprès des Dames que vous y avez vues' (p. 260). Although Lewald's less elegant translation must be due in part to linguistic difficulty, it also seems that the idea that Bluebeard has a room full of dead women is highly problematic for him, and that this is reflected in the awkward sentence structure.

All these details reduce Bluebeard's terrifying aspect in the German texts. On one hand this gentler portrayal of Bluebeard makes the wife's response to him seem less reasonable and more trivial and thus worthy of criticism; on the other, it makes him seem respectable. And Perrault's telling repetition of 'honnête' to describe both Bluebeard and the heroine's second husband is eliminated, since Bertuch translates the term in the first instance as 'ein rechter braver Mann' and in the second as 'sehr rechtschaffen'. Lewald also avoids this repetition by saying first, that the heroine decides with regard to Bluebeard that 'die guten Eigenschaften seines Charakters wären auf jeden Fall bei weitem überwiegend', and second, that her next husband is 'sehr rechtschaffen'. In both cases then, the implication that the quality of 'honnêteté' might be a two-edged one and that all apparently good husbands might be potential murderers is obfuscated. This variation has the effect of legitimizing the behaviour of husbands in general by stressing that they are nothing like Bluebeard, with the result that Perrault's disturbing larger message is tacitly eliminated. In other words, the most crucial and critical ambiguity of Perrault's text, which, by making the two husbands seem alike, opens up the possibility that the *conte* is not a far-fetched tale about exceptional violence but an account of the more violent possibilities inherent in both marriage and civilization, is lost.

Finally, both Bertuch and Lewald omit the two *moralités*. This omission overlooks the puzzling quality of the *moralités*, and may be due in the first place to the belief that Perrault's *contes* must be the product of vernacular wisdom, an idea which gained strength over time. If 'La Barbe bleue' were indeed a folk product, then such consciously 'modern' and intellectualizing *moralités* would appear as an inauthentic addition. Second, the omission may be due to the assumption that the morals merely reiterate the content of the tale itself and are therefore unimportant. If this is the case, then the omission of the morals goes hand in hand with the assumption that the tale is about the evils of uncontrolled (and probably feminine) curiosity, and nothing more sinister than that. So here too, a subversive ambiguity (produced by the discrepancy between Perrault's *conte* and his *moralités*) is lost. Perrault's two translators duly, and possibly unconsciously, strengthen the conventional, superficial interpretation of the *moralités*; in so doing they inculpate the wife, weaken the threat inherent in Bluebeard's character, and thus dull the tale's force. This is precisely what happens too in later indigenous German versions of 'Blaubart'.

A GRIMMER TALE

The Grimms' version departs far more significantly from Perrault's, since its tellers and their editors were not engaged in producing a translation and did not work directly with Perrault's text, and it differs from the French *conte* in five major, interconnected ways. First, the broader societal context is removed and the family ideal propagated by the Grimms is a private one into which society does not obtrude. Second, the power relations within this family are structured differently. Third, the characterization of Bluebeard changes. Fourth, so does that of the wife. Fifth, the atmosphere of the tale no longer involves an ironic realism reflecting contemporary life and mores, because the tale itself takes place in a more sinister, archaic, and magical context. But the Grimms' version nonetheless does reflect contemporary realities, as Perrault's did, albeit more indirectly, since one major aspect of the nineteenth-century ideology of bourgeois family relations involved imagining them as essential, timeless, and separate from public, societal concerns. All these changes help defuse the subversive potential of Perrault's *conte* and develop features that were less prominent in Bertuch's and Lewald's translations.

To begin with, the change in societal context is striking. Perrault's text is located in contemporary polite society and views a sociability in which women as well as men participate as an ideal from which the tale starts (a correctly performed courtship in which the decision is left to the woman) and with which it ends (a successful reintegration of the heroine into society through a new marriage and the establishment of her siblings in equally acceptable social positions). Consequently, the scandal of the secret, forbidden chamber is also an offence against the norms of sociability because it belies the expectations of the wife and her family as to what a marriage should be—a mutually profitable and *public* union of interests. In the *KHM*, however, the bride no longer lives in contemporary polite society but in a dark, spooky wood, a setting especially dangerous for women characters which is popularly imagined today as being traditionally and authentically *märchenhaft* but which in fact breaks with Perrault's earlier version.[19] Although Bluebeard is by now a king, neither he nor his wife exists within a societal framework and the characters appear isolated, since their royalty sets them apart just as the wood sets the bride's family apart. While Bluebeard on his travels is accompanied by 'eine Menge Bediente', once the royal couple reach the castle the servants disappear. Thus, instead of getting married as a means and token of societal intercourse and consolidation, the bride merely moves from one state of solitude to another. Even the dramatic visit of the brothers is no longer motivated by the obligations of normal social intercourse (Perrault's heroine says: 'ils m'ont promis qu'ils me viendraient voir aujourd'hui' (p. 260)) but by some kind of magical connection ('da sprach der jüngste [Bruder]: 'Mir ist als hätt' ich unserer Schwester Stimme gehört'' (p. 288)). Therefore society, and especially female society, both concrete (the bride's female friends, the courtship party, the helpful sister) and abstract (the societal fabric which dictates the events of the tale), has disappeared.

Moreover, the affective and authoritative structures within the family are different. Most significantly, Bluebeard's bride is the only surviving woman in the tale since the mother and sister, who have a key function in Perrault's text, have been removed and replaced by a father and brothers who take precedence in the family hierarchy.[20] Indeed, the Grimm *Märchen* makes this new shift explicit in that it opens by mentioning the *paterfamilias* and his male children first: 'In einem Walde lebte ein Mann, der hatte drei Söhne und eine schöne Tochter' (p. 285). Similarly, while the mother in Perrault leaves the

---

[19] Ruth B. Bottigheimer, *Grimms' Bad Girls and Bold Boys: The Moral and Social Vision of the Tales* (New Haven, Conn.: Yale University Press, 1987), 111.

[20] Citing 'Blaubart' as an example, Bottigheimer identifies in the *KHM* a 'predictable pattern of isolating women in a man's world' (109–10), i.e. a restriction of female roles which was part of a nostalgic desire to abandon a contemporary 'educated and enlightened tradition' for women (and men) and to return to what were perceived to be medieval and early modern mores and social forms.

question of marriage up to her daughters, the Grimms' father is considerably more authoritarian:

ein König . . . bat den Mann, er möchte ihm seine Tochter zur Gemahlin geben. Der Mann war froh, daß seiner Tochter ein solches Glück widerfuhr, und sagte gleich ja; es war auch an dem Freier nichts auszusetzen, als daß er einen ganz blauen Bart hatte, so daß man einen kleinen Schrecken kriegte, sooft man ihn ansah. Das Mädchen erschrak auch anfangs davor und scheute sich, ihn zu heirathen, aber auf Zureden ihres Vaters, willigte es endlich ein. Doch weil es so eine Angst fühlte, ging es erst zu seinen drei Brüdern, nahm sie allein und sagte: 'liebe Brüder, wenn Ihr mich schreien hört, wo ihr auch seyd, so laßt alles stehen und liegen und kommt mir zu Hülfe.' (p. 285)

The woman appears to be afraid of her father, since she takes her brothers aside to tell them of her great fear in private. The word 'wenn' is oddly ambiguous here, meaning either 'if' or 'when', indicating that the woman quite expects to have to scream. Although she confides in her brothers and they appear to find her fear credible, their response is not one of unqualified support: ' "leb wohl, liebe Schwester, wenn wir deine Stimme hören, springen wir auf unsere Pferde, und sind bald bei dir" ' (pp. 285–6). Again, 'wenn' is ambiguous, and the tense ending, where the brothers arrive with only a split second to spare, stresses how potentially unhelpful such a promise might have been. Thus the brothers connive at the father's decision to send their sister away, although it is not clear whether this, too, is due to fear of the father or to agreement with his policy. During her ordeal in Bluebeard's castle, the woman is isolated from her female friends and has no sister or even servants to support her. And the father's exclusive authority over his daughter is maintained even after her marriage and subsequent widowhood, since at the end of the tale the wife does not move on and into further, self-determined societal constellations, as she does in Perrault's version, but is returned to her father's house. Given her father's power to coerce her, her fear of him, and the brothers' disinclination to act as her allies, this is hardly a reassuring conclusion. Finally, although family power structures have become more authoritarian and patriarchal in the Grimms' text, they are also mystified by the emphasis on sibling love as a supernatural redemptive power, since it is their sentimentalized, supernatural, and intuitive hearing that brings the brothers to the rescue.

The passage quoted above also demonstrates how the presentation of Bluebeard has shifted. For instance, the reference to the

mysteriously missing wives is gone, and so the woman's fear is provoked by the blue beard alone, a fact which makes her response seem
less reasonable than in Perrault's text. And while the impression
caused by the blue beard is in Perrault's words 'terrible', here it
produces only a more trivial-sounding 'kleine[r] Schrecken'. The
more profound and uncanny aspects of Bluebeard's frightening
appearance are played down, in that the beard does not seem to
change its hue depending on the beholder's relationship to him, as it
does in Perrault's *conte*, but is rather reduced to an odd physical fact.

Next, the isolated heroine is deprived of her comprehension of the
ways of the world, with the result that she is more helpless and less
autonomous than in Perrault's version. In the Grimms' version, it is
the father not the daughter who is impressed by and knows the value
of material things (in this case a golden coach, which is a residuum
from the opening of Perrault's text—where the heroine's understanding of wealth is more sophisticated).[21] This inability to value material
things appropriately is nearly the cause of her downfall.

Two other indices of the woman's helplessness even within her
own family—which should represent security—are her fear of her
father and inability to protest against his decision. Ruth B.
Bottigheimer has shown how in the *KHM*, speechlessness is increasingly imposed on women and girls by various means. This silencing,
'at odds with . . . tales in the contemporaneous French and English
traditions' (p. 169) becomes a 'paradigm for powerlessness' and indicates a loss of personal and social autonomy (becoming 'unmündig')
(pp. 51–6). On the surface, therefore, the narrative voice of the *KHM*
is concerned to portray the bride as being helpless in the presence of
her father, since she is a dutiful, silent daughter—but only until she
leaves her father's sphere of influence. Once she has done so, she
suddenly becomes an uncontrolled, rampaging, and above all vocal
transgressor. She begins to use direct speech more frequently than
any other character, and ensures her rescue by putting Bluebeard off,
pretending to pray, and calling her brothers—all verbal activities.
The ambivalent position of the bride as regards speech in 'Blaubart'
(first silent, then voluble) also reflects an ambivalence about her
character, since according to Bottigheimer women and girls in the
KHM who speak are likely to be bad. While Bottigheimer refers
principally to later versions of the *KHM*, where such a moralizing

[21] This shift heralds the conservative insistence on the part of Jungian commentators
that a properly 'feminine' woman would not be moved by material issues.

distribution of speech and silence is more marked, it is possible that the beginnings of that development are discernible in 'Blaubart'. According to Bottigheimer, the Grimms knew and used an earlier tradition of thinking about women and silence in which '[Eve's] guilt in Paradise disqualifie[d] her sex from further speech' (p. 170), and the myth of Eve is of course particularly closely linked to the *Blaubartmärchen*. In particular, given this religious context, the woman's deceitful pretence of praying seems to be an impious use of speech, thus confirming moral suspicions about feminine articulacy. Therefore, the bride's extensive and effective use of speech implicitly brands her as vicious with the result that an implicit step is taken towards blaming the woman, which of course legitimizes the father's and the husband's control over her and her punishment.

The Grimms' description of the heroine's transgression strengthens the impression given of her uncontrolled nature. While Perrault's heroine is plagued by curiosity too, her decision to open the forbidden chamber follows a relatively complex intellectual reflection on her part, and the narrator makes it clear that her misbehaviour derives in part from a disregard for the rules of sociability ('sans considérer qu'il était malhonnête de quitter sa compagnie' (p. 259)) rather than a profound moral transgression. In the *KHM*, however, the bride's curiosity is a stronger, more irrational force which overcomes her dramatically:

Es war nun nichts mehr übrig, als die verbotene Kammer, der Schlüssel war von Gold, da gedachte sie, in dieser ist vielleicht das allerkostbarste verschlossen; die Neugierde fing an, sie zu plagen, und sie hätte lieber all das andere nicht gesehen, wenn sie nur gewußt, was in dieser wäre. Eine Zeit lang widerstand sie der Begierde, zuletzt aber ward diese so mächtig, daß sie den Schüssel nahm und zu der Kammer hinging. (pp. 286–7)

The longer, more complex description of the woman's feelings here emphasizes the motif of curiosity more strongly than in Perrault's version—and discredits it more emphatically, too. 'Neugierde' mutates to 'Begierde', a sure sign of female vice. And the new motive which is introduced here (there is no indication whatsoever that Perrault's heroine is looking for further riches) is striking in its denunciatory effect. It confirms that Woman is incapable of understanding material values, a role her father had previously performed on her behalf, since she misjudges their importance, and is duly punished. In the opening of the tale it is made clear that the appreciation and negotiation of material issues is men's business (it is the father who understands the meaning of the golden coach and responds by agreeing to give his daughter in marriage). That idea is confirmed here, for while the passage makes clear that the woman is aware of material values, she does not respond to them appropriately or moderately. That is, her relationship to such values is, again, one of uncontrolled excess. This suspicion justifies both the men's role as the controllers of wealth and the broader *KHM* taboo on the acquisition of money by women, in which 'Blaubart' clearly participates.[22] And the passage quoted not only trivializes the woman's transgression, but indicates too that she is completely dominated by her uncontrolled, destructive desires; and this image of a woman who is overcome by desire is echoed in the Grimms' text by the scene in which the chamber is opened. Perrault describes the opening of the chamber as follows:

D'abord elle ne vit rien, parce que les fenêtres étaient fermées; après quelques moments elle commença à voir que le plancher était tout couvert de sang caillé, et que dans ce sang se miraient les corps de plusieurs femmes mortes et attachées le long des murs . . . (p. 259)

This passage builds up the psychological suspense by revealing only gradually—and then only in the form of indirect reflections—the source of the horror, for in Perrault's description the blood is already clotted. But in the *KHM* we read: 'Da schloß sie auf, und wie die Thüre aufging, schwomm ihr ein Strom Blut entgegen' (p. 287)—which means that in the *KHM* there is no finely judged, gradual increase of horror but rather a sudden impression of irresistible, 'natural' forces ('Strom') that have been unleashed by and are implicitly embodied by the woman.[23]

The Grimms' 'Blaubart' therefore involves a complex narratorial ambivalence regarding the woman, for while she triumphs and profits in the end ('und alle Reichthümer des Blaubarts gehörten ihr' (p. 289)), and while she is a heroine and a figure of identification, all of which should indicate her goodness,[24] she is also suspected of being dangerous, at the mercy of her cataclysmic desires, frivolously covetous, and articulate. These female dangers are countered by a

---

[22] Bottigheimer, *Grimms' Bad Girls and Bold Boys*, 130.

[23] Images of natural, engulfing fluid power are traditionally used to represent the body, its desires, and the unconscious. Cf. Hartmut Böhme, 'Umriß einer Kulturgeschichte des Wassers: Eine Einleitung', in Böhme (ed.), *Kulturgeschichte des Wassers* (Frankfurt am Main: Suhrkamp, 1988), 7–42 (22–5); Klaus Theweleit, *Männerphantasien*, 2 vols. (Reinbek bei Hamburg: Rowohlt, 1980), i. 235–310.

[24] Bottigheimer, *Grimms' Bad Girls and Bold Boys*, 150.

typical feature of the later editions of the *KHM*: the imposition of isolation and silence, an idealized and strongly patriarchal family structure (disaster ensues as soon as women step beyond its confines), and the taboo on the acquisition of wealth by women. As well as articulating a profound uncertainty about Woman, this narratorial ambivalence may also have a more remote origin. 'Blaubart' was collected by the Grimms from the Hassenpflug sisters,[25] and since it is thought by some folklorists that narrators favour protagonists of their own gender, the ambivalence in the Grimms' 'Blaubart' may also be the heteroglossic result of the Grimms' collaboration with their female contributors.[26] All in all, however, this contradictory charac-terization fits in with the general trend whereby the woman in both the *KHM* and the wider Bluebeard tradition is inculpated.[27]

Finally, the narrative tone has changed from the ironically realistic to the magical and mysterious. For instance, the golden coach, which in Perrault's tale is part of a practical and socially comprehensible inventory of Bluebeard's luxurious possessions, makes a sudden, unmotivated, and magical appearance ('Einmal kam ein goldener Wagen mit sechs Pferden . . .'). Moreover, in the Grimms' version material wealth is no longer appreciated as a practical necessity for survival but is implicitly denounced as deceptive because of its association with Bluebeard.

All these shifts combine to alter the meaning of the *Märchen*. The ideal of open sociability is replaced by that of a closed and isolated/isolating family unit in which men mediate between the woman and the outside world. The dominant values here are no longer material ones but sentiment and an adherence to rigid gender roles which distinguish between the 'private' and the 'public' and 'inside' and 'outside' the home, identifying such constructs respectively as feminine and masculine. Disaster ensues when these boundaries are not respected. But these rigid distinctions that were designed to control women and make them dutiful and harmless are accompanied by the subtle implication that Woman is actually out of control and vice-ridden. By displacing the tale in time to an

---

[25] Joannnes Bolte und Georg Polívka, *Anmerkungen zu den Kinder- und Hausmärchen der Brüder Grimm*, 5 vols. (Leipzig: Dieterich'sche Verlagsbuchhandlung Theodor Weichen, 1913–32), i. 404. On the Hassenpflugs, see Heinz Rölleke, 'Alte Marie' in *Enzyklopädie des Märchens*, ed. Kurt Ranke et al., to date 8 vols. (Berlin and New York: de Gruyter, 1977–), i. 380–2.

[26] Bottigheimer, *Grimms' Bad Girls and Bold Boys*, 10.

[27] Ibid. 81–94.

imaginary, feudal, and pre-urban kingdom, and by emphasizing magic, mystery, and symbolism, the impression of 'timelessness' popularly associated with the *Märchen* is generated. But in fact such a telling is very much of its own time, since these shifts correspond to those in Tieck's text, and confirm Suhrbier's suggestion that many versions of the Bluebeard material from the eighteenth and nineteenth centuries dulled the edge of Perrault's text by setting it in the past. The evocation of a timeless past not only invokes the power of a putative history which possesses its authority simply because it is so ancient, but also occludes the possibility that the *status quo* is open to change. In the Grimms' version, therefore, the meaning of 'Blaubart' has changed. From being a tale about a society in which women may act autonomously and be rewarded for it, it has become an account of a world which circumscribes and suspects such actions.

BECHSTEIN: THE TEST OF LOVE

Ludwig Bechstein's codification of the *Blaubartmärchen* certainly had a greater influence on nineteenth-century German literature and culture than the *KHM* version.[28] On the one hand, Bechstein's version is much closer than the Grimms' to Perrault's as regards family constellation and plot. But on the other, Bechstein replaces Perrault's realism with a setting more akin to that of the *KHM*, since his tale, like Tieck's, is set in a fantastic, medieval, feudal world with no ostensibly contemporary detail ('man [nannte] ihn nur Ritter Blaubart, obschon er eigentlich anders hieß, aber sein wahrer Name ist verlorengegangen' (p. 374)). The emphasis on sentimental family ties which marks the *KHM* is also preserved ('diese Geschwister liebten einander sehr zärtlich' (p. 374)), as is the exclusion of society, since in Bechstein's version only the nuclear family, rather than a larger group of friends, is invited to Bluebeard's castle during the courtship. Nonetheless, the bride is no longer isolated and the brothers' rescue is also part of a normal social visit rather than quasi-magical, or based on telepathy as in Tieck's play.[29] While Perrault's

---

[28] 'Blaubart' was included only in the 1812 edition of the *KHM* and Bechstein's *Deutsches Märchenbuch* far outsold the Grimms' *KHM* in the nineteenth century. See Ruth B. Bottigheimer, 'The Publishing History of Grimms' Tales: Reception at the Cash Register', in Donald Haase (ed.), *The Reception of Grimms' Fairy Tales: Responses, Reactions, Revisions* (Detroit: Wayne State University Press, 1993), 78–101.

[29] Bottigheimer points out, in both *Grimms' Bad Girls and Bold Boys* (111) and 'Ludwig

narrative tone is ironic and the Grimms' sinister and magical, Bechstein's narrator, while using suspense, adopts a moralizing and more familiar tone. Bechstein also makes the suspicion towards the bride (which is implicit in the German translations of Perrault's *conte* and in the *KHM*) more explicit, and shifts some blame away from Bluebeard.

On the surface, Bechstein seems to restore some of the woman's autonomy which had been reduced in the *KHM*. Unlike the Grimms, Bechstein makes it clear that the decision to marry is the woman's own, although his formulation implies reluctance: 'endlich [faßte sich] die jüngste der Schwestern ein Herz' (p. 375). Bechstein also lessens the powerless isolation of the wife by restoring her sister as company during the ordeal in Bluebeard's house. Together, the two women defend themselves more actively than the solitary bride does in the *KHM* ('Aber die Frau gewann Mut, warf ihre Zimmertüre ins Schloß und hielt sie fest, und dabei schrie sie samt ihrer Schwester so laut um Hülfe, wie sie beide nur konnten' (p. 377). Yet paradoxically, in other ways, Bechstein also deprives the bride of agency. For instance, if we take the use of direct speech to be some kind of index of the autonomy of a character (as Bottigheimer does with reference to the *KHM*), it is noticeable that while the Grimms' heroine spoke more than Bluebeard himself, here that relationship is reversed. Furthermore, the principal effect of the sister's apparently empowering presence is to highlight the bride's fickle nature and moral weakness. Initially, the bride is impressed by Bluebeard's prohibition and promises to obey him (although she attempts to dodge this test of her moral strength by refusing to accept the key at first, perhaps a sign of moral cowardice), but the sister easily makes the wife break her promise:

Die Frau wollte, obschon sie selbst große Neugier trug, durchaus nicht öffnen, aber die Schwester lachte ob ihrer Bedenklichkeit und meinte, daß Ritter Blaubart darin doch nur aus Eigensinn das Kostbarste und Wertvollste von seinen Schätzen verborgen halte. (pp. 375–6)

While the heroines in Perrault's version and the *KHM* experience a powerful sense of curiosity and undergo an inner struggle with it, this element is greatly weakened in Bechstein's version, where the wife

Bechstein's Fairy Tales: Nineteenth-Century Bestsellers and *Bürgerlichkeit*', *Internationales Archiv für Sozialgeschichte der deutschen Literatur*, 15 (1990), 55–88, that Bechstein's *Märchen* presented a more sociable universe for women than the *KHM*.

simply caves in to her sister's covetous inquisitiveness rather than gratifying an impulse of her own. Thus, it is implied, the wife is morally weak and extremely suggestible. Or rather, she is no longer merely disobedient but so fundamentally, morally bad that Bluebeard calls her 'du schlechte Magd'. In this context the way in which the woman and her predecessors are punished becomes very interesting. While Bertuch and Lewald were squeamish about specifying how exactly the other wives had been murdered, Bechstein emphasizes the act of decapitation far more than his predecessors. Bluebeard warns his wife against entering the room as follows: ' "Ich müßte dir dann mit eigner Hand das Haupt vom Rumpfe trennen!" ' (p. 375). When the room is opened it proves to contain 'ein entsetzlicher Anblick!—die blutigen Häupter aller früheren Frauen Ritter Blaubarts' (p. 376), a gory sight which differs from that encountered by previous heroines, who saw whole corpses. Moreover, the emphasis has shifted here from the dead bodies (which Bluebeard appears not to have kept) to their severed heads. This shift is significant because decapitation is a mode of punishment which is particularly well suited to inquisitive women, for it seems that feminine appropriation of knowledge must be punished in a particularly drastic way, and the loss of the head is the loss of the seat of knowledge. Bechstein must have struck a chord with this detail, for the motif of severed heads was to become very popular in later versions of the material.

The change Bechstein makes in the scene where the forbidden door is opened so that two women are now involved is a further response to the special threat of the 'bad', transgressive woman. This detail makes the point explicitly that the company of women is pernicious and immoral, whereas in the *KHM* such company was simply banished. And for Bechstein, as for the Grimms, there is a conflict between the idea of a transgressive woman and that of an innocent victim who deserves to be rescued. If this conflict is expressed in the *KHM* by an ambivalent narrative tone and a tension between speech and silence, Bechstein solves the problem by making the sister the active, wicked party, thus preserving just enough of the heroine's innocence to justify her rescue. Because there can be no mention of rewarding the sister as happens in Perrault's version, she simply disappears from the narrative as an unsolved problem, like Tieck's Mechtilde. Nonetheless, the heroine still has to be bitterly and legitimately punished for her weakness and Bechstein enigmatically comments: 'Die Frau war erlöst, konnte aber die Folgen ihrer Neugier lange nicht verwinden' (p. 377).[30]

Then again, while Perrault does not pass explicit narratorial judgements in the main body of his narrative, Bechstein does so. Nevertheless, he sends out mixed messages about Bluebeard's character that are similar to Lewald's. At one point, after his crimes have been uncovered, Bluebeard is called 'der böse Mann', but elsewhere he is characterized more positively. For example, the narrative opens with a description that is by no means negative: 'Es war einmal ein gewaltiger Rittersmann, der . . . lebte auf seinem Schlosse herrlich und in Freuden' (p. 374). Furthermore, both Bluebeard's prohibition and his response to its transgression are delivered in terms which, while they are cunning and duplicitous, do affirm a model of marriage in which it is correct for the husband to dictate to his wife in the interest of a harmonious life together:

'Ich muß verreisen und übergebe dir die Obhut über das ganze Schloß, Haus und Hof, mit allem, was dazugehört. Hier sind auch die Schlüssel zu allen Zimmern und Gemächern, in alle diese kannst du zu jeder Zeit eintreten. Aber dieser kleine goldne Schlüssel schließt das hinterste Kabinett am Ende der großen Zimmerreihe. In dieses, meine Teure, muß ich dir verbieten zu gehen, so lieb dir meine Liebe und dein Leben ist. Würdest du dieses Kabinett öffnen, so erwartet dich die schrecklichste Strafe der Neugier.' (p. 375)

The formulation 'muß ich dir verbieten' indicates that Bluebeard is imitating the classic gesture of the 'good' authoritarian father or husband, whereby the speaker makes it clear that he is not responding to some individual urge but acting as the agent of a higher moral instance. Although, following Bluebeard's apparently generous, reasoned speech, the warning 'Ich müßte dir dann mit eigner Hand das Haupt vom Rumpfe trennen!' at first appears incongruous, there is a logic to it, since if Bluebeard's command is reasonable and his wife unreasonable, then her transgression is all the worse and must merit a worse punishment. Furthermore, this prohibition is so forceful that the wife appears criminally silly to disregard it. Bluebeard's response to his wife's transgression affirms his claim to the moral high ground in a formulation which clearly echoes the notion of an originary Fall:

und als er die Flecken am Schlüssel sah, so verwandelten sich alle seine Gebärden . . . 'Alle Gewalt habe ich dir gelassen! Alles war dein! Reich und

---

[30] Cf. Suhrbier, 'Blaubart: Leitbild und Leidfigur', 24.

schön war dein Leben! Und so gering war deine Liebe zu mir, du schlechte Magd, daß du meine einzige geringe Bitte, meinen ernsten Befehl nicht beachtet hast?' (p. 376)

According to this formulation, Bluebeard's prohibition had been reasonable so that his wife is clearly at fault. And the sentimentalization of patriarchal family structures highlighted with reference to the *KHM* is taken further here, since the obedience expected of the wife is no longer described as a form of coercion or even duty, but is now termed 'Liebe'. Thus, part of why the woman is 'schlecht' is her perverse inability or unwillingness to respond to this moral and emotional obligation. The narrator does not intervene to qualify or challenge Bluebeard's attitude. Indeed, he actively affirms Bluebeard's perspective, since, unlike in Perrault's text, it is Bluebeard who first uses the word 'Neugier' and describes curiosity as a punishable crime ('so erwartet dich die schrecklichste Strafe der Neugier'), and the narrator adopts the term and negative judgement only subsequently: 'Die Frau . . . [trug] große Neugier'. Moreover, he says that the forbidden chamber contains 'die blutigen Häupter aller früheren Frauen Ritter Blaubarts, die ebensowenig, wie die jetzige, *dem Drang der Neugier* hatten widerstehen können' (my emphasis). The text closes with a lapidary description of the punishment for this female vice which is, once again, sanctioned by the narrator: 'Die Frau war erlöst, konnte aber die Folgen ihrer Neugier lange nicht verwinden', i.e. the crisis from which the woman has to recover is 'die Folgen *ihrer* Neugier' rather than the cruelty of her husband. The effect of the narrator's adoption of Bluebeard's terminology and moral judgements is to establish Bluebeard very firmly as a moral authority and hence to exculpate him to some degree. If the Grimms' heroine was not fully supported by her brothers, here even the narrator has forsaken her.

CONCLUSION

The development of 'Blaubart' in the classic nineteenth-century versions involves several significant features. My analysis confirms Suhrbier's suggestion that the eighteenth- and nineteenth-century Bluebeard tradition uses distancing devices, since Tieck, the Grimms, and Bechstein all distance the tale both in time and class from their bourgeois present. The social dimension that is so important in

Perrault's version is removed from the later texts, thus isolating the bride and making her appear more helpless. As far as the bride herself is concerned, there is an increasing narratorial ambivalence, and her transgression is miniaturized into curiosity, which in turn becomes a foolish covetousness. Thus, like the children at whom such *Märchen* were increasingly directed, the wife appears immature and in need of education.

The female characters in the texts discussed here are mainly notable for their uncivilized, uncontrolled, and emotional behaviour. Indeed, within the marital constellation the wife is increasingly infantilized and subordinated to a paternal authority figure. In the *KHM* that figure is her father, and in Bechstein's version the husband who delivers legitimized moral judgements speaks like a father to a child. But what is particularly interesting is the way in which the nature of the husband's control over his wife changes. While for Perrault the wife's motive for getting married is material and Bluebeard's hold over her is expressed as physical violence, the Grimms and Bechstein subtly change this situation. Family structures and necessities (such as sibling solidarity or the upholding of authority) are sentimentalized and made into affective and moral issues, so that the wife's obedience to Bechstein's Bluebeard is no longer presented in terms of physical force, but as a moral obligation towards the husband which is called love. Similarly, her punishment is polarized, being on one hand drastically physical but on the other, as Bechstein makes clear, psychological and long-lasting. Conversely, as physical brutality becomes less necessary on Bluebeard's part because more of the responsibility for controlling herself and maintaining the order of his household is imposed on his wife, he is increasingly exculpated. In short, we are here seeing the incipient psychological internalization of power relationships, which renders physical force secondary as a means of control and will in the long run make them superfluous.

This development tallies with Elias's observation in *Über den Prozeß der Zivilisation* that 'civilization' progresses through the transformation and internalization of 'Fremdzwänge' (physical coercion) into 'Selbstzwänge'.[31] Because the degree of internalized control must

---

[31] 'in Wirklichkeit ist es noch ein ganzes Gemisch verschiedener Arten von Gewalt oder Zwang, das in den Menschenräumen zurückbleibt, wenn die körperliche Gewalttat langsam von der offenen Bühne des gesellschaftlichen Alltags zurücktritt und nur noch in vermittelter Form an der Züchtung der Gewohnheiten mitarbeitet': Norbert Elias, *Über den Prozeß der Zivilisation: Soziogenetische und psychogenetische Untersuchungen* (1939), 2 vols. (Frankfurt am Main: Suhrkamp, 1997), ii. 331–2.

become greater in an increasingly complex society, the insistence of the nineteenth-century *Blaubartmärchen* on an increasing internalization of control and punishment on the part of the wife is a reflex of the increasing complexities of social modernization during that period. This shift in interest from body to mind as the locus of control, violence, and punishment was to be of central importance in later Bluebeard texts. And the Grimms' depiction of the wife as an irresistible force of nature letting a flood of blood into the civilized castle contradicts the increasing civilizatory insistence on self-control only apparently. In fact, her unruliness is indispensable for the process of civilization, since it legitimizes ever more stringent sanctions on her behaviour, thus propelling the process of civilization forward since the very essence of that process is ever-increasing control. But paradoxically, this increasing control actively subverts itself by producing its own, threatening opposite. In Bechstein's version of the *Blaubartmärchen*, for instance, the wife knows that chaos can be averted only if she refuses to take the key and submit herself to control. And these patterns also emerge in an alternative, less classic, and forgotten nineteenth-century Bluebeard tradition, even though that tradition seems very different at first sight.

5

THE COLLECTOR:
E. MARLITT, 'BLAUBART'

As well as the short *Märchen* texts discussed in the previous chapter, nineteenth-century Germany also knew another, apparently milder Bluebeard tradition in which physical punishment and decapitation were no longer practised and the narrative material was taken as a vehicle for romantic and/or comic fiction.[1] E[ugenie]. Marlitt's novella 'Blaubart' (1866) (as far as can be ascertained, the first German Bluebeard text to have been published by a woman) is one instance of this alternative tradition.[2] It is a story about psychology rather than about physical force, and as such marks the moment at which 'Blaubart' becomes a distinctly modern narrative.

While differing in many ways from Perrault's seventeenth-century model, Marlitt's text does resemble Perrault's in that it is set in contemporary society rather than a fantastic past. Marlitt's young heroine, Lilli, is caught up in a feud between an old friend of her family, Tante Bärbchen, and Tante Bärbchen's neighbour, Herr von Dorn, who lives on a neighbouring estate—or rather, on a part of the same estate which has been divided because of the feud. Tante Bärbchen and Dorn are in fact related and the two branches of the family were on intimate terms in previous generations.[3] The feud is the result of the alleged theft by Tante Bärbchen's grandfather, Erich Dorn, of a portrait of a young girl by Van Dyck which belonged to the present Herr von Dorn's great-grandfather Hubert. Although the accusation was denied by Erich and never proved (since the

---

[1] e.g. Louis Angély, 'Herr Blaubart oder das geheimnisvolle Kabinett. Posse in Einem Akt, frei nach dem Französischen', in *Vaudevilles und Lustspiele. Theils Originale, Theils Übertragungen, Bearbeitungen*, 3 vols. (Berlin: Cosmar & Krause, 1828), i. 67–123; Julius Roderich Benedix, 'Blaubart. Lustspiel in zwei Aufzügen', *Die deutsche Schaubühne*, 7 (1861); Friedrich Wilhelm Hackländer, 'Der Blaubart', *Über Land und Meer*, 10 (1863).

[2] E. Marlitt (Eugenie John) (1825–87), 'Blaubart', first published in *Die Gartenlaube*, 27–31 (1866); subsequently in *Thüringer Erzählungen* (1869) (Leipzig: Keil, 1886), 107–242, quoted here; and *E. Marlitt's [sic] gesammelte Romane und Novellen*, 10 vols. (Leipzig: Ernst Keil's [sic] Nachfolger, n.d.), x. 263–338.

[3] Dorn's father added the aristocratic 'von' to the family name, estranging the two families further; however the present Herr Dorn chooses to dispense with the 'von', demonstrating family unity and bourgeois solidity.

Van Dyck could not be found in Erich's house), the two families quarrelled and divided their once-communal garden by a hedge, never to speak to each other again.

When Lilli arrives at Tante Bärbchen's house for a holiday, Dorn and Tante Bärbchen are in bitter dispute over the boundary between their territories. This boundary runs through the middle of a summer-house to which Tante Bärbchen lays claim since Lilli has played there since childhood but which Dorn wants to demolish, since it is the only remaining vantage-point from which one garden can be seen from the other. Tante Bärbchen's old woman servant, Dorte, claims that Dorn's desire for increased privacy is due to a mysterious mistress whom he keeps prisoner in his house, and Lilli begins to fantasize about this idea, imagining Dorn as 'der Blaubart, der ein unglückliches Weib gefangen [hält]' (p. 141). Driven by curiosity, Lilli spies on the neighbours at night and glimpses an unhappy and heavily veiled woman with Dorn. In the end, however, Dorn manages to convince Lilli that he is merely the guardian of his invalid, illegitimate half-sister Beatrice. The stolen painting is found in the summer-house, where it had been hidden under the canvas of a painting by Erich Dorn of Orestes and the Furies; the families are then reconciled and Lilli and Dorn become engaged.

So the Bluebeard topos is apparently exploded because it turns out that Dorn is a man of exemplary conduct and character who has no shameful secrets, and in the latter part of the narrative it is Tante Bärbchen herself who becomes the terrifying speaker of prohibitions in place of Dorn, as she misguidedly tries to keep Lilli away from him. Moreover, marriage becomes the harmonious *telos* of the narrative, rather than a problematic beginning which must be overcome. But while Marlitt's plot thus seems to bear little resemblance to the *Märchen*, there are many homologies between Marlitt's text and that model. The constellation of the young, inexperienced woman (Lilli) and the older, wealthy man (Dorn) is reproduced, as is Bluebeard's secret. The notion of the forbidden chamber expands to include all of Dorn's property, since Lilli is forbidden to see inside it. That property contains a woman whom Lilli believes has been badly treated and imprisoned, like the dead women in the *Märchen*. Lilli, like the bride in the *Märchen*, defies the prohibition by opening the window of the summer-house one night to watch Dorn's house and garden. And while she is discovered and fears punishment—first from Dorn and, once she has discovered her attraction for him, from

Tante Bärbchen—her transgression is unexpectedly rewarded at the last minute, with the gratification of her romantic wishes. But finally, there are many inadvertent hints in the text that marriage to Dorn will in fact prove to be as dangerous for Lilli as marriage to a more traditional Bluebeard.

THE RESTORATION OF ORDER

The novella has been read as a confident affirmation of nineteenth-century positivism and civilization, in which the notion of an outwardly respectable, murderous husband could only be the product of servants' and womens' inferior fantasies,[4] in other words, as a conservative text which did not challenge the standards of its time and involved the nineteenth-century suspicion of excessive, inappropriate feminine curiosity and the exculpation of Bluebeard as its main themes. Marlitt's 'Blaubart' seems to take those trends to their logical conclusion, since the murder and the forbidden chamber prove not to exist at all except in the overheated imaginations of Tante Bärbchen's servant, Dorte, and Lilli herself; and Bluebeard's authority is benevolent and legitimate. The novella concludes with Lilli joyfully submitting to that authority: 'Wie trunken hingen [Dorns] Augen an den Lippen des jungen Mädchens, das mit wenigen energischen Worten ihm das Recht auf ihren Besitz einräumte' (p. 239).

On another reading, however, that apparently straightforward progression from ignorance to enlightenment is better described as only the attempted *restoration* of order which is threatened by forces far more frightening and active than mere ignorance. In nineteenth-century versions of the *Blaubartmärchen*—notably the Grimms'—the patriarchal family is supposed to function as the basic unit of social order. Marlitt's 'Blaubart' shows how that unit of order is first disturbed by a threat which is presented as being 'unnatural' and then must be laboriously (and not very successfully) re-established. To begin with, the protagonists' ancestors lived in harmony ('Der Garten wurde gemeinschaftlich benutzt und zur Sommerzeit aß man stets vereint in dem großen Pavillion' (p. 121)), but this state has, as a result of the quarrel, given way to an unnatural hostility within the

⁴ Hartwig Suhrbier, 'Blaubart—Leitbild und Leidfigur', in *Blaubarts Geheimnis: Märchen und Erzählungen, Gedichte und Stücke* (Cologne: Diederichs, 1984), 11–79 (50–1).

family and an equally unnatural division between the sexes. The enmity between the 'Erichs' (represented by Tante Bärbchen) and the 'Huberts' (represented by Dorn) is constantly and emphatically gendered by the use of binary oppositions. Tante Bärbchen's house is a matriarchal universe, dominated by Tante Bärbchen herself and the portrait of her grandmother, Erich Dorn's wife, who taught her to perpetuate the family feud and maintain the family honour. And it is made abundantly clear that this matriarchal side is in the wrong, inasmuch as it represents disorder, superstition, and a lower level of civilization. For instance, in one of many such implicitly programmatic comparisons between Tante Bärbchen's and Dorn's world, the houses of the rival matriarchy and patriarchy are opposed in style and appearance. Tante Bärbchen's house is described as follows:

Es war alt und unschön . . . Und doch lag es so traut und heimlich da, gleichsam auf den grünen Pfühl des Waldes gebettet, der seinen Atem darüber hinwehte, jener Hauch der Romantik, in den sich auch alte, versteckte Jagdschlösser einspinnen. . . . Auf demselben Vorsprung des Berges, nur durch einen hohen, lebendigen Zaun von Tante Bärbchens Besitzung getrennt, erhob sich die brillante Fassade eines neuen Hauses . . . Fast schien es, als verhauche die nordische Luft ihre ganze Kühle und Schärfe an der trennenden grünen Hecke. In Tante Bärbchens Garten strich sie über ehrliche deutsche Kraut- und Kohlhäupter, über ungekünstelten Graswuchs voller hochaufgeschossener Wiesenblumen, und drüben flüsterte sie in den verlockenden Zweigen des Lorbeers . . . Drüben rauschte das Brunnenwasser aus der einfachen Holzröhre in eine uralte, grünbemooste Steinmulde, und hier sprangen Fontänen . . . Man meinte, um jenes alte Dach . . . den ernsten Schatten der deutschen Sage gleiten zu sehen, während drüben ein Stück heiterer südlicher Poesie waltete. (pp. 119–21)

A whole series of binary oppositions is at work here. Tante Bärbchen's old house represents an archaic, anarchic, gothic culture, while Dorn's new house represents a more modern, ordered, classical culture which makes use of superior technology (the fountains as opposed to the wooden water-pipe). Tante Bärbchen's house is described in terms of wild, unformed superstition ('Sage') while Dorn's is described in terms of a more enlightened and formal 'Poesie', a comparison which recalls the literary project described in Chapter 1 of improving on primitive, 'vernacular', and feminine *Märchen* culture in favour of a refined and implicitly masculine elegance. The hedge between the two houses marks a boundary between two stages in civilization in which the patriarchal side is generally superior.

Furthermore, the matriarchal side of the divide is morally as well as aesthetically and practically inferior, since its inhabitants are to blame for perpetuating the family feud and generating the scandalous untruths about Dorn and his sister. Correspondingly, Tante Bärbchen rejects all Dorn's conciliatory advances in the course of the novella and responds increasingly unreasonably to any mention of him and his family. Thus, once Lilli has met the charming and honourable Dorn and suggests to Tante Bärbchen that the dispute could surely be settled calmly, Tante Bärbchen responds violently to this sensible suggestion:

'Komme mir nie wieder mit dergleichen Redensarten, Lilli! Ich bin alt geworden in dem Bewußtsein, daß die Huberts auf unsere Linie einen Flecken geworfen haben, und den Groll und Schmerz darüber nehme ich mit ins Grab . . .' (pp. 175–6)

And the other dominant figure in this matriarchal household is Dorte, who is the principal source of disorderly, superstitious narratives. Dorte's words demonize Dorn, his putative captive mistress and their black servant. For instance, Dorte says of the black servant:

'Gott verzeih mir's, wie nur ein Christenmensch solch ein schwarzes Ungetier um sich leiden mag! Ich erschrecke immer zu Tode, wenn er den Mund aufmacht, und denke an den Walfisch, der den Jonas verschluckt hat.' (p. 138)[5]

Then again, this matriarchal universe is not only disorderly, it somehow (and paradoxically, given the wilder state of the garden and the implication that Tante Bärbchen's world is halted in a regressive, uncivilized state) goes against nature. Much is made of Tante Bärbchen's inappropriately manly appearance, and she is described as being 'verkürzt in ihren *natürlichsten* Rechten' (my emphasis), since, just as the unnatural Amazons in classical mythology lacked one breast, Tante Bärbchen lacks one arm.

Given which, Lilli's step into Dorn's well-kept garden as his fiancée marks a step into a higher level of civilization, or rather, a return to a prelapsarian, civilized paradise. The unnatural division, in conformity with nineteenth-century ideals of complementarity, is overcome by Lilli and Dorn's marriage, as the names of the two

---

[5] Dorte's male counterpart in Tante Bärbchen's house is the manservant Sauer, who criticizes her superstition. The servants' squabbles thematize concisely the increasing suppression and pathologization of the disorderly *Märchentante* in the nineteenth century, as Dorte complains of Sauer's response to her stories: 'da wird doch der Mensch ganz grob . . . und sagt, ich solle nur gleich in den Spittel ziehen; dort glaubten sie noch solches Zeug': *Thüringer Erzählungen*, 153–4.

characters suggest, invoking as they do the very different images of the lily and the thorn. Correspondingly, when Dorn first appears, he is excessively masculine, i.e. aggressive and arrogant, in his behaviour. Soon, however, under the beneficial influence of love, he learns to behave beautifully and teaches Lilli to overcome her exaggerated feminine fantasy. But throughout this process it is clear that Dorn is the dominant instance to which Lilli must conform, and it is his magnaminity, not a true equality, which permits the disorderly, matriarchal world to be incorporated into his. As Lilli says to Tante Bärbchen:

'Wenn er mich nicht verstößt, weil ich ihn in thörichter Überschätzung meiner Kraft tief verwundet habe, so bin ich sein . . . Das Wenige, das wir wissen, oder daß wir vielmehr in uns selbst beschämenderweise vermutet haben, beruht gerade auf einer seiner edelsten Handlungen, du wirst ihm abbitten müssen, so gut wie ich!' (pp. 238–40)

Finally, the restoration of order is thematized by the recovery of the stolen portrait. Van Dyck's work reflects a past, ordered, bourgeois world into which the girl in the portrait with her 'unschuldigen Blumenaugen' fits perfectly. Although she has been hidden by a horrific image from classical mythology for the duration of the unnatural family feud, once order is restored she re-emerges to preside over the new harmony from behind the Orestes painting.

This recuperative account is underpinned by two separate, mythological narratives. First, the plot structure of the novella fits in with the tripartite biblical model of history. As in Genesis, an initial, Edenic state of horticultural harmony issues in a fall from grace. Indeed, the consequences of the originary family quarrel have all the characteristics of Old Testament theology, since the dispute seems to be beyond atonement, with the result that the descendants of the perpetrators not only inherit and perpetuate the hostility but are punished themselves. For instance, Tante Bärbchen, the granddaughter of the accused Erich, was born with only one arm. The narrator comments:

Die böse Welt suchte diese Missethat der Natur in Einklang zu bringen mit dem göttlichen Gesetz: 'Ich will die Sünden der Väter heimsuchen an den Kindern.' Man raunte sich zu, der Vater der Unglücklichen habe einem armen Mädchen die Ehe versprochen und sich dabei vermessen, der Allmächtige solle ihn an Armen und Beinen strafen, wenn er sein Wort nicht halte. Er habe den Schwur gebrochen und das einarmige Kind sei die nothwendige Erfüllung des göttlichen Drohwortes. (p. 118)

And during Bärbchen's childhood one of Hubert's descendants (Dorn's father) teased her in the following significant words:

'Ach, bist du ein häßliches Mädchen! . . . Hast ja nur einen Arm! Das ist *Gottes Gericht* [my emphasis], sagt meine Großmama immer . . . Ihr habt doch das Bild drüben . . . Bilderdieb, Bilderdieb!' (p. 126)

Hubert's female descendants are also physically marked by this history, since Dorn's half-sister, Beatrice, has a terrible, disfiguring, and possibly contagious illness which prevents her from seeing other people. This state of affairs recalls the Genesis narrative according to which the punishment of humanity's originary transgression is clearly marked on the female body (implying, as I have already discussed, that women are to blame). Moreover, this illness recalls the nineteenth-century fear of the transgenerational transmission of syphilis which would also have been interpreted according to this biblical idea (as well as the Grimms' theory that 'Blaubart' may have been about leprosy, an illness associated by sexuality, as we have seen). And strikingly, in a hair-raising tale Tante Bärbchen tells about a suitor who rejected her in her youth on discovering her disability (which she had disguised until then by means of a false arm), she makes implicit but unmistakable connections with the Genesis narrative:

'er [griff] schnell und unversehens nach meiner Hand—es war die linke, falsche . . . er stand vor mir mit einem Gesicht, so weiß, wie der Kalk an der Wand; ich glaube gar, er bekam eine Art von Schwindel oder Ohnmacht vor Schreck und Abscheu. Er stierte mich entsetzt an und schleuderte das unselige Machwerk von Pappe weit von sich, als sei es eine Natter . . . Den Arm . . . habe ich auf der Stelle weggelegt, ich hatte meine Strafe für den Betrug!' (p. 207)

Tante Bärbchen blames herself for deceit (the use of a false arm) rather than her suitor for his insensitivity in the same way that the author of the Fall narrative considers Eve to be at fault for being deceitful when in fact she is duped by God and Satan. Tante Bärbchen even compares her false arm with a 'Natter', thus making connections between her left (or sinister) false arm, Satanic temptation, and the perpetual enmity between Eve's children and the serpent after the Fall. Lilli, too, is more closely involved in this disrupted family history than meets the eye, for the fickle suitor turns out to be her own father. And just as in the Bible, a male redeemer (Dorn) is required to resolve a hereditary enmity, a secular version of original sin. Indeed, not only does Dorn's name recall the New Testament crown of thorns, but he describes his love for Lilli, which he believes to be unrequited, in terms of Christ-like, physical martyrdom: 'Ich kann in diesem Augenblicke noch nicht sagen: "Werden Sie glücklich!" Das hieße sich selbst ans Kreuz schlagen' (p. 237). Similarly, Lilli's name evokes a flower traditionally associated with the Virgin Mary, who in Christian theology redeemed the sins of Eve.

The second mythological narrative which is used to emphasize the restoration of order is classical; more precisely, there are three classical myths in play here, since Tante Bärbchen is associated with a series of powerful female figures from the classics. In particular, she is identified with some anarchic, monstrous, and powerful female figures who are conquered by male figures in the process of classical civilization. In replacing Tante Bärbchen's principles with Dorn's, Marlitt is implicitly referring to the popular nineteenth-century notions that classical patriarchy came to replace a prehistoric matriarchy, and that this process was reflected in classical mythology.

First, Tante Bärbchen wields scissors and is at one point shown spinning at a wheel, instruments and activities traditionally associated with the three Fates or Parcae (in the European tradition, spinning is also closely associated with superstition and feminine, disorderly narrative, and with the German verb 'spinnen' in the sense of telling implausible stories, i.e. what *Märchentanten* like Dorte do).

Second, Tante Bärbchen represents a threatening—or castrating—power since she appears as the mythological Medusa, a connection which is made by the anecdote about the suitor and the false arm. In classical mythology, Medusa's hair consisted of snakes, and this made her appearance so terrifying that all who looked on her turned to stone, which is precisely the effect that Tante Bärbchen's snake-like arm ('Natter') has on her suitor, who 'bekam eine Art von Schwindel oder Ohnmacht vor Schreck und Abscheu' and resembled the 'Kalk an der Wand', that is, a lifeless, mineral substance. Although a missing limb may, through displacement, represent a castrated body, it may also be the projection of a castration fear *provoked* by that body if it is perceived as threatening. Indeed, Freud's reading of Medusa made her into an explicitly castrating instance, whereby the snakes associated with her are images of the phalluses she has thus violently appropriated.[6] In most versions of the myth, Medusa was vanquished by Perseus under the tutelage of Athene, the goddess of wisdom. This is a step from a feminine to a masculine order, for while Athene is female, she was not born of a mother. Neither is she a mother herself; and she stands for virtues generally considered to be masculine, and is often depicted equipped with a helmet and weapons.

Third, Tante Bärbchen is associated with the myth of Orestes and the Furies. At the end of the novella, it turns out that Tante Bärbchen's ancestor *did* steal Hubert's Van Dyck after all and hid it behind a framed painting of Orestes pursued by the Furies that he had executed himself:

Mit flüchtigem Pinsel und einer gewissen Hast gemalt, war [das Gemälde] auffallend verzeichnet in den Proportionen, Fehler, die den Eindruck des Bildes zu einem lächerlichen hätten machen können, wäre nicht der Kopf des Orest gewesen; aber dieses Gesicht hatte etwas Überwältigendes in seinem Ausdruck. Nicht das haarsträubende Entsetzen in den Zügen war es allein, was den widerstrebenden Blick des Beschauers immer wieder fesselte; tiefer noch ergriffen die namenlos bitteren Schmerzen der Reue, welche der sonst ungelenke, steife Maler mit wahrer Meisterschaft diesem Antlitz aufgedrückt hatte. (pp. 157–8)

Orestes was the son of Agamemnon and Clytemnestra, who, together with her lover Aegisthus, murdered her husband. On reaching manhood, Orestes, on the advice of Apollo, murdered his mother to avenge his father. But although this murder was committed on divine advice, Orestes was pursued and driven mad by the Furies who were the 'ministers of the vengeance of the gods', stern female figures (usually three) of a terrible appearance:

They were generally represented with a grim and fearful aspect, with a black and bloody garment, and serpents wreathing around their head instead of hair. They held a burning torch in one hand, and a whip of scorpions in the other, and were always attended by terror, rage, paleness and death.[7]

Orestes's persecution by the Furies ended only when Athene intervened to sanction his matricide before the citizens of Athens and to transform the Furies into the Eumenides, or the 'kindly ones'. And the Furies were in fact even less just than my summary of the Orestes myth makes them appear, since they not only avenged parents

---

[6] Sigmund Freud, 'Die Meduse', in Freud, *Gesammelte Werke*, ed. Anna Freud et al., 18 vols. (London: Imago, 1941), xvii. 45–8 (47).

[7] John Lemprière, *A Classical Dictionary* (London: Routledge & Kegan Paul, 1947), 426–7, 234.

wronged by their children (as is the case here), they also pursued children who did *not* avenge their parents. So even if Orestes had not avenged his father's death by murdering his mother, the Furies would still have pursued him for neglecting to do so. In other words, through Athene's intervention, a contradictory, archaic, matriarchal code of justice is replaced by one that is stable, civic, patriarchal, and superior. That superiority is set out clearly in Aeschylus' *Eumenides*, where Athene defends and vindicates Orestes on the grounds that matricide is a less serious crime than the killing of a husband or father, for mothers are mere vessels, not agents, of procreation, and subordinate to the 'male principle'.[8]

There is a whole series of parallels here with Marlitt's plot, because while the originary crime in this version of 'Blaubart' is the relatively harmless theft of the portrait, Erich's picture superimposes on it the complexities of the Orestes myth. For instance, in classical (and biblical) mythology, crimes like that of Orestes led to a curse in the family which lasted for generations, just as the two families in Marlitt's 'Blaubart' perpetuate their hostility for generations. Although Erich's crime is a good deal more harmless than that of Orestes, the implication here is that Erich is identified with him because Erich, too, committed a crime against family ties and was mercilessly pursued by his conscience ('Reue'). Just as the Furies nearly drove Orestes mad, so Erich at the end of his life is said to have had an 'umdüstertes Gemüt'. By the same token, Tante Bärbchen becomes a kind of Fury who obsessively perpetuates an atavistic family feud and persecutes the descendant of its initiator— ironically, in the belief that he was innocent. Furthermore, in her role as Fury she resembles a castrating Medusa, with snake-like hair, and the fire associated with the Furies is recalled by her attempt at the end of the text to throw the precious painting, as a scapegoat for the family dissent, into the fire. And just as Athene's vindication of Orestes marks the beginning of a new, more civilized judicial order in which the insatiable wrath of the individualistic, anarchic, female Furies is replaced by a more modern public declaration made in law before the (male) Athenian citizens, so too a step is taken into a higher, patriarchal level of civilization at the end of Marlitt's 'Blaubart'.

These mythological narratives turn Tante Bärbchen, who seems

[8] Aeschylus, *Eumenides*, ed. and trans. Anthony J. Podlecki (Warminster: Aris & Phillips, 1989), 103–7.

on the face of things to be a harmless old lady, into an archaic monster whose name echoes the word 'Barbar'. The monstrous images associated with her echo cultural fantasies about a threatening, castrating feminine force which must be suppressed at all costs, imply that feminine authority is unnatural (reflected in Tante Bärbchen's disfigurement), and suggest that Dorn's restoration of order is a welcome and humane triumph of culture. Furthermore, in the myths with which she is associated, female figures—Eve, Clytemnestra, or Mother Nature herself—are blamed for an originary disaster.

THE RETURN OF BLUEBEARD: SUBLIMINAL VIOLENCE

But although the orderly ending of Marlitt's 'Blaubart' is intended to indicate that a monstrous past has been replaced by a benevolent present and future, and that the monster Bluebeard has vanished, this surface text in fact is riddled with contradictions which undermine it. Indeed, Marlitt's novella is remarkable in its inadvertent revelations of disturbing undercurrents. For instance, the 'process of civilization', represented by the engagement between Lilli and Dorn and the imposition of such benevolent and 'masculine' values as reason and discipline (Dorn has been an army officer), may *seem* to suppress violence, but never effaces it. Dorn too is referred to at one point as a 'Barbar', and his rational order proves to have a dark, violent side which seriously jeopardizes the claim that Bluebeard has disappeared from the narrative and that men, civilization and marriage are no longer violent.

The tale of 'Blaubart' represents a conception of gender relations that involves aggression towards the feminine. Such aggression can assume different forms over time, even while it remains fairly consistent in its structure, and it seems to me that the more 'civilized' relationship in Marlitt's 'Blaubart' is the index of just such a formal shift, rather than the elimination of aggression. While Marlitt's model of courtship and marriage seems to be far removed from that in which wives are butchered, the text is still shot through with images of violence and morbid images of femininity that are closely linked with Dorn. While the text employs various strategies, notably splitting off and sublimation, to mask these images, they nevertheless point to a persistent aggression towards the feminine on Dorn's part, or on the part of the text itself, inasmuch as it is itself a vehicle of order that transmits the 'civilized' standards of the day.

While Dorn is capable of aggressive behaviour—for instance, he violently crushes flowers in his hand while talking to Lilli (a classic symbol of defloration)—such behaviour is sanctioned by the narrator, since it is appropriately masculine. But other, more frightening aspects of Dorn's violence are split off from his person in order to preserve his apparent benevolence. For example, when Lilli is seen hiding at night in the summer-house between the two gardens, the demonic black servant, who is easily understood as Dorn's *alter ego*, comes to investigate:

Sie hatte eben mit unsicheren Händen den Riegel vorgeschoben, als draußen der Kies unter seinen Schritten kreischte; er schlug mit der Faust gegen den Laden, daß das alte Holz dröhnte, und stieß in gebrochenem Deutsch einen Schwall von Flüchen und Verwünschungen hervor. Die Finger des jungen Mädchens umschlossen krampfhaft den unteren Riegel und drückten ihn nieder. Dicht neben ihrem Ohr, durch die Spalten der Jalousie klang die heisere Stimme des zornigen Schwarzen, sie meinte, seinen Atem im Gesicht zu fühlen. Ein unsägliches Grauen bemächtigte sich ihrer . . . (p. 149)

After the intense physical horror of this scene, whose associations with rape are heightened by the fact that the text closely associates the summer-house with Lilli's person, a brief sentence follows in which Dorn calls his servant away, and the next sentence reads: 'Es war dies das erste Mal in ihrem Leben, daß sich das junge Mädchen sagen mußte, es habe eine Unannehmlichkeit für Tante Bärbchen herbeigeführt.' This bathetic formulation is such an odd conclusion to draw after a dramatic moment of terror that it draws attention to the fissures in Marlitt's vision, which continually attempts to naturalize the extraordinary by covering it over with the ordinary.

At other points, Dorn's violence is sublimated, notably by means of his repeated association with morbid, feminine images. For one thing, his sister, Beatrice, is dying in his care just as Bluebeard's wives died in their husband's; the alleged happy ending of the novella comes too late for Beatrice, for she 'wandelt mit immer matter werdenden Schritten durch beide Gärten' at the end (p. 241). This description implies that she is dying, so that the surface restoration of order and the reunification of the two gardens have no power to save her. And, of course, Beatrice's own name has connotations of tragic morbidity, for it is the name of the dead beloved in Dante's *Vita nuova* and *The Divine Comedy*.

Furthermore, Dorn is associated with a whole series of deathlike women—who are not human but artistic creations, and this characteristic is of central importance for the new Bluebeard. For instance, a stained-glass window in Dorn's house depicts Romeo and Juliet. On one hand, Dorn can be identified with Romeo, since it is a family feud which keeps him from his beloved Lilli–Juliet. But on the other, it is Dorn himself who angrily smashes the window when he sees Lilli entertaining a male guest of Tante Bärbchen's, because he believes that this encounter challenges his rights over Lilli. This destructive, possessive behaviour recalls that of the family patriarchs in the Romeo and Juliet story more than it does that of Romeo himself. Moreover, the glass image of Juliet brings further meanings into the text:

Das schöne zarte Weib im weißen Atlasgewande da droben, dem die schwarzen Haarwellen über den Busen fluteten . . . hier bog es sich von Licht umflossen, verlangend hernieder und keine rosige Flamme der Scham flog über ihr bleiches Liliengesicht. (p. 140)

This pallid image of Juliet prefigures the tragic death of Shakespeare's heroine, especially since the pale 'Liliengesicht' not only is that of a corpse but evokes too a flower traditionally associated with mourning. The lifelessness of the image is stressed by the phrase 'keine rosige Flamme der Scham', a description which, given the secondary meaning of 'Scham', also represents a desexualization akin to death. In this context, then, the fact that the lily is associated too with the desexualized Virgin Mary seems to be no coincidence. And the description of the Juliet window is followed by one of a statue of a woman in Dorn's garden:

Dort aus dämmerndem Gebüsch leuchtete ein weißes Marmorbild; der schlanke Frauenleib streckte die Arme gen Himmel, als suche er sich angstvoll den Umarmungen des Epheu zu entziehen, der das Piedestal umstrickte. (p. 145)

Like the image of Juliet, the statue is pale and corpse-like; in addition, it is 'angstvoll'. It is desexualized too inasmuch as it is described as attempting to escape the (erotic) embraces of the Dionysian ivy, and at the same time it is *petrified*, that is, its motion seems to have been arrested so that it has become lifeless like Bluebeard's dead women. Here again, we have a deathly image of femininity in Dorn's possession which is hidden away jealously and secretly and so makes him appear like Bluebeard.

It is unsurprising, therefore, that the image of Juliet and the statue are closely linked to that of Beatrice, for at the point in the text where the window is described, it is not clear who or what the 'schönes zartes Weib' is. Indeed, the context initially implies that Dorn's mysterious captive woman is being described, and it transpires only later in the same passage that the narrator is referring to a picture in a window. And the statue and Beatrice are explictly associated in just the same way, since when Beatrice does make her first appearance, she is described as follows: 'Aber schien es nicht, als sei die Marmorstatue plötzlich vom Piedestal herabgestiegen und wandle durch den stillen Laubgang?' (p. 146). Beatrice resembles Juliet and the statue also in that she too appears pale and lifeless; and since the pure, dead child-bride in Dante's writing is her namesake, she too is desexualized.

But the significance of the window is in fact even more threatening than the identification with the dying Beatrice implies. This is because the image of Juliet is identified with Lilli too, and so links Beatrice and Lilli very closely as well. When Dorn is angry he smashes Juliet in a way which implies a murderous violence towards Lilli. And the image of the tragic Beatrice–Juliet is also connected to Lilli through its appearance (for Lilli too is pale and dark and always dressed in white), and especially through the 'bleiches *Lilien*gesicht'. Elsewhere, Lilli's own appearance is described as follows:

die weichen Falten eines hellen Musselins [flossen] um die Gestalt, an der augenscheinlich die Thüringer Luft ihre gerühmte Kraft und Stärke umsonst versucht hatte. Man konnte nichts Zarteres sehen, als diese feinen Glieder, die, eben in sich zusammensinkend, schmal und klein zwischen den Polstern ruhten, scheinbar, ohne dieselben zu drücken. Sah es doch fast aus, als ob selbst die dunklen Flechten am Hinterkopf zu schwer seien für den schlanken Hals; denn das Haupt bog sich stets leicht hintenüber. (pp. 128–9)

This description of a delicate girl in white might also be that of a corpse. Just as the demonic black servant is a projection of Dorn's aggressive unconscious or his diabolical *alter ego*, so Beatrice, linked with Lilli through the image of Juliet, can be seen as Lilli's moribund, dark double. It seems that both women's relationship with Dorn has condemned them to a deathlike appearance or even to death itself, because that relationship involves considerable sublimated aggression that is directed against them. Lilli's deliberate seeking out of Beatrice and pleasurable fascination with such deathlike images implies that she too has internalized this sublimated but deadly aggression against the feminine in herself. At the same time, in an apparently contradictory way, if Beatrice appears to be desexualized through her name, in more subtle ways she does seem to be associated with sex. For instance, she bears the stigma of illegitimacy and may well be suffering from hereditary syphilis, and certainly for most of the narrative she is presented literally and figuratively as a lady of the night, a time which Marlitt descibes in highly sensuous terms. Beatrice may embody those sexual and thanatic aspects of Lilli which she must put to death in order to become Dorn's wife and conform to the rules of Bluebeard's ordered world. In other words, the women most closely associated with Dorn are beautiful, aestheticized images of death or petrification—a new variant on the theme of Bluebeard's dead wives.

THE PSYCHOLOGIZATION OF BLUEBEARD

Clearly, then, despite Marlitt's claims to the contrary, Dorn is a murderous if subtle Bluebeard. Furthermore, the *manner* in which the the *Blaubartmärchen* is evoked in Marlitt's novella is of major interest, since it signals important changes within the tradition; heralds the advent of the modern versions of the twentieth century; and tells us a good deal more about the nature of this new Bluebeard. The *Märchen* reference is not suggested to any characters in the text by any external agent, but emerges independently in the imaginations of both Lilli and Dorn. Dorte only has to describe Dorn as a tyrant who keeps his mistress imprisoned and Lilli immediately thinks of him as 'der Blaubart, der ein unglückliches Weib gefangen [hält]' (p. 282). And when Lilli finally tackles Dorn about his 'captive', he immediately interprets Lilli's inference as follows:

Also Muhmen und Basen erzählen sich . . . von einem weinenden gefangenen Weibe in meinem Hause? Und ich spiele ohne Zweifel in diesem Drama nothgedrungen die Rolle eines Währwolfes oder Blaubartes? (p. 221)[9]

What is interesting here is that Bluebeard springs to mind spontaneously for both characters, who can be assumed, like Marlitt, to have had a standard nineteenth-century upper-middle-class German upbringing. The only difference is that Dorn claims a critical

[9] Jean-Louis G. Picherit associates Bluebeard with werewolves in 'Qui était Barbebleue?', *Neuphilologische Mitteilungen/Bulletin de la société néophilologique/Bulletin of the Modern Language Society*, 89 (1988), 374–7.

distance from the role of Bluebeard and dismisses it as the fantasies of inferior female gossips.

There is an important conclusion to be drawn here. Bluebeard is evidently still irresistibly associated with ideas about unjust, cruel, or dangerous husbands or male lovers, since both protagonists think of him independently and spontaneously. In other words, Bluebeard retained a powerful hold on the later nineteenth-century sensibility as a symbol of destructive masculinity. But at the same time he has undergone a qualitative change, for he is no longer a real character but a fantasy. It seems that, by the later nineteenth century, Bluebeard could be depicted only in terms of an imaginary melodrama and not of real events. Correspondingly, those acts of aggression against Woman or the feminine which were literal in earlier versions of the *Blaubartmärchen* have undergone a qualitative change, and become psychological, not physical—but no less real in their effects. So while the only 'Blutströme' in the text are in Lilli's fantasy and there is no obvious connection between Lilli–Beatrice's mortal illness and Dorn, the references to the *Blaubartmärchen* make an insistent connection between the women's physical weakness and Dorn's sublimated aggression.

In other words, Woman's subjugation to Bluebeard has fundamentally changed. One index of this is the fact that Bluebeard no longer *murders* but *incarcerates* women; furthermore, not only can he dispense with murder, he does not even need to use physical force to imprison his women.[10] Just as Bechstein's Bluebeard called the obedience he expected from his wife 'love', so Bluebeard's power here is described even more strongly, using the idiom of love. And while Bechstein's Bluebeard still principally used physical violence to enforce obedience, Marlitt's Bluebeard uses love alone. Therefore, in Marlitt's version, the Bluebeard material becomes less a commentary on the dark, violent side of the institution of marriage, as Perrault's tale was, than on the dark, violent side of love. So, while on the surface of the novella love is depicted as the greatest good, it also proves to be a new, subtle form of incarceration and violence. For example, Marlitt's narrator remarks of Beatrice, whom Lilli assumes to be an unwilling captive:

Daß jenes gebeugte Weib sein Joch möglicherweise freiwillig trug, weil es seinen

---

[10] This shift is consonant with a general tendency in nineteenth-century versions of the *Blaubartmärchen* towards imprisonment rather than murder.

Kerkermeister liebte, das fiel Lilli nicht im entferntesten ein; sie hatte keine Ahnung von den Widersprüchen und Seltsamkeiten der Liebe . . . (p. 148)

In other words, the narrator takes for granted that love can and does involve feminine masochism and suffering.

In earlier versions of the *Märchen* the house is unequivocally identified with Bluebeard himself as a visible expression of his wealth and power; in later versions, that initially straightforward symbol becomes more complex and psychological. On one hand, the house still represents Bluebeard, his character and his material status, as is evident from the description of Dorn's property above. On the other, there is another domestic interior in the text which is of great symbolic importance—Lilli's summer-house. That building is clearly identified with Lilli's own person, and the central conflict in the novella involves the question of ownership and rights over it. Although the summer-house is morally and traditionally Lilli's because it contains her things, a court judges that Dorn has full legal rights over it and gives him permission to demolish it. Indeed, the demolition actually begins while a terrified Lilli is in the summer-house in a scene which echoes a scenario of assault. Furthermore, while the woman's appropriation of the key in earlier versions represented a certain appropriation of her husband's power, here Lilli has no keys, so the summer-house cannot be locked and her property cannot be protected from Dorn, who effects a violent entry by knocking a hole in the wall and regularly steps through it to spy on Lilli. In other words, a new rivalry develops between Bluebeard and the heroine for control over this crucial symbolic space in which the heroine is seriously disadvantaged (no legal rights, no keys). And it seems that this rivalry is so momentous because the interior of the house has come to stand for the woman herself. Thus, if the woman in earlier versions could be physically imprisoned and threatened by Bluebeard, but remain in other senses quite independent of him, here her autonomy becomes more problematic because the house and the woman come to be identified with one another.

The identification of the woman with the interior of the house is linked, first, to the psychologization of the material, since the interior of the house can also easily be associated with the symbolic interiors of the mind, so that the space which Bluebeard seeks to control is the heroine's *mind* as well as her body. This new type of control takes the form of romantic love. Second, this identification is linked to the increasing identification of Woman in the nineteenth century with

the private sphere. This identification is often expressed in the topo-
graphical terms of 'inside' and 'outside', since in the modern mind
women and their bodies are identified with the interior. As Freud
wrote:

Zimmer im Traume sind zumeist Frauenzimmer . . . Das Interesse, ob das
Zimmer 'offen' oder 'verschlossen' ist, wird in diesem Zusammenhange leicht
verständlich . . . Welcher Schlüssel das Zimmer aufsperrt, braucht dann nicht
ausdrücklich gesagt zu werden . . .[11]

Marlitt's and others' new emphasis on Bluebeard's imprisonment of
his wife seems to parallel the nineteenth-century bourgeois insistence
on the interior as the appropriate location for and symbol of Woman.
But in the nineteenth century, property ownership, and therefore
control of the domestic interior, were still identified with men, as
reflected by the court's verdict that the summer-house is Dorn's
property. That is to say, here the heroine has lost a greater degree of
sovereignty over her own person, which has become subject to
Bluebeard's control in new ways over and above the purely romantic.

   In other words, the shift in interest from body to mind which I
described in my previous chapter has been completed, since
Bluebeard no longer exists as an individual character who does
physical damage at all, but rather as a metaphor for the modern
Symbolic Order which dominates the narrative and controls the
feminine subject in more psychological, insidious, and comprehen-
sive ways. I use this terminology because both Lilli and Dorn have
internalized a frightening, aggressive, patriarchal principle in a way
which makes superfluous the real presence of such a figure, who was
soon to be theorized by Freud (and later by Jacques Lacan) as the
fantastic figure of the castrating, oedipalized father.

   In Marlitt's 'Blaubart', the characters are responding to a law laid
down by their fathers which seems to be inexorable, just as Freud
perceived his subjects to do. In the novella, this is the heritage of
family hostility which began with Hubert and Erich and which
recalls the biblical myth of Cain and Abel, inasmuch as both stories
involve envy between brothers.[12] Once again, however, the divine
Father is at the root of this crime, since he favours Abel over Cain
and so causes Cain's jealousy, which means that this reworking of the

[11] Freud, *Studienausgabe*, ed. Alexander Mitscherlich, Angela Richards, and James
Strachey, 11 vols. (Frankfurt am Main: Fischer, 1989), ii. 349.
   [12] Gen. 4.

Bluebeard narrative redirects the blame for the origin of the conflict onto a purely male lineage. The behaviour of Tante Bärbchen's, Lilli's and Dorn's fathers cast malevolent shadows over later generations too. And in a story told by Dorte a wicked general is carried off at midnight by 'ein ganz schwarzer Herr' (p. 153) for his sins. This story recalls the Don Juan narrative tradition, where the 'Herr' (the dead Commander) is a father-figure. This absent yet omnipotent paternal principle which recalls the absent yet omniscient God in the garden of Eden therefore reinscribes into the narrative the older idea of original sin which was so spectacularly rejected by Perrault. This return to the concept of original sin undermines, too, Dorn's ostensible status as a Christ-like figure, and therefore the superficially redemptive ending.

The transformation of Bluebeard into a ubiquitous psychological principle affects the utopian potential of 'Blaubart', since on a deep level Marlitt's novella expresses profound doubts about the possibility of redemption. These doubts are expressed through the insistence on the malevolent legacy of the fathers and original sin, and are reflected in the complete exclusion of the world beyond the Dorn estate, whose isolation exceeds even that of Bluebeard's house in the *KHM*—for in the Bluebeard tradition, it is from outside the ogre's house that redemption arrives.

Above all, the anti-utopian force of the text is expressed in a profound fear that *all* characters, not only Dorn, may be Bluebeards. At times, Marlitt's 'Blaubart' identifies Tante Bärbchen with the malicious, duplicitous male God who ordains Eve's temptation. Lilli refers to the Genesis narrative explictly when she teases Tante Bärbchen for making Dorn's house a taboo subject: 'Die Äpfel haben [Adam und Eva] nur so gut geschmeckt, weil sie verboten waren' (p. 132). The speaker of the prohibition here is Tante Bärbchen, who therefore acts like God—or, by analogy, Bluebeard himself. In addition, even her name evokes a 'little beard', and she too possesses a Bluebeard chamber, the 'grüne Stube' which 'steckte Jahr aus Jahr ein hinter festgeschlossenen Jalousien und zugeriegelten Thüren' (p. 226), and which contains

einige weibliche Pastellporträts, die eine unkundige tactlose Hand an den Wänden des harmonisch im Renaissancestil gehaltenen Raumes aufgehangen, hatten erblaßte Lippen und Wangen und die einst carmoisinschimmernde Umhüllung der häßlichen, ungebührlich kurzen Taillen war schmutzig-fahl geworden. (pp. 228–9)

This room bears a striking resemblance to Bluebeard's locked chamber in the *Märchen*. Not only are the images of women deathlike, but their arrangement even resembles the way in which Perrault describes the corpses hanging up as though on display. And more shockingly still, Lilli too owns a Bluebeard chamber: the summer-house itself. This has been shut up and left undisturbed in her absence, so this room too is shuttered, dark, and crypt-like:

Alles stand noch unverrückt an seinem Platze, nichts schien berührt worden zu sein während der dreijährigen Abwesenheit des jungen Mädchens. . . . Da saßen sie [Lilli's dolls] noch mit steif ausgestreckten Armen, mühsam in eine sitzende Stelle gezwängt . . . ein großer Hanswurst kauerte trübselig und aus dem kaffeetrinkenden Damenkreise verbannt in der Ecke . . . (p. 156)

This Bluebeard chamber is full of petrified, corpse-like female figures forced into unnatural attitudes. While 'Hanswurst' characters traditionally represent life, vitality, and disorder, in Lilli's secret chamber those principles have been suffocated. And when Dorn surprises Lilli in the summer-house, she is packing her childhood dolls into boxes, an activity which on one level represents Lilli 'putting away childish things' but on another has something funereal about it.

Once Bluebeard has become a psychological idea internalized by all the characters, male and female, in the text, his power is all the greater and, indeed, ubiquitous. And the progression from 'Fremdzwang' to 'Selbstzwang' in the process of civilization, as described by Elias, seems gradually to undermine the utopian impulse of the Bluebeard material.

THE COLLECTOR

One further aspect of Marlitt's account of the psychological internalization and sublimation of Bluebeard's violence in 'civilization' deserves closer attention. This is the insistent link made between Bluebeard and Art. Bluebeard's traditional aggression towards women assumes new forms in Marlitt's text which are linked to morbid, artistic images of femininity (like the stained-glass image of Juliet, Tante Bärbchen's 'grüne Stube', and Lilli's dolls) and which are a new variant on earlier Bluebeards' perverse display of the dead bodies of their wives in the forbidden chamber. Indeed, the central secret of the narrative is no longer a collection of female corpses, which are ugly, frightening, and only briefly glimpsed, but the whereabouts of the hidden portrait which by rights should be proudly displayed. So where the corpses in earlier versions were a shocking secret hidden from the world, the petrified, artistic images of femininity in Marlitt's 'Blaubart' are in the visible, public domain, since the *raison d'être* of a work of art is to be seen, not hidden. This transformation thus signals another change in Bluebeard's deathly arrangements. Because such arrangements are now psychological rather than physical, they have acquired a new respectability and normality, with the result that Bluebeard behaviour can be presented as the unremarkable or positive norm, rather than as antisocial and monstrous.

Such works of art involving images of women are significant for at least three further reasons. First, while Dorn retains his material wealth, as a connoisseur and collector of art, he is a different kind of property-owner from earlier Bluebeards with their opulent homes. Besides being a material capitalist, he is also a cultural capitalist, so Marlitt's insistence on an essentially bourgeois cultural capital as a guarantee of Dorn's human worth reflects the way in which her story, unlike earlier German versions, is closer to Perrault's original in having a solidly upper-middle-class, rather than a feudal, villain.

And second, one further mythological narrative casts light on the transformation of the female corpse into Art. At one point, Dorn threatens Lilli as follows:

'Meinen Sie nicht, daß es ein leichtes für mich sein würde, die Widerspenstige im Fluge hinüberzutragen in mein Haus und dort zurückzuhalten . . . Es wäre nicht das erste Mal, daß es einem kühnen Sterblichen gelungen, eine Nixe zu rauben.' (p. 220)[13]

Dorn gets this poetical fantasy from Lilli's appearance in this scene, in which she is rather oddly dressed as a bridesmaid for a friend's wedding with an implausible water lily, 'lange Schilfblätter', and coral beads in her hair so that she resembles a mermaid. As such, the elusive and fluid Lilli is the antithesis of Dorn's petrified collection of women, and it seems that his desire to kidnap and imprison her would entail her petrification in mid-flight, like the statue. Using an idea elaborated by Theodor Adorno and Max Horkheimer in *Dialektik der Aufklärung*, the mermaid image can be used to understand Bluebeard–Dorn's association with artefacts that resemble dead

---

[13] Dorn is referring to the German title given Shakespeare's anti-feminist play, *The Taming of the Shrew* (c.1594), *Der Widerspenstigen Zähmung*.

women. Adorno and Horkheimer are concerned with an illusory, totalitarian version of the Enlightenment which has fashioned the exclusive, rigid, rationalist, and masculine subject, and identify Homer's Odysseus as a prototype of that subject who

> ist im Leiden mündig geworden. In der Vielfalt der Todesgefahren, in denen er sich durchhalten mußte, hat sich ihm die Einheit des eigenen Lebens, die Identität der Person gehärtet . . . Was Odysseus hinter sich ließ, tritt in die Schattenwelt.[14]

Nonetheless, Odysseus encounters the temptation of the Sirens, who are fascinating precisely because they represent the Other which Odysseus has split off from himself. But the hero of the *Odyssey* has himself restrained by force so that he cannot succumb to the Sirens' temptation, and of this ruse Adorno and Horkheimer write:

> Er hört, aber ohnmächtig an den Mast gebunden, und je größer die Lockung wird, um so stärker läßt er sich fesseln . . . Die Bande, mit denen er sich unwiderruflich an die Praxis gefesselt hat, halten zugleich die Sirenen aus der Praxis fern: ihre Lockung wird zum bloßen Gegenstand der Kontemplation neutralisiert, zur Kunst. (p. 51)

In other words, the civilized subject neutralizes the dangerous mermaid or siren by turning her into a work of art.[15] Analogously, Lilli as mermaid externalizes Dorn's repressed, unconscious impulses which fascinate him. But because, like Odysseus, Dorn cannot relinquish his rational subjectivity and return to the blissful and phantasmagoric whole state of being represented by the mermaid (fluidity vs. plasticity), he fantasizes about capturing her: the result of which would be her transformation into a dead artefact like those in his and Tante Bärbchen's houses.

So despite the prestige Marlitt's 'Blaubart' ostensibly assigns to Art, this is in fact a bleak vision of artistic creativity. The passion and 'wahre Meisterschaft' of the painting of Orestes and the Furies is destroyed to make way for the Van Dyck, which, on the description given, seems to be a more trivial and uninteresting piece of work that was prized by Hubert and Erich for the cultural capital it represented and not for its power (or lack of it). And if in Dante's *Divine Comedy* a transcendent Beatrice has the power to lead the poet safely through

---

[14] Theodor W. Adorno and Max Horkheimer, *Dialektik der Aufklärung* (1947), in Adorno, *Gesammelte Schriften*, ed. Rolf Tiedemann (Frankfurt am Main: Fischer, 1997), iii. 49.

[15] Cf. Hartmut Böhme, 'Umriß einer Kulturgeschichte des Wassers. Eine Einleitung', in Böhme (ed.), *Kulturgeschichte des Wassers* (Frankfurt am Main: Suhrkamp, 1988), 7–42 (23).

Purgatory and into Heaven, here she is dying of bodily, disfiguring disease which implies that the world governed by Bluebeard is worse than purgatorial since it holds out no hope of inspiration through Art and the muse Beatrice. Just as the internalization of Bluebeard's violence undermines the utopian force of 'Blaubart', so too has the art in Bluebeard's world lost any redemptive, utopian potential, and it has become a deathlike object which cannot inspire or redeem—it can only be collected.

And third, therefore, Bluebeard–Dorn, and even Tante Bärbchen and Lilli, since they all collect and display morbid images of women (or in Lilli's case, dolls), are more sinister versions of a typical nineteenth-century figure, the collector. This trait too has been passed down the male line, since the original quarrel was provoked by Hubert's and Erich's 'Sammelleidenschaft'. The collector was the product and promoter of a civilized, enlightened world-view which sought to categorize and display, as evidenced by the nineteeth-century enthusiasm for museums and Linnaeus's scientific categorizations. Through this systematizing activity the collector sought to control his natural and cultural environment, gendered as female.[16] This idea is central to John Fowles's more recent Bluebeard novel, *The Collector* (1963), where it becomes clear that such systematization and collection, whether of butterflies, works of art or real women, ends by killing them. Therefore, the novella inadvertently hints that when Dorn marries—or collects—Lilli, the outcome for her may be fatal.

THE DISRUPTION OF ORDER

On the surface therefore, it appears that Bluebeard's sublimated subjugation of the Other, the feminine and the sexual through the imposition of a rigid, morbid Apollonian Symbolic Order is successful. Nevertheless, as suggested in Chapter 2, experience always resists such ordering; furthermore, it can produce its disruptive opposite. In fact, the irrational, sexual, and monstrous persistently seep through Marlitt's apparently highly controlled text, which is permeated with images of bisexuality, desire, and excess which unsettle the apparently placid surface narrative and the neat binary divisions on

[16] Cf. Elazar Barkan and Ronald Bush (eds.), *Prehistories of the Future: The Primitivist Project and the Culture of Modernism* (Stanford, Calif.: Stanford University Press, 1995).

which it is based. If the novella aims to describe a world which is initially divided into purely masculine and feminine spheres and finally involves their harmonious and complementary reunion (or, on another level, the murderous subjugation of the feminine Other by a rigid, masculine Symbolic Order), it soon becomes clear that this fantasy of exclusive division/subjugation is untenable, since on closer inspection it transpires that neither Dorn's nor Tante Bärbchen's side of the divide has a clearly gendered or consistent identity, as exemplified in Tante Bärbchen's and Lilli's resemblance to Blue-beard, in that they too possess deadly chambers filled with morbid, feminine images.

Similarly, Bluebeard's house and garden have a startling double identity which defies the text's surface binarisms. For example, the description quoted above comparing the order of Dorn's house to the disorder of Tante Bärbchen's betrays a profound uncertainty about the distinction between the two realms, since it begins by describing Tante Bärbchen's house as 'hier' and Dorn's as 'drüben', but inexplicably reverses this relationship half-way through the passage, so that Tante Bärbchen's house is suddenly 'drüben' and Dorn's 'hier', before complicating matters further by switching back once again.

Furthermore, at night Dorn's garden becomes the scene of blurred identities, unreliable boundaries between the animate and the inanimate, Dionysian gender shifts, and utopian, feminine desire. For instance, in her role as God/Bluebeard, Tante Bärbchen seeks to prohibit Lilli from finding out more about her neighbours with the following words:

'Ich bitte dich, Kind . . . sieh nicht dort hinüber. Ich stelle dir die eine Bedingung—aber in vollem Ernst—daß du während deines Hierseins thust, als höre da drüben mit dem Zaun die Welt auf . . . Was dort lärmt, schwatzt und geigt, darf für dich nicht existieren . . .' (p. 115)

Tante Bärbchen's formulation sets out the basic premiss of the 'process of civilization' which is the offensive exclusion of disorder: 'daß du . . . thust, als höre da drüben mit dem Zaun die Welt auf.' The formulation reads like a description of the forbidden unconscious, and its topography corresponds with Freud's paradoxical territorial metaphor for the unconscious, 'das innere Ausland',[17]

---

[17] Quoted in Hartmut Böhme and Gernot Böhme, *Das Andere der Vernunft: Zur Entwicklung von Rationalitätsstrukturen am Beispiel Kants* (Frankfurt am Main: Suhrkamp, 1983), 17.

because, equally contradictorily, the world behind the hedge is in reality part of the same estate as Tante Bärbchen's more disordered garden. The sounds described by Tante Bärbchen are mysterious, unclearly defined disturbances, and while 'geig[en]' refers to Dorn playing the cello, that verb is odd here since it does not usually apply to cello-playing. While on the surface it may be interpreted as Tante Bärbchen's attempt to dismiss the playing as mere fiddling, the image also has demonic overtones. So because Tante Bärbchen is here stylizing Dorn's garden as the unconscious, her words involve a reversal of the binary description of the two houses according to which Tante Bärbchen's initially seemed far the wilder. And this reversal, which disturbingly makes Dorn's garden into a realm of disorder, is exemplified by the statue there. That statue is more than an image of death, since it too involves a dramatically subversive aspect. To begin with, it is described as '*der* Frauenleib' (my emphasis), i.e. with a masculine noun and the pronoun 'er', and its form is described in phallic terms emerging out of a 'Gebüsch'. It is also covered in ivy, the plant sacred to Dionysus, a disruptive deity who had bisexual aspects and whose worship included cross-dressing as well as debauchery and carnival. In other words, the statue also stands for those irrational aspects of experience which the novella seeks to eliminate, and embodies a threatening (bi)sexuality and a resistance to ordered, binary gender divisions.[18]

The novella's classical subtexts are similarly problematic, despite the initial impression they give of imposing order on chaos. While Tante Bärbchen resembles the monstrous Medusa vanquished by Perseus under the protection of Athene, and while this mythological subtext works on one level to strengthen the masculine/feminine binarism set up by the text, at another level it undermines it. For while at one level Athene is a phallic goddess who is committed to imposing a rational (masculine) order on (feminine) chaos, in fact her mythological origins are less clear-cut, since according to the earliest sources she was a Medusan figure herself, and the Gorgon's head she carried on her shield to terrify her enemies was her own.[19] On another account, Athene herself was responsible for making the once lovely Medusa, of whom she was jealous in a typically vengeful,

---

[18] The image of the walking female statue emerges too as a prelude to a sexual threat and destruction in Leopold von Sacher-Masoch's *Venus im Pelz* (1869), and therefore may well embody some compelling contemporary fear.

[19] Jacques Le Rider, *Modernity and Crises of Identity: Culture and Society in Fin-de-Siècle Vienna* (1990), trans. Rosemary Morris (Cambridge: Polity Press, 1993), 150.

irrational, and 'feminine', way, into a monster. All of which means that Tante Bärbchen as God, Bluebeard, Medusa, and Athene all rolled into one unites frightening, aggressive masculine and feminine powers in a manner which contradicts the most basic binarism informing Marlitt's surface narrative.

As a result of all this instability, any ordered conclusion will always be fragile, as in the Orestes myth where the Furies may have turned into 'kindly' Eumenides but they may turn back into Furies at any moment (according to some classical sources, the 'kindly' appellation was in fact merely ironic). Furthermore, at the ostensibly happy ending of Marlitt's 'Blaubart' (which cannot be happy for Beatrice and may well not be so for Lilli), the compulsive tying up of all the disorderly loose ends reads like overcompensation for a suspicion that the irrational is far from being suppressed by the apparently rational order imposed by Dorn.

I suggested in Chapter 2 that the very process of division and suppression of the Other which is involved in the imposition of a rationalist order is problematic because this very procedure of separation and division in fact *produces* the frightening, irrational Other.[20] This too proves to be the case with Marlitt's 'Blaubart', since the family feud, for instance, takes place not over some uncivilized object or issue but over the Van Dyck painting which symbolizes order both in its content (the docile young girl) and in its meaning as a bourgeois status symbol. Similarly, the moment of Medusan horror experienced by Tante Bärbchen's suitor is provoked by so civilized and normalizing an artefact as the false arm. And even the ordered conclusion to the novella throws up disorder. The *mise en abyme* involved in Tante Bärbchen's irrational, philistine attempt to burn the Van Dyck painting and its rescue by Dorn constitutes a new eruption of the crisis which had just been so carefully resolved. And the very last sentence in the text returns to Dorte's disruptive narratives and quarrels:

[Sauer] ist noch viel unduldsamer gegen Dortes haarsträubende Teufels-geschichten geworden, seit er weiß, daß der Neger—nach ihrer ehemaligen Behauptung ein Sohn der Hölle—das treueste und ehrlichste Herz unter der Sonne hat. (p. 242)

Dorte is in no way cured of her extravagant imagination; further-more, the disruptive antagonism between Dorte and Sauer con-

---

[20] Cf. Böhme and Böhme, *Das Andere der Vernunft*.

cerning her narratives has *escalated*, not ceased. Or in other words, domestic disorder has actually been stimulated by the attempt to impose a more civilized order.

'WAS DORT LÄRMT, SCHWATZT UND GEIGT . . .': A UTOPIAN SUBTEXT

Finally, the apparently morbid, rigid order imposed by Bluebeard is challenged too by a utopian subtext. In Chapter 1, it was suggested that *Märchen* told in a feminine voice may have an eccentric relationship to the 'process of civilization' and its control mechanisms. Marlitt's 'Blaubart' can also be scrutinized for such features, which constitute a weak but distinctly pro-feminine counterpoint of desire to the dominant narrative of stabilization in nineteenth-century German texts. This subtext recalls the utopian force of Perrault's earlier text by re-evaluating feminine desire and fantasy positively, which were negatively evaluated in the Grimm *Märchen*, for instance.[21]

While the Grimms and Bechstein also took a certain voyeuristic interest in the wife's fear and curiosity, there is a pro-feminine bias in Marlitt's narrative focus on Lilli and her thoughts. Lilli's confident articulacy is affirmed in a way which challenges the Grimmian norm of female speechlessness.[22] In a broader sense, too, the narrative voices Lilli's experience, since Marlitt turns the *Blaubartmärchen* into an extensive expression of feminine subjectivity, not only in the exposition of Lilli's conscious thoughts but also in the form of her partially unconscious fantasies and desires.

These fantasies and desires prove surprisingly resistant to prohibitions—and rewarding. Lilli's moment of transgression (corresponding to the wife's opening of the forbidden chamber in the *Märchen*) is described not in terms of fear and horror, but of pleasure for which she is not punished and which eventually leads to the gratification of her desires. In the scene in question, Lilli hides in the summer-house at night to observe Dorn's house:

Da lag es vor ihr, das mondbeglänzte Schloß des Blaubarts, und all jener bestrickende, geheimnißvolle [*sic*] Zauber, hinter welchem in dem schauerlichen

---

[21] Ruth B. Bottigheimer, *Grimms' Bad Girls and Bold Boys: The Moral and Social Vision of the Tales* (New Haven, Conn.: Yale University Press, 1987).

[22] Ibid. 51–6.

Märchen Blutströme rieseln, er stieg auch hier aus fremdartigen Blüthenkelchen
. . . (p. 144)

This quotation is followed by a long and rhapsodic description of the scene in terms of enchantment and 'Sehnsucht', as a secret 'Wunderwelt'. While the magic proves illusory in the rationalist conclusion of the novella, this scene is nonetheless of key importance to the text, since it expresses Lilli's desires and fantasies and as such is the matrix of all later romantic developments. While on one hand the scene is shot through with subliminally masochistic imagery (Lilli's fantasy about blood), such imagery competes in her mind with a less destructive female sexual symbolism ('fremdartige Blüthenkelche') and more active and conscious ideas. For instance, Lilli also fantasizes about rescuing Beatrice in an access of proto-feminist solidarity.

Tante Bärbchen says of Dorn's garden: 'Was dort lärmt, schwatzt und geigt, darf für dich nicht existieren . . .' (p. 115). But just as those unconscious areas of experience which the modern, civilized subject has to fence off remain irresistibly fascinating, so too do the 'lärmen', 'schwatzen', and 'geigen' which resonate with Lilli's own *Nachtseite* (*Nacht-Saite*). Tante Bärbchen's description of these sounds tallies with Julia Kristeva's characterization of the 'semiotic', the pre-linguistic, unconscious energy which can seep into conscious experience via music and non-verbal sound like nonsense and glossolalia ('schwatzen').[23] Kristeva associates these with the feminine, both metaphorically, because they, like femininity, are 'Other', and literally also, because she believes such experience to be particularly associated with the female body and thus more accessible to feminine experience. Accordingly, she characterizes the 'semiotic' as being typical of utopian, non-logocentric, feminine artistic production, a notion which tallies with my argument that Marlitt's 'Blaubart' gives expression, albeit at a very deep level, to feminine desire and fantasy.

A study by Jutta Schönberg (1986) endorses the argument that Marlitt's 'Blaubart' can be read as a positive re-evaluation of feminine experience and desire.[24] Schönberg argues (although without referring to 'Blaubart') that the fantasies and daydreams of Marlitt's heroines were highly unorthodox for the mid-nineteenth century, since they broke out of the conventional, passive patterns

---

[23] Julia Kristeva, *La Révolution du langage poétique* (Paris: Seuil, 1974).

[24] Jutta Schönberg, *Frauenrolle und Roman: Studien zu den Romanen der Eugenie Marlitt* (Frankfurt am Main: Lang, 1986), 64–5, with reference to Freud's 'Der Dichter und das Phantasieren' (1908).

described by Freud as 'female', and represented certain 'male', and therefore transgressive, desires and ambitions. 'Blaubart' can certainly be read as a positive expression of unconventional feminine desire and fantasy because of the powerful images of bisexuality that are, for instance, linked with the strangely attractive Beatrice and the statue. So here, as in Perrault's *conte*, feminine curiosity is productive and utopian, revealing as it does to Lilli all kinds of anarchic pleasures and possibilities.

But at another level, Marlitt's plot is murderous, so that the success of Lilli's libidinal enterprise is equivocal. Lilli's initially polymorphous desire solidifies in the course of the narrative into a conventional subjugation to Dorn. The major problem and paradox here is that it is precisely the fulfilment of *active* desire which marks the end of Lilli's independent subjectivity and turns her into a *passive* object, like Dorn's statue which seems both to be dead *and* fleeing from its own sexuality. This is because, as Schönberg observes, the nineteenth-century ideal of marriage was based on a complementary binarism in which men were active subjects and women passive objects. Yet the complex texture of Marlitt's novella does show that that constricting ideal is fissured and open to desire and the unconscious.

CONCLUSION

Marlitt's apparently superficial, if entertaining, 'Blaubart' encodes some major changes in the *Blaubartmärchen*. Violent force is replaced by the constraints of love; and what used to be a shameful secret is made visible and yet invisible, as a work of art; at another level, the whole notion of secrecy is transferred onto the genre of the novella itself, which is a kind of detective story, a genre which comes to be associated with later Bluebeard versions. As the process of civilization advances, the shift of interest from the body to the mind progresses too, and requires an increasingly watchful occlusion of the body and its scandals such as desire and death. Dorn as the new, civilized Bluebeard collects artistic representations of women which are attempts to distance and control the scandalous difference inherent in the feminine. And Tante Bärbchen and Lilli too, as possessors of Bluebeard chambers, have internalized this system of control in what must be a damaging way. In other words, Bluebeard's aggressive activity has been sublimated into the work of artistic production, which includes the task of controlling the feminine—the Sirens, Medusa, and the Furies in particular—and neutralizing art's utopian potential too.[25]

And yet the efficiency of this strategy of control is doubtful, since Bluebeard's activities are clearly revealed to be absurd. Control of another kind of difference, too, is at stake in Marlitt's shift away from murder and towards the contemplation of aesthetic images: the control of death,[26] since the very fact of death is the major contradiction of a civilization which valued such ideas as the control and perfection of the human body and lasting progress. Therefore, the murderous collector's task of control is ultimately self-defeating, as in Fowles's novel, when the female protagonist, Miranda ('she who is to be admired', not locked away), dies in Bluebeard's captivity, as does Beatrice–Lilli here. Therefore, the collector's activity becomes repetitive, serial, and meaningless, just like Bluebeard's murders. What is more, this new Bluebeard order continues to be countered by other forms of disorder and an (albeit imperfect) utopian desire. And it is this theme of desire introduced by Marlitt which, above all, was to fascinate the early twentieth century.

[25] Like a painter, Perseus catches Medusa's image, turning her into a harmless object of contemplation.

[26] Cf. Elisabeth Bronfen, *Over Her Dead Body: Death, Femininity and the Aesthetic* (Manchester: Manchester University Press, 1993). Bronfen argues that the nineteenth-century 'obsession' with portraying beautiful female corpses expressed a particular, modern anxiety about mortality, as an earlier, intimate and organic understanding of death was lost. Woman and Death made a compelling symbolic match with which to deal with the fear of death because both are imagined as Other, and the image of the beautiful dead woman obscured the fear of death by aestheticizing it.

6

'DER GUTE BLAUBART': BLUEBEARD AT THE TURN OF THE CENTURY

> . . . *sieben*, du blühende Todeskandidatin, sind dir vorangeeilt auf diesem Pfad in den Tartarus! Laß dir das zum Troste gereichen und suche nicht durch diese flehentlichen Blicke noch meine Qualen ins Ungeheuere zu steigern.
>
>   Du stirbst nicht um *deiner*, du stirbst um *meiner* Sünden willen!— Aus Notwehr gegen mich begehe ich blutenden Herzens den siebenten Gattenmord. Es liegt etwas Tragisches in der Rolle des *Blaubart*. Ich glaube, seine ermordeten Frauen insgesamt litten nicht soviel wie er beim Erwürgen jeder einzelnen.[1]

In Frank Wedekind's play *Frühlings Erwachen* (1891), the teenager Hänschen Rilow performs a melodramatic monologue in the lavatory as he flushes away a reproduction of Palma Vecchio's nude Venus. Hänschen reveals that his interest in the Venus image is less aesthetic and intellectual than sexual and masturbatory, since he addresses the image of the woman as a lover and reveals that the Venus is the latest in a long line of such reproductions which he had first treasured and then destroyed. Hänschen stylizes this collection of images as his harem and its serial destruction as *crimes passionnels* or sexual murders. This scene in *Frühlings Erwachen* may be read both as an anticipation and, paradoxically, as a parody of the sea change evident in versions of the Bluebeard material written by men from 1905 onward in Germany. Not only did the years 1905–1913 produce an unusual quantity of Bluebeard texts, but these texts are also remarkable in their unprecedented, merciless, and consistent savagery towards women characters. This development is all the more startling given the contemporary emergence of quite different interpretations of the Bluebeard material elsewhere in Europe; and it seems that the German authors in question were consciously reacting against such interpretations. Moreover, while the number of such texts decreased after the Great War, the new interpretation of the

---

[1] Frank Wedekind, 'Frühlings Erwachen: Eine Kindertragödie' (1891), in *Werke in drei Bänden*, ed. Manfred Hahn, 3 vols. (Berlin: Aufbau, 1969), i. 95–165.

Bluebeard material which exploded onto the German stage at the turn of the century came to dominate later German workings of 'Blaubart'.

CASTLES OF THE MIND

E. Marlitt's 'Blaubart' encoded a utopian (albeit fragile) expression of feminine desire and touched upon the possibility of making the Bluebeard material into a subtle statement about some limited feminine empowerment through the articulacy ascribed to the heroine. Precisely this theme of feminine empowerment is central to two French operas of the late nineteenth and early twentieth centuries: Jacques Offenbach's (music) and Henri Meilhac's and Ludovic Halévy's (libretto) operetta (1866) *Barbe-bleue* and Paul Dukas's (music) and Maurice Maeterlinck's (libretto) *Ariane et Barbe-bleue* (1907), both of which would have been known to cultivated German audiences around the turn of the century.[2] In Offenbach/ Meilhac/Halévy's farce, Bluebeard is a merry widower who, in order to be able to marry a series of wives, orders his alchemist to murder them as and when necessary. But at the end of the operetta it transpires that the alchemist has merely been drugging the women and then admitting them to his own harem. Thus, the women's survival allows a happy ending. This operetta was part of the apparently milder nineteenth-century tradition in which women were spared, and it both prefigured and helped to establish the twentieth-century concern with Bluebeard as a ladykiller in the figurative rather than the literal sense. But while Maeterlinck's and Dukas's opera of thirty years later preserved the challenge to masculine authority, in other respects it is strikingly different from the farce.

Ariane et Barbe-bleue is not only a deadly serious parable about liberation and the psychology of oppression, it also presents these issues in gender-specific terms, thus making a strong, potentially feminist statement. The courageous Ariane enters Bluebeard's castle with the sole object of freeing Bluebeard's five imprisoned wives on the principle: 'D'abord il faut désobéir: c'est le premier devoir quand l'ordre est menaçant et ne s'explique pas.—Les autres ont eu tort et

---

[2] Libretto written by Maeterlinck in 1899–1902, first performed in Paris in 1907. Text included with the recording directed by Armin Jordan (Paris: Erato Disques, 1984).

les voilà perdues pour avoir hésité' (p. 7). Although the five wives are freed by Ariane, in the end they prefer their imprisonment to Ariane's 'monde inondé d'espérance' (p. 75) to which she returns alone. In other words, Maeterlinck and Dukas present the Bluebeard plot as a psychological issue in which liberation is a question not of physical constraint but of pyschological coercion, since the women have internalized the laws of their imprisonment. But while the conclusion of the opera is therefore in some respects pessimistic, it nonetheless holds open the utopian moment of a world filled with hope.

Further dimensions are added to the libretto by a classical narrative, since Ariane's name and actions recall Ariadne, in classical mythology the daughter of King Minos of Crete who enabled Theseus to escape from the labyrinth by laying a trail of thread. While Theseus escaped with Ariadne from Crete and married her as he had promised, he subsequently abandoned her on the island of Naxos. So while Ariadne/Ariane knows and has power over labyrinthine secrets (in the modern text, the secrets of Bluebeard's dark underground fortress) she is not rewarded for the generous and subversive use of her knowledge and is abandoned by those whom she rescued. Some sources state, however, that Ariadne later became the wife of Dionysus, a mythological narrative which has a more contemporary resonance too, since at the turn of the century Ariadne was celebrated, notably by Nietzsche, as the embodiment of Dionysian Woman.[3] Given which, *Ariane et Barbe-bleue* can also be read as an attempt to smash up the frozen, Apollonian reign of Bluebeard which is symbolized by his treasure chambers full of jewels. These possess the colours of nature but not its vitality, whereas the Dionysian Ariane, who is associated with the fluid, thundering sea that washes around the castle walls, threatens to sweep away the rigid prohibitions and values which hold up those very walls.

While *Ariane et Barbe-bleue* enjoyed great popularity when first performed, is an acknowledged masterpiece, and was a very influential work at the time, it is not well known today, and this occlusion may very well be due to the work's explosive, potentially feminist treatment of the Bluebeard material.[4] The way it handles this

---

[3] John Lemprière, *A Classical Dictionary* (London: Routledge & Kegan Paul, 1947), 74; Jacques Le Rider, *Modernity and Crises of Identity: Culture and Society in Fin-de-Siècle Vienna*, trans. Rosemary Morris (Cambridge: Polity Press, 1993), 147–61, esp. 157–61.

[4] Michael Stegemann, 'Ariane et Barbe-Bleue', in Attila Csampai and Dietmar Holland (eds.), *Der Opernführer* (Hamburg: Hoffmann & Campe, 1989), 954–7 (955); cf. Klaus

material is consistently described by critics as being incomprehensible, whereas in fact the force of the plot ('Niemand will befreit
werden. Befreiung bedrückt, weil sie das Unbekannte ist')[5] is very
simple. Thus the widely read philosophical popularizer Wilhelm
Bölsche's claim in 1899 that the work is a 'Sphinxproblem' is, given
the connotations of the legendary sphinx, a defensive response to its
feminist potential.[6]

Dukas's and Maeterlinck's opera influenced another tremendously
important Bluebeard opera from the first decade of the twentieth
century which has been celebrated by such writers as George Steiner
as a seminal modern text:[7] Béla Bartók's (music) and Béla Balász's
(libretto) Hungarian opera *A kékszakállú herceg vára* (*Duke Bluebeard's
Castle*) (1910–11).[8] *Duke Bluebeard's Castle* is a key work in the development of atonal music as well as the first major opera to be written in
Hungarian, and like *Ariane et Barbe-bleue*, its plot challenges conventional interpretations of the *Blaubartmärchen*, albeit with key
differences. Here, Judith has fallen in love with the brooding Bluebeard and left her home, family and fiancé in order to follow him to
his dark, tragic castle because she believes that her love will redeem
him.

At first she is the dominant figure, both musically and in the
action, and Bluebeard's response to her is ambivalent, for he lets her
in and allows her to explore his castle by opening a series of doors at
her request. While he tries to warn Judith against doing this he does
not actively attempt to stop her or send her away. Judith becomes
increasingly frightened by what she finds, since all Bluebeard's

Angermann, 'Zur Aufführungsgeschichte', in Klaus Angermann et al. (eds.), *Ariane et Barbe-
Bleue. Programmheft zur Neuinszenierung* (Hamburg: Hamburgische Staatsoper, 1997), 36–7.
However, international interest in the opera has been somewhat rekindled from the 1970s
onward.

[5] Dukas, quoted in Angermann, 'Zur Aufführungsgeschichte', 7.

[6] Quoted in Hartwig Suhrbier, 'Blaubart: Leitbild und Leidfigur', in Suhrbier (ed.),
Blaubarts Geheimnis: Märchen und Erzählungen, Gedichte und Stücke (Cologne: Diederichs, 1984),
11–79 (57). Uncomprehending responses to the opera are not limited to the nineteenth
century; cf. Harriet Angell Hobson Mowshowitz, 'Bluebeard and French Literature',
Ph.D. thesis (University of Michigan, 1970), 92; Stegemann, 'Ariane et Barbe-Bleue', 955;
and the cover of the Erato recording, which shows a late nineteenth-century illustration to
Perrault's tale, the classic image of Bluebeard holding his wife by the hair and preparing to
decapitate her, which is at odds with the themes and events of Maeterlinck's work.

[7] George Steiner, *In Bluebeard's Castle: Some Notes Towards the Definition of Culture* (London:
Faber & Faber, 1971).

[8] Hungarian libretto (1910) and English translation by John Lloyd Davies in *The Stage
Works of Béla Bart a*, ed. Nicholas John (London: John Calder, 1991), 45–60, music composed in 1911, and revised up to the première in 1918.

possessions are spattered with blood and the penultimate door opens onto a pool of tears, Bluebeard's inner life. As this happens, so Bluebeard becomes increasingly dominant musically. When the final door is opened, it reveals Bluebeard's three previous wives who have not been murdered as Judith feared. Rather, they are alive, beautiful, and grandly adorned, but mute and more like statues than women, as though they were petrified aspects of Bluebeard's memory. Judith realizes in horror that she now belongs in this memorial gallery as well and takes her place there, apparently willingly. And in contrast to the ending of *Ariane et Barbe-bleue*, where the heroine has the last word and departs from the castle amid imagery of natural light, Balász's libretto ends with Bluebeard saying 'Now all shall be darkness . . ./Darkness . . . darkness' and the stage direction: '*Complete darkness, and Bluebeard disappears in it*' (p. 60). There is no chance of rescue for Judith, and that finality is emphasized by the fact that all four women are associated with times of day and that she, as the last, is associated with Night, the close of that series. On one level, the implication might be that love ends by trapping women; on another, that Judith's very desire to discover more about Bluebeard in order to redeem him must tragically lead to the end of their relationship and her transformation into a reified memory.

This work shares many features with *Ariane et Barbe-bleue*: the emphasis on the opening of a series of doors; the initially confident heroine and the initially passive hero; the aesthetics of colour and ornament typical of the period; the transformation of Bluebeard's castle into a castle of the mind; and the conflict staged between a feminine, Dionysian vitality and a masculine, Apollonian rigor mortis. But where *Ariane et Barbe-bleue* focuses on the women's psyches, the later work explores Bluebeard's psyche. Moreover, the conclusion of *Duke Bluebeard's Castle* has none of the utopian possibilities of Maeterlinck's and Dukas's opera, and is to my knowledge the first Bluebeard text in the European tradition to resist any utopian perspective whatsoever. These two major differences may have contributed to the celebrity of *Duke Bluebeard's Castle*, since the twentieth century had an avid interest not in Bluebeard's wife, but in Bluebeard himself; and since the fatalistic, non-utopian analysis of the relationship between Bluebeard and his wife or lover would also become a typical feature of many twentieth-century reworkings of the material. It may be that the opera reflects that profound sense of cultural pessimism which afflicted Europe as the Great War came

closer (indeed, the opera's Prologue refers to war (p. 46)). Or it may
be that, at the start of the century of women's liberation, the fatalism
of *Duke Bluebeard's Castle* acted as a tacitly reassuring reaffirmation of
the status quo in the face of the unprecedented changes heralded by
the women's movement. Such changes and threats are represented in
the opera by Judith's name. Like Perrault's version of 'Bluebeard',
the Apocryphal story of Judith and Holofernes is an inversion of the
biblical myth of the Fall, since Judith tempts and punishes
Holofernes.[9] Or it may be that *Duke Bluebeard's Castle* is less an outright rejection of the changes and role reversals heralded by the
women's movement than an exploration of a masculine psyche's
complex response to those changes, embodied in Judith. While
Ariane discovered that it is not easy to liberate women, Duke Bluebeard shows that men cannot be liberated either from the accoutre-
ments of civilization or from the castles in which they imprison
themselves at such great human cost. Just as in *Ariane et Barbe-bleue*,
the problem of freedom is couched in psychological rather than
physical terms; but here, it proves to be insoluble.

'SIE WOLLTEN IHN ALS MÖRDER': CONTEMPORARY CRITICISM

In 1909 Paul Wiegler published an essay entitled 'Der gute Blaubart'
which summarized the plots of Offenbach's operetta, *Ariane et Barbe-
bleue* and Anatole France's *Les sept femmes de Barbe-bleue* (1907) (which
made rationalist fun of the Bluebeard material and its supernatural
overtones by presenting Bluebeard not as a murderer but as the
victim of his scheming last wife). Wiegler concluded dismissively:

Nie haben die Deutschen ein solches Bedürfnis gefühlt, den bretonischen Ritter,
der sie wie in Wahlverwandtschaft anzog, durch Empfindsamkeit zu sühnen. Sie
wollten ihn als Mörder. Sie ließen dem Stoff seine Konturen und das
Barbarische, das der deutschen Gier entgegenkommt, Sinnliches und Geistiges
zu vermählen.[10]

Wiegler is criticizing what he perceived as the French weakening of
the original force of the material, which he believed, paradoxically,
to be based on French history but expressed most authentically in
Ludwig Tieck's play *Ritter Blaubart* (1797) and the 'deutsche Blaubart-

---

[9] Judith 8–13.
[10] 'Der gute Blaubart', *Die neue Rundschau*, 20 (4) (1909), 1679–80 (1679).

Atmosphäre' created by Herbert Eulenberg in his play of the same title (1905). According to Wiegler, Tieck's and Eulenberg's German versions of the material are superior because they are more faithful to a putative, ancient original, that is, they are more bloodthirsty and apparently historical in their setting. In Eulenberg's neo-Romantic play, which recalls Tieck's in several ways, the medieval setting is restored for a family drama in which Bluebeard Raul, an intro-spective, violent man who has already murdered five wives, marries Judith. Once he has submitted her to the test of the forbidden chamber and murdered her, he seduces her younger sister Agnes and is finally murdered by his in-laws. This play became a *cause célèbre* in its time; was called 'die . . . bedeutsamste dramatische Fassung der Märchenidee und zugleich das literarische Denkmal einer anbrechenden neuen Epoche';[11] and made into an opera with music by Ernst Nikolaus von Reznicek (1920) that is now as forgotten as the play itself. Wiegler read Eulenberg's play jubilantly as a crucial correction to Maeterlinck's opera, and contemporary interest in Eulenberg's play suggests that it was instrumental in helping to initiate the German Bluebeard vogue discussed here.[12] Furthermore, Eulenberg's play may well have influenced Balász's and Bartók's opera of five years later, since the two texts share, for instance, a concern with Bluebeard's psyche and memory, and the unusual symbolic name Judith.

Similarly, in 1911–12 Karl Schoßleitner, writing on 'Das Blaubart-Thema' in the periodical *Der Brenner*, wrote of Maeterlinck's libretto: 'Maeterlinck scheint sich um das eigentliche Blaubart-Thema nicht zu bekümmern.'[13] This 'eigentliches Thema' was, according to Schoßleitner, Bluebeard himself, whom Schoßleitner, like Wiegler, believed to be a historical figure. Schoßleitner assumed that in the Bluebeard material the male protagonists are

das Primäre und Ausschlaggebende, die Frauen nur die Reflexe und die Spiegel dieser Männer, nicht viel mehr als ihre Opfer, sie sind das Bestimmte, nicht das Bestimmende und kommen somit nur sekundär in Betracht. Es sind vor allem männliche Probleme, Probleme des Mannes, und seiner Schilderung muß der größte Raum zugewiesen werden. (pp. 514–15)

[11] Leopold Schmidt, 'Rezniceks *Ritter Blaubart*', *Berliner Tageblatt*, 57 (31 Jan. 1920). The fact that Berlin's most important daily newspaper sent Schmidt to Darmstadt illustrates the contemporary celebrity of Reznicek's opera.

[12] Cf. Helgard Bruhns, *Herbert Eulenberg: Drama, Dramatik, Wirkung* (Frankfurt am Main: Akademische Verlagsgesellschaft, 1974), 153–5.

[13] *Der Brenner*, 4 (15) (1911–12), 513–26.

By thus criticizing Maeterlinck, Schoßleitner was concerned to draw attention to his own short story 'Prinz Blaubart' (published in the same journal as his essay), which, like Eulenberg's play, involves real murders, a fictional feudal setting, and a focus on Bluebeard to the neglect of the female characters. Here, the Prince is the son of King Bluebeard, who has murdered many wives and is now dying himself. A nameless woman comes to the Prince ostensibly as a lover, but in reality she has been sent by her brother to murder him in revenge for their mother, who was killed by Bluebeard senior. But instead the woman and the Prince fall in love, and he drives her to suicide because he finds the possibility of such a close relationship terrifying and threatening. Prince Bluebeard's fear, combined with a contradictory desire for closeness to women, then causes him to embark on a career of serial sexual murder and finally to destroy himself and his kingdom.

The commentaries by Wiegler and Schoßleitner share many features. Although both vociferously claimed that their understanding of the material was superior to that of Maeterlinck and other writers, their claims were in fact based on a faulty understanding of the Bluebeard tradition, contradicting as they did the contemporary avant-garde, classic, and comic Bluebeard traditions. Yet both writers were very concerned with a notion of literary authenticity—which proves to be quite spurious. For example, Wiegler's citation of Tieck as a more authentic author is misleading, since the play from which he quotes in all seriousness is a nonsensical parody in which Tieck's comically stupid Bluebeard has little of either the 'Sinnliches' or the 'Geistiges' which Wiegler believes to mark the true Bluebeard figure. Similarly, for Schoßleitner the main inauthenticity of *Ariane et Barbe-bleue* lies in its focus on female characters. This, too, is a serious misapprehension of the Bluebeard tradition, since until the turn of the century it was in fact the woman protagonist who had been 'das Primäre und Ausschlaggebende', with Bluebeard himself taking a secondary role.

Furthermore, where, for Schoßleitner, the most authentic ('eigentlich') issue in the *Blaubartmärchen* was the question of why Bluebeard murders his wives, that issue had never been previously thematized in the Bluebeard material. This new focus went hand in hand with a new attitude towards Bluebeard's character, since Schoßleitner displays an explicit admiration and sympathy for the serial murderer who kills a woman precisely because he loves her;

and Wiegler admires the combination of 'Sinnliches' and 'Geistiges' in such a murderer: 'der *gute* Blaubart' (my emphasis). A further common element was an extreme marginalization of the women characters. For example, Schoßleitner accepted the murder of women as a normal occurrence, writing in a casual tone: 'daß einer eine Frau tötet, weil er sie unerträglich findet und nichts mehr von ihr wissen will, könnte auch sonst vorkommen' (p. 515). And yet in order to legitimize his interpretation of the Bluebeard material, Wiegler appealed to ideas of gender equality, describing France's version of the material as 'misogyn'. The mental operation whereby Wiegler could assume that Eulenberg's version, with its descriptions of Bluebeard's desire to kill his wife ('Sie soll wimmern vor Angst; ihr Blut soll mir über die Hände rieseln, ihre Augen zerbrechen . . .') and in which seven women die, must be more women-friendly than France's, in which the wives are *not* murdered, is striking.

Wiegler's and Schoßleitner's theories diverge so clearly from the Bluebeard tradition which they would have known that their inaccuracies are very revealing. The two essays actually twist the facts in order to express a new but consistent set of ideas about the Bluebeard material (which Leopold Schmidt also endorsed in reviewing Reznicek's opera).[14] Because, in the German Bluebeard versions which these critics consider superior, no challenge is made to Bluebeard's murderous authority, these versions are actually rewriting the Bluebeard tradition as a narrative about masculinity in which female characters are mere 'Spiegel', 'Reflexe', or 'Opfer' and in which murder is, perversely, considered acceptable. They also typify the nasty series of German Bluebeard texts from this period. Essentially, these critics are reiterating in deadly earnest the ironic monologue which Wedekind had ascribed to Hänschen Rilow some years before; and this means that the writers had an urgent interest in promoting their ideas by appealing to such powerful, albeit fallacious notions as national authenticity, historical truth, and original meaning. Indeed, given their strenuous rhetorical efforts, Wiegler's and Schoßleitner's motivation for redefining the Bluebeard tradition

---

[14] Schmidt too wrote that Eulenberg's treatment of the masculine psyche was 'de[r] eigentlich[e], geheim[e] Sinn der Sage', noting: 'Wie Lohengrin stellt [Blaubart] das Verbot als Prüfstein der Treue auf und geht daran zugrunde, daß er sich nicht so geliebt sieht, wie seine Natur es verlangt. Die sadistische Form der Gefühlsauslösung wird . . . gewissermaßen nur zu einer Begleiterscheinung.' Schmidt makes Bluebeard appear heroic by comparing him with Lohengrin; by idealizing his crime as a particularly intense form of love; and by reducing his destruction of women to a 'Begleiterscheinung'.

must go further than the simple desire to promote new literary texts.

NEW GERMAN TEXTS

The group of new literary texts under discussion here consists of Eulenberg's *Ritter Blaubart: Ein Märchenstück in fünf Aufzügen* (1905),[15] Georg Trakl's fragmentary 'Blaubart: Ein Puppenspiel' (1910),[16] Schoßleitner's own 'Prinz Blaubart' (1911),[17] Reinhard Koester's poem 'Ritter Blaubart' (1911),[18] Alfred Döblin's 'Der Ritter Blaubart' (1911),[19] El Hor's short prose text 'Ritter Blaubart' (1913),[20] and Georg Kaiser's play *Gilles et Jeanne* which followed in 1922 and shares many concerns with the earlier texts,[21] as does Hänschen Rilow's monologue quoted above.

Koester's poem of nine lines is a brief psychogram of a super-Bluebeard who loves and desires more than other men do; it is this very capacity for immense desire which drives him to kill women when he realizes that his own self is dissolving in the sexual union. El Hor's short prose text consists mainly of a short dialogue between Bluebeard and a nameless woman in which he informs her that he is going to kill her. The woman, who is smitten (!) by an irrational, unconditional, and masochistic love for Bluebeard, is delighted, and the sadistic Bluebeard realizes that she would suffer more if he were to imprison her. Consequently, the woman dies in his dungeons, writing in blood on her clothes: 'Ich liebe dich, mein lieber Herr.' Bluebeard has been unable to destroy her persistent, sickening love and is therefore, like Schoßleitner's prince, driven to suicide himself. Although Döblin's story is the most complex and ambiguous of these texts and comes closest to preserving a meaningful feminine presence, the Bluebeard figure, Baron Paolo di Selvi, remains the

---

[15] Herbert Eulenberg, *Ausgewählte Werke in fünf Bänden*, 5 vols. (Stuttgart: Engelhorn, 1925), ii. 271–324.

[16] *Dichtungen und Briefe. Historisch-kritische Ausgabe*, ed. Walther Killy und Hans Szklenar, 2 vols. (Salzburg: Otto Müller Verlag, 1969), i. 435–45.

[17] Karl Schoßleitner, 'Prinz Blaubart', *Der Brenner*, 3 (7 and 8) (June–Dec. 1911), 203–22 and 247–62.

[18] *Pan*, 1 (16) (1911), 527; also in Suhrbier, *Blaubarts Geheimnis*, 160.

[19] *Erzählungen aus fünf Jahrzehnten* (Olten: Walter, 1979), 76–86.

[20] *Saturn*, 3, no. 7 (1913), 201–3; also in Suhrbier, *Blaubarts Geheimnis*, 160–1.

[21] *Werke*, ed. Walther Hude, 6 vols. (Frankfurt am Main: Propyläen Verlag/Ullstein, 1972), v. 746–811.

main character. In the course of a journey around the world, Paolo mysteriously disappears while on land and is found in a wounded, pitiful state on a cliff edge by the sea. He abandons his travels and builds a castle near where he was found in which three successive wives mysteriously die. But these women are succeeded by the adventuress Miß Ilsebill who discovers a secret chamber in the castle and learns from an old man that Paolo

habe sich mit Leib und Seele einem bösen Untier verkauft. Das läge aus Urzeiten auf dem alten Meeresgrunde, dort auf der Heide; in der Klippe hause es und brauche alle paar Jahre einen Menschen. Es klänge wie ein Märchen und sei doch wahr. (p. 83)

Ilsebill falls ill and plans to leave and destroy the accursed castle behind her. But before she can implement this plan, she is attacked in the castle by 'ein grauenhaftes Meeresungeheuer' and disappears into thin air, or rather, into mist described as 'der Mantel der Mutter Gottes'.[22] Paolo also disappears and, in a brief postscript, is said to have died years later in America, fighting the Indians. In Trakl's fragment, which is marked by an atmosphere of excessive fear and horror, two members of Bluebeard's retinue, an old man and a young boy, discuss Bluebeard's marriage to the fifteen-year-old Elisabeth. This is followed by a dialogue between Bluebeard and Elisabeth in which she expresses sexual desire, and this prompts Blaubart to kill her in what is evidently a sexual murder. And finally, Kaiser returns to the historical theory of origin which linked Bluebeard to Gilles de Rais and portrays Gilles as being plagued by unrequited desire for the virginal Jeanne so that, in his frustration, he accuses her of witchcraft, thus ensuring her execution. Later, Gilles employs an alchemist to recall Jeanne from the dead, but the alchemist tricks him by kidnapping six young women and disguising them as Jeanne. Gilles kills each of these women in turn and is finally caught, but when he confesses before a religious tribunal, he is celebrated as a hero by all present and goes to the stake 'für alle'.

TIME AND TOPOGRAPHY

One striking feature shared by these German texts, *Ariane et Barbe-bleue*, and *Duke Bluebeard's Castle* is their temporal and topographic

---

[22] A reference to 'Marienkind' (*KHM* 3, i. 36–41), which involves the brutal punishment of a young girl for her curiosity.

setting: a fantastic past, as Wiegler demanded. In most cases (Eulenberg, El Hor, Schoßleitner, Trakl, and Koester) this is the pseudo-
medieval world of Tieck, and Kaiser uses the French Middle Ages as
his setting to similar effect.[23] Döblin's short story is less easy to
categorize in this respect, since it is set in a fantastic world which contains modern as well as apparently archaic elements. Nonetheless,
like the other texts, Döblin's story creates an apparently timeless
fantasticism, since in the *Märchen*, the evocation of a distant, romantic
past has traditionally gone hand in hand with the desire to create
an illusion of timelessness and therefore universal validity. And in
stylizing himself as Othello or Heliogabalus, Hänschen Rilow also
creates just such a fantastic past while at the same time satirizing
such inaccurate, sensational uses of a fictional past when taken as a
model for the present by blatantly mixing up the myth, history, and
literature of many periods.

The reasons for this consistent evocation of a fantastic past are as
follows. First, just as Wilhelm Grimm's nostalgic editorial interventions in the *KHM* one hundred years before were a rejection of a
disturbing modernity, so these texts are a reaction to an increasingly
threatening, technological modernity accompanied by all kinds of
societal and symbolic changes. Second, setting the *Blaubartmärchen* in
the 'past' deflects attention from the contemporary relevance of its
gender politics. Third, to set these texts in the past is to imbue them
with the (spurious) authority of historical authenticity and thus seemingly timeless values, as Wiegler sought to do. Indeed, at the turn of
the century there was a strong tendency towards such an assertion of
timeless values among those writers and thinkers who sought to deny
the threats of modernity, not least that stemming from the contemporary *Frauenbewegung*. The cultural historian Christina von Braun
describes how prominent theoreticians of the time were concerned to
pronounce 'neue "Urgesetze" über die Geschlechter . . . Gesetze, die
erheblich dazu beitrugen, das Bewußtsein von der Geschichtlichkeit
aller Geschlechtsbilder auszulöschen'.[24]

The topographies of these texts are also strikingly similar. While,
as Suhrbier has shown, it was only in the eighteenth and nineteenth
centuries that the *Blaubartmärchen* began to be set in a medieval castle,

[23] No temporal setting is indicated by Koester, but the title 'Ritter Blaubart' evokes a
past, feudal world.
[24] Christina von Braun, *Die schamlose Schönheit des Vergangenen: Zum Verhältnis von Geschlecht
und Geschichte* (Frankfurt am Main: Verlag Neue Kritik, 1989), 10–11.

that convention was fully established by the turn of the century (in the texts by Eulenberg, El Hor, Schoßleitner, Trakl, Kaiser, and Döblin—for although Paolo's castle in Döblin's story is newly built, it has the spookiness of a classic *Märchen* castle). *Ariane et Barbe-bleue* and *Duke Bluebeard's Castle* also use this setting. Suhrbier notes the use of the aristocratic castle as another strategy for deflecting attention from contemporary bourgeois man (p. 27). Nevertheless, the topos has other implications too, notably, as an increasingly important symbol of psychological issues, as prefigured in Marlitt's 'Blaubart'. For instance, Balász's and Bartók's opera is not merely entitled *Duke Bluebeard*, but *Duke Bluebeard's Castle*, and in Balázs's libretto the castle takes on psychological characteristics of its own. Judith exclaims:

> All your castle lies in darkness!
> *She feels her way on. She shudders*
> It is wet here my beloved.
> What's this liquid in your castle?
> Is it weeping? Is it weeping? (p. 48)

And when Judith approaches the first door, the castle expresses itself as in the following stage direction (and echoed in the music itself):

She hammers on the door. As though in reply, a cavernous sigh is heard, like night winds sighing down long, dismal corridors

Judith responds by saying:

> Ah! Ah! What was that? What was sighing?
> Who was sighing? Tell me Bluebeard!
> It's your castle! It's your castle! It's your castle! (p. 49)

Here, Bluebeard's castle represents Bluebeard's psyche, since the rooms that Judith opens not only contain his property but also function as symbols of his state of mind and his past. That identification of Bluebeard's psyche with his castle is also central to the German texts in question here. For instance, in Eulenberg's play a character says of Bluebeard's castle: 'da graute es mir, wie auf einmal . . . dies Schloß auf uns zusprang, mit den düstern Fenstern, die uns antierten' (p. 277). The dark windows are the windows of Bluebeard Raul's soul. Similarly, in Schoßleitner's text the architecture of the castle reflects the souls of the King and the Prince, for it is full of statues of the women they have killed and the King has designed a grave for himself in its grounds which the Prince describes as follows:

'Siehst du dort in der Mitte den Tempelbau mit den Gestalten, die säulengleich ein mächtiges Behältnis tragen, wie einen großen Sarg?—Den hat mein Vater sich errichten lassen, als seine Ruhestatt nach dem Leben, und die Gestalten sind die Marmorbilder seiner letzten Frauen.' (p. 247)

Among other possibilities, this consistent use of the castle as a symbol for Bluebeard's psyche anticipates Jacques Lacan's image of the fortress for the inner reaches of the human subject (and the fortifications around it as neuroses).[25]

This explains why, in texts where Bluebeard is destroyed, his castle is destroyed too. In El Hor's castle, the persistent love of the dead woman is said to permeate the castle: 'Da spürte [der Ritter], daß alle Mauern und Winkel von ihrer Liebe durchsickert waren' (p. 161). In order to purge himself of this love, Bluebeard has to destroy not only himself but the castle also. Similarly, at the end of Schoßleitner's narrative, when Prince Bluebeard takes his own life, he destroys his castle and the neighbouring town too for good measure. Ilsebill also plans to burn down Paolo's castle, as do Raul's in-laws in Eulenberg's play.

Moreover, the locations and topographies of these castles are all similar. The castles tend to be located on elevated sites, especially cliffs, and/or to be surrounded by, or be near, water, especially the sea, and in Kaiser's play too, the forest around Gilles's castle is described as a 'Grünmeer'. And while there is no indication in the texts of Perrault, Grimm, and Bechstein that the forbidden chamber or other important parts of Bluebeard's house are underground, this feature is emphasized in the texts in question here.[26] In *Duke Bluebeard's Castle*, the opening stage directions specify that to enter the castle Bluebeard and Judith must *descend* a long flight of stairs, not *ascend* them, as might seem more usual in a castle. In Döblin's story, the ominous secret room which Ilsebill discovers is not part of the castle structure itself, but dug deep into the cliff behind it; and in Eulenberg's play, the forbidden chamber is also underground. Gilles's murders take place in a cellar, and the prison in *Ariane et*

---

[25] Jacques Lacan, 'Le Stade du miroir comme formateur de la fonction du je' (paper given 1936, published 1949), in *Écrits* (Paris: Seuil, 1966), 93–100 (97–8).

[26] In Perrault's text the wife does run downstairs to open the forbidden room. However, that room is on the ground floor, a contemporary detail, since in seventeenth-century France, the ground-floor suite of rooms in a grand bourgeois home was generally 'Monsieur' 's domain. In 'Das Mordschloß' (*KHM, Anhang* 14, ii. 477–9), the dismembered corpses are kept in the cellar; the murder in 'Der Räuberbräutigam' (*KHM* 40) also takes place in the cellar.

Barbe-bleue is also subterranean. Equally strikingly, when these castles (and sometimes Bluebeard) are destroyed, which happens frequently, the agent is fire.

While medieval-style castles are often imagined as standing on high vantage-points, having capacious dungeons and being destructible only by fire, this persistent emphasis is conspicuous. The relocation of the forbidden chamber underground is closely linked with the reinvention of the castle as a symbol of the masculine psyche, since underground spaces are traditionally used in literature to represent the secret regions of the mind.[27] Given which, the cliffs, water, and fire are particularly interesting. I have argued that the *Blaubartmärchen* can be read as a history of the civilized subject, which is gendered as masculine and constitutes itself by marking itself off from and violently controlling all that it perceives to be its Other, both inside and outside itself. Where that civilized self is often imagined as armoured, solid, and defensive ('gepanzert', in the terminology used by Klaus Theweleit, and like the association of Dorn with an Apollonian plasticity in Marlitt's 'Blaubart'), the Other tends to be fluid.[28] The castles in question here involve precisely such imagery, being strongly identified with Bluebeard himself and fortified against the uncivilized, disturbing water outside. In *Ariane et Barbe-bleue*, for example, one of the imprisoned women, Sélysette, expresses her fear of that water when Ariane tries to open the prison doors: 'Non, non, n'y touchez pas, on dit que c'est la mer qui baigne les murailles! . . . Les grandes vagues vont entrer!' (p. 37). In Döblin's 'Ritter Blaubart', a sea-monster destroys Paolo's wives—which is to say that the monster represents Paolo's unconscious destructive drives that he has split off from his civilized self and are therefore imagined as belonging to the Other, i.e. the watery element beyond the castle walls. Moreover, when things are discovered within the castle walls that threaten the order of its master, they must be banished into the alien element. So when Eulenberg's Raul discovers a friend *in flagrante* with his first wife, he murders that friend and throws the corpse into the lake in front of his castle. Raul recalls:

Das entsetzlichste war, daß [die Leiche] wieder emporkam am andern Morgen

---

[27] e.g. E. T. A. Hoffmann, 'Die Bergwerke zu Falun' (1819), in *Poetische Werke* (12 vols., Berlin: de Gruyter, 1957), v. 197–228.

[28] Klaus Theweleit, *Männerphantasien*, 2 vols. (Reinbek bei Hamburg: Rowohlt, 1980), i. 311. Hartmut Böhme, *Kulturgeschichte des Wassers* (Frankfurt am Main: Suhrkamp, 1988), 7–42.

und ans Licht auftauchte und die Sonne anstierte . . . Und dreimal noch mußte ich sie niederschießen, eh sie zu schwer wurde für den Tag und für ewig untertauchte und zu Boden sank. Nur der Teich ward seit dem Tage schwarz und morastig. (p. 283)

Raul was attempting to eliminate what he saw as a disturbing, alien force from his castle: that is, the friend (or *alter ego*) who represents an uncontrolled libido—Raul's own. The disturbing friend not only has to be killed and thrown out bodily, he also has to be repressed: i.e. sunk in water which is as dark and unpleasant as the unconscious itself and situated outside the castle, beyond the bounds of the conscious mind.

The fact that fire seems to be the only appropriate means of destroying Bluebeard's castle may be explained partially by the *Märchen* tradition which the authors invoke, since in the related *KHM* 46, 'Fitchers Vogel' (i. 219–23), the *Hexenmeister* and his household are also burnt to death. In 'Marienkind' (*KHM* 3), too, the heroine only narrowly escapes that fate. Furthermore, fire is an appropriate medium for Bluebeard's (self-)destruction, since it is traditionally connoted as masculine and opposed to the 'feminine' element water. And in the Grimm *Märchen*, fire is an element over which male characters, but not females, have power, and this would reinforce the marked emphasis which these texts lay on masculinity.[29] Finally, being burnt was a traditional punishment for heresy and witchcraft: that is, for crimes which concerned the soul rather than the body. Thus, the burning of the castle and Bluebeard along with it ties in with my observations about the increasing psychologization of Bluebeard texts during the High Modernist period.

There has been a distinct and major change in the topography of the Bluebeard material. Where Bluebeard's house in earlier versions was important as material proof of Bluebeard's wealth and social status, and was identified in Marlitt's text as a feminine interior, in these texts it has become a cipher for Bluebeard's psyche, thus continuing the shift in interest from the material to the mental. The projection of Bluebeard's psyche onto his castle also continues the development whereby 'Bluebeard' becomes an abstract principle that can be internalized by literary characters. The same projection is also a means of separating the values for which Bluebeard stands from the character of Bluebeard and making them into a super-

---

[29] Ruth B. Bottigheimer, *Grimms' Bad Girls and Bold Boys: The Moral and Social Vision of the Tales* (New Haven, Conn.: Yale University Press, 1987), 25–8.

individual, ubiquitous Symbolic Order, provoking a need to destroy the castle alongside Bluebeard himself.

BLUEBEARD'S WOMEN

Just as the settings in the texts in question share significant similarities, so do Bluebeard's women, and the most distinctive of these is their dispensability and marginality: they are no longer the central object of narrative interest which they were in earlier versions of the material. Hänschen's 'lovers' are not women at all, but cheap, dispensable mass reproductions of paintings, that is to say, easily available, replaceable images that are at several removes from the women who modelled for them. In this respect, too, Hänschen's monologue is a clairvoyant parody of the Bluebeard texts in question here. The secondary function of Bluebeard's lovers is reflected, for instance, in their namelessness; and in Koester's poem there is not even a specific female character but a series of generic women: 'Er liebte viele— aber keiner/gab er die ganze Seele her.' And even in the cases where the women *are* named (Eulenberg, Döblin, Kaiser), their characterization remains schematic, stereotypical, or inconsistent. Nonetheless, the texts blame the women either directly or indirectly for their own fate and that of Bluebeard.

The women who are directly blamed include Bluebeard's mother. In Eulenberg's play, Raul says: 'Meine Mutter hat mich verhätschelt, und mein Vater hat mich gepeitscht, und beide haben mich vergiftet zum Leben' (p. 284). Schoßleitner's Prince, addressing his dead father, says:

'Das hast du schlecht gemacht! . . . Du hast mir keine gute Mutter ausgesucht! Von ihr kam dieses sklavenhafte Niedrigsein, das mich hinunterzwingt[,] mich klein zu machen und mich anzuschmiegen.' (p. 253)

This condemnation of the parents perpetuates the constellation in Marlitt's 'Blaubart' where the action comes to be dominated by an absent, fantastical, proto-Freudian father-figure, although here, the sons give their mothers a disproportionate amount of the blame.[30]

But most significantly, it is now Bluebeard's lovers who take the blame. In almost all cases Bluebeard's women are his lovers, no

---

[30] The prince's outburst echoes Otto Weininger's *Geschlecht und Charakter: Eine prinzipielle Untersuchung* (1903) (Munich: Matthes & Seitz, 1980), 280–313.

longer his wives, and the fact that this is so both helps to inculpate them and contributes to Bluebeard's glamorous status as an outsider who rejects conventional morality. If Marlitt's text marked the shift where 'Blaubart' became a critique of love, not marriage, these newer German texts refer principally to sex. So in earlier versions of the *Blaubartmärchen*, the suggestion that the wife might have committed a sexual transgression which deserves punishment is only latently present, if at all. But here, the fact that these women run off with Bluebeard illicitly turns them for the first time in the history of the material into sexual transgressors who are worthy of condemnation and punishment. By going with Bluebeard without the sanction of marriage, the women forfeit their social status and so can be more easily marginalized both morally and socially. And since Bluebeard's lovers are drawn to him voluntarily, by love and desire rather than familial coercion or material expediency, they may be presumed to take more of the responsibility for their own fate and to derive some pleasure from it.

Indeed, the major characteristic shared by most of these women is an irresistible fascination with Bluebeard. While in earlier versions women felt suspicion towards Bluebeard, here they are infatuated with him. Indeed, Bluebeard's attraction is so strong that he needs to make no effort to attract these women, as he did in the earlier versions by Perrault, Tieck, and Marlitt, for instance. In some cases the women feel sorry for him and wish to redeem him from his tragic state. But in all cases this is a masochistic attachment, often provoked by a show of strength or aggression on Bluebeard's part. In Schoß-leitner's story, the following dialogue takes place between the prince and the woman:

'Ich zwinge dich und halte dich in den Armen und tue, was ich will mit dir!'
Ihr kam es von den Lippen wie verhauchend: 'Küsse mich! du Starker, du! . . .'
Und dann das Eine wiederum und fort und fort: 'Küsse mich! küsse mich!'
(p. 214)

And in El Hor's text the dialogue runs as follows:

'Wirst du mich töten?'
'Ja.'
'Warum tötest du die Frauen?'
'Frag nicht.'
'Wann wirst du mich töten?'
'Fürchtest du dich?'
'Nein—ich liebe dich dafür.' (pp. 160–1)

These women consciously put themselves in danger in order to fulfil their excessive desire to be with Bluebeard and to be oppressed, even hurt by him.

In some cases the inculpation of the women is even more explicit. The woman in Schoßleitner's story contributes to her own downfall by first encountering the Prince with the intention of murdering him. Eulenberg's Raul portrays himself with much pathos as the victim of his first wife's infidelity: 'Ich war jung und meine Seele stand noch voll Sonne. Da fand ich mein Weib hier bei ihm' (p. 283). Raul's later wives are put to the test of the forbidden chamber as a pathological reaction to the trauma of that first marriage, and while Raul is waiting to discover whether Judith has obeyed him, he expresses his fear as follows: 'Ich muß sie prüfen. Ich glaube mich sonst von neuem genarrt.—*Er wischt sich den Schaum vom Munde.* . . . Soll ich wieder warten, bis ich den Buhlen bei ihr finde!' (pp. 305–6). The obedience test appears to Raul as a perfect justification for murder which applies to all future wives: 'Die erste hatte mich betrogen, und wie ich die andern prüfte, da täuschten sie mich alle. Eine mußte sterben, die andern wollten sterben' (p. 321).

In other words, the notion that women are to blame permeates all these texts. In Döblin's story, the peasant who tells Ilsebill about the sea-monster (which seems to be more female than male, a fact which also inculpates the feminine) adds: 'Wäre nicht bei den Frauen jetzt die Unzucht und Gottlosigkeit so groß, so wäre der arme Ritter befreit von dem Tier' (p.83). And in Kaiser's play, Gilles says:

die Dörfer bersten von Dirnen, die erbärmlich seufzen nach Männern. Mich schmerzt das Wehleiden! Schaffe sie her—es soll ihnen nicht wieder nach einem Bräutigam schmachten! (p. 784)

At the same time, Gilles had Jeanne executed for refusing him. And while Hänschen says that Venus must die for his sins and not hers, he also blames her for his deed: 'Du saugst mir den Mark aus den Knochen . . . Du bist mir zu anspruchsvoll in deiner unmenschlichen Bescheidenheit, zu aufreibend mit deinen unbeweglichen Glied-maßen!' (p. 125). In all cases, then, it seems that sex and Woman, whatever she does, are linked and that she must be punished for this association, either for provoking Bluebeard's sexuality, for respond-ing to her own, or indeed for not responding to Bluebeard's advances.

While these women's lives become less important morally, their deaths and the sight of dead women become absolutely central, but without the conventional, aesthetically appealing transformation of that sight into clearly recognizable works of art in the text, as in Marlitt's 'Blaubart'.[31] Thus, while the late nineteenth century had moved away from murder and towards other, apparently less physical forms of female suffering and punishment, the texts in question here return to and revolve around murder in an unprecedented way. This seems to be part of the nostalgic desire to return to what were erroneously perceived to be earlier, more authentic uses of the 'Blaubart' material as recommended by Wiegler. Eulenberg's play dwells in horrible detail on the corpses of the dead wives kept in the cellar, as in the following stage direction for example: '*Ein Kellergewölbe im Schloß, kahl und kalt. Nur hinten auf einem Vorsprung der Mauer liegen auf weißen Schüsseln fünf blutige verweste Frauenköpfe*' (p. 286). Trakl's fragment ends with the following stage direction: 'Er zerrt sie in die Tiefe. Man hört einen gellenden Schrei. Dann tiefe Stille. Nach einiger Zeit erscheint Blaubart, bluttriefend, und trunken außer sich' (p. 445). Koester's poem ends with the lapidary formulation '[er] [e]rschlug sie', which gains its force from its position at the close, and as the main clause and resolution of a longer sentence which begins with two sub-clauses. In El Hor's text the woman dies imprisoned by Bluebeard, leaving a message written in blood on her clothes. And in Kaiser's play, not only is Jeanne burnt at the stake on Gilles's malicious testimony, but he murders six further women in the cellar of his castle and plans a seventh murder. While his murders are not displayed, they are described fully and ecstatically. Similarly, while Schoßleitner spares his readers the sight of real corpses and the woman protagonist commits suicide, Bluebeard's castle is littered with statues of dead wives, and the fact that they were brutally murdered is stressed. Döblin's 'Ritter Blaubart' is to some extent an exception, since Paolo does not murder his women and Ilsebill dissolves into mist rather than dying. However, the other three women die sinister, untimely deaths; the reader sees the corpses; and the implication is that Paolo is somehow to blame.

Thus, murder and dead women come to be the central focus of these texts in an unprecedented, voyeuristic and sadistic manner. And not only is murder restored to new importance, it comes to mark a narrative closure in ways which again break with the Bluebeard

[31] Exceptionally, in Schoßleitner's text the prince and his father, like Marlitt's Dorn, have statues made of their dead women, thus dispensing with the need to keep the corpses.

tradition. While earlier versions in which the last woman survived ended with an emancipatory, utopian, or at least open moment, here, that openness is eliminated, since in practically all cases all the women, including the last, are killed. Also, Bluebeard himself dies in most cases. There is thus a shift from a comedic plot structure (as in Perrault's text, which ends with a new series of marriages) to a tragic plot structure, and as in tragedy, that shift is accompanied by a new interest in character rather than in the logic of the plot, traditionally the province of comedy. But the new tragic hero and central psychological subject is no longer the woman protagonist, but Bluebeard himself.

'EIN BEWEINENSWERTER MENSCH': BLUEBEARD AS TRAGIC HERO

While earlier versions of 'Blaubart' focused on the wife's actions, character, and chances of escape, with Bluebeard fulfilling a principally mechanical function in the plot, in this new group of Bluebeard texts that relationship is reversed, as Schoßleitner demanded. The role of transgressor is transferred from the disobedient woman to the homicidal Bluebeard, and his murders are flagrant, sexualized, and far more sensational and destructive transgressions than the wife's in earlier Bluebeard versions. And yet Bluebeard's transgressions are treated with more reverence. Hänschen says: 'Es liegt etwas Tragisches in der Rolle des *Blaubart*. Ich glaube, seine ermordeten Frauen insgesamt litten nicht soviel wie er . . .'. When Eulenberg's Raul dies, another character says: 'Es war ein beweinenswerter Mensch, der da sterben mußte' (p. 324), and this, not regret for the two lost sisters, is the dominant note in the speaker's feelings at the close of the play, despite the fact that he is the women's bereaved brother. The focus in Koester's poem is exclusively on Bluebeard's suffering in love; and El Hor's narrative sympathy and interest are also with Bluebeard. Schoßleitner's Prince 'sprach von seiner Einsamkeit, seiner Verlassenheit und seiner großen Sehnsucht' (p. 212), and in his essay, Schoßleitner portrays the 'Blaubart-Typus' as a tragic man:

Daß er gerade dort die stärkste Notwendigkeit fühlt zu töten, wo es ihm am schwersten fällt, gerade *die* Frau zu töten, die am besten zu ihm passen würde, die er am meisten liebt . . . Wenn sogar dieser Fall tragisch endet, dann ist überhaupt keine Rettung mehr zu erwarten, denn jener Frauen, die weniger zu ihm passen, die er weniger liebt, wird er sich noch viel leichter entledigen. (pp. 516–17)

The tragedy lies in the fact that Bluebeard loses the woman he loves, rather than in the fact that several women are killed, a deadly serious reiteration of Hänschen's comic comment that Bluebeard suffers more than all his women put together.

Indeed, Bluebeard's fatal flaw—the desire to murder—acquires a tragic grandeur so that he becomes a hero in a world which fails to understand him. He is distinguished by his challenge to the norms of that inferior world and also, as Wiegler demanded, by his superior spiritual capacities and sensuality. Schoßleitner's Prince complains that 'Das Leben will das Mittelmaß' (p. 249), and Eulenberg's Raul is a philosopher of death who rejects all conventional morality, saying: 'Wir hassen uns alle. Wir sind nur zu feige oder zu faul, es uns zu sagen' (p. 282). His murders provide privileged existential insight: 'Durch Blut sehen wir in alles hinein. Jedes Messer schließt das Rätsel des Blutes auf' (p. 283). Gilles is also larger than life and contemptuous of the rest of the world:

Das Land verdorrt vor der Pest, die ich ausschütte. Öde zerstampft Dörfer und Städte. Die letzte Kratur [sic] scheucht sich in karges Gebirge und glast in Eis. Ich bin übrig—und vom First meines Hauses lästere ich meinen hohnlachenden Triumph auf die wächserne Wüstenei! (p. 783)

This superhuman, misanthropic perspective is also that of the mad Roman emperor Heliogabalus whom Hänschen invokes; and all these Bluebeards are unconditionally admired for their murderous acts of resistance against a mediocre world. When Gilles confesses, the Papal Nuncio announces:

Kein Henker!!—keine Fessel!!—es ist mehr geschehen, als unsere Verdammnis sühnt!! Ein Mensch bekannte sich!! Wer ist nicht seinesgleichen?! . . . jeder brennt mit Gilles, der für alle verbrennt!!!! (p. 811)

This formulation elevates Gilles to a Christ-like status, just like Marlitt's Dorn, but the Nuncio's boundless admiration may be less for Gilles's confession than for his whole, grand, murderous career, with which the Nuncio may tacitly wish to identify himself.

In some cases, a further tragic motif is provided by Bluebeard's paradoxical desire for redemption through his lovers. The struggle of the wife with her curiosity in earlier versions of the *Blaubartmärchen* is replaced by Bluebeard's struggle with his desires both to kill and spare his wives, although this is not a straightforward role reversal but an escalation, since his actions are more drastic and destructive than those of the wife. Bluebeard's hope for redemption is expressed by Eulenberg and Schoßleitner, implied by Döblin, and central to *Duke Bluebeard's Castle*. While the women in question are convinced of their ability to redeem Bluebeard, he knows that both he and they are doomed. Nevertheless, he may hope weakly against this knowledge. Eulenberg's Raul says: 'laß sie unschuldig sein. Mich ekelt vor dem Blut'—so that his concern seems to be less with Judith's survival and more with his distaste at the process of murdering her. This ambivalent desire for redemption is strongest in the case of Döblin's Paolo, who attempts ineffectually to make Ilsebill leave, telling her, 'am besten, sie ginge fort von hier'. Indeed, the projection of Paolo's murderous instincts onto the apparently independent, sentient sea-monster indicates that his dilemma has split him completely.

But not all Bluebeards have such ambivalent feelings. Schoßleitner's Prince does not struggle long with the insight that he must kill his lover, and his desire to kill other women involves no hesitation. Koester's and El Hor's protagonists feel no such ambivalence either. Only in one text is the wife's regret at having been disobedient replaced with remorse on the part of Bluebeard, since Trakl's Bluebeard collapses in front of a crucifix after murdering Elisabeth. On the whole, however, it is difficult to discern remorse in these protagonists—not least because their regrets, inasmuch as they are expressed at all, are more often self-centred. For instance, while Kaiser's Gilles wishes to bring Jeanne back to life, this is due to his continued desire for her, and he shows no remorse whatsoever over the other women he murdered.

Nonetheless, Bluebeard the tragic hero suffers after his murders because he is plagued by a new problem: memory, concomitantly with the period's great interest in that theme.[32] In Eulenberg's play, Bluebeard is tortured by the memory of his earlier wives, as is El Hor's Blaubart, who cannot shake off the love of the dead woman. Paolo also falls into a deep depression after the loss of three wives, and Gilles is plagued by the memory of Jeanne. Indeed, in Kaiser's

---

[32] Cf. Weininger, *Geschlecht und Charakter*, 145–81; Freud, *Die Traumdeutung* (1900), in *Studienausgabe*, ed. Alexander Mitscherlich, Angela Richards, and James Strachey, 11 vols. (Frankfurt am Main: Suhrkamp, 1989), ii, and other writings; and Nietzsche's reflections on memory in *Zur Genealogie der Moral* (1887), in *Werke in zwei Bänden*, ed. Karl Schlechta and Ivo Frenzel, 2 vols. (Munich: Hanser, 1967), ii. 175–288. Cf. my article '*In Blaubarts Schatten*: Murder, *Märchen* and Memory', *German Life and Letters*, 50 (1997), 491–507.

play memory not only makes Bluebeard suffer, it provokes his sub-
sequent murders, since they all take place as Gilles attempts to recall
Jeanne from the dead. And memory also emerges clearly in *Duke
Bluebeard's Castle*. One critic wrote of the closing scene:

[Judith] sieht sich konfrontiert mit den zu Geschichte geronnenen früheren
Frauen Blaubarts . . . Das Geheimnis der letzten beiden Türen [zur Seele des
Mannes] ist die bittere Wahrheit, daß . . . die in der Seele verhüllten
Erinnerungen . . . mit niemandem geteilt werden können. Judith wird so zur
Erinnerung einer erträumten Liebe . . .[33]

On this reading, Bluebeard's memory is deadening, melancholic,
and can affect not only its subject but also others around it.[34] The
same is true of the other Bluebeard characters, all of whom have a
melancholic memory indicating an inability to mourn normally.

Bluebeard's new status as a tragic hero makes the texts' endings
ambivalent. Traditionally, his antisocial behaviour was punished by
summary execution, which was endorsed by the narrators. Here,
however, his superiority puts him above normal moral standards,
with the result that summary execution takes place only in Eulenberg's play. Kaiser's protagonist is formally condemned to death, but
we do not see him go to the stake. Rather, the text ends with him in a
triumphant posture, and in both Eulenberg's and Kaiser's texts
Bluebeard is praised, not condemned, by his executioners. Although
in El Hor's text Bluebeard decides to commit suicide by fire, the text
does not end with his death, but only with his waiting for it, so again
the sight of his demise is avoided. While Döblin's Paolo dies by
violence, it is years later in an ostensibly unrelated, heroic, and only
indirectly reported incident. Schoßleitner's Bluebeard stages an
elaborate suicide which also involves the deaths of all his subjects.
There is no mention of punishment in Koester's poem, just as the
end of Balázs's and Bartók's opera remains open and Bluebeard is
not physically punished. And in Trakl's fragment it is impossible to
tell what Bluebeard's end might have been. Thus, even in those cases
where Bluebeard is said to die, either his corpse is seldom shown or
the texts end before his death. Such ambivalent endings reflect
Bluebeard's new status as an admirable, heroic figure who should
neither be humiliated nor experience public or private censure

---

[33] Dietmar Holland, 'Herzog Blaubarts Burg', in Csampai and Holland, *Der Opernführer*,
1049.
[34] Mourning which refuses to relinquish its object is, in Freudian terms, melancholic.
See Freud, 'Trauer und Melancholie' (1915), in *Studienausgabe*, iii. 193–212.

because conventional moral standards do not apply to him, bringing him into close proximity with the Nietzschean *Übermensch*, a cult figure of the same period. At the same time, such endings map with the observation that these new versions of Bluebeard are tragic and non-utopian since there is no foreseeable end to the murderous cycle, except through violence done to the self.

BLUEBEARD/DON JUAN/*LUSTMÖRDER*

While in earlier versions of 'Blaubart' the wife's curiosity could be interpreted as a sexual transgression only very speculatively, in these turn-of-the-century versions sexuality is an explicit issue, since Bluebeard is not only heroic and admirable but also very sexy. Interestingly, these characteristics are shared by another celebrated literary figure who haunted thinking about masculinity around the turn of the century, and what is more, came to be identified with the figure of Bluebeard: Don Juan (as foreshadowed by Marlitt).[35] Don Juan, too, emerged at the beginnings of European modernity in the seventeenth century, at the same time as the *conquistadores* who set out to rule the world.[36] In this period, dreams of the conquest and control of Nature were also developed, as was the utopian notion that man could learn to control mortality and the human body.[37] In Don Juan narratives, this ultimate conquest was symbolized in the conquest of the substance which, more than any other, has been a symbol of the corporeal and material: the female body. Thus, there is a homology between Don Juan's conquests of women and his victory over bodily mortality when he summons up the dead Commander. In 1896, Wedekind wrote an essay on the restitution of the original ending of Mozart's *Don Giovanni* on stage, an ending which dispenses with the usual moral condemnation of the eponymous hero and was not usually performed in the nineteenth century. Here, he praised the figure of Don Giovanni as an instance of '*übermenschlicher Genuß-fähigkeit*' (Wedekind's emphasis):

[35] Weininger wrote: 'der Don Juan [ist] der einzige Mensch, vor dem [das Weib] bis zum Grunde zittert': *Geschlecht und Charakter*, 400–1. Cf. my thesis 'The Blaubartmärchen and Its Reception in German Literature of the Nineteenth and Twentieth Centuries', D.Phil. thesis (Oxford, 1998), 252. Cf. Jürgen Wertheimer, *Don Juan and Blaubart: Erotische Serientäter in der Literatur* (Munich: C. H. Beck, 1999). Due to its recent appearance, it has not been possible to include a discussion of this study in the present work.

[36] Cf. von Braun, *Die schamlose Schönheit des Vergangenen*, 37.

[37] Cf. Carolyn Merchant, *The Death of Nature: Women, Ecology and the Scientific Revolution* (New York: HarperCollins, 1983).

Don Giovanni, im moraltrunkenen Deutschland längst ein psychiatrisches-kriminelles Schreckgespenst geworden, rehabilitiert sich als *Heros*. . . . Aus der neubelebten Originalfassung erwächst [den Damen] keine höhere Aufgabe, als zur Verherrlichung des *Unverwüstlichen* schön zu singen, . . . Mit welcher Herzenswärme würde Friedrich Nietzsche, wenn ihm das Glück noch vergönnt wäre, den Wiedererwecker des Don Giovanni zu seiner mutigen Tat beglück-wünschen![38]

And in another piece on Don Giovanni, this time a fictional inter-view, the narrator/interviewer desires to emulate him as a 'Genuß-mensch' and asks him for advice on conquering women. This advice (which is ironically taken) consists of a simple physical and mental schema according to which women may be classified and seen as being interchangeable and marginal.[39]

Similarities between Don Juan and Bluebeard are evident. Blue-beard, too, emerged at the beginning of modernity. He sets out on his own travels of discovery (to the woman's house to court her and then again on a journey during which the woman submits to her curiosity). The motif of the journey is used in many Bluebeard texts of the period, as though it were a prerequisite of the Bluebeard character to travel.[40] Bluebeard also eliminates real women and replaces them with idealized, aesthetic images, just as Don Juan seems to be pursuing not real women but some impossible ideal which excludes them.[41] The display of dead women with their clotted blood in Perrault's forbidden chamber and the euphemistic substitu-tion of those corpses with statues and other works of art in such later texts as Marlitt's resemble Don Juan's stone guest: lifeless, petrified, and petrifying. And Wedekind's two essays also show that his percep-tion of Don Juan is close to contemporary ideas about Bluebeard. Both figures are admirable because their sensuality is superhuman and because they disregard both conventional morality and women, making them into mere elements in an autistic schema for Don Juan's/Bluebeard's self-gratification. Finally, in Wedekind's estima-tion, Don Juan becomes a philosopher, just as Bluebeard does for Wiegler, Schoßleitner, and others.

But one difference remains between the two traditions. If Don Juan uses sexuality in order to conquer femininity and metonym-

---

[38] Wedekind, 'Don Giovanni', in *Werke in drei Bänden*, iii. 170–1 (170).

[39] 'Interview: Don Giovanni', ibid. 182–7.

[40] Cf. Marga Passon, *Blaubart* (Berlin: Ullstein, 1929); Georg Freiherr von Ompteda, *Der neue Blaubart* (Berlin: Fleischel, 1919).

[41] Cf. von Braun, *Die schamlose Schönheit des Vergangenen*, 40.

ically rule the world, Bluebeard uses murder. Nevertheless, around 1900 this important difference began to be disregarded and the figures of Bluebeard and Don Juan explicitly identified. In a short article on Bluebeard published in 1883, K. Hofmann noted:

Nach den Sprichwörtersammlungen des sechzehnten Jahrhunderts bedeutet Blaubart einen Mann, der einen dichten schwarzen Bart hat. Nach der Meinung jener Zeit wurde ein solcher *Blaubart* für einen gebornen [*sic*] *Don Juan* und *Frauenverführer* gehalten.[42]

Because Hofmann does not cite his sources it may well be, especially in the case of his second claim, that he is presenting a very contemporary idea in the guise of historical fact, as Wiegler and Schoßleitner did. In his essay, Schoßleitner also associated Bluebeard and Don Juan:

daß einer die Frau, zu der er in erotischer Beziehung gestanden hat, *tötet*, scheint für den Blaubart-Typus charakteristisch, daß einer nacheinander mit *mehreren* Frauen erotische Beziehungen eingeht für den Don Juan kennzeichnend. Die Mehrheit der Beziehungen bringt es wieder mit sich, daß der Don Juan eine Frau nach der anderen verläßt, und zwar umso entschiedener, je stärker ihn ein neues Erlebnis anreizt und entflammt; er möchte sie am liebsten völlig abtun und vergessen und *tötet* sie gleichsam *in sich*. Der Blaubart, der sie wirklich und körperlich tötet, scheint nach dieser Betrachtung nur die physische Konsequenz zu ziehen, und insoferne er nicht bloß eine Frau, sondern eine Mehrheit von Frauen tötet, gleichzeitig den Don Juan-Typus in sich zu schließen. (pp. 513–14)

Schmidt wrote in his review of Eulenberg/Reznicek's Bluebeard opera that its protagonist was 'donjuanhaft'; and the origins of Balázs's libretto *Duke Bluebeard's Castle*, too, lay in an unfinished earlier stage work entitled *Don Juan and Bluebeard*.[43] For these writers then, Bluebeard is an 'erotischer Unhold'; and in sexualizing Bluebeard, they introduced an influential new dimension into this *Märchen* tradition.

As Hofmann anticipated, the blue beard comes into its own as a symbol in this new, sexualized treatment of the Bluebeard material.[44]

---

[42] 'Über die älteste Quelle der Blaubartsage', *Romanische Forschungen*, 1 (1883), 434–5 (434).

[43] Paul Banks, 'Images of the Self: Duke Bluebeard's Castle', in John, *The Stage Works of Béla Bartók*.

[44] Weininger said about beards: 'Die Wirkung des männlichen Bartes auf die Frau ist . . . psychologisch ein vollständiges, und nur in der Intensität geschwächtes, *Abbild* der Wirkung des männlichen Gliedes selbst' (*Geschlecht und Charakter*, 338–9); and of the colour blue: '*Blau* ist die Farbe der Freude und Seligkeit des höchsten Lebens' (quoted by Gerald Stieg, 'Otto Weiningers Blendung: Weininger, Karl Kraus und der Brenner-Kreis', in *Otto*

In earlier versions, the blue beard could only be understood either as a joke (Tieck) or as a mystery (Perrault). While the Grimms suggested that a 'Blaubart' might be a 'Starkbärtiger', they implied no obviously sexual connotation. From Hofmann onward, however, the beard suddenly acquired an evident, realistic meaning: that of a potent, sexualized, and dangerous masculinity anticipated even by Marlitt's Lilli:

Waren auch jene männlich schönen Züge dort unergründlich für ihren unerfahrenen Blick, so schwebte doch in der That, als untrügliches Warnungszeichen, ein tiefer, blauer Hauch um das Kinn und den unteren Teil der Wangen . . . (p. 299)

Similarly, in El Hor's text:

Sein Bart war spitz zugeschnitten und so glatt und glänzend wie ein schwarzes Pantherfell, mit einem stahlblauen Schimmer darauf . . . . Da lachte sie und fing mit der hohlen Hand das Regenwasser auf, das aus seinem Bart tropfte und trank es. (pp. 160–1)[45]

In the association of Don Juan and Bluebeard, then, serial love affairs and serial murders become perversely condensed into sexual murder. Eulenberg's Raul finds sadistic pleasure in such murder and looks forward to it; and Prinz Blaubart's murders are described by Schoßleitner as follows:

Er schlürfte ihr [his lovers'] Vertrauen in sich ein wie etwas ihm Versagtes, nie Erlebtes und sog sich niemals satt an dieser glaubensvollen Liebe der Betrogenen, denn er blieb immer noch im Innersten verschlossen und gepanzert wie zuvor und stieß mit ausgesuchter Sicherheit den schlanken Dolch in ihren Jubelruf der brünstigsten Entladung, daß sie im höchsten Augenblick der Lust verröchelten. (p. 257)

In Koester's poem, Bluebeard also murders 'im Lustgenießen', and Trakl's Bluebeard announces that he will kill Elisabeth as follows:

> Lust peitschen Haß, Verwesung und Tod
> . . . soll ich dich Kindlein ganz besitzen—
> Muß ich, Gott will's den Hals dir schlitzen!
> Du Taube, und trinken dein Blut so rot

Weininger: Werk und Wirkung, ed. Jacques Le Rider and Norbert Leser (Vienna: Österreichischer Bundesverlag, 1984), 59–67 (62)).

[45] This motif is a commonplace in twentieth-century texts, e.g. Barbara König, 'Nepomuk', in *Blaubärtchen: Märchen und Geschichten für neugierige Leser*, ed. Felicitas Feilhauer (Munich: Hanser, 1990), 149–70 (149).

Und deinen zuckenden, schäumenden Tod!
Und saugen aus deinem Eingeweid
Deine Scham und deine Jungfräulichkeit. (p. 444)

Kaiser's Gilles also murders his victims after he has raped them and declares: 'jetzt will ich töten!!!! . . . Ich schwinge die furchtbare Geissel aus Genuß und Verderben' (p. 783).

One speculative reason for this unprecedented sexualization of Bluebeard's murders may be related to the argument that secrecy in sexual matters came to be increasingly important in nineteenth-century education and that such secrecy generated more curiosity— so that, in turn, ever more secrets were required to reinforce the silence surrounding sexuality.[46] In other words, the notions of the secret and sexuality became closely identified. The Bluebeard narrative is an account of the production of secrets, so, as the very notion of the secret became associated with sex in the nineteenth century, the secrets of the *Blaubartmärchen* could be increasingly associated with sex for the children who were brought up in that period, and grew up to be the authors of these early twentieth-century texts. Such an association of Bluebeard's secret with sex comes over, albeit in comical form, in Hänschen's monologue. Hänschen is aware of the need for secrecy for his rendezvous with Venus, since he conducts his monologue in the lavatory, presumably the most secret place he could find. Furthermore, the taboo on masturbation has frightened him into destroying the evidence and temptation represented by the picture, a destruction which he stylizes in aggressive terms as murder. Thus, secrecy is transformed into aggression.

In conclusion, since Don Juan's serial love affairs are condensed in this period with Bluebeard's serial murders, murder acquires a less serious aspect and becomes a heroic game for a 'Genußmensch', thus implying that the difference between a love affair and sexual murder is quantitive and not qualitative. Yet for the women characters the qualitative difference between the end of a love affair and being murdered is considerable. This point of view demonstrates how absolutely the male protagonist has become the centre of attention,

---

[46] In *La Volonté de savoir* (Paris: Gallimard, 1976), Michel Foucault argued that the nineteenth-century production of sexual secrets did not so much *suppress* sexuality as *generate* it in its modern form. The secrecy imposed upon the sexual subject is productive: not only of more secrets, but of fantasies and cultural narratives, just as Hänschen produces a narrative in which he becomes a heroic sexual murderer.

since it is only from his point of view that certain similarities could be perceived. Once again, Hänschen's monologue comically exemplifies the autism of Bluebeard as a sexual murderer, who in this case is able to suspend disbelief and thus 'forget' that the figure he is addressing is not a woman but a picture. And Bluebeard's transformation into an irresistible lover became quickly accepted in the twentieth century.[47]

THE AETIOLOGY OF THE CRIMES

It was in the late nineteenth and early twentieth centuries that scholarly searches for the origins of Bluebeard's crimes began in earnest, since it was in that period that secondary articles began to appear which sought to explain the *Blaubartmärchen* and to establish its purportedly correct meaning, content, and origin, beginning with Hofmann's article of 1883 quoted above. Such writings reflected a new interest in the figure of Bluebeard himself and perpetuated the attempts to exculpate him by providing (pseudo-)rational explanations for his behaviour and making it appear humanly comprehensible, or even normal, by grounding it, for instance, in social practice. In this respect such secondary texts are very similar to the primary texts being discussed in this chapter, since they too focus sympathetically on the motives for Bluebeard's crime and make it appear rational or worthy of pity. Such rationalist secondary literature is part of the systematic, ordering thinking described in the previous chapter, where the activity of collecting formed part of a relentlessly logical attempt to order, explain, and subjugate the world and experience.

Furthermore, such literary and scholarly searches for origins are a further variant on the theme of the secret in the *Blaubartmärchen*. While in Marlitt's 'Blaubart' the Bluebeard theme of the production of secrets was transposed into the genre of the novella which became a detective story, in the primary and secondary texts produced around the turn of the century the search for secrets focuses on the figure of Bluebeard himself as a mystery that has to be unravelled. In earlier versions of the *Märchen* the killing remained enigmatic, and if an explanation was given, it tended to be that the wife must be

---

[47] e.g. Gerd Winkler, *Mike Blaubart* (Frankfurt am Main: Heine, 1968); Dieter Hildebrandt, *Blaubart Mitte 40* (Hamburg: Hoffmann & Campe, 1977).

punished for her curiosity, or perhaps for some more obscure reason. But the authors of these texts attempt to provide a logical explanation for Bluebeard's apparently illogical crimes, and one aspect of this new, more forensic interest is the tendency to focus on the death of the first woman in order to explain why the series of murders began (in the texts by Eulenberg, Schoßleitner, and Kaiser). Here, the detective work is undertaken not by the reader or by characters in the text (as in Marlitt's novella), but by the authors themselves. Thus, Eulenberg's drama is, to my knowledge, the first Bluebeard text to use psychological explanations for Bluebeard's killings (possibly with the exception of Tieck's *Die sieben Weiber des Blaubarts*; however, it can be argued that the psychology of that text's Bluebeard is more limited, and that its author is more interested in literary theoretical than psychological motivations[48]). Furthermore, while not all these authors were Freudians or otherwise committed to psychoanalysis (Schoßleitner denounces such approaches), the contemporary discovery of psychoanalysis and the unconscious provided them with new, apparently scientific models for their rationalist detective work. Bluebeard, in this context, represented a fascinating condensation of criminal and analysand as fantasized by Freud.[49]

At first sight the texts in question seem to present a simple, schematic view of gender relations and sexual murder in which women are the willing, masochistic objects of violence and the male hero is sadistic and psychologically complex. But this binary view is too simple, and is contradicted by powerful and disturbing undercurrents in the texts which recall those in Marlitt's novella. In fact, Bluebeard senses that the traditional masculine/feminine binarism on which his subjectivity is based is precarious, and this realization precipitates within him a profound and violent crisis of masculinity. Indeed, Bluebeard's inability to suppress his loss of confident selfhood causes this issue to become the major focus of interest in the texts being discussed here. According to Schoßleitner's essay:

---

[48] Ludwig Tieck, *Die sieben Weiber des Blaubart* (1797), in *Ludwig Tieck's* [sic] *Schriften*, 28 vols. (Berlin: Reimer, 1828), ix. 89–242.

[49] Freud imagined the psychoanalyst as a detective, perceiving 'eine Analogie zwischen dem Verbrecher und dem Hysteriker', in 'Tatbestandsdiagnostik und Psychoanalyse' (1906), quoted in Jacques Le Rider, *Der Fall Otto Weininger: Wurzeln des Antifeminismus und Antisemitismus*, trans. Dieter Hornig (Munich: Löcker, 1985), 174. Cf. Michel Foucault, *Surveiller et punir: la naissance de la prison* (Paris: Gallimard, 1975), in which, conversely, the modern transformation of the criminal into a psychiatric or psychological case is discussed.

Alle Sinnlichkeit erscheint ihm wie ein Heruntersteigen, wie etwas Feindliches, das ihn seiner stolzen Sicherheit und Ruhe zu berauben droht, wogegen man ankämpfen muß: und so dünkt ihm das Weib etwas Gegnerisches und Feindliches, weil es ihm die Verkörperung der Sinnlichkeit bedeutet und seine eigenen Sinne entflammt. Er tötet sie, weil er sie geliebt hat, weil sie ihn entwürzelt und rächt sich gleichsam an ihr für dies und für seine Enttäuschung. (p. 519)

Correspondingly, in the story itself the Prince expresses feelings of mistrust towards the woman who has revealed his vulnerability:

'Wirst du auch immer zu mir halten? Du? Und immer treu zu mir? . . . Es ist ja eine Abkehr von sich selbst, ein Sklavendienst an etwas außer mir . . . All diese Liebe, diese hingeopferte Anschmiegsamkeit und und dieses Hinströmen und Verfließen—: ein rasend geiler Mörderlust am eigenen Selbst, ein Taumel durch Vernichtungstode unseres Selbstgefühls.' (p. 220)

The Prince solves this problem by turning his 'geile Mörderlust' against his lover and becoming like his murderous father. In *Gilles et Jeanne*, Gilles has Jeanne executed for resisting him, but later he murders a series of women because they do *not* resist:

knallend fällt die Rüstung auseinander—Leib von Weib bietet sich an—ich versinke—ich sterbe—!! . . . Ich sterbe nicht!!!! Kein Ende mit mir—kein Chaos mit mir!! Die Luft birst nicht in Donner—das Sein birst nicht in Atome!! Nicht Untergang zu Verlöschen—nicht Tod zu Vergehen!!!! . . . ich übersehe das platte Liebeslager—ich taste an die dornige Haut der Geliebten—der Ekel führt meine Hände—und die Hände verrichten ihr Werk wie zwei Henker!!!! (p. 782)

Hänschen 'murders' Venus because he fears the damage to his physical and mental health caused by masturbation, and Koester's poem sums up Bluebeard's motive succinctly:

> Und sah er sich im Lustgenießen,
> nach dem sein Blut verzweifelt schrie,
> in eine Frau hinüberfliessen—
> erschlug er sie.

In Trakl's fragment, Elisabeth's description of her own desire challenges and frightens Bluebeard. In Eulenberg's play Raul fears sexual betrayal, which he sees as an existential challenge to his identity. El Hor's Bluebeard feels that he has been permeated by an alien element—the woman's love; and Paolo's sense of self in the face of sexual relationships is so disturbed that it splits into two—Paolo and the sea-monster.

In each case, Bluebeard fears for the integrity of his self which he perceives to be under threat. In the case of Gilles, the vehemence of Bluebeard's denial that he is experiencing a loss of selfhood is telling and unconvincing: 'Ich sterbe nicht!!!!', following as it does the equally emphatic claim: 'ich versinke—ich sterbe—!!' In each case that threat involves sexuality—most often the sexual act itself—and Bluebeard responds to it by attacking the woman who has catalysed the threat.

This consistent fear of a losing a stable selfhood in the sexual act is repeatedly expressed by means of fluid imagery. Eulenberg's Prince fears a 'Hinströmen' and 'Verfliessen' and Koester's protagonist a 'hinüberfliessen'. El Hor's Bluebeard is pursued by a love which 'sickert' and 'klebt' and Trakl's fragment also involves fluid imagery: Elisabeth, too, spills her wine 'wie Blut', and Blaubart says, 'Wie stehen dir die schimmernden Tränen gut!' (p. 442). Elisabeth describes her own desire in these terms:

> Trink meine Glut,
> Bist du nicht durstig nach meinem Blut,
> Nach meiner brennenden Haare Flut? (p. 443)

Gilles also speaks of his fear of 'Versinken' and 'Vergehen' (meaning fluid dissolution). Hänschen's fear is likewise expressed in fluid images: 'Aber du saugst mir den Mark aus den Knochen', and he is afraid that his brain will melt 'wie ein Butterkloß'. The native element of Paolo's monster is the watery ocean; and not only are Raul's murders linked to the dark pool outside his castle, but he literally foams at the mouth when contemplating murder.

Such a consistent use of the fluid metaphor in connection with the threat to Bluebeard's selfhood is revealing as to the precise nature of that threat. I described above how these Bluebeard texts stage the manner in which the civilized, masculine self, which imagines itself to be solid and 'gepanzert' like Bluebeard's castle, marks itself off from the fluid, feminine Other.[50] Consequently, it is no coincidence that Gilles's fear is provoked when 'knallend fällt die Rüstung auseinander', and that Schoßleitner's Prince knows that he is making himself vulnerable by removing the protective 'Panzer' he always wears for fear of betrayal. These Bluebeards all realize that the 'Panzerung' of the masculine self is vulnerable and repeatedly broken

---

[50] Weininger wrote: '*Die Frau lebt stets, auch wenn sie allein ist, in einem Zustand der* **Verschmolzenheit** *mit allen Menschen, die sie kennt* . . . Dieses Verschmolzensein ist etwas durchaus *Sexuelles*' (*Geschlecht und Charakter*, 256, Weininger's emphases).

through by desire so that they are compelled to turn against their lovers who seem both to incorporate and provoke desire. But because this act of aggression is directed against the signified rather than the signifier, the murder must be continually repeated. In Freudian terms, such serial killing represents the compulsive repetition of a response to a profound repressed trauma that constantly re-emerges (like Raul's murdered friend persistently floating back up to the top of the pond into which Raul threw him), and this trauma is Bluebeard's discovery of the non-integrity of the self. Or in Lacanian terms, to constantly attack the signifier and not the signified, as Bluebeard does here, is a marker of neurosis—here, it seems, of a profound cultural neurosis about masculinity which permeates a whole group of texts.[51]

But there is worse to come, for Bluebeard senses that he is threatened not only by forces outside himself which provoke his desire and fear, but also by forces that are an inalienable part of himself. Not only does the ocean wash around the castle walls, but Balász's Judith also recognizes that the walls *inside* Bluebeard's castle are 'oozing water'; in *Ariane et Barbe-bleue* an underground river flows *through* Bluebeard's dungeon; and Paolo's sea-monster looks feminine and appears within the castle itself, because that castle is located on land which used to be covered by the sea which has now retreated. In other words, the 'feminine' or the 'Other' is *inside* as well as *outside* Bluebeard. A rigorous division of Self and Other is therefore not possible and Bluebeard is consistently confronted with his own 'fluid', 'feminine' unconscious, his libido, and other aspects of himself identified as somehow irrational. So his attempts to control or repress the Other by serial murder are doomed to failure.

And just to make Bluebeard's crisis of masculine identity even more drastic, the texts in question also involve some odd gender role reversals so that he finds himself in the role formerly occupied by the woman in the *Märchen*—as a sexual transgressor, as the psychological focus of interest, and as the victim of psychological circumstances beyond the control of himself, his lovers, or his parents. In Marlitt's *Blaubart*, the interior of a building became the locus of the conflict between Bluebeard and his wife. In the texts being discussed here, this conflict seems at first sight to be diminished, since the identification of Bluebeard with his castle is stressed to the exclusion of any sense that the woman or women might have a stake in that place.

---

[51] Jacques Lacan, 'Subversion du sujet et dialectique du désir dans l'inconscient freudien', in *Écrits*, 793–827.

Nevertheless, the emphatic identification of Bluebeard with his castle does not resolve the symbolic conflict, but rather exacerbates it, since the identification of his psyche with his domain is synonymous with his identification with that classic modern symbol of the feminine, the interior. Consequently, only a dramatic act of destruction or self-destruction will completely end Bluebeard's crisis,[52] since in order to eliminate the alien feminine from his castle/mind, Bluebeard must destroy himself as well. The consistent emphasis on destruction by fire involves a further level of gender trouble, because in the *Märchen* tradition death by fire is a punishment often reserved for transgressive women.[53] Given which, it is entirely appropriate that one of Hänschen's fantastic self-stylizations in his monologue should be as Heliogabalus, the degenerate, adolescent Roman emperor of whom Lemprière writes:

to bestow more dignity upon the sex, . . . [he] chose a senate of women, over which his mother presided, and prescribed all the modes and fashions which prevailed in the empire. . . . and not satisfied with following the plain laws of nature, he professed himself to be a woman, and gave himself up to one of his officers. (p. 269)

Such confusion fits well with the slipping of gender boundaries in the texts here.

Bluebeard's crisis is made worse by the fact that the women characters (like Heliogabalus' mother) often behave in transgressive ways which challenge conventional notions of femininity, thus revealing their bisexuality which is so disturbing for Bluebeard himself. In Eulenberg's play, Judith is disobedient in opening the forbidden chamber and such disobedience may be interpreted as a case of mimetic rivalry in which the woman, by making use of the phallic key, challenges traditional gender boundaries. Not only is this scenario replicated in Eulenberg's play, but Judith's very name emphasizes this possibility by recalling the biblical heroine who assumes a masculine role and decapitates Holofernes with his own sword, which conveniently hangs over his bed where he has attempted to seduce her. Then again, after Judith's death Raul elopes with her sister Agnes, whose name suggests that she is an even more stereotypically innocent girl than Judith. But Agnes's elopement undermines that stereotype, because in doing so she

---

[52] Cf. Theweleit, *Männerphantasien*, i. 245–50.
[53] Bottigheimer, *Grimms' Bad Girls and Bold Boys*, 27–9.

compromises her social status and her virtue by claiming the traditionally masculine prerogative of travelling about unchaperoned. And the ending of the text emphasizes Agnes's ambivalent status because although she is not killed by Bluebeard, she is not rescued by her male relatives either. Rather, the last we see of her is described as follows: '*Man sieht Agnes über den Söller jagen und sich hinunterstürzen*' (p. 322). Now, while this stage direction disposes of Agnes for the rest of the action, the significant fact is that we neither witness her death nor see her corpse, which means that she, like Tieck's Mechtilde, the disruptive sister in Bechstein's *Märchen*, and Helmina von Boschau in Karl Hans Strobl's *Madame Blaubart* (1929), successfully challenges the traditional possibilities reserved for women at the end of the *Blaubartmärchen*: punishment, death, or rescue. Indeed, at the end of the play it is more certain that Raul is dead than the two women, and that moral judgements may be passed on him.

Döblin's Ilsebill has a symbolic name, too, which recalls the woman in *KHM* 19, 'Von dem Fischer un syner Fru', who represents a threat to the conventional order of things. In this story, a fish promises to grant a fisherman wishes, and indeed his wife, Ilsebill, wishes her way out of poverty and misery, only to fall back into it when her husband and the fish decide that she has become too greedy.[54] Döblin's Ilsebill is metaphorically greedy inasmuch as she makes use of such masculine rights as free and unchaperoned movement and the public expression of sensuality; for instance, she eats chocolate and eyes up Paolo at a race course. Consequently she, like her namesake, incurs punishment by a monster from the deep. In Schoßleitner's story, the woman surrenders the poison—a traditionally feminine instrument of murder—she had brought for Prince Bluebeard but keeps a (phallic) dagger and attempts to stab the Prince with it. And in Kaiser's play, the threat of the transgressive, unfeminine female is at its most evident, since Jeanne appears equipped with armour and a sword. No wonder, therefore, that Bluebeard's masculinity is threatened by these women.

In short, these texts are dealing with a crisis of a masculinity which has become aware of its non-integrity, its persistent openness to desire, and the constant possibility that it may take on 'feminine' roles while apparently female figures may suddenly become bisexual

---

[54] *KHM*, i. 119–27. Cf. Günter Grass's novel *Der Butt* (Frankfurt am Main: Fischer, 1977), a response to the *Neue Frauenbewegung* of the 1970s based on *KHM* 19, where the female protagonist is called Ilsebill.

or masculine. This crisis is experienced in so profound a way that it is expressed in terms of tragedy and can be temporarily and compulsively alleviated only by sadistic attacks on women who represent the incontrollable Other within and outside the threatened male subject. While earlier versions permitted the wife to transgress gender boundaries and thus to break out of a cycle of violence in a manner which was positively evaluated, here such transgression is no longer seen as positive, but rather as negative and frightening. And while Perrault's version championed women, these texts express a savagery towards women which exceeds anything the nineteenth century had to offer.

CONCLUSIONS AND CONTINUITIES

It seems to me that the crisis of masculinity experienced by Bluebeard was precipitated by the fear of modernity and its attendant disruptions that is evident in Wiegler's essay. This theory is endorsed, for instance, by the fact that where these Bluebeard figures have fathers, their relationships with them are highly problematic and, as in Marlitt's 'Blaubart', the fathers leave a malevolent legacy. Commenting on the contemporary phenomenon of Expressionism, Richard Sheppard reminds us that the motif of a conflict between sons and fathers becomes culturally important at times of social and symbolic upheaval, such as the period in question in Germany:

On the one hand, the father-figure who, by his absence or presence, dominates so many expressionist texts, was clearly the literary hypostasis of the alliance, peculiar to Germany around the Great War, between old, semi-feudal power and new, capitalist power. On the other hand, German society during the same period was fraught with inner contradictions and clearly suffered from a deep-seated fear that this patriarchal constellation, notwithstanding its apparently monumental weight, was fragile, threatened by the sons . . . The proclamation by Nietzsche's Madman of the Death of God perfectly encapsulates this paradoxical situation: the source of authority still exists and wields power over men's unconscious, but that authority, being unreal, is disappearing as that source decays.[55]

That 'monumental weight' recalls Don Juan's stone dead yet un-

[55] Richard Sheppard, 'Unholy Families: The Oedipal Psychopathology of Four Expressionist *Ich-Dramen*', in Richard Sheppard (ed.), *New Ways in Germanistik* (Oxford: Berg, 1990), 164–91 (167).

cannily animate Commander, the father's massive sarcophagus built
to dominate the castle grounds in Schoßleitner's text, and the son's
hatred of his dying father's authority and refusal to be like him—
which nonetheless ends in the tragic inevitability of imitation. This
'unreal authority' can be likened to Lacan's notion of the Symbolic
Order which proved useful in describing the psychologization of the
Bluebeard material in Marlitt's work. The fact that the ultimate
source of patriarchal authority, God, has been pronounced dead
leads, among other things, to a more desperate and aggressive insistence on masculine authority on the part of these Bluebeards. The
patriarchal order, under the corrosive pressure of modernity,
responds by asserting its seemingly disappearing authority with a
violence which needs to be constantly repeated, and is very much of
its time.

This new insistence on seriality is a characteristic feature of
Modernist culture. For instance, this period saw the rise of the
serial detective story in which evil constantly emerges, and must be
repeatedly countered—usually by a celibate detective, since sex and
evil seem to correlate consistently. The new interest in seriality was
also expressed, for instance, in Freud's book *Jenseits des Lustprinzips*
(1920), in which, prompted by such modern phenomena as war
neuroses arising from the Great War, he identified a compulsion to
repeat trauma which defied the creative pleasure principle. From
this, Freud deduced that a primitive and regressive death drive must
lie at the heart of the human psyche, which produces a sadism like
that of Bluebeard. Such interest in the repetition of evil marks the
twentieth century as a whole and the Bluebeard tradition in particular, and seems to be a response to the new problems posed by Evil
after the collapse of a Christian cosmogony, in which Evil was either
explicable or redeemable. After the death of God, Evil was no longer
containable, and this idea is clearly reflected in twentieth-century
treatments of the Bluebeard material which frequently focus on a
pathological seriality.

Moreover, modernity at the turn of the century involved more
than the threat of the *Frauenbewegung*, for in contemporary conservative thought it was also a commonplace to imagine modernity
itself as being immoral and corrupt, and to identify it as Jewish,
feminine, or both.[56] As the reactionary philosopher Otto Weininger

---

[56] David Luft, 'Otto Weininger als Figur des Fin de siècle' and Jean-Michel Palmier,
'Otto Weininger, Wien und die Moderne', both in Jacques Le Rider and Norbert Leser

wrote in his phenomenally influential classic *Geschlecht und Charakter* (1903):

Unsere Zeit, die nicht nur die jüdischeste, sondern auch die weibischeste [*sic*] aller Zeiten ist; die Zeit, für welche die Kunst nur ein Schweißtuch ihrer Stimmungen abgibt, die den künstlerischen Drang aus den Spielen der Tiere abgeleitet hat; die Zeit des leichtgläubigsten Anarchismus, die Zeit ohne Sinn für Recht und Staat, die Zeit der Gattungs-Ethik, die Zeit der seichtesten unter allen denkbaren Geschichtsauffassungen (des historischen Materialismus), die Zeit des Kapitalismus und des Marxismus, die Zeit, in der Geschichte, Leben, Wissenschaft, alles nur mehr Ökonomie und Technik ist; die Zeit, die das Genie für eine Form des Irrsinns erklärt hat, die aber auch keinen großen Künstler, keinen einzigen großen Philosophen mehr besitzt, die Zeit der geringsten Originalität und der größten Originalitätshascherei; die Zeit, die an die Stelle des Ideals der Jungfräulichkeit den Kultus der Demi-Vierge gesetzt hat: *diese Zeit hat auch den Ruhm, die erste zu sein, welche den Koitus bejaht und angebetet hat.* (p. 441)

Many of the authors discussed in this chapter would have known Weininger's ideas, and all of them were responding in the same way to a modernity that was gendered in their minds as sexualized and feminine.[57] Consequently, these perceived threats provoked a defensive reaction that involved a defiant and misogynistic assertion of masculinity. This was certainly the case with Weininger, who imagined that the past was superior to the present because it had involved a more manly masculinity; by the same token, Bluebeard as imagined by Wiegler and Schoßleitner is a perfect instance of such nostalgic ideals legitimized by an imaginary past.

But Weininger proposed a more fanciful solution to the ills of a feminized modernity than a mere return to the past. In his view, the only possible way to redeem the situation would be for women to overcome their womanhood: 'wenn alle Weiblichkeit Unsittlichkeit ist, so muß das Weib aufhören Weib zu sein, und Mann werden' (p. 452). This elimination of the feminine is Bluebeard's project too. But while Weininger argued that the cultural and moral crisis of the modern, feminized world must be overcome by the self-sacrifice of Woman, Bluebeard achieves that end by a violence which is persistently linked with ideas about female sacrifice, as seen in Chapter 3.

(eds.), *Otto Weininger: Werk und Wirkung* (Vienna: Österreichischer Bundesverlag, 1984), 71–9 and 80–95 respectively; and Le Rider, *Modernity and Crises of Identity*, 77–161.

[57] Schoßleitner's texts appeared in *Der Brenner*, a journal in which Weininger's work was widely discussed and which Trakl also read. Stieg writes: 'im *Brenner* werden die schreckenerregendsten Wirkungen von . . . Weininger publiziert' (62–3); and Palmier refers to the influence of these debates on Balász ('Otto Weininger', 83–4).

And while Weininger accepted that the elimination of femininity would result in the extinction of the human race, that resolution of the contemporary cultural crisis could not, in his view, come too soon. Just as the vision at the end of *Geschlecht und Charakter* is apocalyptic, so the denial of the feminine in the Bluebeard texts can end only in catastrophe, with the murder of women and sometimes also with the destruction of Bluebeard himself, a scenario which leaves open no future perspective.

This group of texts marks important developments in the German Bluebeard tradition. There are continuities like the inculpation of the women and the exculpation of Bluebeard, but most striking is the drastic shift in interest towards Bluebeard himself, and the new focus on brutal, serial murder, rather than the more subtle issue of curiosity. On the surface, this new interest in physical violence appears to indicate a return to the Bluebeard tradition pre-dating Marlitt's purely psychological tale of suspense. In fact, however, the psychological emphasis in these texts is more intense than ever, since the authors are extremely interested in Bluebeard's autistic and frightened subjectivity as the source of violence. It seems to me that these texts are, even more than Marlitt's, centrally interested in the subject of civilization as represented by Bluebeard. In the modernist period, that subject undergoes tremendous pressure which forces him to reveal his weaknesses and fissures. In other words, the crises of modernity reveal fundamental contradictions and flaws in the civilized subject and indeed, the very project of civilization, and so in these cases the subject of civilization responds with desperate, gendered violence. This serial violence can only be halted by the destruction of Bluebeard, the civilized subject, himself. And in these tests, the utopian force of the material seems at last to have quite disappeared.

7

'ICH . . . VERLIEß DAS HAUS IM MORGENGRAUEN': BLUEBEARD IN THE LATER TWENTIETH CENTURY

BLAUBART. Erich, mein Freund . . . sag's: in welchem Jahrhundert befinden wir uns jetzt?
ERICH. Fünfzehntes, glaub' ich.
BLAUBART. Da müssen wir uns aber beeilen, damit wir schleunigst ins zwanzigste kommen![1]

After the extraordinary popularity of 'Blaubart' in the early twentieth century, the appeal of that *Märchen* subsequently diminished. It is in the course of the twentieth century that the selective suppression of the tale described in Chapter 2 took place, whereby the Bluebeard material changed from being both adults' and children's literature to more strictly adult material. This development seems to be, at least in part, due to those changes which took place at the turn of the century. Because the texts discussed in the previous chapter turned 'Blaubart' into a savage tale about sadism, seriality, and psychology, it was no longer considered suitable for children. In more recent decades, however, a remarkable number of authors have returned inquisitively to the Bluebeard material, and once again it has been given characteristically contemporary forms.

'VOM ARMEN BB': BLUEBEARD IN RECENT MEN'S WRITING

Bluebeard goes comparatively silent in the middle years of the century only to be rediscovered in its last three decades. Moreover, there has been an efflorescence of new Bluebeard works since the mid-1980s. If the development of the *Märchen* correlates with broader social and cultural developments, then there may be a straightforward explanation for this pattern. While during the middle years of the century Europe was preoccupied with some monstrous

[1] Gerd Winkler, *Mike Blaubart* (television film), 1967; quotation from *Gerd Winklers Mike Blaubart* (Frankfurt am Main: Heine, 1968), 84.

political Bluebeards and their very real chambers of horrors, from 1967–8 onward a later generation began to respond to and attempt to deal with the legacy of that period. One form which that response took was the emergence of a women's movement that had profound social and symbolic consequences. It seems to me that this newfound interest in the Bluebeard material, which had traditionally addressed gender issues, was a response by both sexes (albeit in some cases very indirectly) to a new critical awareness of a patriarchal society which could produce megalomaniacs like Stalin and Hitler.

All but one of the eleven original German works from the postwar period listed in Hartwig Suhrbier's bibliography (1984) are by men, and the texts (with a few exceptions) share certain tendencies.[2] They implicitly respond both to the broader historical crises described above and more specifically to the *Neue Frauenbewegung*. These texts focus on the Bluebeard figure and marginalize the female characters, and tend to develop the early twentieth-century conception of Bluebeard as the misunderstood victim of society, women, or a hostile cosmos, a concern that is replicated, for example, in the title of Suhrbier's essay, 'Blaubart—Leitbild und Leidfigur'. Thus the protagonist of Janosch's 'Blaubart' (1972) is a victim of his own ugliness and a superficial society.[3] Hildebrandt's protagonist in *Blaubart Mitte 40* (1977) is the victim of a mysterious murder plot which threatens him and kills off his seven girlfriends one by one, and although he is innocent, he comes to be suspected of these murders himself.[4] Frisch's *Blaubart* (1982) is a victim of existential guilt and emotional suffering, and Rühmkorf's Bluebeard in 'Blaubarts letzte Reise' (1982) of a repressive upbringing.[5] In all cases, the characterization of Bluebeard as a victim is a new variant on his exculpation. But in several of these texts Bluebeard is no longer the anomaly, the exceptional being or the *Übermensch* he often was in earlier writing, but has come to resemble Everyman.

---

[2] Hartwig Suhrbier, *Blaubarts Geheimnis: Märchen und Erzählungen, Gedichte und Stücke* (Cologne: Diederichs, 1984), 211–22.

[3] Janosch (ps. Horst Eckart), 'Blaubart', in *Janosch erzählt Grimms Märchen und zeichnet für Kinder von heute* (Weinheim: Beltz & Gelberg, 1972), 161–4.

[4] Dieter Hildebrandt, *Blaubart Mitte 40* (Hamburg: Hoffmann & Campe, 1977). Cf. my article ' "Du bist in einem Mörderhaus": Representing German History through the *Märchen* of "Blaubart" and "Der Räuberbräutigam" in Works by Dieter Hildebrandt and Helma Sanders-Brahms', in Mary Fulbrook and Martin Swales (eds.), *Representing the German Nation* (Manchester: Manchester University Press, 2000), 118–35.

[5] Max Frisch, *Blaubart* (Frankfurt am Main: Suhrkamp, 1982) (also as a radio play, Süddeutscher Rundfunk/Westdeutscher Rundfunk, 4 Nov. 1982).

Concomitantly, these texts involve a suspicion that women are powerful yet incomprehensible beings who make Bluebeard their victim. In Hildebrandt's thriller, the murderer is Bluebeard's ex-wife; in Frisch's novella, Bluebeard's six wives all leave him; in Janosch's 'Blaubart', the innocent suitor Bluebeard is rejected by a series of shallow women who are put off by his ugliness, so that the final woman in the series, who does marry him, must be put through a long, transferred punishment before she can benefit in any way from her marriage; and in Rühmkorf's story, Bluebeard's twisted mother is at the root of all the murders and fully deserves her violent end. As a result, women characters in these texts are often the objects of physical violence. While Bluebeard is an out-and-out serial killer only in h.c. artmann's poems (1958) (which belong firmly in the *fin-de-siècle* tradition) and in Rühmkorf's story, in Hildebrandt's novel and Frisch's novella, too, the murder of women is central. Alternatively, Bluebeard may be presented as a metaphorical ladykiller. In Hildebrandt's novel and Winkler's play Bluebeard is a Don Juan type; and even Frisch's existentially tortured protagonist is a serial husband.

Where the women characters are not murdered or blamed, they may be mocked or made to look foolish; and some of these texts imply that, at heart, modern women secretly hanker after some nostalgic ideal of masculinity. When Winkler's superman Blaubart is the object of a police search for kidnapping and suspected murder, the female colleagues of the woman he has ravished defend him and turn against the police:

ZWEITES MÄDCHEN. Dabei—dabei—...
ERSTES MÄDCHEN.   —dabei war kein Mann in meinem ganzen verhunzten Leben so nett zu mir—
ZWEITES MÄDCHEN. —wie er.
ERSTES MÄDCHEN. So entschieden und sicher.
ZWEITES MÄDCHEN. So zärtlich und sympathisch. . . .
ERSTES MÄDCHEN. Werden Sie ihre Hunde auf ihn hetzen?
KOMMISSAR (off). Wenn es sein muß: ja.
ZWEITES MÄDCHEN. Oh, wie schrecklich!
ERSTES MÄDCHEN. Das können Sie doch nicht tun, sie mit ihrem hinter-hältigen Lächeln! (pp. 29–30)

Similarly, Hildebrandt describes one of Bluebeard's liberated lovers as follows:

Linda war ein Mädchen für alles, für alles, was gerade in der Welt an der Reihe ist: Marxismus, Feminismus, Zen-Buddhismus, romantisches Erbe, neuen Konservatismus. Er hatte mit ihr schon eine Menge Weltanschauungen durch-

gemacht und viele Aggressionen erlebt, . . . Einmal, als sie vor lauter Emanzi-
pationsfuror fast häßlich geworden war, lagen sie im Bett, und sie sagte, mit
einem plötzlichen Lachen: 'Du, ich glaub, ich spinne. Unterdrück mich noch ein
bißchen.' (pp. 68–9)

In other words, while these texts as a group come nowhere near the
horror and sadism of the *fin de siècle* texts, they do use 'Blaubart' to
describe or reassert a model of masculinity which is threatened by
major changes.

'ZIMMER IM TRAUME SIND ZUMEIST FRAUENZIMMER':[6] INSIDE *DAS HAUS DER KRANKHEITEN*

Hildebrandt's *Blaubart Mitte 40* appeared in 1977. Coincidentally,
although it was written in 1958, Unica Zürn's Surrealist text *Das Haus
der Krankheiten: Geschichten und Bilder einer Gelbsucht* was also first
published (posthumously) in 1977, and takes issue with precisely such
masculinist ideas as those which underpin Hildebrandt's novel.[7] At
first sight Zürn's text seems to fall outside the explicitly feminist
agenda of the 1970s because of its apparently private and apolitical
themes, but in fact it deals with the gender issues so hotly debated in
those years and anticipates more explicitly political writing by
women which followed decades later—and indeed exceeds many
such texts in its sophistication.

Das Haus der Krankheiten is a curious text, both formally and
thematically. It takes the form of a diary consisting of ten chapters of
varying length and seventeen illustrations. The narrator states that
this shape was dictated not by formal or generic criteria, but by the
demands of sickness: 'Ich weiß . . . warum ich dieses Buch anfertige:
um noch eine Weile krank zu sein. Ich kann jeden Tag neue, leere
Seiten hineinlegen, die beschrieben werden müssen, und so lange
werde ich krank bleiben' (p. 71). This formulation expresses the
fundamental dilemma experienced by the narrator, since she is ill
and has been in the house of sicknesses, which resembles a hospital
and sometimes a prison, for almost a year (p. 56). This house has the
topography of a female body, since the rooms are called 'das

---

[6] Sigmund Freud, *Die Traumdeutung* (1900), in Freud, *Studienausgabe*, ed. Alexander
Mitscherlich, Angela Richards, and James Strachey, 11 vols. (Frankfurt am Main: Fischer,
1989), ii. 348.
[7] Unica Zürn, 'Das Haus der Krankheiten. Geschichten und Bilder einer Gelbsucht'
(1958), in Zürn, *Gesamtausgabe*, ed. Günter Bose and Erich Brinkmann, 8 vols. (Berlin:
Brinkmann & Bose, 1988–   ), iv. 1. 43–78.

Kopfgewölbe', 'die Busenstube', and so forth, a manner of representing the body identified by Freud in *Die Traumdeutung* (1900) as typical of dream logic (a highly privileged sphere of experience, according to the Surrealists).[8] On one hand, the state of illness is magical, visionary, and pleasurable; on the other, as the narrator recuperates she begins to feel obliged to leave the house and take up her old activities and duties once more. At the end of the text she is confronted with a choice. If she stays longer in the house of sickness, she will be condemned to stay for ever; but if she leaves, it is for a less magical, possibly hostile world.

In the first chapter, we are introduced to the narrator and the bizarre condition which afflicts her: the 'Herzen in [ihren] Augen' have been shot out by someone she calls her 'Todfeind'. While this condition does not affect her vision, it means that her gaze is always drawn to a point in the distance, on the left of the horizon, where she knows her 'Todfeind' must be. This chapter also introduces the narrator's unsympathetic, authoritarian physician, Dr Mortimer, who runs the house of sicknesses and dispenses narcotic injections. In the second chapter the narrator describes him as her 'eigener Tod' in person, and goes on to reflect on the 'Todfeind' who is apparently a different character and who, it transpires, is also the narrator's lover:

Dieser Mensch, der mich wissen ließ, daß er mich liebt, verfolgt mich mit seiner Liebe auf so rächende Art und Weise, daß ich einem seiner zukünftigen Angriffe erliegen werde. . . . Ich beklage mich bitter darüber, daß Liebe und Haß so dicht beieinander liegen. (p. 56)

The 'Todfeind'/lover has two important attributes or manifestations: a white eagle and a red scorpion, which to some extent embody respectively his positive and negative aspects. The third chapter describes how the narrator is tempted to believe that she is better and to leave the house of sicknesses, but knows that this would be detrimental. The fourth chapter consists of reflections on violence in love and the narrator's conviction that 'Ewig das Opfer zu sein, ist mein Schicksal'. The savagery of these thoughts and images is striking, since her lover's violence is symbolized by the phallic act of stabbing, 'das Messer im Herzen' (p. 61). The narrator's own position, on the other hand, is one of constant masochism, and she expresses frustration with her heart and its 'widerlichen, weiblichen Charakter'. Nonetheless, she defends love as a 'Segen' and accepts that she will

---

[8] Freud, *Studienausgabe*, ii. 106.

never escape it. The fifth chapter, 'Verbotene Zimmer', describes some of the rooms in the house, including two which the narrator may not enter: the 'Raum der Herzen' and the 'Zimmer der Augen'. She says of the latter:

Auch Augen gehören zuweilen zu den 'verbotenen Zimmern'. . . . Ich habe oft eine furchtbare Lust nach verbotenen Augen. Wenn ich mich nicht mehr beherrschen kann, blicke ich hinein, wenn ich sicher sein kann, daß es die anderen Augen nicht merken. Aber auch das ist stets mit der größten Gefahr verbunden und geht schon leicht in die Richtung der schwarzen Magie, die ich, da ich sie am eigenen Leibe erfuhr, um jeden Preis einem anderen ersparen möchte. Das Zimmer der Augen im Haus der Krankheiten wird für mich eines Tages—das ahne ich schon—das Zimmer des Ritters Blaubart werden. Man wird sehen, was das geben wird. Mir ahnt nichts Gutes. (p. 65)

The narrator did once look through the keyhole of this room and meet the eyes of her 'Todfeind' within, but narrowly escaped harm. In the sixth chapter, the 'Saal der Bäuche' and the 'Busenstube' are described, both of which disgust the narrator because of their overtly physical nature and, it is implied, their particular associations with the female body. In the seventh chapter, despite the appeal of the 'Haus der Krankheiten', the narrator decides to leave. This she does in the following chapter, but the uninspiring, depressing outside world drives her back to the house of sicknesses. In the eighth chapter, the narrator describes her split mental state, wanting both to be inside and outside the house; and in the ninth chapter Dr Mortimer confronts her with the choice of leaving or being condemned to stay for ever. Dr Mortimer is transformed into an aggressive, grotesque, military officer, the sight of whom so horrifies the narrator that she decides to leave. The tenth, final chapter describes her last night in the 'Haus der Krankheiten', when she finally finds the courage to enter the 'Zimmer der Augen'. There, she finds the following objects: her own 'Augenherzen' on a silver plate, which spring back into her eyes (it has already been hinted that Dr Mortimer might have been the true thief); a red scorpion which threatens her and which she crushes; and a wax doll in her own image, transfixed with pins, which she throws onto the fire. A white eagle flies in through the window, looks the narrator in the eyes and embraces her before flying back to the left of the horizon where the 'Todfeind'/lover resides, leaving an ecstatic smile hanging (Cheshire Cat-like) in the air. The narrator concludes: 'Ich war getröstet und verließ das Haus im Morgengrauen' (p. 78).

Das Haus der Krankheiten does not appear in Bluebeard biblio-graphies, since its title does not include any reference to the *Märchen*. Indeed, the reference to 'Ritter Blaubart' quoted above is the only explicit one in this text. This text nonetheless fits neatly into the Bluebeard tradition. First, although the text's loose, diaristic form is not one commonly associated with the *Märchen* tradition, frag-mentary reference to *Märchen* is a characteristic aspect of the tradition both during and after the Modernist period, reflecting the notion that simple linear and closed narratives, as *Märchen* are often believed to be, can no longer be written. As the narrator of Rilke's *Malte Laurids Brigge* (1910) says, with reference to just such an ideal of narrative: 'Daß man erzählte, wirklich erzählte, das muß vor meiner Zeit gewesen sein.'[9] Zürn's narrator strikes the same note: 'Wo ist das alte Fräulein hin verschwunden, das mich als junges Mädchen betreute und mir so viel . . . erzählte . . .?' (p. 72). Nevertheless, despite this loss, the text privileges the idea of the *Märchen* and an associated, supportive narrative community, for it involves the unexplained, fleeting, yet crucial presence of a helper figure: '. . . der weißhaarige Herr, der mir die Märchensuppen meiner Kindheit von neuem und immer wieder Löffel für Löffel einflößte. . . . es war mir, als kostete ich vom Salz des Lebens' (p. 156). And when Dr Mortimer refuses to grant the narrator a final wish, he rages:

'Die Geschichten, die sich die Leute von der Erfüllung ihrer letzten Wünsche erzählen, sind Märchen, . . . nichts als Märchen. Mir als Arzt wurden im Laufe meiner Praxis eine Menge letzter Wünsche vorgetragen. Ich gebe in diesen Fällen eine beruhigende Injektion. Letzte Wünsche'—wieder stampfte er klirrend auf den Boden und krähte—'werden nicht erfüllt! Das wäre ein Verstoß gegen die Hausordnung und ein Verbrechen der Ärzte gegen die Menschlich-keit.' (pp. 74–5)

In other words, *Märchen* are the antithesis of the oppressive, medical/military 'Hausordnung'.

Second, motifs specifically connected with the *Blaubartmärchen* are emphasized, e.g. through colour symbolism, which is consistently important in Zürn's writing (cf. the '*Gelb*sucht' in the title). Thus, the 'Märchensuppe' described above is served in a *blue* dish and because this colour is used elsewhere in the text *only* to describe the eyes of the 'Todfeind'/lover and in the name of 'Ritter Blaubart' himself, it

---

[9] Rainer Maria Rilke, *Die Aufzeichnungen des Malte Laurids Brigge* (1910) (Leipzig: Insel, 1958), 185. On the fragmentation of the *Märchen* in Modernism, see Thomas Eicher (ed.), *Märchen und Moderne: Fallbeispiele einer intertextuellen Relation* (Münster: Lit, 1996).

makes an intimate link between apparently disparate elements in the narrative.

Third, and most importantly, there are structural parallels between the *Blaubartmärchen* and *Das Haus der Krankheiten*. In both narratives, the female protagonist finds herself in a mysterious house ruled by a male authority figure in which a room is forbidden her. Although the ruler of Zürn's house is more difficult to identify than the character of Bluebeard in the *Märchen*, two powerful male figures whom we can associate with Bluebeard feature in *Das Haus der Krankheiten*: the double figure of the 'Todfeind'/lover and Dr Mortimer. In the *Märchen*, Bluebeard is both the heroine's physically violent enemy *and* her lover or husband and similarly, Zürn's double figure of the 'Todfeind'/lover reproduces that dual role. And although Dr Mortimer is a separate character, he, like Bluebeard, rules in the house and speaks perverse prohibitions, notably in the chapter entitled 'Ein *aufschluß*reiches Gespräch' (my emphasis), a title which is a very apt pun in this context. He has death in his name (*Mort*imer) and is apostrophized as the narrator's 'eigener Tod'. Nevertheless, it is also implied at times that he may himself be another aspect of the 'Todfeind'/lover figure. It appears, for instance, that it is he who has removed the narrator's 'Augenherzen' even though the 'Todfeind', believed to be far away behind the horizon, is said to be the culprit. Just as the 'Todfeind' is linked to the deadly, phallic 'Messer im Herzen', so Mortimer is habitually armed with a narcotically phallic syringe. At another point the 'Todfeind' is called 'der Meister-schütze', since it is thought that he actually shot out the narrator's eyes with a pistol, and Mortimer has a pistol too. Moreover, Mortimer is like the positive incarnation of the narrator's lover because he sometimes resembles 'einem Menschen, der mir [the narrator] sehr teuer gewesen war . . .' (p. 50).

But despite these resemblances, the text makes it clear that no simple identifications can be made between Mortimer, the 'Todfeind'/lover, and 'Ritter Blaubart'. Mortimer is not the true ruler of the house but rather a 'Gehaltsempfänger'; the 'Todfeind'/lover is absent; and the third authority figure, 'Ritter Blaubart', is an analogy rather than a sentient presence ('Das Zimmer der Augen . . . wird für mich . . . das Zimmer des Ritters Blaubart'). So it seems that, as in Marlitt's text, Bluebeard is a way of naming an abstract, intuitively grasped Symbolic Order. Consequently, the other male figures in the text are merely its agents or avatars.

In the *Märchen*, the secret chamber contains knowledge—female corpses—which is forbidden to the woman. Paradoxically, that knowledge is both dangerous and empowering, because the discovery of the bodies both puts the woman in danger and precipitates the end of Bluebeard's cycle of violence. In *Das Haus der Krankheiten* the narrator, like Bluebeard's wife, is tempted in a manner which has sexual undertones ('furchtbare Lust'), and she enters the room knowing that great danger is involved. Here she finds, *inter alia*, a mutilated image of her own body (the doll), which, like the dead wives in earlier versions, prefigures her own death. She also meets the wrath of her enemy/lover in the threatening form of a red scorpion. Nevertheless, she finds the strength to kill it and is rewarded with the restoration of her 'Augenherzen', i.e. the physical and emotional integrity which had been denied her in Bluebeard's house, a restoration which allows her to leave the house. But while Zürn's text seems to end on a note of hope, this conclusion is in fact problematic, like Perrault's with its deeply ambiguous repetition of 'honnête', since there is a crucial semantic ambiguity in the apparently simple phrase 'ich verließ das Haus im Morgen*grauen*' (my emphasis).

The events in the 'Zimmer der Augen', or Bluebeard's chamber, are central to the meaning of *Das Haus der Krankheiten*, not least because Zürn makes a persistent link between vision and love. For instance, the narrator's eyes do not have a round iris but are marked by the classic symbol of love, the heart, a condensed dream image which looks forward to the Lacanian notion that desire is located in the gaze.[10] In *Das Haus der Krankheiten*, too, vision is the source of desire—and it is precisely this faculty which the 'Todfeind' has denied the narrator. This explains the significance of the 'Zimmer der Augen', since vision and the concomitant ability to love or desire are the content of the forbidden chamber. On regaining her vision, the narrator is able to encounter her Beloved, an act which gives her the courage to leave the magical yet debilitating house of sicknesses.

But why should the heroine be denied her vision and the ability to love and desire? Why is she scared to death of her lover and why are love and desire so very dangerous for her? Who is this Bluebeard who

---

[10] Jacques Lacan, *Les Quatre Concepts fondamentaux de la psychanalyse* (Paris: Seuil, 1973). Lacan did not develop this theory fully until the 1960s, i.e. after *Das Haus der Krankheiten* was written, but a shared intellectual background accounts for its similarity to Zürn's writing. Zürn's text 'MistAKE' is dedicated to 'Monsieur le prof/LACAN/U.Z./fou de joie–', in *Gesamtausgabe*, iv. 2, 408–15.

does not match exactly any specific figure in the text? And what is the nature of the order he enforces? In order to arrive at more precise answers to these questions, an excursus on Surrealist theories of vision, desire, and artistic practice as expounded by Zürn's collaborator and companion Hans Bellmer is revealing.

'ABOLIR LE MUR QUI SÉPARE LA FEMME DE SON IMAGE': SURREALIST AESTHETICS, HANS BELLMER, AND *L'ANATOMIE DE L'IMAGE*[11]

Das Haus der Krankheiten was written in the theoretical context of an European intellectual and artistic avant-garde which involved Surrealism and Lacanian psychoanalysis, two major schools of thought in the twentieth century. Zürn's work developed in collaboration with her Parisian Surrealist contemporaries, Bellmer in particular; and both Zürn's and Bellmer's work and thinking evolved in close connection with Lacan's.[12]

Surrealist theory elevates Woman to the highest poetic status as Muse and medium by virtue of her perceived closer relationship to the highly valued spheres of childhood, Nature, and the Unconscious. It also emphatically identifies both the creative act and the gaze of desire as masculine, thus excluding the feminine subject from the inseparable practices of creativity and desire.[13] This theoretical context produces a curious, painful, and split self-reflexivity in the work of Zürn and other women Surrealists, and that dilemma permeates *Das Haus der Krankheiten*, since the image of the house itself

---

[11] Hans Bellmer, *Petite Anatomie de l'inconscient physique ou l'anatomie de l'image* (1957) (Paris: Eric Losfeld, 1977).

[12] Lacan's first publications were in the Surrealist journal *Minotaure*, and he praised *L'Anatomie de l'image*. On links between psychoanalysis and Surrealism and Lacan's part in that tradition, see Elisabeth Roudinesco, *Jacques Lacan & Co.: A History of Psychoanalysis in France, 1925–1985*, trans. Jeffrey Mehlman (London: Free Association Books, 1990); Elizabeth Wright, *Psychoanalytic Criticism: Theory in Practice*, 2nd rev. edn. (London: Routledge, 1987), 118. On Bellmer and Lacan, see Malcolm Bowie, *Lacan* (London: Fontana, 1991), 251; Peter Webb with Robert Short, *Hans Bellmer* (London: Quartet Books, 1985), 161–79 (178); Sigrid Weigel, 'Hans Bellmer Unica Zürn—Junggesellenmaschinen und die Magie des Imaginären', in Inge Stephan and Sigrid Weigel (eds.), *Weiblichkeit und Avantgarde* (Hamburg: Argument, 1987), 187–230.

[13] Cf. Whitney Chadwick, *Women Artists and the Surrealist Movement* (London: Thames & Hudson, 1985); Gwen Raaberg, 'The Problematics of Women and Surrealism'; Rudolf E. Kuenzli, 'Surrealism and Misogyny'; Robert J. Belton, 'Speaking with Forked Tongues: "Male" Discourse in "Female" Surrealism?', all in Mary Ann Caws, Rudolf E. Kuenzli, and Gwen Raaberg (eds.), *Surrealism and Women* (Cambridge, Mass.: MIT Press, 1991), 1–10; 17–25 and 50–62 respectively; Weigel, 'Hans Bellmer Unica Zürn'.

is a kind of self-portrait which is identified with the narrator even though she is simultaneously alienated from it. Bellmer's treatise *L'Anatomie de l'image*, in setting out key aspects of such theories in an extreme manner, can be taken as a paradigmatic expression of these central Surrealist concerns, since discussions of Surrealism frequently cite Bellmer's project as the most characteristic manifestation of that movement's project of recovering (masculine) desire in art.[14] And Bellmer's project can also be seen as a kind of Bluebeard thinking.

'LES IMAGES DU MOI': THE MALE ARTIST AND LOVER

In *L'Anatomie de l'image*, Bellmer sets out the way in which he perceives the human body and psyche and explains how such perceptions influence art. Essentially, he claims that the body and psyche are inseparable because the individual subject cannot see his own—or any other—body objectively, so that bodies become merely images onto which psychological patterns are projected. Consequently, the body is a malleable, protean, and psychological entity rather than a fixed, physical one, since it changes according to psychological demands. Indeed, such physical sensations as pain or desire may be displaced from one part of the body to another, creating a fantastic virtual anatomy which is superimposed on the real, as in a toothache sufferer's transfer of pain from his tooth to his clenched fist (p. 11), or in some cases of hysteria, where the sufferers effectively rearrange their anatomy according to psychological demands, so that for instance a hysteric might imagine that she is seeing with her nose (p. 15). In other words, the relationship between the parts of the human body is metonymic. And in extreme cases of pain, hysteria, or similar states, the subject can take this psycho-physical reversibility even further, creating its own virtual *Doppelgänger* onto which physical sensation is projected. Therefore, Bellmer believes that the real human body always appears incomplete to the subject who inhabits it (or, in Lacanian terms, the subject is organized around a central lack).[15] He sums up: 'démonstration est faite de la présence d'une

---

[14] Cf. most of the studies in n. 13.

[15] Bellmer anticipates Lacan's essay 'La Signification du phallus', first published in 1958, one year after *L'Anatomie de l'image*. In *Écrits* (Paris: Seuil, 1966), 685–95. See also Wright, *Psychoanalytic Criticism*, 117. Of Lacan's published works, Bellmer must have relied on 'Le Stade du miroir comme formateur de la fonction du je' (paper given 1936, published 1949), and 'L'Aggressivité en psychanalyse' (1948), *Écrits*, 101–24.

réalité incomplète à laquelle est opposée son image par l'intervention d'un élément moteur condensant le réel et le virtuel en une unité supérieure' (p. 25).

Bellmer goes on to apply this crucial insight to desire. Although the lover's own body seems to him a 'réalité incomplète', he may achieve an illusion of completeness by unconsciously projecting his own image onto his object of desire, which can then reflect his own image back to him in a more satisfactory way. Therefore, desire is a process which is visual, and, in the last analysis, self-referential because all the lover perceives is an image of himself and his own desire, not his beloved at all.[16] Given which, Bellmer argues:

Il est certain qu'on ne se demandait pas assez sérieusement jusqu'à présent, dans quelle mesure l'image de la femme désirée serait prédéterminée par l'image de l'homme qui désire, donc en dernier lieu par une série de projections du phallus, qui allaient en détail de la femme vers son ensemble. (pp. 30–2)

Bellmer considers this 'predetermination' total, illustrating his point with drawings in which a monster phallus is superimposed onto and obscures female nudes.[17] In short, Bellmer describes the exercise of desire as the exclusive prerogative of the masculine subject which uses and erases a feminine object to produce its own phallic image and thus provide itself with an illusion of plenitude.

In his treatise, Bellmer proposes to undertake a thorough investigation of these processes in order to gain greater insight into what he calls the 'anatomy of desire', and describes that exploration as follows:

Dès que la femme sera au niveau de sa vocation experimentale, accessible aux permutations, aux promesses algébriques, subsceptible de céder aux caprices transsubstantiels, dès qu'elle sera extensible, rétrécible, à l'épiderme et aux jointures préservées des inconvénients naturels du montage et du démontage— on nous renseignera définitivement sur l'anatomie du désir, mieux que ne le fait la pratique de l'amour. (p. 38)

By this, Bellmer means that Woman is mere educational, experimental, and endlessly manipulable material, from which it follows that the male lover and the male artist are essentially the same because each constantly rearranges images of the female body in his own image. Consequently, according to Bellmer, the ideal means of

---

[16] Cf. Lacan's notion of the 'scopic drive'. See Wright, *Psychoanalytic Criticism*, 117–21.

[17] Cf. Lacan, 'La Signification du phallus'; and Weigel, 'Hans Bellmer Unica Zürn', 202–3.

exploring the 'anatomy of desire' is through art (or his own art, at least), because it is a concrete, visual representation of such psychological processes. He summarizes these ideas most clearly and succinctly when he says:

Le Nôtre: Comme le jardinier oblige le buis à vivre sous forme de boule, de cône, de cube, l'homme impose à l'image de la femme ses élémentaires certitudes, les habitudes géométriques et algébriques de sa pensée. (p. 41)

The imposition of masculine desire, just like the imposition of stylized artistic form on an image of a woman, is said to be like the way in which very formal gardening in the style of Le Nôtre forces an artificial, implicitly masculine order on an implicitly feminine Nature. For a Surrealist, that is, a member of a movement which claimed to see conventional order as oppressive and to celebrate the destruction of all such conventional standards, such a statement seems incongruous. (Indeed, it might be argued that Bellmer's statement indicates the stark limits of Surrealism's claims to be subversive.)

Finally, Bellmer makes a leap from visual art to language: 'le corps est comparable à une phrase qui vous inviterait à la désarticuler, pour que se recomposent, à travers une série d'anagrammes sans fin, ses contenus véritables' (pp. 43–4). He means that verbal art functions in exactly the same manner as visual art, except that in the former it is not visual images of the body which are dismembered and rearranged, but language itself. He also wrote, in the afterword to a collection of anagrams and drawings by Zürn: 'Auch der Satz ist wie ein Körper, der uns einzuladen scheint, ihn zu zergliedern, damit sich in einer endlosen Reihe von Anagrammen aufs Neue fügt, was er in Wahrheit enthält.'[18] This proposition is the exact reverse of that in *L'Anatomie de l'image*; and this reversibility demonstrates how alike Bellmer perceives art and language to be.

By implication, therefore, Bellmer's concepts of the masculine gaze, artistic practice, and theoretical exploration are incontestably violent ('zergliedern'), and in *L'Anatomie de l'image* he makes this aggression explicit by equating the artist with the sexual criminal and glorifying the active mutilation of the female body in the name of art:

Pour avoir des preuves objectives [of the workings of desire], on aura recours par conséquent à l'artisan criminel par la passion la plus humainement sensible et la plus belle, celle d'abolir le mur qui sépare la femme de son image. D'après le

---

[18] In Bellmer's afterword to Zürn's volume *Hexentexte* (1954), in Zürn, *Das Weisse mit dem roten Punkt: Texte und Zeichnungen*, ed. Inge Morgenroth (Frankfurt am Main: Ullstein, 1988), 223–4 (223).

souvenir exact que nous gardons d'un certain document photographique, un homme, pour transformer sa victime, avait étroitement ficelé ses cuisses, ses épaules, sa poitrine, d'un fil de fer serré, entrecroisé à tout hasard, provoquant des bousuflures de chair, des triangles sphériques irréguliers, allongeant des plis, des lèvres malpropres, multipliant des seins jamais vus en des emplacements inavouables. (pp. 39–40)

Unsurprisingly, Bellmer's visual work represents violence, for instance, the dismembered dolls in the photographic collections *Die Puppe* (1934), *Les Jeux de la poupée* (1949), and the photograph of a cruelly deformed and constricted 'Unica' (1958), a nude wrapped up in string or wire as described in *L'Anatomie de l'image*. (1958, it should be noted, was one year after the appearance of *L'Anatomie de l'image* as well as the year in which *Das Haus der Krankheiten* was written.[19])

Comparisons can be made between Bellmer's work, the Bluebeard of Marlitt's novella, and the *fin-de-siècle* anti-feminist vogue. First, the masculine subject—Bluebeard, the lover, or the artist—is the centre of all interest and activity. Like the Victorian Bluebeard collector, Bellmer's interest consists in undertaking a brutally rational and deadly classification of defunct, dismembered objects which have been (violently) torn out of their contexts in the name of science ('l'homme impose à l'image de la femme ses élémentaires certitudes, les habitudes géométriques et algébriques de sa pensée'). Second, the feminine object is quite marginal—to the point of being violently effaced under the sign of the phallus—and useful only as a means of helping the masculine subject to constitute itself and fend off a sense of incompleteness. This is a radicalized version of the crisis of masculine identity experienced at the turn of the century. Like the women in Bluebeard's chamber, women figure in Bellmer's treatise only as petrified objects of violence and dismemberment, as dolls, that is, as extreme, miniaturized versions of the works of art collected by Marlitt's Dorn, that serve merely to reflect, and be effaced by, phallic desire. Third, just as I observed in my two previous chapters that violence and control were becoming increasingly psychologized, here that process is taken further still, because Bellmer sees the physical world and physical violence as being purely subordinate to (rather than merely being influenced by) psychological processes. The violence involved has become more pervasive than it was at the

---

[19] Photograph reproduced in Webb and Short, *Hans Bellmer*, 232 and Weigel, 'Hans Bellmer Unica Zürn', 190. Webb and Short stress Bellmer's emphasis on Zürn's resemblance to his Doll, 216–21.

turn of the century. Then, Bluebeard murdered only in states of extreme fear and crisis and was in all ways an exceptional man. But according to Bellmer, such violence and dismemberment is ubiquitous, a fundamental truth of masculinity. Violence against the feminine is practised not only by criminals or extraordinary men, but by all masculine subjects when gazing on an object of desire; and indeed, more sweepingly still, by all users of language, since, according to Bellmer, the very manipulation of language is like the dismembering of bodies.[20]

Reading *L'Anatomie de l'image* in the light of 'Blaubart' gives a new twist to the structural similarities between 'Blaubart' and the Genesis narrative in respect of the inevitability of evil and original sin because, just as in the Old Testament original sin was ubiquitous, here, language is ubiquitous because it forms the human subject. And because language according to Bellmer is inherently violent, the ideas in his treatise amount to a reinscription of the myth of original sin in the sense of a pervasive, damaging legacy of the fathers which they can never evade (Lacan describes the ubiquitous Symbolic Order as being initiated by the 'Name of the Father').[21] Just as the protagonist of Frisch's *Blaubart* has become Everyman, tortured by a universal, existential guilt, and just as Winkler's *Mike Blaubart* ends with the slogan: 'Männer, werdet wie Blaubart!', in Bellmer's thinking all men are Bluebeard, and this is to be accepted, even approved of. In other words, in Bellmer's work the proliferation and internalization of subliminally violent forms of control and regulation as described by Elias and Foucault reach new extremes from which there is allegedly no escape. Consequently, the potentially utopian conclusion of Perrault's tale where a cycle of violence may be broken is, by implication, no longer available.

'ABOLIR . . . LA FEMME': WOMEN AS OBJECTS AND SUBJECTS

Bellmer does not develop the implications of this theory for the Surrealist woman. Indeed, Surrealism as a whole, like Lacanian

---

[20] According to Lacan too, the use of narrative itself is a compulsive repetition of the traumatic fantasy of the fragmented body which underlies the formative mirror stage and the painful emergence of the unified subject into language, enforced by the threat of castration (dismemberment and wounding). Lacan, 'Le Stade du miroir'; and Wright, *Psychoanalytic Criticism*, 113.

[21] See Lacan, 'L'Instance de la lettre dans l'inconscient ou la raison depuis Freud' (1957), in *Écrits*, 493–528.

psychoanalysis, prefers to imagine Woman as a sublime mystery. Nevertheless, Bellmer's theory has two major consequences for the Surrealist woman. First, the female body is effectively erased by the masculine gaze and desire. Second, subjectivity, desire, and artistic enterprise are gendered as so emphatically masculine that women are excluded from being subjects, lovers, and artists. Given which, the Surrealist woman is the object not only of external but also of internal violence. She must contend with two distinct yet theoretically linked threats of dismemberment. The first is the dismembering gaze of the artist or lover, and the second is her own, already fragmentary, precarious, subjective state which precludes her from being an artist or a lover in the conventional (i.e. masculine) sense. Her subjectivity is at best uncertain and at worst disunified, chaotic, or psychotic, since the simple, stabilizing option of projecting the male phallic desire onto a malleable female beloved is not available to the Surrealist woman. Consequently, the psychotic doubling against which Bellmer warns is more likely to happen to her.

This kind of theory produces a curious split self-reflexivity in the work of Surrealist women. Sigrid Weigel points out that there are some (albeit rare) expressions of frustration with this state of affairs—or rather, with the state of femininity itself—in Zürn's *œuvre*. For instance, the narrator of *Notizen einer Blutarmen* (1957–8), being forced to project her gaze onto herself and not outward, says: 'Ich habe mich in mir um und umgedreht und mich behorcht und betrachtet. Dabei habe ich mich so satt bekommen. Wäre ich ein Mann, hätte ich aus diesem Zustand vielleicht ein Werk geschaffen.'[22] In *Das Haus der Krankheiten*, the narrator expresses distaste at her femininity, which she experiences as masochistic and as condemning her to be an object of her lover's violence:

Mein Herz, von dem ich nichts halte, . . . ist seitdem noch oft durchlöchert worden. So, als machte ihm das gar nichts aus, will es immer von neuem die Zielscheibe sein. Das ist verächtlich. Ich beachte mein Herz nicht mehr. . . . Es hat einen widerlichen, weiblichen Charakter. (pp. 61–2)

It is also significant that she expresses distaste at the 'Busenstube' and the 'Saal der Bäuche', both rooms representing parts of the body strongly associated with physical femininity.

For Surrealist women artists, the essential problem lies in the

---

[22] Zürn, *Gesamtausgabe*, iv. 1, 25–42 (39), and quoted in Weigel, 'Hans Bellmer Unica Zürn', 217.

fact that, according to Surrealist theory, the mainspring of artistic creativity is the projection of desire onto the work of art. But because that projection is gendered as masculine and because its object is a stylized female, not a male body (there is no tradition of male nudes painted by Surrealist women, and the theoretical insistence on heterosexuality was so strong that representations of same-sex desire did not appear to be a powerful alternative for them), desire cannot be expressed in terms of the usual iconography but has to be diffused or displaced. One possible solution to this double-bind lies in an aesthetic of self-portraiture and autobiography, as described by Whitney Chadwick with reference to Surrealist women artists' uneasy self-portraits,[23] where the painter becomes her own Muse. Similarly, Weigel observes that while Bellmer's artistic practice involved blurring the divisions between 'la femme et son image', i.e. stylizing womanhood artistically and excessively, Zürn had recourse to a more autobiographical practice: she blurred the divisions between her life and work and adapted the former to correspond to the images of the latter (p. 210). In other words, Zürn turns inwards and simultaneously becomes her own subject and object. *Das Haus der Krankheiten* may be read as just such a fraught, fictional self-portrait, created in a theoretical universe where an all-powerful but invisible Bluebeard holds sway, eliminating and dismembering Woman and forcing her back onto her own fragile resources.

DAS HAUS DER KRANKHEITEN AS A RESPONSE TO L'ANATOMIE DE L'IMAGE

Zürn did not reject the theoretical contexts of Surrealism and Lacanian psychoanalysis, but acknowledged the difficulties they caused for her as artist and lover and tried to work out utopian solutions within their confines. Similarly, her narrator in *Das Haus der Krankheiten* does not reject love, even though it is harmful to her, but seeks subversive ways of encountering it. Indeed, *Das Haus der Krankheiten* not only maps with the ideas set out in *L'Anatomie de l'image*, it can even be read as a response to that treatise from a feminine subject position.

First, while *L'Anatomie* evolved over many years, it was published when *Das Haus der Krankheiten* was being written and the photograph

---

[23] *Women Artists and the Surrealist Movement.*

entitled 'Unica' described above made. Second, just as Lacan saw *L'Anatomie* as the confirmation of his theories, so too was Zürn a disciple of Lacan. Third, the two texts share *topoi* and features. For instance, in *Das Haus der Krankheiten* we find a mutilated doll made in the narrator's image which recalls Bellmer's mutilated dolls that were intended to resemble Zürn. Moreover, just as a threatening, red scorpion occurs in *Das Haus der Krankheiten*, so Bellmer's text has the following epigraph: ' "Le scorpion guérit le scorpion" PARACELSE' (p. 11). For Bellmer, the Paracelsian scorpion represents positively productive, narcissistic doubling. But in *Das Haus der Krankheiten* the scorpion appears in the 'Zimmer der Augen' *after* the narrator has transgressed by entering, and it threatens her. This suggests that the same image is adapted to stand for a negative, aggressive masculine principle associated with the 'Todfeind' and 'Ritter Blaubart'. Finally, just as Bellmer praises the anagram because it resembles the bodily rearrangements he describes in *L'Anatomie*, so too are the aesthetics of *Das Haus der Krankheiten* metaphorically anagrammatic inasmuch as the 'Haus der Krankheiten' is a large, dismembered body which is constantly rearranged by the narrator. Formally, too, the text is an anagrammatic montage since the narrator can add pages to it at will, and the associations between the pictures and individual diary entries are loose (as in the loose-leaf book in which she says she is writing) and potentially rearrangeable. Moreover, the work makes intertextual connections with some of Zürn's own anagrams, and with elements and characters in her other texts in a way which suggests that these texts, too, have an anagrammatic relation to one another and could be reshuffled at will.

Thus, *Das Haus der Krankheiten* exemplifies the double-bind in which the Surrealist woman finds herself under the thrall of theories like Bellmer's. Indeed, Zürn's narrator speaks from the precise point of view of the woman in *L'Anatomie de l'image*. She has lost her 'Augenherzen', or in other words, she is prohibited by her terms of reference from projecting her gaze outwards onto her lover, so she projects her gaze inwards onto herself, creating an odd, anagrammatical self-portrait that resembles Bellmer's Dolls. She partially identifies with and is partially alienated from this self-portrait, since the house itself and her own person are under the control of the deathly, dismembering Dr Mortimer, that is to say, a constricting, masculinist theory. And although the aesthetic of anagrammatic self-portraiture, infused with a residual, but subversive desire, allows the narrator to become a Surrealist artist, this kind of self-doubling is insecure and perpetually open to crisis.

Despite these dangers, however, a sense of subjective coherence is achieved by the narrator in the final chapter of *Das Haus der Krankheiten* where she violates the rigid rules of the house by venturing into the forbidden domain of vision and is rewarded by the recovery of her 'Augenherzen'. These she finds lying on a silver plate, over whose reflective surface she bends, and when she does so, her fear of psychosis or physical fragmentation is allayed by this image of the mirror, which in Lacanian theory provides a specular (if fragile) guarantee of physical wholeness.[24] This transgression and its reward implies that although the order in Bluebeard's house is damaging, it is less stable than it claims to be and may be subverted by an unexpected (albeit short-lived) challenge.

The narrator also finds strategies which enable her to encounter her lover, despite her awareness of the threat which is posed to her by her lover's gaze and/or physical presence and which means that she cannot encounter him directly. First, she uses the idea of distance, a motif which recurs throughout her writing and which is evident here in the positioning of the lover 'in der linken Ferne'. Second, once she has experienced a moment of integration in the 'Zimmer der Augen' through the recovery of her 'Augenherzen', she can encounter her lover eye to eye. Third, this encounter is achieved by the narrator's splitting up of the lover into several figures: the eagle, the scorpion, and Dr Mortimer, a strategy which permits her to defy and destroy the negative aspects of her lover (Mortimer and the scorpion) while retaining his more positive aspects (the eagle).[25] Given the utter passivity that Bellmer assigns to the Surrealist woman, such a move is a surprisingly active strategy of resistance.

In conclusion, Zürn makes use of the *Blaubartmärchen* in two ways. First, she uses the image of 'Ritter Blaubart' to encapsulate the double-bind into which the theories of *L'Anatomie de l'image* force the Surrealist woman. Moreover, given the close connection between Bellmer, Zürn, and Lacan, we are justified in identifying Zürn's 'Ritter Blaubart' with Lacan's Symbolic Order, which, in his view at least, was inescapable.[26] Second, Zürn's reference to the Bluebeard

---

[24] Lacan, 'Le Stade du miroir'.

[25] This division into positive and negative aspects is nonetheless tenuous and relative; cf. Zürn's illustration, 'Das Haus der Krankheiten', 54.

[26] Lacan adapted his concept of the Symbolic Order from Claude Lévi-Strauss's work on exogamous kinship structures and the exchange of women in *Les Structures élémentaires de*

Märchen involves a powerfully utopian charge, since the imprisoned narrator uses *Märchen* to encourage and empower herself. Specifically, she uses the model of the *Blaubartmärchen* not only to *describe* her position but also to *criticize* it, and as a blueprint for resistance, since the *Märchen* suggests that to transgress into the 'Zimmer der Augen'/ Bluebeard's chamber will bring rewards, as in the tale's early versions.

BLUEBEARD IN *DAS HAUS DER KRANKHEITEN*

Das Haus der Krankheiten takes up the *Blaubartmärchen*'s salient features of gendered oppression, subversion, and reward, as well as some other features of earlier texts. At the same time, there are new developments here too. Formally, *Das Haus der Krankheiten* involves a fragmentary reception of the perceived traditional *Märchen* form which typifies many texts of the postwar period. While this was nothing new in itself (for instance, Theodor Fontane's novel *Graf Petöfy* (1884) involves a brief reference to 'Blaubart'),[27] this feature of more recent literature nonetheless signals a change in a literary culture which had lost a good deal of its traditional faith in reliable, monolithic narratives and, concomitantly, in a unified selfhood like the coherent subject of emancipation assumed by Perrault.

Zürn's text not only confirms Elias's idea (affirmed by Foucault) that in the modern period, power relationships and social control are gradually transposed from the physical to the psychological sphere, it also takes that development still further. If, in the nineteenth and early twentieth centuries, Bluebeard's house and the heroine were increasingly isolated from society, then Zürn's text involves an even more radical kind of isolation since the house of sicknesses, i.e. the narrator's own body and mind, is a totally private world into which 'external' realities do not obtrude at all, so that such apparently sentient characters as Dr Mortimer are figments of the narrator's mind. This is because Zürn is using the same idea as Bellmer in

la parenté (1947). With reference to 'Blaubart' this is a most interesting connection, for just as the term 'Symbolic Order' was first used by Lévi-Strauss to describe the exchange of women between families and then transformed into a psychoanalytic concept, so too does 'Blaubart' in the nineteenth century involve an exogamous marriage forced onto the heroine, and in the twentieth, a psychoanalytic idea.

[27] *Werke, Schriften und Briefe*, ed. Walter Keitel and Helmuth Nürnberger, 20 vols. (Munich: Hanser, 1970), i. 685–866 (760).

L'Anatomie de l'image according to which the body is a psychological creation that blots out the Real. Accordingly, the material, physical world has completely disappeared, thus absolutely radicalizing the traditional theme of the heroine's isolation from her family and/or society.

So, in the virtual universe of the house of sicknesses, Bluebeard's violence is purely psychological. In the early twentieth century, his actions were motivated by an anonymous, super-personal Symbolic Order. Here, however, he is no longer even an individual character who represents that Order, but has become absent, simply a shifter that names something far more abstract which has been internalized and literally embodied by the narrator.[28] In other words, Bluebeard no longer exists outside of and separately from the woman protagonist, but is inside her, a part of herself.[29] Consequently, the central *topos* of Bluebeard's house has become superfluous, since he no longer requires a house into which he can entice the heroine, because the order he represents has been internalized so fully by Zürn's narrator that her own body is Bluebeard's house, from which there can be no escape. Given which, this Bluebeard order involves a permanent crisis of subjectivity for the narrator. Furthermore, his violence is no longer anomalous or unusual, and thus potentially reprehensible, as earlier authors perceived it to be. Rather, as I discussed above with reference to Bellmer's ideas, it is an all-pervasive, existential condition, since it runs through love, vision and language. But while such violence is existential and universal, it remains gendered, so that the feminine subject must fear that: 'Ewig das Opfer zu sein, ist mein Schicksal' (p. 61).

Although Bluebeard has become an abstract shifter, his avatar Dr Mortimer, in whom the persona of a medical man has been superimposed onto that of a military officer, is interesting for two reasons. First, Freud stressed in *Die Traumdeutung* that dreams tend to represent objects and ideas by means of condensing one thing with another, and this is a technique which is much used in *Das Haus der Krankheiten*: indeed, Mortimer himself consists of a series of condensations. This condensation involves images of Death, the 'Todfeind', the lover, the doctor, and the officer. If texts by male

---

[28] Cf. Lacan, 'L'Instance de la lettre'; Wright, *Psychoanalytic Criticism*, 109–13.

[29] In Lacanian terms, the narrator has taken up her place in the Symbolic Order. That is, she herself has become and internalized the phallus, the representative of the Father's Law, the very support of the Symbolic Order.

authors from the 1960s onward tended to stress seriality or splitting as a way of representing Woman, i.e. fragmenting her into a series of figures in order to display her various characteristics individually, Zürn's strategy of condensing various masculine figures into one (Dr Mortimer) is a reversal of that technique whereby various diverse ideas are brought together in order to give a sense of the nature of the Symbolic Order as a whole.

Second, while the portrayal of Bluebeard as a military man had occurred in earlier texts (e.g. Marlitt's and Kaiser's), by making Mortimer a medical doctor Zürn is combining a familiar aspect of the portrayal of Bluebeard with something new. In the traditional *Märchen*, Bluebeard's house is a space owned by Bluebeard on which power conflicts are enacted. But in Zürn's text, the image of the interior of Bluebeard's house is condensed with that of the female body which is ruled by an evil doctor. Thus it is implied that a further aspect of the oppressive, violent Symbolic Order involves medicine, a science that is ostensibly concerned with healing. Indeed, the presence and nature of Dr Mortimer implies a new critique, from a feminine point of view, of the practice of modern medicine as being oppressive, patriarchal, and analogous in its workings to military activity and scientific collecting. This new dimension to the catalogue of Bluebeard's activities dovetails with a certain feminist critique of modern medicine which argues that it is essentially a patriarchal practice, being male-dominated, exclusionary to women as practitioners, and unsympathetic both to women patients and to alternative, female-identified care for the body and mind.[30]

Yet despite all these dangers the house of sicknesses is also a place of magic and visions, and as such has many positive aspects. Indeed, when the narrator leaves, her artistic production (in the form of the diary and illustrations) stops, so that it seems that the Symbolic Order as manifested in 'das Haus der Krankheiten' gives the narrator some (masochistic) pleasure and even encourages her creativity.[31] This may

---

[30] Carolyn Merchant, *The Death of Nature: Women, Ecology and the Scientific Revolution* (1980) (New York: HarperCollins, 1983), 152–5.

[31] It is at the very moment of the subject's possession of the beloved that artistic and linguistic production, and the magic of the *Haus der Krankheiten*, stop. Cf. Lacan's reflections on the notion that to possess the object of desire, i.e. the signifier, is always to lose contact with the Symbolic, that is, with desire, language and subjectivity, in 'Le Séminaire sur "La Lettre volée"', in *Écrits*, 11–61. The dilemma of Zürn's narrator as to whether she should leave the house and so stop producing her text also recalls Freudian images of the hysteric woman who resists treatment and healing, and in whom hysteria itself is a distorted work of

be due to the perceived inevitability of that Order, and finding pleasure in it may be part of the narrator's way of coming to terms with her predicament—just as Marlitt's Lilli also found pleasure in accepting the romantic inevitability of her highly suspect marriage to Dorn.

But more positively, Zürn's narrator also discovers that the Bluebeard Symbolic Order is less monolithic than it claims to be. If, in early twentieth-century texts, the Symbolic Order was associated with images of huge, oppressive, and rigid stone monuments, here it is associated with a house whose contours are far more unstable and shifting. Similarly, Bluebeard's agent, Dr Mortimer, is not a deadly serious figure like those presented by Marlitt and the *fin-de-siècle* authors, but somewhat ridiculous, like the traditional medical villain of melodrama. And the narrator succeeds in finding the courage to challenge the Symbolic Order and operate her own strategies within it. This then permits her, if not to topple that order, then at least to subvert it for her own purposes—or even simply to abandon it, by leaving the house of sicknesses and walking away, as she does at the end of the text. Neither the house itself nor Mortimer has the power to stop her. So, while she cannot express her desire in conventional ways, that desire is nonetheless present and slips through the strictures of Bluebeard's order, prefiguring the way in which Lacanian theory in the 1960s came to imagine Woman as being always in excess of the order which binds her.[32] The text has an open ending, and its utopianism consists precisely in its open-endedness and ability, notwithstanding the weight of Bellmer's theory, to demonstrate how the feminine subject is constantly 'en procès' and resistant to any reductive classifications or fixed identifications *à la* Bluebeard.[33]

CONNECTIONS WITH OTHER RECENT BLUEBEARD TEXTS

Finally, Zürn's text is interesting too in that it shares a remarkable series of features with a further group of Bluebeard texts by women

art (cf. Roudinesco, *Jacques Lacan & Co.*, 6; and Sigmund Freud and Josef Breuer, *Studien über Hysterie* (1893) (Frankfurt am Main: Fischer, 1970)).

[32] Jacqueline Rose, 'Introduction II', in Jacques Lacan and the *École Freudienne, Feminine Sexuality*, ed. Juliet Mitchell and Jacqueline Rose (London: Macmillan, 1982), 27–57 (51).

[33] Cf. Julia Kristeva's concept of the 'sujet en procès', in *La Révolution du langage poétique* (Paris: Seuil, 1974), 19.

authors which were produced from around 1968 onwards.[34] In Ingeborg Bachmann's fragmentary novel customarily known as *Der Fall Franza*, also first published posthumously, in 1977, the eponymous protagonist suffers a mental and physical breakdown as a result of her marriage to Jordan, a psychiatrist who conducts destructive experiments on her.[35] In order to escape Jordan and all she associates with him, Franza escapes to Africa, where she attempts to identify with the post-colonial people in the expectation of some kind of release. But instead, after what seems to be a sexual assault by a white man at the Pyramids, she dies. Franza refers to her own marriage as a 'Blaubartehe' (ii. 207, 247), and she uses the figure of Bluebeard and his chamber to make connections with the Holocaust and the gas chambers. In Karin Struck's novel *Blaubarts Schatten* (1991), the protagonist, Lily, has a series of abusive relationships with men, beginning with her father.[36] One of her lovers drives her to terminate a pregnancy, an act which she later comes to regard as murder of what she calls the 'unborn child'. While Lily begins her narrative by considering 'Blaubart' as a synonym for patriarchal power and Bluebeard's chamber as being full of women who have been defeated by that power, her experiences lead her to realize that women, too, are equally guilty in the so-called crime of abortion and to draw analogies between women's acceptance of abortion, and women's complicity in National Socialist genocide. In Elisabeth Reichart's short story 'Die Kammer' (1992), the protagonist Andrea suffers from a neurotic eye complaint which makes her intermittently blind.[37] This, it transpires, is the result of childhood abuse at the hands of her father, who, like Bluebeard, kept her locked up in a 'Kammer', and it seems in turn that the father's behaviour goes back to his experience of National Socialism and the Holocaust, even though we learn nothing more about his relationship to that historical event.

These texts share similarities in terms of both form and theme. Formally, each of them breaks up canonical expectations of the *Märchen* by presenting the *Blaubartmärchen* as a series of fleeting

[34] Cf. my article '*In Blaubarts Schatten*: Murder, *Märchen* and Memory', *German Life and Letters*, 50 (1997), 491–507; also in Margaret Littler (ed.), *Gendering German Studies: New Perspectives on German Literature and Culture* (Oxford: Blackwell, 1997), 113–29.

[35] While the text has usually been known as *Der Fall Franza*, the scholarly edition of 1995 gives it the title *Das Buch Franza*, in *Todesarten-Projekt*, ed. Monika Albrecht and Dirk Göttsche, 4 vols. (Munich: Piper, 1995), ii.

[36] Karin Struck, *Blaubarts Schatten* (Munich: List, 1991).

[37] In *La Valse* (Salzburg: Otto Müller, 1992), 81–97.

references or fragments embedded in a longer, epic narrative. And with the exception of Struck's novel, which has an evident Bluebeard allusion in its title, these texts fall outside canonical discussions of the Bluebeard tale too because they do not refer obviously to Bluebeard in their titles. There are also many thematic similarities. All these texts are narrated from the point of view of a female protagonist, thus giving a voice to a character (Bluebeard's wife or lover) who has traditionally often been silenced. More fundamentally, too, the women characters in these texts speak in an unconventional way because they no longer appear as straightforwardly unified, self-identical subjects, as Perrault assumed his heroine to be. Rather, their voices reveal a complex, fragmented subjectivity, which is reflected in fragmented narrative forms. Next, just as Zürn presented 'Ritter Blaubart' as a shifter representing a set of psychological and aesthetic rules, these texts likewise all envisage Bluebeard not as a person but as an oppressive, internalized *psychological* principle or Symbolic Order. This Order is clearly damaging, since in each case the stability of the female protagonist is called into question and the themes of mental disturbance or illness are very much to the fore. And while these texts do not exclude real violence and abuse, they also suggest how such issues fit into a broader psychological scheme of things, and how they are internalized and perpetuated by individual subjects, both men and women.

At the same time, these later texts develop Zürn's presentation of 'Blaubart' further, by making connections between the more obviously political and the seemingly private, that is, between those structures which are psychologically and sometimes physically damaging to women and girls and other, similar forms of oppression which underpinned by a hyper-rational, Bluebeard way of thinking. The technique of condensation is very important here, because 'Blaubart' becomes a cipher for many forms of authoritarian oppression which can stand for more than one such system at once and draw attention to their perceived similarities.

For instance, one idea persistently linked with Bluebeard in these texts is militarism, and military figures come to be condensed, via Bluebeard, with modern-day medical figures. The women in all these texts are patients who have to deal with male doctors who are at best impersonal and at worst knowing murderers. *Der Fall Franza* even involves a former Nazi doctor who was responsible for terrible crimes in the concentration camps. Then again, while Bluebeard's house was traditionally the space in which power struggles are enacted, and while the power struggle between Perrault's Bluebeard and the heroine was enacted in a house which symbolized material property and legal marriage, in Zürn's and Struck's texts the female body itself is explicitly described as a house. In all cases, what is at stake is power over the woman's body and mind through gynaecology, narcotic drugs, or psycho-pharmaceuticals: control of women is characterized as medical, psychiatric, or psychoanalytical and all three practices are viewed with suspicion as another oppressive, barbarically rationalizing principle which is especially antagonistic to women. And from this insight it is a short step to a critique of the traditionally masculine institution of medicine, which, although usually considered to be an aspect of order and progress, proves to be violent and cause disorder, just like the Bluebeard systems in earlier texts. It is the very application of medical practice to Franza which makes her ill and in turn legitimizes ever more intrusive medical control over her. So while Franza's life with her physician husband is outwardly ordered, it actually makes her terminally ill, and she comes to call it a 'Dschungel inmitten der Zivilisation', thus bringing together the normally separate ideas of civilization and disorder, and showing their conventional distinction to be fictional.

Moreover, all these texts make the connection between the figure of Bluebeard, National Socialism, and genocide, phenomena that are shown to be linked with militarism, rigorous organization, and medicine (e.g. in the form of eugenics in Struck's text). In short, therefore, Bluebeard as medical or military man or party official comes to stand, too, for Fascism or, more precisely, for oppressive ways of thinking which can end in Fascism. Bluebeard can also stand for the lasting and destructive legacy of Fascism and genocide which haunts later generations, as in Reichart's and Bachmann's texts, which deal with what Bachmann called the 'Spätschaden' of the Holocaust.

These texts also make use of the ambiguities in the 'Blaubart' model (e.g. the wife's willingness to marry Bluebeard and her responsibility for her own actions in opening the door) in order to avoid simplistic distinctions between men as perpetrators and women as victims of violence. All the texts blur such boundaries and make it clear that the female protagonists are complicit in the Bluebeard system(s). Because the Bluebeard order has been internalized by the women protagonists, it not only damages them but involves them and makes them complicit in it, through their own masochism or by perpetuating and imposing that order on others (Andrea's fear of transmitting her own psychological damage to her children; Lily's abortion; and Franza as a white woman in Africa is necessarily associated with colonial forces).

In other words, in the period after National Socialism all aspects of traditional 'civilization' had to be re-examined, both because many of them had been deeply implicated in the Fascist project and, on a deeper level, because all aspects of civilization had to be interrogated in new ways in an attempt to understand how it could throw up such manifest horror. So these later texts by women use the figure of Bluebeard in order to undertake a complex exploration of a series of historical problems: the restrictive discourses of medicine, colonialism, and Fascism with all their terrible consequences, as well as the psychological and physical oppression of women.

Finally, how does this group of texts compare with that group of texts by male authors from the same period discussed at the start of this chapter? Formally, the texts by women tend to be different in that they are more fragmented and less easily identifiable as Bluebeard texts. While women characters have little or nothing to say in the texts discussed above, in these texts by women the female protagonist is the centre of attention. Nevertheless, she seems to be a different kind of subject from the male protagonists of the texts by men, inasmuch as both her narrative and her subjectivity are 'in process' rather than fixed. Yet at the same time both groups of texts are reflexes of one phenomenon: expressions of a new unease with the social and symbolic status quo that was provoked at a deep level by the horrors of the middle years of the twentieth century and expressed with particular reference to a feminist awareness and critique of society. Texts by women tend, however, to problematize the psychology of the characters more and, in response to the idea that the 'personal is political', to be more concerned to relate that psychology to history and society, with varying degrees of persuasiveness. Unlike the male authors, the women make Bluebeard into an abstract principle rather than an individual character. Therefore, in the later decades of the twentieth century, the *Blaubartmärchen* is still used to address difficult issues involving—but also going beyond—gender politics. As I have argued, the *Märchen* has traditionally been a useful way of addressing disturbing or scandalous issues because it permits an indirect presentation. In the late twentieth century, that potential takes on a particular significance as the *Märchen* is used by Bachmann and Reichart to approach the problem of representing Auschwitz, around which they impose a taboo.[38] In this respect Bachmann and Reichart take their place in a literary tradition which dealt critically with the possibility of representing Auschwitz naturalistically.

Perrault's 'La Barbe bleue' was utopian in that it showed how an apparently perpetual cycle of violence could be broken and so reversed the Genesis narrative of the Fall of Man which had led to an unbroken cycle of lasting evil and original sin. Given that they are responding to a historical catastrophe of shocking dimensions, it is not surprising that Bachmann and Reichart should perpetuate the twentieth-century trend set by Bartók's opera whereby Perrault's utopian ending is replaced by fatalistic closure. It seems that the legacy of the twentieth century makes such utopianism increasingly unavailable. Reichart's 'Die Kammer' and Bachmann's *Der Fall Franza* make it clear that the crimes of earlier generations continue to weigh inevitably and heavily on later generations like a new kind of original sin. And yet other texts, like Struck's *Blaubarts Schatten* and Zürn's *Das Haus der Krankheiten*, do hold out a hope, however tenuous and open to threat, that even the most pervasive of oppressive orders, those which structure both body and soul, can be, if not broken open, at least displaced or evaded.

[38] Bachmann, '[Auf das Opfer darf keiner sich berufen]', in *Werke*, ed. Christine Koschel, Inge von Weidenbaum, and Clemens Münster, 4 vols. (Munich: Piper, 1978), iv. 335. In 'Die Kammer' Reichart writes of the deportation of victims to the East: '[die Reise], die jenseits der Worte bleiben muß, weil kein Wort sie bannen kann' (106). Cf. e.g. *Lyrik nach Auschwitz? Adorno und die Dichter*, ed. Petra Kiedaisch (Stuttgart: Reclam, 1995).

8

BLAUBARTS SCHATTEN:
SOME CONCLUSIONS

THE CHANGING SIGNIFICANCE OF 'BLAUBART'

'Blaubart' texts from the last 300 years can be read as reflections of both contemporary gender politics and the process of civilization. In the late seventeenth century, Perrault used 'La Barbe bleue' to describe the dark obverse of the *grand renfermement* in France, the rise of the *père terrible*, and the predicament of women without legal and property rights in marriage. In the nineteenth century the tale was used by authors as different as the Brothers Grimm and E. Marlitt to affirm, rather than challenge, the familial authority of the father or husband. The early twentieth century witnessed the production of a different kind of text which presented Bluebeard as a Don Juan-like hero, and glorified the act of murder as well as his sexuality.

By the late twentieth century the focus had moved to different, very contemporary issues in gender politics and power relations, for instance, the practice of modern medicine which is criticized by some authors for denying women access to their own bodies and psyches. Elisabeth Reichart's 'Die Kammer' (1992) uses the *Blaubartmärchen*'s theme of a dangerous secret behind an outwardly harmonious exterior to describe, among other things, hidden abuse in the family, a major social concern of the 1990s. Reichart's text thus challenges the bourgeois ideal of the family headed by a father as a place of safety. In December 1997 the prestigious Volksbühne in Berlin premièred a new Bluebeard work, Walter Bickmann's *Blaubart. Die letzten Männer*, which also transposes 'Blaubart' into contemporary life.[1] Partly inspired by a documentary, the play highlights the modern phenomenon of the surreptitious importation of women from poor countries as so-called wives or concubines—in effect, unpaid domestic and sexual servants—for conservative Western men who find that the expectations of modern Western women regarding married life no longer correspond to their own. The play's title

---

[1] Walter Bickmann, *Blaubart—Die letzten Männer*, Volksbühne am Rosa-Luxemburg-Platz, Berlin, première 16 Dec. 1997.

echoes these characters' feeling that they represent a last bastion of real, endangered manliness. This play is, like earlier versions of the *Märchen*, a story in which women find themselves transported by material necessity into a relationship in an alien environment where the balance of power is seriously weighted against them and they have no access to family support or legal rights; but those themes are given distinctive contemporary form. In this period, therefore, the characterization of Bluebeard changes correspondingly. He is no longer a remarkable ogre, but is often either an oppressive abstract principle or sometimes a very ordinary man who feels beleaguered, like Bickmann's protagonists. Indeed, Bluebeard often appears as a weak or helpless victim in the 1980s and 1990s, for example in Max Frisch's *Blaubart* (1984), although this development does not seem to temper the bleakness of the material's presentation of gender relations or aggression against the feminine.

Yet despite these important shifts in meaning, a striking aspect of the Bluebeard tradition's tracing of gender politics in the modern period is precisely its consistency. By this I mean the lack of variation in the basic plot and constellation of characters—the aggressive, oppressive, often powerful male character or principle displaying, or attempting to display, aggression towards or authority over a female character. While it might be expected that such a tale as Bluebeard would provide tremendous scope for authors to play with role reversals and surprising twists to that basic plot, very few do so. For example, only one text seems to perform the apparently obvious reversal whereby Bluebeard is a wife who victimizes her husband, Karl Hans Strobl's *Madame Blaubart* of 1929. Strobl's text remains an exception, apart from Dieter Hildebrandt's *Blaubart Mitte 40* (1977) where Bluebeard's ex-wife is the real murderer; Günter Grass's *Ein Weites Feld* (1995) discussed below; and perhaps Karin Struck's *Blaubarts Schatten* (1991) which makes explicit that women can be Bluebeards too in terminating pregnancies. (Nonetheless, Struck insists that such behaviour on the part of women is the result of their oppression by male Bluebeards.)

Similarly, it is seldom that the potential victims of Bluebeard are anything but nubile, attractive, or sexualized. There seems to be only one instance of Bluebeard killing a male character in the context of a homosexual relationship, in Marga Passon's *Blaubart* (1925), which has Bluebeard performing sexual attacks on women and children too. Such symbolic reversals and omnivorous appetites on the part of

Bluebeard characters might again seem to be an obvious option for authors, especially given that the historical figure of Gilles de Rais, so frequently identified with Bluebeard, was charged with the murder of children. However, this is not the case, with the exception of two texts about Gilles, Karl Felix von Schlichtegroll's *Gilles de Rais. Das Urbild des Blaubart* (1938) and Hans Natonek's *Blaubarts letzte Liebe* (1988). It would appear that there is something very compelling about Perrault's plot and constellation of characters, which appeals remarkably persistently to the imagination and remains convincing over centuries in such a way that alterations seem inappropriate or unappealing. Such consistency suggests that Bluebeard and his symbolic meanings—as the authoritarian husband or father—have always wielded great power.

Second, 'Blaubart' traces the problematic process of civilization in the modern period in Germany, since Bluebeard can be understood as a representative of the modern, civilized subject, and his female counterpart often appears as the Other of civilization. This situation reflects the facts that the ideal subject of civilization has traditionally been the male individual of the dominant class, and that therefore the situation of women in civilization can be ambivalent. This identification of Bluebeard with the civilized subject leads to sustained attempts by commentators and literary authors to exculpate, legitimize, or even glorify his morally problematic behaviour. But it is revealed that this subject's project of civilization is increasingly prone to crisis so that, after an increase in confidence which culminates in the mid-nineteenth century with E. Marlitt's 'Blaubart', he undergoes a severe crisis in the twentieth century, especially its second half. This experience of the twentieth century cast increasing theoretical doubt on the assumed simplicity, sovereignty, and superiority of the enlightened subject of civilization, his technologies, and his social and psychological orders; and this doubt was reinforced by the events of the mid-century, notably National Socialism, the Holocaust and their legacy.

My readings confirm Norbert Elias's contention that the process of civilization involves an ever more pervasive imposition of order through its gradual transformation from 'Fremdzwang' to 'Selbstzwang', as a result of which control and authority are increasingly internalized by both men and women. This means that brute physical control becomes increasingly superfluous so that, while Perrault's Bluebeard is a real character who physically butchers women, from

Marlitt's novella onward he increasingly disappears as a character in his own right and becomes the personification of a Symbolic Order or an internalized, psychological principle. Moreover, that Symbolic Order comes to be identified with many of the structures and processes of civilization, such as conventional aesthetics or an obsession with excessive order and classification, all of which are experienced as subliminal or manifest forms of violence. While Perrault's Bluebeard is terrifying and dangerous, his reign of terror is ended and the cycle of violence broken once he has been killed. But the transformation of Bluebeard into a Symbolic Order means that violence has become psychological and is thereby normalized as well as made more invisible and pervasive; and so the utopian potential of the original tale is seriously jeopardized. In later texts, where Bluebeard becomes an abstract principle, he no longer appears to be the subject of civilization. Rather, that relationship is reversed so that the victim or intended victim becomes the subject of civilization struggling with cruel cultural imperatives, and therefore potentially dangerous herself or himself, as in Andrea's fear of harming her children in 'Die Kammer'.

Nevertheless, the imposition of order identified with Bluebeard is no straightforward matter because in fact it constantly produces its own Other and opposites, so that such order is always fragile and threatened by chaos or rebellion, often embodied in the female protagonist. And so, paradoxically, it is at the apparent apotheosis of Bluebeard's order, in Unica Zürn's *Das Haus der Krankheiten*, a text which is informed by Lacanian ideas about a violent, phallocentric, and absolutely ubiquitous Symbolic Order, that Bluebeard's rule is in fact most easily defied. No longer restricted by the rules of a fantastic, feudal patriarchy, the heroine simply walks out of Bluebeard's castle. Thus, contrary to what one might expect, 'Blaubart' does not lose its utopian potential for Zürn.

BLUEBEARD AND NATIONAL IDENTITY

A third important theme runs through the Bluebeard tradition, that of national identity. That theme has been present in the Bluebeard tradition since its inception, alongside the emergence of the civilized subject as described by Elias (and, in a different way, by Perrault), which went hand in hand with the emergence of the modern nation-state. That emergent nation-state invested the concept of the nation with important meanings, and such issues appear still to resonate throughout the material, which has two separate strands. One strand explicitly emphasizes that Bluebeard is not German; the other affirms that he must be.

At the start of the former strand, the Grimms were sensitive to the cultural implications of Bluebeard's nationality when they excluded him from the *KHM* on account of being French. Many authors followed the Grimms' lead, suspecting that the villainous Bluebeard could not be a German. For example, Alexander von Ungern-Starnberg's 'Blaubart' (1850) is a Frenchified fraud. Armand Vestris's *Blaubart: Grosses romantisch-pantomimisches Ballet* (1832) is set in Arabia. In 1866, Marlitt identified Bluebeard–Dorn with his black servant or *alter ego*, characterized by the womanservant Dorte as a semi-civilized (Othello-like) 'Mohr'. For Passon, Bluebeard is an 'asiatischer Titan', that is, half English and half Indian and certainly not German. Like Dorn, Passon's Bluebeard has a demonic black servant for good measure. Gerd Winkler's Mike Blaubart (1968) is a 'Deutsch-Amerikaner'. This tendency to orientalize Bluebeard or otherwise ensure that he is a foreigner can be understood not only as part of a European tradition, prevalent above all in England, in which Bluebeard is an 'Oriental', but also as an attempt to distance Bluebeard and his practices from the author's own surroundings.[2] (In the case of Winkler, however, Mike Blaubart's American connections are intended to make him appear more glamorous.)

The latter strand is equally well established and posits an intimate connection between the murderous Bluebeard and German identity. Tieck's influential works of 1797 locate the material very firmly in Germany, as did the Grimms initially, and such authors as Franz Pocci (1845, 1859) and Ernst Maier (1852). It is to this tradition that Paul Wiegler confidently referred in 1909:

Nie haben die Deutschen ein solches Bedürfnis gefühlt, den bretonischen Ritter, der sie wie in Wahlverwandtschaft anzog, durch Empfindsamkeit zu sühnen. Sie wollten ihn als Mörder. Sie ließen dem Stoff seine Konturen und das Barbarische, das der deutschen Gier entgegenkommt, Sinnliches und Geistiges zu vermählen.[3]

While Wiegler acknowledges historical theories of origin which associated Bluebeard with the Breton Gilles de Rais, he is emphasizing

---

[2] Cf. Hartwig Suhrbier, 'Blaubart: Leitbild und Leidfigur', in Suhrbier (ed.), *Blaubarts Geheimnis: Märchen und Erzählungen, Gedichte und Stücke* (Cologne: Diederichs, 1984), 11–79 (36).

[3] 'Der gute Blaubart', *Die neue Rundschau*, 20 (4) (1909), 1679–80 (1679).

that, symbolically, the most grisly variants of the tale are truly indigenous to Germany. And Winkler's Mike Blaubart, while he initially
seems to be a 'Deutsch-Amerikaner', in an address to his wives finally
confesses to a more disturbing identity in a manner which, although
parodic, echoes Wiegler's statement:

BLAUBART. Ja, ja, das wollen wir auskosten, dachtet Ihr, obendrein heißt er noch
'Mike', das klingt ja so amerikanisch, und die Amerikaner, die sind ja nicht
so, die haben gar kein Talent zum Blaubart. Fehlanzeige, meine Damen, ich
bin aus keinem Comic-Strip entsprungen! Ich denke und fühle urdeutsch.
Und deswegen muß ich jetzt ein kleines Massenblutbad anrichten . . .

*Mike hat sich während seines Ausbruchs in einen regelrechten Rausch hineingesteigert; in der
Sprache klingt das am Ende an die hysterischen Ausbrüche des Adolf Hitler an.*[4]

Most recently, in Bickmann's *Blaubart. Die letzten Männer*, the Bluebeard protagonists are emphatically German in a manner which is
highlighted by their selection of wives from other parts of the world,
who are divided from them most conspicuously by the lack of a
common language.

Mike Blaubart's words resonate too with a trend in post-1945
German texts, which has Bluebeard as being not alien to Germany or
German culture but deeply rooted there, and symbolically linked to
German history of the mid-twentieth century in particular. Such
recent versions of 'Blaubart' often address two major, interrelated
issues in German history. First, the tale may be used to illuminate the
history and the legacy of National Socialism and the Holocaust, as
in the texts by Bachmann, Struck, and Reichart discussed in the
previous chapter. Helma Sanders-Brahms's film *Deutschland, bleiche
Mutter* (1979) also uses the variant tale 'Der Räuberbräutigam' to
suggest that the 'Mörderhaus' in which the *Märchen* heroine's future
husband lives is identified with a Germany which contains ruined
extermination camps and where the past is suppressed.[5] In such
versions, Bluebeard is identified with the National Socialist past with
its gas chambers and the forbidden chambers of its repressed
memory. This is coherent symbolism because the Bluebeard tale
itself has traditionally been used to describe the attempted erasure of
perceived difference or Otherness, an idea which is often represented

---

[4] Gerd Winkler, *Mike Blaubart* (1967) (Frankfurt am Main: Heine, 1968), 80.
[5] Cf. my article ' "Du bist in einem Mörderhaus": Representing German History
through the *Märchen* of "Blaubart" and "Der Räuberbräutigam" in Works by Dieter
Hildebrandt and Helma Sanders-Brahms', in Mary Fulbrook and Martin Swales (eds.),
Representing the German Nation (Manchester: Manchester University Press, 2000), 118–35.

metonymically, if deeply problematically, in European culture as Woman. Such erasure of perceived difference was also the aim of the genocidal policies of National Socialism. A different variation on that theme of using 'Blaubart' to encode the National Socialist past and its consequences is provided by Dieter Hildebrandt's novel *Blaubart Mitte 40* (1977), in which the eponymous protagonist embodies an emblematic West German biography, and the outward successes and the inner psychological problems of the Economic Miracle. Here, the repressed history is that of the protagonist's traumatic experiences as a Soviet prisoner of war.

Second, 'Blaubart' has been used by authors to comment on the division of Germany after 1945 and reunification after 1989. For instance, the GDR author Helga Schubert's short story 'Das verbotene Zimmer' (1982) is written from the point of view of an East German narrator who has viewed West Berlin as a 'verbotenes Zimmer' which is tantalizingly near for her in East Berlin, but forbidden.[6] The narrator gains permission to go to West Berlin for a day in order to conduct research for a literary project and visit the house in which she was born, and the text consists of her impressions of West Berlin, which she finds alienating in many respects.

There may be some subtle criticism here of either the Eastern or Western bloc for prohibiting access to the territory of their Cold War rival, thus making it into a closed forbidden space, but the Bluebeard analogy remains tantalizingly equivocal, such that it is not clear whom the narrator considers to be the Bluebeard of the piece. For Schubert, as in the texts discussed in Chapter 7, Bluebeard is no longer an individual character or agent, but in this case an anonymous historical imperative which has made West Berlin into a forbidden chamber for East Berliners. But while Schubert shows no interest in identifying Bluebeard, she does identify her narrator with Bluebeard's bride, since she does enter the forbidden chamber—which proves to contain only the woman's own past, and no nasty surprises. Bluebeard's threat is thus exploded by revealing his chamber to be empty, a strategy which subverts Perrault's plot in a manner not unlike Tieck's *Die sieben Weiber des Blaubart*, where the forbidden chamber is empty too. One interpretation of Schubert's text may be, then, that despite the prohibitions of history and national and political boundaries, there is in fact nothing to fear from

---

[6] Helga Schubert, 'Das verbotene Zimmer', in *Das verbotene Zimmer* (Darmstadt: Luchterhand, 1982), 81–97.

the threatening images of political Otherness deployed for propagandistic purposes in the Cold War.

Karin Struck's *Blaubarts Schatten* (1991) also uses 'Blaubart' to illustrate her view of the postwar division of Germany. Struck's narrator suggests that Germany has resembled a dismembered body which, in tandem with the healing of the narrator's psyche around the time of the *Wende*, is also restored from its dismembered state. And a more perplexing text, Wolfgang Rohner-Radegast's fragment *Vetter Blaubart oder wie die wohl drüben* (1995), also uses the Bluebeard motif in an experimental narrative about German–German relationships and border crossings, in which 'Vetter Blaubart' appears to belong in the GDR (and is, incidentally, a doctor and a ladykiller).[7]

In 1995, Günter Grass's ambitious *Wende* novel *Ein weites Feld* (1995) made references to the Bluebeard material too in its thirteenth, fourteenth, and fifteenth chapters which describe a central symbolic event, the wedding of the East German Martha Wuttke to the West German Heinz-Martin Grundmann in September 1990.[8] In these chapters, references to Jacques Offenbach's *Barbe-bleue. Opéra bouffe en trois actes* (1867) recur in the description of the wedding breakfast, for the party is held in the Prenzlauer Berg restaurant Offenbachstuben, where the dishes are named after the composer's works. Those dishes include one named 'Ritter Blaubart' (although not ordered by the wedding party, for it is rejected by the bride's mother as being in poor taste, a choice which the bride's father regrets, noting, 'dabei hätte [Ritter Blaubarts] Wiederholungstätergeschichte eine Menge Anspielungen erlaubt' (p. 290)).

That subtle subtext has many resonances. For instance, it echoes the bride's doubts as to the wisdom of forgoing her career for married life without paid employment and the surrender of her financial and professional independence to her wealthy, powerful husband, analogous to the critique of bourgeois marriage in some Bluebeard texts. Such a critique has particular significance in the context of the *Wende* and its impact on the lives of GDR women, many of whom lost the professional and material independence they had had in the GDR.[9] In this context the way in which the main dish on the menu, the 'Entenbrust Schöne Helena' (by virtue of its feminine name asso-

---

[7] Wolfgang Rohner-Radegast, *Vetter Blaubart oder wie die wohl drüben* (Karlsruhe: Literarische Gesellschaft Karlsruhe und Arbeitskreis Neue Literatur, 1995).

[8] Günter Grass, *Ein weites Feld* (Göttingen: Steidl, 1995), 260–317.

[9] Elizabeth Boa and Janet Wharton (eds.), *Women and the Wende: Social Effects and Cultural Reflections of the German Unification Process* (Amsterdam: Rodopi, 1994).

ciated with the bride) is devoured by the guests, is slightly unnerving, recalling as it does Bluebeard's slaughter (and in some cases consumption) of his wife.

On another level, Martha and Heinz-Martin are a variant on the familiar literary topos of the star-crossed couple which embodies inter-German history from 1962 to 1989.[10] In this light, the rich, rapacious widower bridegroom Bluebeard is associated with the rich, widowed property developer Heinz-Martin Grundmann (*nomen est omen*) who aims to make a financial killing in—or cannibalistically gobble up—the 'neue Bundesländer'. The potential of the union to descend into conflict, as in the *Märchen*, is great, as illustrated by the East–West row which develops between the guests, and which prompts Grass's protagonist, Fonty, the father of the bride, to comment: 'Nun soll aber schleunigst das Dessert auf den Tisch und die beim Glaubensstreit erhitzten Gemüter ein wenig abkühlen, sonst mißrät uns die Hochzeit zum Schlachtfest bei dem am Ende doch noch "Ritter Blaubart" auftischt' (p. 307). However, the reference to the operetta, where the wife survives, introduces a comic aspect and prefigures the couple's role reversal to come.[11]

Finally, the most recent of these texts is Ingo Schramm's *Wende* novel *Fitchers Blau* (1996),[12] whose title refers to the variant 'Fitchers Vogel' which the Grimms considered more German than 'Blaubart', an appropriate detail in the context of the text's analysis of contemporary German identity. The main plot of this complex, dystopian novel involves two disturbed protagonists, Karl and Janni, who grew up in East Berlin without knowing one another. Janni rebels and emigrates to the West in the mid-1980s. She first meets Karl in the days following German reunification in November 1990, when he is on the run from opportunist criminals. Karl joins Janni in street fights with the police and defending squatted houses. The couple meet a man in the Underground who identifies them both as his children, revealing their relationship to be incestuous, and the inconclusive ending suggests that Janni has been severely injured (and may even be dying) in a clash with the police, and Karl attempts to attack a young child for no discernible reason.

---

[10] e.g. Christa Wolf's novel *Der geteilte Himmel* (1963); Margarethe von Trotta's film *Das Versprechen* (1995).

[11] Interestingly too in this episode, Fonty cites Theodor Fontane's novel *Graf Petöfy* (1884), which makes explicit reference to 'Blaubart' but, like Offenbach's operetta, reverses its plot, inasmuch as the eponymous hero turns out not to be a Bluebeard at all.

[12] Ingo Schramm, *Fitchers Blau. Poetischer Roman* (Berlin: Verlag Volk & Welt, 1996).

In addition, there is a separate, central section of narrative in which the father's own story is told. He was ten years old in 1945 and grew up a fanatically loyal Party member in the GDR, becoming (in a now familiar pattern in modern Bluebeard narratives) a medical doctor. He founded two families with the intention of conducting comparative experiments on the children Karl and Janni, and, while terrorizing the children, made their respective mothers tell them the tale 'Fitchers Blau'. The father sees the fortuitous meeting of his two children as the confirmation of his theories about them: they have been drawn together by 'die Stimme des Bluts'. The text is permeated with references to German Romantic literature, notably Novalis's *Heinrich von Ofterdingen* with its *blaue Blume*, but loses all aspects of the Grimms' happy ending to 'Fitchers Vogel'. Janni and Karl have been irredeemably damaged by their cruel, authoritarian father, who is identified with the authoritarian GDR state and, more subtly, with the National Socialist past, through his insane eugenic experiments which seek to release 'die Stimme des Bluts'.

In different ways, all these texts make connections between the figure of Bluebeard and the weight of German history, notably the National Socialist period and its consequences, including the division of Germany. Bluebeard represents a certain conception of the German nation itself, which cannot tolerate perceived difference and seeks to erase it as in the Holocaust; or he can stand for the intolerant authoritarianism of the GDR (Schramm); or even the damaging, ulti- mately murderous repressions underlying the outward success of the West German economic miracle (Sanders-Brahms and Hildebrandt). Just as Bluebeard or the robber bridegroom are shadowy, powerful, masculine figures, who embody social and symbolic authority and against whom victims are helpless, the texts discussed here show protagonists in the thrall of political, implicitly patriarchal authority. That authority may be the dead weight of history; more specula- tively, the dominance of Bluebeard or the robber in texts like Schramm's or Hildebrandt's may symbolize the suggestion of some thinkers that the traditionally passive relationship of many Germans to authority may have been a contributory factor to the rise of authoritarian National Socialist ideology.[13]

---

[13] On the complexities of such a theory, see e.g. Theodor W. Adorno, 'Erziehung nach Auschwitz' (1966), in *Gesammelte Schriften*, ed. Rolf Tiedemann, 20 vols. (Frankfurt am Main: Suhrkamp, 1997), x. 2, 674–90 (677–8).

HISTORICAL PATTERNS

While these shifts in meaning and contemporary interest in 'Blaubart' disprove traditional notions about the timelessness, the formally
static nature, and the regressive, nostalgic nature of the *Märchen*, it
would be misleading to imply that 'Blaubart' has enjoyed consistent
popularity in Germany since the eighteenth century. The pattern is
more differentiated. While there was a more unbroken interest in
'Blaubart' in the nineteenth century, in the twentieth century
Bluebeard texts tend to cluster, notably around 1905–25, especially
1905–13, and from 1968 to the present. And within that second
period the tale gained a new lease of life after 1989. This suggests
that, certainly in the last hundred years, 'Blaubart' has been used at
times of cultural unease or change, often in stabilizing ways. Just as
the tale formed part of the Grimms' nostalgic project which involved
a regression from the disturbing present of the early nineteenth
century, the same is true of the work of authors who used the
Blaubartmärchen in the period preceding the Great War, and again,
although more subtly, in the decades following 1968, when some
texts like Winkler's *Mike Blaubart* present nostalgic ideals of gender
roles. These latter two periods witnessed the rise of strong women's
movements and were, more broadly, marked by an unease with
modernity. But after 1968 also, women writers also came to use the
material in order to respond from a different, less nostalgic point of
view to such change. In addition, as the terms of the German debate
on the legacy of the mid-twentieth century shifted after the fall of the
Berlin Wall, so further possibilities of literary interpretation emerged.

GENERIC AND FORMAL CHARACTERISTICS OF THE TEXTS

The 'Blaubart' material is not only thematically diverse, it is also
formally heterogeneous. Of the eighty or so German primary texts
collected in the bibliography to this study, the most frequently occur-
ring genre is the short story or novella, followed by the drama, and
only then the classic *Märchen*. Indeed, only some twelve of these texts
conform to the traditional *Märchen* genre, and only one of those is an
original product of the last fifty years. Since Perrault, then, 'Blaubart'
has had a long tradition of being told in many forms, and what is
thought of as the classic *Märchen*—the short prose narrative—is only

the most celebrated of these. In fact, it seems that even in the nineteenth century, a period which is imagined as being the heyday of the traditional *Märchen* in Germany, there was never one fixed *Märchen* form.

Different forms proliferated parallel to, and even in advance of, the best-known tradition of short prose *Märchen* during the eighteenth and nineteenth centuries. These included poetry (F. W. Gotter's verses 'Blaubart. Eine Romanze' of 1772) and, most notably, drama. There is a strong and consistent tradition of Bluebeard plays, beginning with Ludwig Tieck's *Ritter Blaubart* (1797), so that modern dramatic works like Bickmann's, or Dea Loher's new play *Blaubart—Hoffnung der Frauen* (1997), are in no sense formal innovations or new departures, but rather continue a tradition of putting 'Blaubart' on the stage which in fact pre-dated the classic nineteenth-century German *Märchen* versions.[14] More unexpectedly, perhaps, there is a similar, major and unbroken tradition of comic texts, perpetuated by Gerd Winkler's television play for example. Despite the murders involved in Dieter Hildebrandt's thriller *Blaubart Mitte 40* (1977), that work continues the tradition of light reading described with reference to Marlitt's 'Blaubart'. And the recent cabaret piece *Blaubarts Orchester* (1993) performed at the Kammerspiele in Hamburg continues a significant tradition of musical and operatic settings of 'Blaubart', which dates back to *Raoul Barbe-bleue* by Michel-Jean Sédaine and André Ernesto Modeste Grétry (1789), and in the early twentieth century, Ernst Nikolaus von Reznicek's opera based on Herbert Eulenberg's play *Ritter Blaubart* (1920).

So, because the classic *Märchen* is only a small part of the Bluebeard tradition, this study would, if it had focused on classic *Märchen* alone, have been limited to a meagre and fairly monologic corpus of texts. To appreciate the breadth and complexity of the German Bluebeard tradition, it is necessary to discard such narrowly generic concerns and investigate in broader and more associative ways the use of names, motifs, and plot structures which are related to this extremely diverse narrative tradition. The tradition's formal and generic heterogeneity also indicates that it is erroneous to imagine that an originally formally consistent tradition of *Märchen* became

[14] Dea Loher, *Blaubart—Hoffnung der Frauen* (a reference to the title of Oskar Kokoschka's play *Mörder—Hoffnung der Frauen* (1907, first published 1910)), Residenztheater, Munich, première 26 Nov. 1997, published as *Manhattan Medea. Blaubart—Hoffnung der Frauen* (Frankfurt am Main: Verlag der Autoren, 1999). For programme and reviews, see the Bibliography.

fragmented over time. In fact, the formal diversity of the Bluebeard literature of the twentieth century is simply a continuation of an earlier heterogeneity. It is only with hindsight that the Bluebeard material has been organized and evaluated around a central, formally consistent canon *à la KHM*.

THE BLUEBEARD CANON

Three criteria may be used to determine the way in which the canon is constituted. First, the canon includes the texts which are most frequently included in anthologies and similar collections; for example, new versions of 'Blaubart' often preface the new text with one of the classic versions. Winkler's *Mike Blaubart* uses Bechstein's text in this way. Second, the canon includes those texts which are routinely cited in reference works, bibliographies, and secondary literature. And a third element in canonization is the accessibility of Bluebeard texts for literary analysis and inclusion in bibliographies and studies. By accessibility I mean both the availability of texts in libraries and archives and the ease of identifying them as Bluebeard texts. For instance, if there is no reference to 'Blaubart' in the title, the text immediately becomes less recognizable and is unlikely to make its way into systematic catalogues, bibliographies, and Bluebeard studies.

In Bluebeard anthologies and other collections of texts, Perrault's text is included by far the most frequently, followed by the Grimms', with Bechstein's a little way behind. Second, reference works and commentaries also refer most often by far to the classic versions by Perrault and the Grimms, but perceive Bechstein's version to be epigonal. Very often, the Grimms' alternative to 'Blaubart', 'Fitchers Vogel', is also included, but the similarly related 'Der Räuberbräutigam' is mentioned less frequently. Only very few reference works and bibliographies aim to include an overview of literary Bluebeard texts as opposed to classic *Märchen*. The major sources of this type are the *Enzyklopädie des Märchens*, Elisabeth Frenzel's *Stoffe der Weltliteratur*, and Hartwig Suhrbier's anthology *Blaubarts Geheimnis*.[15] Apart from the classic *Märchen*, the *Enzyklopädie des Märchens* mentions

---

[15] Kurt Ranke et al. (eds.), *Enzyklopädie des Märchens: Handwörterbuch zur historischen und vergleichenden Erzählforschung*, to date 8 vols. (Berlin: de Gruyter, 1975); Elisabeth Frenzel, *Stoffe der Weltliteratur*, 8th edn. (Stuttgart: Kröner, 1992), 107–11.

Tieck, Bechstein, the eighteenth-century opera by Grétry and Sédaine, Offenbach, Maeterlinck, Bartók, and Suhrbier's edition of Friedrich II. Similarly, apart from the classic *Märchen*, possible early historical sources, and texts outside the German tradition, Frenzel includes works by Tieck, Eulenberg, Reznicek, Döblin, Kaiser, Rühmkorf, Frisch, and Struck. And Suhrbier's anthology is particularly important, since this collection itself has not only become canonical but has come itself to help define the canon, since it is the only easily available, broad-ranging collection of literary Bluebeard texts and as such is routinely cited by later commentators. Suhrbier's bibliography is large, and in his accompanying anthology and essay he covers a broad range of texts. However, the German texts he selects for inclusion in his anthology tend towards the murderous, not the comedic strand of the tradition. Other secondary literature on individual, literary 'Blaubart' texts apart from the classic *Märchen* is very limited, with the most frequently discussed authors being those who are well known for their other work, such as Tieck and Frisch.

Third, the accessibility and availability of Bluebeard texts is important, as we can see, for instance, with reference to the texts produced at the turn of the century. While the texts discussed in Chapter 6 are not the only Bluebeard texts from the period in question, it is significant that they are the ones which have become to some degree canonized. The thematically homogeneous group of texts analysed in that chapter is relatively accessible through anthologies, notably Suhrbier's, inclusion in editions of collected works, as in the case of Eulenberg or Trakl, and the storing of such serious-minded journals as *Der Brenner* or *Die neue Rundschau* in libraries. While the other Bluebeard texts from the period are mentioned in bibliographies, they are difficult, if not impossible, to find. But according to Suhrbier's brief summaries of some of those texts, it seems that they are more indebted to the nineteenth-century comedic and romantic Bluebeard variants. In other words then, the murderous and misogynistic texts have been canonized, but not the milder comedies.

Therefore, there are biases in the Bluebeard canon. These are, first, towards the classic *Märchen* versions. Second, texts make their way into the canon by virtue of being by writers who are well known for the rest of their *œuvre* (Tieck, Kaiser, Frisch et al.), to whom collected works and so on are devoted, and who are mentioned in reference works. Third, the canon involves texts whose initial context of publication means that they make their way into libraries and archives more easily. For a text to become canonised, it helps if its author is part of a literary élite (such as the *Brennerkreis*) which has the means of promoting its status, for instance through a journal of high culture like *Der Brenner*, where Karl Schoßleitner's 'Prinz Blaubart' appeared. *Der Brenner* is more often included in library collections than, say, the more lowbrow nineteenth-century illustrated magazine *Über Land und Meer*, which ran a now completely forgotten 'Blaubart' serial by F. W. Hackländer in the 1860s.[16] Fourth, the canon includes texts which contain explicit references to 'Blaubart' in their titles. This is important because the content of texts with such titles often seems to be distinctive and may reveal a narratorial identification with Bluebeard, as in the texts discussed in Chapter 6. And fifth, the tone and content of the texts play a role, since serious texts, tragedies and texts involving murder get into the canon most frequently.

Consequently, the canon does not reflect those genres which were actually most common in the Bluebeard tradition, which were the drama, the novella, and the short story. Neither does it reflect the major importance of comedy. Moreover, it does not take account of the contemporary popularity and influence of individual Bluebeard texts. For instance, Bechstein's version of 'Blaubart' was more popular and frequently read in the nineteenth century than the Grimms', but commentators on the *Märchen* consider the Grimms' to be the more important text. Similarly, Marlitt's 'Blaubart' must have reached a far broader audience and touched a contemporary nerve more than Trakl's fragmentary *Puppenspiel* can have done, for while the former text was serialized in the widely read periodical *Die Gartenlaube* and went into foreign-language translations and many editions as a book, the latter text was never completed, published only posthumously, and has tended only ever to be read by academics. Yet Trakl's Bluebeard fragment is far more accessible than Marlitt's novella because there is a recent critical edition of Trakl's writing but no similar edition of Marlitt which would be bought as a matter of course by university libraries.

It seems that the canon is a self-perpetuating phenomenon, which will therefore naturally privilege writers who are already well known and literary forms which are considered prestigious like the Grimmian *Märchen*. The fact that the excluded texts tend to be comic

---

[16] Friedrich Wilhelm Hackländer, 'Der Blaubart', *Über Land und Meer*, 10 (38–40) (1863), 593–95, 609–11, and 625–7 respectively. The Deutsches Literaturarchiv in Marbach am Neckar does not keep *Über Land und Meer*, but it does have *Der Brenner*.

and not cast in the classic *Märchen* form must be partly due to the convention whereby comic, light, or romantic texts are considered *ipso facto* trivial. But on a deeper level, it may be that the canon is biased against the rewarding or triumph of women—or even their very survival. Perrault's original text has utopian potential because it depicts the overthrow of a tyrant and the breaking of a cycle of violence, symbolized by the survival of the heroine and the classic comic finale of reward and multiple marriage. But the best-known texts weaken that potential, as in the case of the greater popularity of the tragic opera *Duke Bluebeard's Castle* over that of the more utopian *Ariane et Barbe-bleue*. And even Marlitt's *Blaubart*, with its ultimately submissive heroine, is better known and more easily available than Julius Roderich Benedix's contemporary *Lustspiel* of the same title, in which the charming, clever Rosamunde lays bare men's folly in suspecting women of being more curious than themselves, and in submitting them to authority born of jealousy. And Rosamunde not only triumphs in that battle of wits, she is rewarded with a husband, without surrendering her autonomy like Marlitt's Lilli, whose folly has to be exposed and who must profess her submission before gaining a mate.

So the canonical bias towards more earnest, violent, or tragic texts involves scepticism towards ideas of subversion and change, often symbolized by the survival of women or the undermining of patriarchal power relations. This canon, which is conservative in the way it valorizes forms it considers traditional, also fails to bring out the utopianism and challenge to traditional, patriarchal gender roles which are so important in Perrault's text. This conclusion maps with the observation that the *Märchen* tends to be popularly identified as a regressive, normative, and conservative form; and that that identification is actually a product of the canon rather than an accurate reflection of the nature of the material involved, since here, for instance, comedy, less likely to be fatalistic in its outcome, is left out.

GENDER AND THE CANON

The opening chapter of this study suggested that the *Märchen* canon is gendered in that it has traditionally been biased towards patriarchal values and/or men writers, because, among other reasons, the originary 'script' of the genre and German folklore as laid down by

Herder emphasized the virtues of masculinity and patrilinearity. It has been argued that texts by women often tend to drop out of the canon both because they do not measure up to such a patrilinear ideal and because they are more likely to reflect alternative, eccentric experiences of dominant culture and authority.

At first sight, that expectation that women writers will be excluded from the canon seems not to be borne out by the evidence collected in this thesis, because the Bluebeard canon excludes a large body of work by both men and women authors and seems to be constituted according to apparently non-gender-specific criteria like form and genre, for instance the use of the classic *Märchen* form. So, since comedies tend to be excluded, this is principally to the detriment of men writers like Benedix, since they wrote more Bluebeard comedies than women did. And at the same time, because *Märchen* are *inter alia* associated with children's literature and popular culture, they are often not thought to belong to high culture and therefore tend not to be conserved in the way that apparently more serious texts are. This is as true of texts by men as it is of work by women. For example, while collected editions of the writings of F. W. Hackländer, Moriz Hartmann, and August Lewald exist, none includes these authors' versions of 'Blaubart', which were considered too trivial to be included. For instance, the 'Vorwort der Herausgeber' in Moriz Hartmann's *Gesammelte Werke* (1874) states:

Die Gesammtausgabe der Dichtungen und Schriften Moritz Hartmanns, . . . wird . . . Alles umfassen, was der Dichter auf dem Gebiet der Poesie, der Novellistik und der höheren Unterhaltungsliteratur *Nennenswertes* geschaffen hat. [my emphasis][17]

According to these editors *Märchen* are not 'nennenswert', although ironically it is Hartmann's *Märchen* and not other parts of his *œuvre* which have recently been reissued and which form the basis of his reputation today. Moreover, despite the fact that the tale of 'Bluebeard' seems to have originated with the influence of a woman writer, Marie-Jeanne Lhéritier, on Perrault, of all the texts in the bibliography to this study, only an unexpectedly small proportion (sixteen or so) are by women authors. Only one of these texts was produced before 1900, and only two or three further such texts were published before the 1970s. Since 1990, however, at least seven new

---

[17] Moriz Hartmann, *Gesammelte Werke*, ed. Ludwig Bamber and Wilhelm Vollmer, 10 vols. (Stuttgart: Cotta, 1874), vol. i, pp. iii–x (p. iii).

Bluebeard texts by women writers have appeared. It seems therefore that in recent years more women writers have been inspired to take a creative interest in 'Blaubart'.

Until very recently, therefore, 'Blaubart' must have failed to interest women writers and feminist critics, since there is also a surprising dearth of feminist secondary work on 'Blaubart'. First, general circumstances traditionally made writing more difficult for women than men in Germany;[18] second, the nature of the canon as it developed may not have appealed to women writers, since the Bluebeard canon became increasingly masculinized in its content with the passing of time. In many texts there was a defamation and marginalization of the women characters and a glorification of Bluebeard, who became an identificatory figure for men authors. The texts analysed in this study, however, suggest that for women writers, the heroine or other women characters are more likely to be figures of identification, so that the emphasis in the canonical *Blaubartmärchen* on violence and the inculpation, murder, and imprisonment of women (rather than escape, reward, and triumph), as well as the heroine's morally suspicious character in some versions, might have limited the material's appeal for women writers. We may conclude that it is not correct to suggest that there is a significantly large body of writing by women which has been unjustly ignored. Rather, the canon may simply reflect the real situation of women writers in this tradition, rather than excluding them to a disproportionate extent.

And yet, without in any way contradicting the above conclusions, in some respects the canon is gendered to the disadvantage of women writers. It is certainly striking that Lhéritier's founding text has been forgotten, or has been attributed to Perrault; that no texts by women have made their way into the canon at all; and that the major texts which are all by men (except, paradoxically, for Perrault's and perhaps Tieck's) do all stand for patriarchal values, or have been traditionally read as doing so. Certainly, too, the texts by women writers discussed in this thesis have been more difficult to identify and find than the texts by men. Even the chapter on Marlitt's 'Blaubart', which is included in Marlitt's *Gesammelte Werke* (undated, presumably

---

[18] Cf. Sigrid Weigel, 'Der schielende Blick: Thesen zur Geschichte weiblicher Schreibpraxis', in Inge Stephan and Sigrid Weigel, *Die verborgene Frau: Sechs Beiträge zu einer feministischen Literaturwissenschaft* (Berlin: Argument, 1983), 83–137, or *Deutsche Literatur von Frauen. Zweiter Band. Neunzehntes und zwanzigstes Jahrhundert*, ed. Gisela Brinker-Gabler (Munich: Beck, 1988).

late nineteenth century) and Suhrbier's bibliography was due to the providential discovery of the text in a private library. The same is true of Zürn's and Reichart's texts, found by a process of serendipity rather than by means of systematic bibliographical searches. And the one German Bluebeard work by a woman produced after 1917 and listed by Suhrbier, Pina Bausch's *Blaubart. Beim Anhören einer Tonbandaufnahme von Béla Bartóks Oper 'Herzog Blaubarts Burg'* (1977), being a live dance performance, cannot be preserved in the same way as a published text. Works by men which appeared as one-off performances, like Gerd Winkler's television play or Frisch's radio version of his *Blaubart*, seem more likely to be backed up with the publication of a book. And other twentieth-century texts by women are unavailable in published form (Hermynia Zur Mühlen's typescript, Barbara Köhler's manuscript).

I therefore suggest that the canon is gendered for six reasons. First, since the canonical Bluebeard authors are in many cases canonical by virtue of the fact that they are already famous, this weights the canon against women writers who are, given German cultural traditions, less likely to be known and therefore not subjects of critical editions and so forth. Bachmann is an apparent exception here, but of course her *Franza* novel slips out of the 'Blaubart' canon for other reasons. Second, the texts' status in the canon can be a question of where they were first published, for example in more prestigious journals likely to be collected by libraries. Such journals, like *Der Brenner*, were often in the hands of groups who considered themselves to be arbiters of high culture, and such cultural power has customarily been in the hands of men. Third, it may well be that more Bluebeard texts were produced by women, but that they have not survived, or at least not in a way which makes them visible to researchers. This has often been the fate of writing by women, because it has been considered trivial. *Märchen* or comic or romantic literature by women are doubly open to such a judgement. The respectable *Märchen* is conventionally imagined to be patrilinear in its descent, another factor which discredits such writing by women. So such apparently trivial and therefore ephemeral texts may not have made their way into libraries and catalogues. Fourth, other texts may have disappeared because they do not refer to 'Blaubart' in obvious ways, for example through their titles. While this point may seem self-evident, it is important given the findings in Chapter 7, which noted the existence of a whole series of texts by male authors which referred explicitly to 'Blaubart' in their titles, while few of the literary texts by women did so. Instead, those texts (e.g. Bachmann's *Das Buch Franza*) referred to the *Blaubartmärchen* in more oblique ways. This suggests that in the postwar period at least male authors may have tended to respond differently from and more emphatically than women authors to the identificatory possibilities held out by the figure of Bluebeard himself. The same patterns may have obtained in earlier literary production also, with the result that Bluebeard texts by women became invisible. And fifth and sixth, the form and content of the texts play a role, since many of the Bluebeard texts by women examined here are strikingly similar in certain aspects of their form and content. Those aspects differ from the best-known canonical versions of the material, and therefore such material is likely to be considered eccentric or inauthentic and therefore excluded.

DIFFERENT VOICES?

Chapter 1 of this study presented arguments by feminist critics that *Märchen* by women are likely to be different from canonical texts, and eccentric to, or subversive of, canonical values, a proposition which may now be re-examined with reference to the evidence collected in this book. I stress here that to suggest that writing by women may differ from that in the canon is not to suggest that women use the material fundamentally or consistently differently from men, or that any such thing as an essential feminine aesthetic exists. While in practice the canon is made up of texts by men, there are many non-canonical texts by men too, because male authors also use the material in challenging ways. That is, I am not arguing that women's writing is inherently different from men's, but rather that the Bluebeard material provides a good test case which shows that historical circumstances are likely (but not bound) to provoke features in writing by women which are especially likely to exclude them from the canon. Conversely, since the Bluebeard canon as I have defined it is broad and diverse, I do not claim here that all the texts included in it are consistently and diametrically opposed, in the same ways, to texts by women, partly because the canonical texts differ greatly from one another and may contain what might be called non-canonical aspects too. Rather, it seems that many of the texts by women writers have certain consistent features which are different from consistent features of many texts in the canon, rather than all canonical texts *en bloc*.

First, while the canon privileges the classic *Märchen* form, none of the texts by women discussed in this study fits in with received ideas of what a *Blaubartmärchen* should be formally, that is, a classic Grimmian *Märchen*. Rather, they are all longer, often fragmentary prose narratives which do not strive for narrative closure. While Marlitt's novella is an exception in that it does tend towards closure, it has otherwise little in common formally with the classic texts of the nineteenth century. And while Struck uses the *Märchen* reference conventionally in one way because she, like the Grimms, is aiming to produce an 'Erziehungsbuch', in other ways, for instance in the text's defiance of closure and monologic narrative, her novel too deviates formally from the canonical *Märchen*. In sum, it might be argued that this group of writers' more problematic relationship to a form which taught patriarchal values is often reflected in an alternative, often fragmented narrative technique.

Second, how do women authors handle the figure of Bluebeard? Nineteenth-century canonical texts evince unease regarding Bluebeard's murders and seek to exculpate him in subtle ways. For instance, the Grimms introduce an authoritarian *paterfamilias* into their text who behaves much as Bluebeard does but is allegedly good; and Bechstein's narrator implicitly affirms Bluebeard's moral judgements. This tendency takes a different tack at the turn of the century, where Bluebeard becomes a stronger focalizer for a series of avantgarde authors. In that period, he is legitimized not by being a moral authority in his family but by being an outlaw Don Juan who is exculpated by his superhuman qualities. This kind of focalization persists in those postwar texts where Bluebeard is exculpated because he is presented as a victim. In other words, in many canonical texts attempts are often made to recuperate aspects of Bluebeard.

The treatment of Bluebeard in texts by women differs in two ways. While Marlitt's Lilli does love Bluebeard–Dorn, for later women writers he has no positive aspects to be recuperated. Where the idea of Bluebeard is associated with an individual character, that character is viewed from without and (with the exception of Marlitt's Dorn) with little sympathy. While characters associated with Bluebeard may still be attractive by virtue of their power or prestige, like Franza's husband, Jordan, in Bachmann's novel, that attraction is viewed critically. And even in the case of Marlitt's text, Dorn can only be viewed positively because all the characters believe that he is *not* Bluebeard, i.e. it is not Bluebeard who is being glorified, but a man who is distinguished by the narrator and characters precisely because they believe he is not Bluebeard.

Furthermore, and very significantly, if in the canonical texts Bluebeard appears as an individual character, he does not do so in any of the texts by women. Not only do women authors, including Marlitt, have difficulty seeing Bluebeard as a focalizer, they in fact resist seeing him as an individual character, that is, a human being, at all. Rather, he appears as a disembodied idea or principle, or else as a fantastic figure in whom many images are condensed (e.g. the lover, doctor, and military officer in *Das Haus der Krankheiten*). In other words, women writers tend to dehumanise, de-individualize and deconstruct the idea of Bluebeard and use him to make connections between apparently separate things (e.g. love and medicine in *Das Haus der Krankheiten* or love and collecting in Marlitt's 'Blaubart'). It could be said that women authors' perception of Bluebeard involves a certain theorization—and thus, potentially, a politicization—of the individual Bluebeard figure described by the canon, because such a theorization permits the texts to make connections between the individual and the general.

Third, the portrayal of the woman protagonist also varies. While in Perrault's text she is the focus of relatively sympathetic attention, in the nineteenth-century canon she comes to appear morally suspicious and to stand for a threatening Other. That tendency persists during the twentieth century so that the woman is increasingly marginalized, objectified, and imagined as emotional, uncontrolled, and to blame for her own fate. She is also increasingly perceived as being sexually threatening, a further element leading to her inculpation and punishment. For instance, the female victim in Frisch's *Blaubart* is killed in a sexual murder. Because she has rejected the status of a good bourgeois wife and subsequently become a prostitute and, more scandalously still, has done so voluntarily rather than through material desperation, Frisch is fitting her into a clichéd tradition of thinking about prostitutes which assumes first that they are sure to become victims of sexual violence and second that they are wicked and so deserve or invite punishment because they have voluntarily made themselves sexually available. Frisch's plot is a modern continuation of the frequent punishment of transgressive women in the Bluebeard tradition. But in texts by women writers, the portrayal of the female protagonist is often different. Where other authors use Bluebeard as a focalizer, the women authors use the heroine of 'Blaubart' in a like manner. All the texts examined give a voice to Bluebeard's wife in a way which contrasts with the Grimms' attempts at silencing her, Bechstein's emphasis on her weakness, and the dominance of the male hero in the twentieth century. Correspondingly, the modern fascination with seriality which is dominant in some other texts becomes less important in texts by women since their texts are told from the point of view of the woman protagonist, so that there tends to be one woman at the centre of the texts, rather than a series of them at the margins. Indeed, seriality is replaced in the texts by women by the motif of a central female character who engages not with a series of individual men but with *one* Bluebeard principle or figure which may be made up of several layers or condensations, as described above. And if some of the canonical texts make the point that women invite violence by being wanton, wicked, or masochistic, the texts by women (apart from Marlitt's) redress the balance of blame by making clear that Bluebeard is the criminal, not his wife. Nevertheless, at the same time the texts by women tend to avoid any clear binary schema of victim and perpetrator, since their analysis of women's complicity in Bluebeard's crime is comparatively complex. Women writers not only show that women's complicity in the Bluebeard order or masochism are fraught and contradictory, but they acknowledge (in the case of Marlitt), or even (in the later texts) try to provide an explanation of, the way in which the circumstances of women's lives can generate complicity and masochism. So if Perrault could assume a coherent feminine subject of emancipation, women writers describe a more complex, fragmented, or split subjectivity which makes the heroine's liberation more problematic as well.

Fourth, the nature of the control exerted by Bluebeard varies. In canonical texts, that control tends to be physical and violent, so that murder, physical incarceration and force are central to the plot up to the present day. In the texts by women writers, only two of the women characters die (Beatrice and Franza), and in both cases this is not the result of direct, brutal murder or literal imprisonment, but a delayed effect of the lives the women have led in the shadow of their father (in the case of Beatrice, who seems to be most strongly affected by her heredity and the family curse brought about by her male ancestors) or husband (in the case of Franza). In texts by women there is little or no physical restriction, threat, or violence because the women characters are subject instead to less tangible controls which operate psychologically. This means that the texts by women look beyond individual force for more subtle, psychological patterns of behaviour, which once again are broader in nature and connect the individual and the general. The women writers' analysis of the process of civilization is more subtle, too, in that they identify the shift from 'Fremdzwang' to 'Selbstzwang' more clearly, and fit that shift explicitly into its historical context, that is, like Perrault, to a contemporary setting.

Fifth, the two groups of authors handle the issues of history, time-lessness, and nostalgia differently. The traditional association of the *Märchen* with a lost past is, at least in the case of the *Blaubartmärchen*, related to the way the *Märchen* is used at a time of crisis. Often (although less frequently after 1968) the form is used to invoke a fantastical past and its ideals in order to ward off the perceived threats of the present. And after 1968 too, some of the canonical texts invoke the past in that they promote nostalgic gender ideals. But this is not the case with non-canonical texts and especially with texts by women, since, without exception, the texts by women are set in the present and use 'Blaubart' to examine that present critically, although this critique is unintentional in Marlitt's 'Blaubart'.

Sixth, the utopian or subversive impulses of 'Blaubart' vary. In canonical texts, the utopian impulse is increasingly covered over by the increasingly emphatic punishment of the heroine in the classic nineteenth-century versions, and then the focus on seriality at the turn of the century; this precludes the possibility of breaking the violent cycle, so that the *fin-de-siècle* texts are the first to deny any utopian possibility. This tendency is visible in later twentieth-century mainstream texts too, like Frisch's. In contrast, the texts by women are more complex in their mix of utopianism and fatalism. It seems that women writers are interested not only in showing the nature and workings of the Bluebeard order but also in exploring ways of sub-verting it, albeit with varying and fraught conclusions. Similarly, many canonical texts seek to reassert a threatened, patriarchal status quo and nostalgic ideals of masculinity; but the later texts by women especially tend to use 'Blaubart' not in order to affirm the status quo of gender politics and traditional ideals of masculinity but to criticize them.

Seventh, feminist critics have argued that women writers who use *Märchen* material often refer positively and subversively to the traditional notion of a feminine narrative community, or to the image of the *Märchentante*, who was increasingly demonized in canonical *Märchen* in the modern period. Marlitt's text includes two such demonic woman narrator figures: the servant Dorte with her disruptive gossip and Tante Bärbchen, who says equally disruptive things and also spins, a typical occupation for such a figure. The narrator's attitude towards these two figures is highly ambivalent, but they are important for generating the subversive undertones of the text. In fact, it is the stereotypical, chattering old servant Dorte who unmasks Dorn for what he is, a true Bluebeard, whereas everyone else is set on denying that fact. But while Zürn's text embraces the notion of a supportive narrative community more forcefully, it also makes the point that that community includes both male and female helpers.

Bachmann's Franza appears to be isolated from any such supportive community until after her death, but she too uses the *Märchen* in an attempt—albeit a failed one—to produce a redemptive narrative for herself and so explain and overcome her predicament. And Struck cites Bachmann's *Der Fall Franza* explicitly in her novel *Blaubarts Schatten* in order to lend weight to her argument. Struck is re-creating intertextually the traditional concept of the supportive, feminine narrative community on behalf of her protagonist, who has no immediate access to a supportive, feminine community in a man's world. While a consistent vision of a supportive, subversive and feminine community is not presented in these texts, narrative community involving the female voice is important, and those voices can be subversive. In addition, the way the texts give a voice to Bluebeard's wife make that character herself into a disruptive teller of tales.

In conclusion, the *Märchen* is a less objective and timeless form than is popularly thought; the German canon not only fails to cover the complexity and diversity of the literature in question but also favours masculinist values; and many women authors do tend to handle the *Blaubartmärchen* differently from canonical authors, who are more likely to be men. For all these reasons, and by virtue of its powerful themes too, 'Blaubart' provides many insights into civilization, difference—of nationality or gender—and utopia.

And the tale reminds us of issues nearer home than literature. In

1993 Jill Hague and Ellen Malos wrote that 'between 90 and 97 per cent of domestic violence is perpetrated against women by men':[19]

On 14 April 1990, *The Times* reported that a half [*sic*] of all women murdered in Britain were killed by their husbands or lovers, by far the largest single category of women victims. Homicide statistics consistently reveal that between 40 and 45 per cent of women victims . . . are murdered by their partners. . . . A study published in 1993 by Middlesex University found that one in ten of the women they interviewed had experienced violence from their partners in the previous twelve months; and in a 1992 report, the Women's Aid Federation (England), . . . estimated in support of other studies that up to one in four women may on occasion experience violence in their sexual relationships with men. Severe, repeated and systematic violence is clearly less common, but it has been estimated to occur in at least five in a hundred marriages in Britain. In a 1985 survey by *Woman* magazine, one in four women who anonymously reported such violence had told no one else about it. (pp. 6–12)

Strikingly, the title of a recent study on domestic violence refers explicitly to Bluebeard, in a way which makes clear that this figure still encodes urgent and very real contemporary meanings.[20] At a time when hidden abuses of power in the home have by no means been checked, the critical and utopian potential of the Bluebeard material is of continued importance for a literary criticism whose goal is ultimately to make connections with a transformative political practice.

[19] Jill Hague and Ellen Malos, *Domestic Violence: Action for Change* (Cheltenham: New Clarion Press, 1993), 4.
[20] J. W. E. Sheptycki, *Rapacious Bluebeards and Chivalrous Knights: A Sociolinguistic View of Policing Women Battering* (Edinburgh: University of Edinburgh New Waverley Papers, 1995).

BIBLIOGRAPHY

PRIMARY TEXTS: 'BLAUBART'

ANGÉLY, Louis, 'Herr Blaubart oder das geheimnisvolle Kabinett. Posse in Einem Akt, frei nach dem Französischen', in *Vaudevilles und Lustspiele. Theils Originale, Theils Übertragungen, Bearbeitungen*, 3 vols. (Berlin: Cosmar & Krause, 1828), i. 67–123.

ARTMANN, h. c., 'blauboad 1', in *med ana schwoazzn dintn* (Salzburg: Otto Müller, 1958), 17.

—— 'blauboad 2', in *med ana schwoazzn dintn* (Salzburg: Otto Müller, 1958), 18.

BACHMANN, Ingeborg, 'Das Buch Franza', in *Todesarten-Projekt*, ed. Monika Albrecht and Dirk Göttsche, 4 vols. (Munich: Piper, 1995), ii.

BALÁSZ, Béla, 'Duke Bluebeard's Castle' (1910–11, première 24 May 1918), trans. John Lloyd Davies, in *The Stage Works of Béla Bartók*, ed. Nicholas John (London: Calder, 1991), 45–60.

BAUER, Wolfgang Maria, *Blaubart, von der Sehnsucht der Kaltblütler* (première 5 December 1998, Schauspielhaus Graz).

BECHSTEIN, Ludwig, 'Das Märchen vom Ritter Blaubart' (1845), in *Deutsches Märchenbuch*, ed. Hans-Heino Ewers (Stuttgart: Reclam, 1996), 374–7.

BENEDIX, Julius Roderich, 'Blaubart. Lustspiel in zwei Aufzügen', *Die deutsche Schaubühne*, 7 (1861), 2–27.

BERTUCH, Friedrich Justin, 'Blaubart', in *Die Blaue [sic] Bibliothek aller Nationen*, ed. and trans. Friedrich Justin Bertuch, 12 vols. (Gotha: Ettinger, 1790–1800), i. 13–21.

BICKMANN, Walter, *Blaubart—Die letzten Männer* (première 16 Dec. 1997, Volksbühne, Berlin).

BLASCHEK, Ulrike, *Märchen vom Blaubart* (Frankfurt am Main: Fischer, 1989).

VON CRAMER, Heinz, 'Ritter Blaubart', in *Märchen, Sagen und Abenteuer auf alten Bilderbogen neu erzählt von Autoren unserer Zeit*, ed. Jochen Jung (Munich: Moos, 1974), 26–8.

DÖBLIN, Alfred, 'Der Ritter Blaubart' (1911), in *Erzählungen aus fünf Jahrzehnten* (Olten: Walter, 1979), 76–86.

EL HOR, 'Ritter Blaubart', *Saturn*, 3 (1913), 201–3; also in *Blaubarts Geheimnis*, ed. Hartwig Suhrbier (Cologne: Diederichs, 1984), 160–1.

EULENBERG, Herbert, 'Ritter Blaubart', in *Ausgewählte Werke in fünf Bänden*, 5 vols. (Stuttgart: Engelhorn, 1925), ii. 271–324.

---

* This bibliography is not intended to supersede Hartwig Suhrbier's bibliography of 1984 since, while it contains items omitted by Suhrbier and items published after 1984, it does not include items listed by Suhrbier to which I did not have access.

FEILHAUER, Felicitas, *Blaubärtchen: Märchen und Geschichten für neugierige Leser* (Munich: Hanser, 1990).

FOWLES, John, *The Collector* (London: Pan, 1963).

FRIEDRICH II, König von Preußen, *Das Buch Blaubart. Eine Satire* (1779), ed. Hartwig Suhrbier (Frankfurt am Main: Insel, 1987).

FRISCH, Max, *Blaubart* (Frankfurt am Main: Suhrkamp, 1982).

GOTTER, Friedrich Wilhelm, 'Blaubart. Eine Romanze' (1772), in *Gedichte*, 3 vols. (Gotha: Ettinger, 1787), i. 47–56.

GRIMM, Jacob, and GRIMM, Wilhelm, 'Blaubart' (1812), no. 62 in *Kinder- und Hausmärchen. Gesammelt durch die Brüder Grimm. Vergrößerter Nachdruck der zweibändigen Erstausgabe von 1812 und 1815*, ed. Heinz Rölleke and Ulrike Marquardt, 3 vols. (Göttingen: Vandenhoeck & Ruprecht, 1986), i. 285–9; also in *Kinder- und Hausmärchen* (1857), ed. Heinz Rölleke, 3 vols. (Stuttgart: Reclam, 1980), ii. 465–8.

————— 'Marienkind', in *Kinder- und Hausmärchen* (1857), ed. Heinz Rölleke, 3 vols. (Stuttgart: Reclam, 1980), i. 36–41.

HACKLÄNDER, Friedrich Wilhelm, 'Der Blaubart', *Über Land und Meer*, 10 (38–40) (1863), 593–5; 609–11; 625–7.

HARTMANN, Moriz, 'Blaubart' (1867), in *Märchen nach Perrault neu erzählt von Moriz Hartmann. Illustrirt von Gustave Doré* (Hamburg: Broschek, 1966), 149–62.

HEIDENREICH, Elke, 'Blaubart und ich', in *Blaubärtchen: Märchen und Geschichten für neugierige Leser*, ed. Felicitas Feilhauer (Munich: Hanser, 1990), 25–32.

HILDEBRANDT, Dieter, *Blaubart Mitte 40* (Hamburg: Hoffmann & Campe, 1977).

HUYSMANS, Joris Karl, *Là-bas* (1891) (Paris: Gallimard, 1985).

JANOSCH (ps. Horst Eckart), 'Blaubart', in *Janosch erzählt Grimms Märchen und zeichnet für Kinder von heute* (Weinheim: Beltz & Gelberg, 1972), 161–4.

JOHANSEN, Hanna, 'Der Wüstling', in *Blaubärtchen: Märchen und Geschichten für neugierige Leser*, ed. Felicitas Feilhauer (Munich: Hanser, 1990), 89–98.

KAISER, Georg, 'Gilles und Jeanne' (1922), in *Werke*, ed. Walther Hude, 6 vols. (Frankfurt am Main: Propyläen Verlag and Ullstein, 1972), v. 746–811.

KÖHLER, Barbara, 'Blaubarts Zimmer', unpublished ms.

KÖNIG, Barbara, 'Nepomuk', in *Blaubärtchen: Märchen und Geschichten für neugierige Leser*, ed. Felicitas Feilhauer (Munich: Hanser, 1990), 149–70.

KOESTER, Reinhard, 'Ritter Blaubart', *Pan*, 1 (1911), 527; also in *Blaubarts Geheimnis*, ed. Hartwig Suhrbier (Cologne: Diederichs, 1984), 160.

KREINER, Otto, 'In Herzog Blaubarts Burg', *Neue Zürcher Zeitung, Fernausgabe* (1982), 27.

KRÜGER, Michael, 'Die Blaubart-Stiftung', in *Blaubärtchen: Märchen und Geschichten für neugierige Leser*, ed. Felicitas Feilhauer (Munich: Hanser, 1990), 185–207.

LAUSCH, Ernst, 'Vom Ritter Blaubart', in *Das Buch der schönsten Kinder- und Volksmärchen, Sagen und Schwänke* (Leipzig: Otto Spamer, 1876), 221–4.

LEWALD, August, 'Blaubart', in *Blaue Mährchen für alte und junge Kinder* (Stuttgart: Scheible, 1837), 267–8.

LOHER, Dea, *Manhattan Medea*. *Blaubart—Hoffnung der Frauen* (Frankfurt am Main: Verlag der Autoren, 1999).

MAETERLINCK, Maurice, and DUKAS, Paul, *Ariane et Barbe-bleue* (1901, première 10 May 1907) (Paris: Erato Disques, 1984).

MAIER, Ernst, 'König Blaubart' (1852), in *Deutsche Volksmärchen aus Schwaben* (Hildesheim: Olms, 1977), 134–7.

MARLITT, E., 'Blaubart', in *Die Gartenlaube*, 27, 417–20; 28, 433–6; 29, 449–52, 30 465–8; 31, 481–7 (1866); *Thüringer Erzählungen* (Leipzig: Keil, 1866), 107–242; *E. Marlitt's [sic] gesammelte Romane und Novellen*, 10 vols. (Leipzig: Keil's [sic] Nachfolger, n.d.), x. 263–338.

MEWIS, Marianne, *Blaubart* (Stuttgart: Engelhorn, 1917).

MÜLLER, Heiner, 'Selbstkritik 2 zerbrochner Schlüssel', in *Werke*, 3 vols. to date, ed. Frank Hörningk (Frankfurt am Main: Suhrkamp, 1998), i. 235.

NATONEK, Hans, *Blaubarts letzte Liebe* (Vienna: Zsolnay, 1988).

OMPTEDA, Georg Freiherr von, *Der neue Blaubart* (Berlin: Fleischel, 1919).

PASSON, Marga, *Blaubart* (Berlin: Ullstein, 1925).

PERRAULT, Charles, 'La Barbe bleue' (1697), in *Contes*, ed. Jean-Pierre Collinet (Paris: Gallimard, 1981), 147–54; also in *Contes*, ed. Marc Soriano (Paris: Flammarion, 1989), 257–62.

PIWITT, Hermann Peter, 'Ritter Blaubart', *diskus*, 7 (1957), 9.

POCCI, Franz Graf von, 'Blaubart. Ein furchtbares Spektakelstück aus dem finstern Mittelalter in drei Aufzügen' (1859), in *Franz Poccis sämtliche Kasperkomödien*, 3 vols. (Munich: Etzold, 1909), i. 95–126.

—— 'Blaubart. Ein Märchen erzählt und gezeichnet von F. Pocci' (1845), in *Die gesamte Druckgraphik*, ed. Marianne Bernhard (Herrsching: Pawlak, n.d.), 150–8.

REICHART, Elisabeth, 'Die Kammer', in *La Valse* (Salzburg: Otto Müller, 1992), 81–97.

VON REZNICEK, Ernst Nikolaus, *Ritter Blaubart* (Vienna: Universal-Edition, 1920).

ROHNER-RADEGAST, Wolfgang, *Vetter Blaubart oder wie die wohl drüben* (Karlsruhe: Literarische Gesellschaft Karlsruhe und Arbeitskreis Neue Literatur, 1995).

RÜHMKORF, Peter, 'Blaubarts letzte Reise', in *Der Hüter des Misthaufens: Aufgeklärte Märchen* (Reinbek bei Hamburg: Rowohlt, 1983), 110–22.

VON SACHER-MASOCH, Leopold, 'Ein harmloser Blaubart', in *Falscher Hermelin: Kleine Geschichten aus der Bühnenwelt* (Leipzig: Ernst Julius Günther, 1873), 81–91.

SANDERS-BRAHMS, Helma, *Deutschland, bleiche Mutter* (film) (1980).

—— *Deutschland, bleiche Mutter: Film-Erzählung* (Reinbek bei Hamburg: Rowohlt, 1980).

VON SCHLICHTEGROLL, Carl Felix, *Gilles de Rais: Das Urbild des Blaubart* (Leipzig: Leipziger Verlag, 1908).

SCHMIDT, Arno, 'Die 10 Kammern des Blaubart', in *Trommler beim Zaren* (Karlsruhe: Stahlberg, 1966), 243–52.

SCHOßLEITNER, Karl, 'Prinz Blaubart', *Der Brenner*, 3 (7, 8) (1911), 203–22; 247–62.

SCHRAMM, Ingo, *Fitchers Blau* (Berlin: Verlag Volk und Welt, 1996).

SCHUBERT, Helga, 'Das verbotene Zimmer', in *Das verbotene Zimmer* (Darmstadt: Luchterhand, 1982), 81–97.

STROBL, Karl Hans, *Madame Blaubart* (Leipzig: Singer, 1929).

STRUCK, Karin, *Blaubarts Schatten* (Munich: List, 1991).

STRUCK, Thomas, TUKUR, Ulrich, and WALLER, Ulrich, *Blaubarts Orchester* (première 8 Jan. 1993, Schmidts Tivoli, Hamburg).

SUHRBIER, Hartwig, *Blaubarts Geheimnis: Märchen und Erzählungen, Gedichte und Stücke* (Cologne: Diederichs, 1984).

TIECK, Ludwig, 'Der Blaubart. Ein Märchen in fünf Akten' (1797), in *Schriften*, ed. Manfred Frank et al., 12 vols. (Frankfurt am Main: Deutscher Klassiker Verlag, 1985), vi. 394–438.

—— 'Die sieben Weiber des Blaubart' (1797), in *Ludwig Tieck's* [*sic*] *Schriften*, 28 vols. (Berlin: Riemer, 1828), ix. 89–242.

TRAKL, Georg, 'Blaubart. Ein Puppenspiel' (1910), in *Dichtungen und Briefe. Historisch-kritische Ausgabe*, ed. Walther Killy and Hans Szklenar, 2 vols. (Salzburg: Otto Müller, 1969), i. 435–45.

VON UNGERN-STARNBERG, Alexander, 'Blaubart' (1850), in *Braune Märchen* (Bonn: Bouvier, 1977), 127–39.

VESTRIS, Armand, *Blaubart. Großes romantisch-pantomimisches Ballett in drei Abtheilungen* (Berlin: Lassar, 1832).

WESTENHOLZ, Friedrich Freiherr von, *Blaubart: Lustspiel in zwei Aufzügen* (Stuttgart: Frommann, 1895).

WINKLER, Gerd, *Mike Blaubart* (1967) (Frankfurt am Main: Heine, 1968).

ZIMMERMANN, Joachim, 'Ritter Blaubart. Nach Perrault', in *Alte Märchen mit der Feder erzählt von Max Slevogt, in Worte gefaßt von Joachim Zimmermann* (Berlin: Propyläen-Verlag, 1920).

ZUR MÜHLEN, Hermynia, 'Das verbotene Zimmer', Bundesarchiv Potsdam, *Pariser Tageszeitung* archive, no. 280 (n.d.), 9–13.

ZÜRN, Unica, 'Das Haus der Krankheiten: Geschichten und Bilder einer Gelbsucht', in *Gesamtausgabe*, ed. Günter Bose and Erich Brinkmann, 8 vols. (Berlin: Brinkmann & Bose, 1988–   ), iv. 1, 43–78.

FURTHER ANTHOLOGIES

AUERBACH, Nina, and KNOEPFLMACHER, Ulrich C. (eds), *Forbidden Journeys: Fairy Tales and Fantasies by Victorian Women Writers* (Chicago and London: University of Chicago Press, 1992).

TEGETTHOFF, Folke (ed.), *Das rot-weiss-rote Wolkenschiff: Märchen aus unserer Zeit* (Vienna: Österreichischer Bundesverlag, 1985).

TETZNER, Lisa (ed.), *Die schönsten Märchen der Welt für 365 und einen Tag*, 12 vols. (Darmstadt and Neuwied: Luchterhand, 1981).

ZIPES, Jack D. (ed.), *Don't Bet on the Prince: Contemporary Fairy Tales in North America and England* (New York: Methuen, 1986).

FURTHER PRIMARY TEXTS

AESCHYLUS, *Eumenides*, ed. and trans. Anthony J. Podlecki (Warminster: Aris & Phillips, 1989).

The Arabian Nights, ed. Muhsin Mahdi, trans. Husain Haddawy (New York: Norton, 1990).

VON ARNIM, Bettine, and VON ARNIM, Gisela, *Das Leben der Hochgräfin Gritta von Rattenzuhausbeiuns: Erste vollständige Ausgabe, mit 17 Zeichnungen von Gisela von Arnim und Hermann Grimm*, ed. Shawn Jarvis (Frankfurt am Main: Insel, 1987).

VON ARNIM, Gisela, *Märchenbriefe an Achim*, ed. Shawn Jarvis (Frankfurt am Main: Insel, 1991).

ARP, Hans, *Gesammelte Gedichte*, ed. Marguerite Arp-Hagenbach and Peter Schifferli, 3 vols. (Zurich: Limes, 1963).

BACHMANN, Ingeborg, *Werke*, ed. Christine Koschel, Inge von Weidenbaum, and Clemens Münster, 4 vols. (Munich: Piper, 1978).

—— *Todesarten-Projekt*, ed. Monika Albrecht and Dirk Göttsche, 4 vols. (Munich: Piper, 1995).

BECKER, Jurek, *Jakob der Lügner* (Frankfurt am Main: Suhrkamp, 1969).

BELLMER, Hans, *Petite Anatomie de l'inconscient physique ou l'anatomie de l'image* (1957) (Paris: Eric Losfeld, 1977).

BRUSTELLIN, Alf, SINKEL, Bernhard, FASSBINDER, Rainer Werner, KLUGE, Alexander, MAINKA, Maximiliane, REITZ, Edgar, MAINKA-JELLINGHAUS, Beate, SCHUBERT, Peter, CLOOS, Hans-Peter, RUPÉ, Katja, and SCHLÖNDORFF, Volker, *Deutschland im Herbst* (film) (1978).

CAMPION, Jane, *The Piano* (1993) (London: Bloomsbury, 1993).

ENDE, Michael, *Die unendliche Geschichte* (Stuttgart: Thienemann, 1979).

FONTANE, Theodor, *Werke, Schriften und Briefe*, ed. Walter Keitel and Helmuth Nürnberger, 20 vols. (Munich: Hanser, 1970).

FRISCHMUTH, Barbara, *Die Mystifikationen der Sophie Silber* (1976) (Munich: Heyne, 1993).

VON GOETHE, Johann Wolfgang, *Werke, Kommentare und Register: Hamburger Ausgabe*, ed. Erich Trunz, 14 vols. (Munich: Beck, 1981).

GRASS, Günter, *Der Butt* (Frankfurt am Main: Fischer, 1977).

—— *Die Rättin* (Darmstadt: Luchterhand, 1986).

—— *Ein weites Feld* (Göttingen: Steidl, 1995).

HOFFMANN, E. T. A., *Sämtliche Werke*, ed. Wulf Segebrecht and Hartmut Steinecke, 6 vols. (Frankfurt am Main: Deutscher Klassiker Verlag, 1985).

JELINEK, Elfriede, *Die Liebhaberinnen* (Reinbek bei Hamburg: Rowohlt, 1975).

LASKER-SCHÜLER, Else, *Gesammelte Werke in einem Band*, ed. Sigrid Bauschinger (Munich: Artemis & Winkler, 1991).

LINDSAY, Joan, *Picnic at Hanging Rock* (Harlow: Longman, 1968).

MERIAN, Svende, *Der Tod des Märchenprinzen* (Reinbek bei Hamburg: Rowohlt, 1980).

MORGNER, Irmtraud, *Hochzeit in Konstantinopel* (Frankfurt am Main: Luchterhand, 1968).

—— *Leben und Abenteuer der Trobadora Beatriz nach Zeugnissen ihrer Spielfrau Laura* (Berlin: Aufbau, 1974).

NOVALIS (Friedrich von Hardenberg), *Heinrich von Ofterdingen und andere dichterische Schriften* (1802) (Cologne: Könemann, 1996).

PALMEN, Connie, *The Laws*, trans. Richard Huijing (London: Minerva, 1992).

RILKE, Rainer Maria, *Die Aufzeichnungen des Malte Laurids Brigge* (1910) (Leipzig: Insel, 1958).

SANDER, Helke, *Die Geschichten der drei Damen K.* (Munich: Frauenbuchverlag, 1987).

SCHLEGEL, Friedrich, *Lucinde* (1799) (Berlin: Ullstein, 1980).

WEDEKIND, Frank, *Werke in drei Bänden*, ed. Manfred Hahn, 3 vols. (Berlin: Aufbau, 1969).

WOLF, Christa, *Kein Ort. Nirgends* (1979) (Berlin: Aufbau, 1980).

ZÜRN, Unica, *Das Weisse mit dem roten Punkt: Texte und Zeichnungen*, ed. Inge Morgenroth (Frankfurt am Main and Berlin: Ullstein, 1988).

—— *Der Mann im Jasmin* (Berlin: Ullstein, 1992).

SECONDARY TEXTS

AARNE, Antti, and THOMPSON, Stith, *Motif-Index of Folk Literature*, 6 vols. (Copenhagen: Rosenkilde and Bagger, 1958).

ADORNO, Theodor W., *Gesammelte Schriften*, ed. Rolf Tiedemann, 20 vols. (Frankfurt am Main: Suhrkamp, 1997).

ALLEN, Ann Taylor, 'The March Through the Institutions: Women's Studies in the United States and West and East Germany', *Signs*, 22 (1996), 152–80.

ANGERMANN, Klaus, CORDES, Annedore, and GOTTSCHALK, Frank (eds.), *Ariane et Barbe-bleue*, opera programme (Hamburg: Hamburger Staatsoper, 1997) .

ANTHONY, William Wilton, 'The Narration of the Marvelous in the Late Eighteenth-Century German *Märchen*', Ph.D. dissertation (Baltimore: Johns Hopkins University, 1982).

AZIZA, Claude, OLIVIERI, Claude, and SCTRICK, Robert, *Dictionnaire des symboles et des thèmes littéraires* (Paris: Nathan, 1978).

BAADER, Renate, *Dames de lettres: Autorinnen des preziösen, hocharistokratischen und 'modernen' Salons (1649–1698)* (Stuttgart: Metzler, 1986).

BACCHILEGA, Cristina, 'Folk and Literary Narrative in a Postmodern Context: The Case of the *Märchen*', *Fabula*, 29 (1988), 302–16.

—— *Postmodern Fairy Tales: Gender and Narrative Strategies* (Philadephia: University of Pennsylvania Press, 1997).

BÄCHTOLD-STÄUBLI, Hanns, and HOFFMANN-KRAYER, E., *Handwörterbuch des deutschen Aberglaubens*, 10 vols. (Berlin: de Gruyter, 1927–42).

BÄUERLE, Dorothea, 'Das nachromantische Kunstmärchen in der deutschen Dichtung', Ph.D. dissertation (Würzburg, 1937).

BAKHTIN, Mikhail M., *Problems of Dostoevsky's Poetics* (Ann Arbor, Mich.: Ardis, 1973).

BARKAN, Elazar, and BUSH, Ronald (eds.), *Prehistories of the Future: The Primitivist Project and the Culture of Modernism* (Stanford, Calif.: Stanford University Press, 1995).

BARTHES, Roland, *Image—Music—Text*, trans. Stephen Heath (London: Fontana, 1977).

BARZ, Helmut, *Blaubart: Wenn einer vernichtet, was er liebt* (Zurich: Kreuz, 1987).

BATAILLE, Georges, *Le Procès de Gilles de Rais* (Paris: Pauvert, 1972).

BAUSINGER, Hermann, *Märchen, Phantasie und Wirklichkeit* (Frankfurt am Main: Dipa, 1985).

DE BEAUVOIR, Simone, *Le Deuxième Sexe* (1949), 2 vols. (Paris: Gallimard, 1976).

VON BEIT, Hedwig, *Symbolik des Märchens*, 2 vols. (Berne: Francke, 1960).

BELTON, Robert J., 'Speaking With Forked Tongues: "Male" Discourse in "Female" Surrealism?', in Mary Ann Caws, Rudolf E. Kuenzli, and Gwen Raaberg (eds.), *Surrealism and Women* (Cambridge, Mass.: MIT Press, 1991), 60–2.

BENJAMIN, Walter, *Gesammelte Schriften*, ed. Rolf Tiedemann and Hermann Schweppenhäuser, 7 vols. (Frankfurt am Main: Suhrkamp, 1991).

BETTELHEIM, Bruno, *The Uses of Enchantment: The Meaning and Importance of Fairy Tales* (London: Thames & Hudson, 1976).

BLACKWELL, Jeannine, 'Fractured Fairy Tales: German Women Authors and the Grimm Tradition', *Germanic Review*, 62 (1987), 162–74.

BÖHME, Hartmut (ed.), *Kulturgeschichte des Wassers* (Frankfurt am Main: Suhrkamp, 1988).

——and BÖHME, Gernot, *Das Andere der Vernunft: Zur Entwicklung von Rationalitäts-strukturen am Beispiel Kants* (Frankfurt am Main: Suhrkamp, 1985).

BOHDE, Rebecca Sue, 'The German *Märchen* from 1970 to 1985: Versions of a Literary Genre in Areas of Topical Interest', Ph.D. Dissertation (Ann Arbor: Dissertation Abstracts International, 1992).

BOLTE, Johannes, and POLÍVKA, Georg (eds.), *Anmerkungen zu den Kinder- und Hausmärchen der Brüder Grimm*, 5 vols. (Leipzig: Dieterich'sche Verlagsbuchhandlung Theodor Weichen, 1913–32).

BOSSARD, Eugène, *Gilles de Rais Maréchal de France dit Barbe-Bleue* (1885) (Paris: Champion, 1886).

BOTTIGHEIMER, Ruth B. (ed.), *Fairy Tales and Society: Illusion, Allusion and Paradigm* (Philadelphia: University of Pennsylvania Press, 1986).

——*Grimms' Bad Girls and Bold Boys: The Moral and Social Vision of the Tales* (New Haven, Conn.: Yale University Press, 1987).

——'The Face of Evil', *Fabula*, 29 (1988), 326–35.

——'Bettelheims Hexe: Die fragwürdige Beziehung zwischen Märchen und

Psychoanalyse', *Psychotherapie—Psychosomatik—Medizinische Psychologie*, 39 (1989), 294–9.

——'Ludwig Bechstein's Fairy Tales: Nineteenth-Century Bestsellers and *Bürgerlichkeit*', *Internationales Archiv für Sozialgeschichte der deutschen Literatur*, 15 (1990), 55–88.

——'The Publishing History of Grimms' Tales: Reception at the Cash Register', in Donald Haase (ed.), *The Reception of Grimms' Fairy Tales: Responses, Reactions, Revisions* (Detroit: Wayne State University Press, 1993), 78–101.

BOUCHARD, Alain, *Les Grandes Croniques de la Bretaigne Composées en l'an 1514* (1514) (Nantes: Société des Bibliophiles Bretons et de l'histoire de la Bretagne, 1886).

BOWIE, Malcolm, *Lacan* (London: Fontana, 1991).

VON BRAUN, Christina, *Die schamlose Schönheit des Vergangenen: Zum Verhältnis von Geschlecht und Geschichte* (Frankfurt am Main: Neue Kritik, 1989).

BRINKER-GABLER, Gisela, *Deutsche Literatur von Frauen. Zweiter Band. Neunzehntes und zwanzigstes Jahrhundert* (Munich: Beck, 1988).

BRONFEN, Elisabeth, *Over Her Dead Body: Death, Femininity and the Aesthetic* (Manchester: Manchester University Press, 1993).

BRUHNS, Helgard, *Herbert Eulenberg: Drama, Dramatik, Wirkung* (Frankfurt am Main: Akademische Verlagsgesellschaft, 1974).

CAMPE, Joachim Heinrich, *Wörterbuch der deutschen Sprache*, 4 vols. (Brunswick: Schulbuchhandlung, 1807–11).

CAWS, Mary Ann, KUENZLI, Rudolf E., and RAABERG, Gwen (eds.), *Surrealism and Women* (Cambridge, Mass.: MIT Press, 1991).

Centre National de la Recherche Scientifique, *Trésor de la langue française: Dictionnaire da la langue du 19e et du 20e siècle (1789–1960)*, 16 vols. (Paris: Éditions du CNRS and Gallimard, 1971–94).

CHADWICK, Whitney, *Women Artists and the Surrealist Movement* (London: Thames & Hudson, 1985).

CIXOUS, Hélène, 'Castration or Decapitation?', trans. Annette Kuhn, *Signs*, 7 (1981), 41–55.

CRONAN ROSE, Ellen, 'Through the Looking Glass: When Women Tell Fairy Tales', in Elizabeth Abel, Marianne Hirsch, and Elizabeth Langland (eds.), *The Voyage In: Fictions of Female Development* (Hanover, NH: University Press of New England, 1983), 209–27.

CSAMPAI, Attila, and HOLLAND, Dietmar, *Der Opernführer* (Hamburg: Hoffmann & Campe, 1989).

DAHLKE, Birgit, *Papierboot: Autorinnen der DDR—inoffiziell publiziert* (Würzburg: Königshausen & Neumann, 1997).

DAVIES, Mererid Puw, '*In Blaubarts Schatten*: Murder, *Märchen* and Memory', *German Life and Letters*, 50 (1997), 491–507.

——' "Du bist in einem Mörderhaus": Representing German History Through the *Märchen* of "Blaubart" and "Der Räuberbräutigam" in Works by Dieter

Hildebrandt and Helma Sanders-Brahms', in Mary Fulbrook and Martin Swales (eds.) *Representing the German Nation* (Manchester: Manchester University Press, 2000), 118–35.

DAVIES, Mererid Puw, 'The *Blaubartmärchen* and Its Reception in German Literature of the Nineteenth and Twentieth Centuries', D.Phil. thesis (Oxford, 1998).

DELARUE, Paul, and TÉNÈZE, Marie Louise, *Le Conte populaire français*, 4 vols. (Paris: Érasme, 1957).

DENNELER, Iris, 'Blaubart ab. Zur Aktualität eines alten Märchens', *Lendemains*, 53 (1989), 119–25.

DOUTREPONT, Georges, *Les Types populaires de la littérature française* (Brussels: Lamertin, 1926–7).

DROSS, Annemarie, 'Blaubarts Schloß steht im Wald', in Brigitte Wartmann (ed.), *Weiblich-Männlich: Kulturgeschichtliche Spuren einer verdrängten Weiblichkeit* (Berlin: Ästhetik & Kommunikation, 1980), 134–49.

DWORKIN, Andrea, *Woman Hating* (New York: Plume, 1974).

EICHER, Thomas (ed.), *Märchen und Moderne: Fallbeispiele einer intertextuellen Relation* (Münster: Lit, 1996).

ELIAS, Norbert, *Über den Prozeß der Zivilisation: Soziogenetische und Psychogenetische Untersuchungen* (1939) (Frankfurt am Main: Suhrkamp, 1997).

ELLIS, John M., *One Fairy Tale Too Many* (Chicago: University of Chicago Press, 1983).

EWE, Brigitte, 'Das Kunstmärchen in der Jugendliteratur des 20. Jahrhunderts', Ph.D. Dissertation (Munich: 1965).

FEHLING, Detlev, *Amor und Psyche: Die Schöpfung des Apuleius und ihre Einwirkung auf das Märchen. Eine Kritik der romantischen Märchentheorie* (Mainz: Akademie der Wissenschaften und der Literatur, 1977).

FILZ, Walter, *Es war einmal . . . Elemente des Märchens in der deutschen Literatur der siebziger Jahre* (Frankfurt am Main: Lang, 1989).

FINK, Gonthier-Louis, *Naissance et apogée du conte merveilleux en Allemagne 1740–1800* (Paris: Belles Lettres, 1966).

FOUCAULT, Michel, *Surveiller et punir: naissance de la prison* (Paris: Gallimard, 1975).

—— *La Volonté de savoir* (Paris: Gallimard, 1976).

Fox, Jennifer, 'The Creator Gods: Romantic Nationalism and the En-Gendermment of Women in Folklore', in Susan Tower Hollis, Linda Pershing, and M. Jane Young (eds.), *Feminist Theory and the Study of Folklore* (Urbana: University of Illinois Press, 1993), 29–40.

FRENZEL, Elisabeth, *Stoffe der Weltliteratur*, 8th edn. (Stuttgart: Kröner, 1992).

FREUD, Sigmund, *Gesammelte Werke*, ed. Anna Freud et al., 18 vols. (London: Imago, 1941).

—— *Studienausgabe*, ed. Alexander Mitscherlich, Angela Richards, and James Strachey, 11 vols. (Frankfurt am Main: Fischer, 1989).

FREVERT, Ute, *Frauen-Geschichte: Zwischen Bürgerlicher Verbesserung und Neuer Weiblichkeit* (Frankfurt am Main: Suhrkamp, 1986).

FUNCKE, E. W., 'Das Märchen in Deutschland heute', *Acta Germanica*, 15 (1982), 131–47.

GERCKE, Hans (ed.), *Blau: Farbe der Ferne* (Heidelberg: Wunderhorn, 1990).

GILBERT, Sandra M., and GUBAR, Susan, *The Madwoman in the Attic: The Woman Writer and the Nineteenth-Century Literary Imagination* (New Haven, Conn.: Yale University Press, 1979).

GÖTTNER-ABENDROTH, Heide, *Die Göttin und ihr Heros: Die matriarchalen Religionen in Mythos, Märchen und Dichtung* (Munich: Frauenoffensive, 1980).

GRACE, Sherrill E., 'Courting Bluebeard with Bartók, Atwood and Fowles: Modern Treatments of the Bluebeard Theme', *Journal of Modern Literature*, 11 (1984), 245–62.

GRÄTZ, Manfred, *Das Märchen in der deutschen Aufklärung* (Stuttgart: Metzler, 1988).

GRIMM, Jacob, and GRIMM, Wilhelm, *Deutsches Wörterbuch* (Leipzig: Hirzel, 1804–78).

HAASE, Donald (ed.), *The Reception of Grimms' Fairy Tales: Responses, Reactions, Revisions* (Detroit: Wayne State University Press, 1993).

HAGUE, Jill, and MALOS, Ellen, *Domestic Violence: Action for Change* (Cheltenham: New Clarion Press, 1993).

HECKMANN, Emil, 'Blaubart: Ein Beitrag zur vergleichenden Märchenforschung', Ph.D. dissertation (Heidelberg, 1930) (Schwetzingen: Moch, 1932).

HERZOG, Josef, *Die Märchentypen des 'Ritter Blaubart' und Fitchervogel* (Würzburg: Triltsch, 1937).

HOFMANN, K., 'Über die älteste Quelle der Blaubartsage', *Romanische Forschungen*, 1 (1883), 434–5.

HOLBEK, Bengt, *Interpretation of Fairy Tales* (Helsinki: Suomalainen Tiedeakatemia, 1987).

HOLLAND, Dietmar, 'Herzog Blaubarts Burg', in Attila Csampai and Dietmar Holland (eds.), *Der Opernführer* (Hamburg: Hoffmann & Campe, 1989), 1047–51.

HOLLIS, Susan Tower, PERSHING, Linda, and YOUNG, M. Jane (eds.), *Feminist Theory and the Study of Folklore* (Urbana: University of Illinois Press, 1993).

HOLZ, Friedrich, 'Die Mädchenräuberballade', Ph.D. dissertation (Heidelberg, 1929).

IRIGARAY, Luce, *This Sex Which Is Not One*, trans. Catherine Porter (Ithaca, NY: Cornell University Press, 1985).

JACKSON, Rosemary, *Fantasy: The Literature of Subversion* (London: Routledge, 1981).

JACOBY, Mario, 'Märcheninterpretation aus der Sicht C.G. Jungs: Überlegungen zu einer tiefenpsychologischen Hermeneutik', in Mario Jacoby, Verena Kast, and Ingrid Riedel (eds.), *Das Böse im Märchen* (1978) (Fellbach: Bonz, 1980), 12–23.

JARVIS, Shawn C., 'Spare the Rod and Spoil the Child: Bettine's *Das Leben der Hochgräfin Gritta von Rattenzuhausbeiuns*', *Women in German Yearbook*, 3 (1986), 77–91.

—— 'Literary Legerdemain and the Märchen Tradition of Nineteenth-Century Women Authors', Ph.D. dissertation (University of Minnesota, 1990).

JOHN, Nicholas (ed.), *Königskinder or The Prince and the Goosegirl* (London: ENO, 1991).

——(ed.), *The Stage Works of Béla Bartók* (London: Calder, 1991).

KANT, Immanuel, 'Beobachtungen über das Gefühl des Schönen und Erhabenen', in Kant, *Werke*, ed. Ernst Cassirer et al., 11 vols. (Berlin: Bruno Cassirer, 1922), ii, 243–300.

KAST, Verena, 'Der Blaubart: Zum Problem des destruktiven Animus', in Mario Jacoby, Verena Kast and Ingrid Riedel (eds.), *Das Böse in Märchen* (Fellbach: Bonz, 1980), 90–108.

KERR, Alfred, 'Deutsches Drama', *Die neue Rundschau*, 18 (1) (1907), 113–18.

KIEDAISCH, Petra (ed.), *Lyrik nach Auschwitz? Adorno und die Dichter* (Stuttgart: Reclam, 1995).

KINDL, Ulrike, 'Blaubarts Mord-Motiv oder: Wie neugierig darf Märchen-deutung sein?', *Lendemains*, 53 (1989), 111–17.

KÖHLER-ZÜLCH, Ines, 'Who Are the Tellers? Statements by Collectors and Authors', *Fabula*, 38 (1997), 199–209.

KRETSCHMER, Paul, 'Das Märchen vom Blaubart', *Mitteilungen der anthropologischen Gesellschaft*, 31 (1901), 62–70.

KRISTEVA, Julia, *La Révolution du langage poétique* (Paris: Seuil, 1974).

——'Word, Dialogue and Novel', in *The Kristeva Reader*, ed. Toril Moi (Oxford: Blackwell, 1986), 34–61.

KRÖMER, Wolfgang, 'Märchen, Legende, phantastische Geschichte—oder der bittere Unernst als Wesenszug der Moderne', *Sprachkunst*, 15 (1984), 212–26.

KUENZLI, Rudolf E., 'Surrealism and Misogyny', in Mary Ann Caws, Rudolf E. Kuenzli, and Gwen Raaberg (eds.), *Surrealism and Women* (Cambridge, Mass.: London: MIT Press, 1991), 17–25.

LACAN, Jacques, *Écrits* (Paris: Seuil, 1966).

——*Les Quatre concepts fondamentaux de la psychanalyse* (Paris: Seuil, 1973).

——*Le Séminaire livre XX: Encore*, ed. Jacques-Alain Miller (Paris: Seuil, 1975).

——and the *École Freudienne, Feminine Sexuality*, ed. Juliet Mitchell and Jacqueline Rose (London: Macmillan, 1982).

LAGANE, René, and NIOBET, Georges (eds.), *Grand Larousse de la langue française*, 7 vols. (Paris: Larousse, 1971–8).

LANGE, Sigrid (ed.), *Ob die Weiber Menschen sind: Geschlechterdebatten um 1800* (Leipzig: Reclam, 1992).

LE GRAND, Albert, *Les Vies des Saints de la Bretaigne Armorique* (1636–7), 5th edn. (Quimper: J. Salaun, 1901).

LEMPRIÈRE, John, *A Classical Dictionary* (London: Routledge & Kegan Paul, 1948).

LE RIDER, Jacques, *Der Fall Otto Weininger: Wurzeln des Antifeminismus und Antisemitismus*, trans. Dieter Hornig (Munich: Löcker, 1985).

——*Modernity and Crises of Identity: Culture and Society in Fin-de-Siècle Vienna*, trans. Rosemary Morris (Cambridge: Polity Press, 1990).

——and LESER, Norbert (eds.), *Otto Weininger: Werk und Wirkung* (Vienna: Österreichischer Bundesverlag, 1984).

LEWIS, Philip, *Seeing Through the Mother Goose Tales: Visual Turns in Perrault* (Stanford, Calif.: Stanford University Press, 1996).

LOCHMANN, Angelika, and OVERATH, Angelika (eds.), *Das blaue Buch: Lesarten einer Farbe* (Nördlingen: Greno, 1988).

LUFT, David, 'Otto Weininger als Figur des Fin de Siècle', in Jacques Le Rider and Norbert Leser (eds.), *Otto Weiniger: Werk und Wirkung* (Vienna: Österreichischer Bundesverlag, 1984), 71–9.

LÜTHI, Max, *Das europäische Volksmärchen* (Berne: Francke, 1960).

—— *Märchen*, rev. Heinz Rölleke (Stuttgart: Metzler, 1962).

—— *Das Volksmärchen als Dichtung: Ästhetik und Anthropologie* (Düsseldorf: Diederichs, 1975).

LUNDELL, Torborg, 'Gender-Related Biases in the Type and Motif Indexes of Aarne and Thompson', in Ruth B. Bottigheimer (ed.), *Fairy Tales and Society: Illusion, Allusion and Paradigm* (Philadelphia: University of Pennsylvania Press, 1986), 149–64.

MACCULLOCH, J. A., *The Childhood of Fiction* (London: Murray, 1905).

MACKENSEN, Lutz, and BOLTE, Johannes (eds.), *Handwörterbuch des deutschen Märchens*, 2 vols. (Berlin: de Gruyter, 1930–3).

McGLATHERY, James M. (ed.), *The Brothers Grimm and Folktale* (Urbana: University of Illinois Press, 1989).

—— *Grimms' Fairy Tales: A History of Criticism on a Popular Classic* (Columbia, SC: Camden House, 1993).

MENNINGHAUS, Winfried, *Lob des Unsinns: Über Kant, Tieck und Blaubart* (Frankfurt am Main: Suhrkamp, 1995).

MERCHANT, Carolyn, *The Death of Nature: Women, Ecology and the Scientific Revolution* (New York: HarperCollins, 1983).

MERKEL, Ingrid, 'Wirklichkeit im romantischen Märchen', *Colloquia Germanica*, 3 (1969), 162–83.

METZLER, Michael M., and MOMMSEN, Katharina (eds.), *Fairy Tales as Ways of Knowing: Essays on Märchen in Psychology, Society and Literature* (Berne: Lang, 1981).

MOI, Toril, *Sexual/Textual Politics* (London: Routledge, 1985).

MOWSHOWITZ, Harriet Angell Hobson, 'Bluebeard and French Literature', Ph.D. dissertation (University of Michigan, 1970).

NIETZSCHE, Friedrich, *Werke in zwei Bänden*, ed. Ivo Frenzel and Karl Schlechta, 2 vols. (Munich: Hanser, 1987).

NIXON, Lucia, 'Gender Bias in Archaeology', in Léonie J. Archer, Susan Fischler, and Maria Wyke (eds.), *Women in Ancient Societies: An Illusion of the Night* (London: Macmillan, 1994), 1–23.

OVERATH, Angelika, 'Azurne Scherben', *Merkur*, 38 (1984), 619–28.

PALMIER, Jean-Michel, 'Otto Weiniger, Wien und die Moderne', in Jacques Le Rider and Norbert Leser (eds.), *Otto Weiniger: Werk und Wirkung* (Vienna: Österreichischer Bundesverlag, 1984), 80–95.

Pancritius, Marie, 'Aus mutterrechtlicher Zeit: Blaubart', *Anthropos*, 25 (1930), 879–909.

Picherit, Jean-Louis, 'Qui était Barbe bleue?', *Neuphilologische Mitteilungen / Bulletin de la Société Néophilologique / Bulletin of the Modern Language Society*, 89 (1988), 374–7.

Pomeroy, Sarah B., 'Selected Bibliography on Women in Antiquity', *Arethusa*, 6 (1973), 127–57.

Pröpstl, Ellen, 'Neuromantische Prosamärchendichtung', Ph.D. dissertation (Munich, 1950).

Raaberg, Gwen, 'The Problematics of Women and Surrealism', in Mary Ann Caws, Rudolf E. Kuenzli, and Gwen Raaberg (eds.), *Surrealism and Women* (Cambridge, Mass.: MIT Press, 1991), 1–10.

Ramm, Klaus, 'Blaubart vor [*sic*] der Krummen Lanke im Radio. Gerhard Rühm', in Klaus Schöning (ed.), *Hörspielmacher: Autorenporträts und Essays* (Königstein im Taunus: Athenäum, 1983), 163–8.

Ranke, Kurt, et al. (eds.), *Enzyklopädie des Märchens: Handwörterbuch zur historischen und vergleichenden Erzählforschung*, to date 8 vols. (Berlin: de Gruyter, 1975–   ).

Rebel, Hermann, 'Why Not "Old Marie" . . . Or Someone Very Much Like Her? A Reassessment of the Question about the Grimms' Contributor from a Social Historical Perspective', *Social History*, 13 (1988), 1–24.

Röhrich, Lutz, *Lexikon der sprichwörtlichen Redensarten*, 2 vols. (Freiburg im Breisgau: Herder, 1973).

Rölleke, Heinz, *Die älteste Märchensammlung der Brüder Grimm: Synopse der hand-schriftlichen Urfassung von 1810 und der Erstdrücke von 1812* (Cologny-Genève: Fondation Martin Bodmer, 1975).

——'Die "stockhessischen" Märchen der "alten Marie": Das Ende eines Mythos um die frühesten *KHM*-Fassungen der Brüder Grimm', *Germanisch-Romanische Monatsschrift*, 25 (1975), 74–86.

——'Die Frau in den Märchen der Brüder Grimm', in Sigrid Früh and Rainer Wehse (eds.), *Die Frau im Märchen* (Kassel: Europäische Märchengesellschaft / Röth, 1985), 72–88.

Roudinesco, Elisabeth, *Jacques Lacan & Co.: A History of Psychoanalysis in France, 1925–1985*, trans. Jeffrey Mehlman (London: Free Association Books, 1990).

Rowe, Karen E., 'To Spin a Yarn: The Female Voice in Folklore and Fairy Tale', in Ruth B. Bottigheimer (ed.), *Fairy Tales and Society: Illusion, Allusion and Paradigm* (Philadelphia: University of Pennsylvania Press, 1986), 53–74.

Rutschky, Katharina (ed.), *Schwarze Pädagogik: Quellen zur Naturgeschichte der bürger-lichen Erziehung* (Frankfurt am Main: Ullstein, 1977).

Saintyves, Pierre, *Les Contes de Perrault et leurs récits parallèles, leurs origines* (Paris: Librairie Critique, 1923).

Scherf, Walter, *Lexikon der Zaubermärchen* (Stuttgart: Kröner, 1982).

——*Das Märchenlexikon* (Munich: Beck, 1995).

SCHMITT, Franz Anselm, *Stoff- und Motivgeschichte der deutschen Literatur* (Berlin: de Gruyter, 1976).

SCHMITZ-KÖSTER, Dorothee, 'Hexen, Weltfahrer und die schöne Melusine: Annäherung an Irmtraud Morgner', in Kristine von Soden (ed.), *Irmtraud Morgners hexische Weltfahrt: Eine Zeitmontage* (Berlin: Elefanten Press, 1991), 6–16.

SCHÖNBERG, Jutta, *Frauenrolle und Roman: Studien zu den Romanen der Eugenie Marlitt* (Frankfurt am Main: Lang, 1986).

SCHOßLEITNER, Karl, 'Das Blaubart-Thema', *Der Brenner*, 4 (15) (1911–12), 513–26.

SCHWARZER, Alice, *Der 'kleine Unterschied' und seine großen Folgen: Frauen über sich: Beginn einer Befreiung* (Frankfurt am Main: Fischer, 1975).

—— *Warum gerade sie? Weibliche Rebellen: 15 Begegnungen mit berühmten Frauen* (Frankfurt am Main: Luchterhand, 1989).

SEIFERT, Lewis C., *Fairy Tales, Sexuality and Gender in France 1690–1715: Nostalgic Utopias* (Cambridge: Cambridge University Press, 1996).

SHEPPARD, Richard, 'Unholy Families: The Oedipal Psychopathology of Four Expressionist *Ich-Dramen*', in Richard Sheppard (ed.), *New Ways in Germanistik* (Oxford: Berg, 1990), 164–91.

SHEPTYCKI, J. W. E., *Rapacious Bluebeards and Chivalrous Knights: A Sociolinguistic View of Policing Woman Battering* (Edinburgh: Edinburgh University New Waverley Papers, 1995).

SHUMAN, Amy, 'Gender and Genre', in Susan Tower Hollis, Linda Pershing, and M. Jane Young (eds.), *Feminist Theory and the Study of Folklore* (Urbana and Chicago: University of Illinois Press, 1993), 71–85.

SILVERMAN, Kaja, *The Subject of Semiotics* (Oxford and New York: Oxford University Press, 1983).

SKRINE, Peter, 'Elsa Bernstein and *Königskinder*', in *Königskinder or The Prince and the Goosegirl*, ed. Nicholas John (London: ENO, 1990).

SORIANO, Marc, *Les Contes de Perrault: culture savante et traditions populaires* (Paris: Gallimard, 1968).

SPÖRK, Ingrid, 'Das Bild der Frau im Märchen', in Beate Frakele, Elisabeth List, and Gertrude Pauritsch (eds.), *Über Frauenleben, Männerwelt und Wissenschaft: Österreichische Texte zur Frauenforschung* (Vienna: Verlag für Gesellschaftskritik, 1987), 121–42.

STEGEMANN, Michael, 'Ariane et Barbe-Bleue', in Attila Csampai and Dietmar Holland (eds.), *Der Opernführer* (Hamburg: Hoffmann & Campe, 1989), 954–7.

STIEG, Gerald, 'Otto Weiningers Blendung: Weininger, Karl Kraus und der Brenner-Kreis', in *Otto Weininger: Werk und Wirkung*, ed. Jacques Le Rider and Norbert Leser (Vienna: Österreichischer Bundesverlag, 1984), 59–67.

STEINCHEN, Renate, 'Märchenerzählerin und Schneewittchen—Zwei Frauenbilder in einer deutschen Märchensammlung: Zur Rekonstruktion der Entstehungsgeschichte Grimmscher Märchenfiguren im Kontext sozial- und kulturhistorischer Entwicklung', in Barbara Schaeffer-Hegel and Brigitte Wartmann (eds.), *Mythos Frau: Projektionen und Inszenierungen im Patriarchat* (Berlin: Publica, 1984), 280–308.

STEINER, George, *In Bluebeard's Castle* (London: Faber & Faber, 1971).

STONE, Kay F., 'Feminist Approaches to the Interpretation of Fairy Tales', in Ruth B. Bottigheimer (ed.), *Fairy Tales and Society: Illusion, Allusion and Paradigm* (Philadelphia: University of Pennsylvania Press, 1986), 229–36.

SUHRBIER, Hartwig, 'Blaubart—Leitbild und Leidfigur', in Hartwig Suhrbier (ed.), *Blaubarts Geheimnis: Märchen und Erzählungen, Gedichte und Stücke* (Cologne: Diederichs, 1984), 11–79.

TATAR, Maria M., *The Hard Facts of the Grimms' Fairy Tales* (Princeton, NJ: Princeton University Press, 1987).

—— *Off With Their Heads! Fairy Tales and the Culture of Childhood* (Princeton, NJ: Princeton University Press, 1992).

THEWELEIT, Klaus, *Männerphantasien*, 2 vols. (Reinbek bei Hamburg: Rowohlt, 1980).

TIEDKE, Marion (ed.), *Blaubart—Hoffnung der Frauen*, theatre programme (Munich: Bayerisches Staatsschauspiel, 1997, no. 59).

TISMAR, Jens, *Das deutsche Kunstmärchen im 20. Jahrhundert* (Stuttgart: Metzler, 1981).

VELLAY-VALLANTIN, Charlotte, *L'Histoire des contes* (Paris: Fayard, 1992).

VON FRANZ, Marie-Luise, *Problems of the Feminine in Fairy Tales* (New York: Spring, 1972).

WAELTI-WALTERS, Jennifer, *Fairy Tales and the Female Imagination* (St Albans, Vt.: Eden, 1982).

WALDSTEIN, Edith, 'Romantic Revolution and Female Collectivity: Bettina von Arnim's *Gritta*', *Women in German Yearbook*, 3 (1986), 92–101.

WARNER, Marina, *From the Beast to the Blonde: On Fairy Tales and Their Tellers* (London: Chatto & Windus, 1994).

WEBB, Peter, and SHORT, Robert, *Hans Bellmer* (London: Quartet, 1985).

WEIGEL, Sigrid, 'Der schielende Blick: Thesen zur Geschichte weiblicher Schreibpraxis', in Inge Stephan and Sigrid Weigel, *Die verborgene Frau: Sechs Beiträge zu einer feministischen Literaturwissenschaft* (Berlin: Argument, 1983), 83–137.

—— 'Hans Bellmer Unica Zürn—Junggesellenmaschinen und die Magie des Imaginären', in Inge Stephan and Sigrid Weigel (eds.), *Weiblichkeit und Avantgarde* (Hamburg: Argument, 1987), 187–230.

WEILLER, Edith, *Max Weber und die literarische Moderne: Ambivalente Begegnungen zweier Kulturen* (Stuttgart: Metzler, 1994).

WEININGER, Otto, *Geschlecht und Charakter: Eine prinzipielle Untersuchung* (1903) (Munich: Matthes & Seitz, 1980).

WERTHEIMER, Jürgen, *Don Juan und Blaubart: Erotische Serientäter in der Literatur* (Munich: C. H. Beck, 1999).

WIEGLER, Paul, 'Der gute Blaubart', *Die neue Rundschau*, 20 (4) (1909), 1679–80.

WRIGHT, Elizabeth, *Psychoanalytic Criticism: Theory in Practice* (London: Routledge, 1987).

WÜHRL, Paul-Wolfgang, *Das deutsche Kunstmärchen: Geschichte, Botschaft und Erzählstrukturen* (Heidelberg: Quelle & Meyer, 1984).

WÜRZBACH, Natascha, 'Feministische Forschung in Literaturwissenschaft und Volkskunde: Neue Fragestellungen und Probleme der Theoriebildung', in Sigrid Früh and Rainer Wehse (eds.), *Die Frau im Märchen* (Kassel: Europäische Märchengesellschaft/Röth, 1985), 192–214.

ZIPES, Jack D., 'The Revolutionary Rise of the Romantic Fairy Tale in Germany', *Studies in Romanticism*, 16 (1977), 409–50.

——*Breaking the Magic Spell: Radical Theories of Folk and Fairy Tales* (Austin: University of Texas Press, 1979).

——'Der Prinz wird nicht kommen: Feministische Märchen und Kulturkritik in den USA und England', in Sigrid Früh and Rainer Wehse (eds.), *Die Frau im Märchen* (Kassel: Europäische Märchengesellschaft/Röth, 1985), 174–92.

——'The Grimms and the German Obsession with Fairy Tales', in Ruth B. Bottigheimer (ed.), *Fairy Tales and Society: Illusion, Allusion and Paradigm* (Philadelphia: University of Pennsylvania Press, 1986), 271–95.

——'Marxists and the Illumination of Folk and Fairy Tales', in Ruth B. Bottigheimer (ed.), *Fairy Tales and Society: Illusion, Allusion and Paradigm* (Philadelphia: University of Pennsylvania Press, 1986), 237–43.

——*The Brothers Grimm: From Enchanted Forests to the Modern World* (London: Routledge, 1988).

——*Fairy Tales and the Art of Subversion: The Classic Genre for Children and the Process of Civilisation* (London: Routledge, 1991).

——'The Struggle for the Grimms' Throne: The Legacy of the Grimms' Tales in the FRG and GDR since 1945', in Donald Haase (ed.), *The Reception of Grimms' Fairy Tales: Responses, Reactions, Revisions* (Detroit: Wayne State University Press, 1993), 167–206.

REVIEWS IN NEWSPAPERS AND JOURNALS

(Page references are not given in the following sections because these details are based on dossiers of photocopies without full references kindly provided by the Hamburger Staatsoper and Münchner Residenztheater.)

SCHMIDT, Leopold, 'Rezniceks *Ritter Blaubart*', *Berliner Tageblatt*, 57 (1920).

On *Ariane et Barbe-bleue*, dir. Anja Sündermann (Hamburg, 1997)

BERNDT, Hans, *Handelsblatt*, 7 and 8 Nov. 1997.

KESTING, Jürgen, *Opernwelt*, Dec. 1997.

272   BIBLIOGRAPHY

KÖNIGSDORF, Jörg, *Tagesspiegel* (Berlin), 6 Nov. 1997.
KRIEGER, Gottfried, *Hamburger Morgenpost*, 30 Oct. 1997.
PINTER, Eva, *Neue Zürcher Zeitung*, 5 Nov. 1997.
SÖRING, Helmut, *Hamburger Abendblatt*, 23 Oct. 1997.

On Dea Loher, *Blaubart—Hoffnung der Frauen* (Munich, 1997)

Anon., *Bayernkurier*, 6 Dec. 1997.
DULTZ, Sabine, *Münchner Merkur*, 28 Nov. 1997.
KAISER, Joachim, *Süddeutsche Zeitung*, 27 Nov. 1997.
KOHSE, Petra, *die tageszeitung*, 29 and 30 Nov. 1997.
LAAGES, Michael, NDR 3, 27 Nov. 1997.
LÖFFLER, Sigrid, *Die Zeit*, 5 Dec. 1997.
MEYER-ARLT, Ronald, *Freitag*, 28 Nov. 1997.
MICHALZIK, Peter, *Frankfurter Rundschau*, 2 Dec. 1997.
PRESTELE, Charly, *Morgen*, 29 Dec. 1997.
STADELMAIER, Gerhard, *Frankfurter Allgemeine Zeitung*, 28 Nov. 1997.
WENGIEREK, Reinhard, *Die Welt*, 28 Nov. 1997.

INDEX